Recognition
and
Revelation

CARLETON LIBRARY SERIES

The Carleton Library Series publishes books about Canadian economics, geography, history, politics, public policy, society and culture, and related topics, in the form of leading new scholarship and reprints of classics in these fields. The series is funded by Carleton University, published by McGill-Queen's University Press, and is under the guidance of the Carleton Library Series Editorial Board, which consists of faculty members of Carleton University. Suggestions and proposals for manuscripts and new editions of classic works are welcome and may be directed to the Carleton Library Series Editorial Board c/o the Library, Carleton University, Ottawa K1S 5B6, at cls@carleton.ca, or on the web at www.carleton.ca/cls.

CLS *board members*: John Clarke, Ross Eaman, Jennifer Henderson, Paul Litt, Laura Macdonald, Jody Mason, Stanley Winer, Barry Wright

240 *Tax, Order, and Good Government*
A New Political History of Canada,
1867–1917
E.A. Heaman

241 Catharine Parr Traill's *The Female*
Emigrant's Guide
Cooking with a Canadian Classic
Edited by Nathalie Cooke and
Fiona Lucas

242 *Tug of War*
Surveillance Capitalism, Military
Contracting, and the Rise of the
Security State
Jocelyn Wills

243 *The Hand of God*
Claude Ryan and the Fate of Canadian
Liberalism, 1925–1971
Michael Gauvreau

244 *Report on Social Security for Canada*
(New Edition)
Leonard Marsh

245 *Like Everyone Else but Different*
The Paradoxical Success of Canadian
Jews, Second Edition
Morton Weinfeld with Randal F.
Schnoor and Michelle Shames

246 *Beardmore*
The Viking Hoax That Rewrote History
Douglas Hunter

247 *Stanley's Dream*
The Medical Expedition to
Easter Island
Jacalyn Duffin

248 *Change and Continuity*
Canadian Political Economy in the
New Millennium
Edited by Mark P. Thomas,
Leah F. Vosko, Carlo Fanelli,
and Olena Lyubchenko

249 *Home Feelings*
Liberal Citizenship and the Canadian
Reading Camp Movement
Jody Mason

250 *The Art of Sharing*
The Richer versus the Poorer Provinces
since Confederation
Mary Janigan

251 *Recognition and Revelation*
Short Nonfiction Writings
Margaret Laurence
Edited by Nora Foster Stovel

Recognition and Revelation

Short Nonfiction Writings

MARGARET LAURENCE

Edited by
Nora Foster Stovel

Carleton Library Series 251

McGill-Queen's University Press
Montreal & Kingston • London • Chicago

ISBN 978-0-2280-0346-5 (cloth)
ISBN 978-0-2280-0347-2 (paper)
ISBN 978-0-2280-0475-2 (ePDF)
ISBN 978-0-2280-0476-9 (ePUB)

Legal deposit third quarter 2020
Bibliothèque nationale du Québec

Printed in Canada on acid-free paper that is 100% ancient forest free
(100% post-consumer recycled), processed chlorine free

Funded by the   Financé par le
Government   gouvernement
of Canada   du Canada

Canada

Canada Council   Conseil des arts
for the Arts   du Canada

We acknowledge the support of the Canada Council for the Arts.

Nous remercions le Conseil des arts du Canada de son soutien.

Library and Archives Canada Cataloguing in Publication

Title: Recognition and revelation : short nonfiction writings / Margaret Laurence ;
   edited by Nora Foster Stovel.
Names: Laurence, Margaret, author. | Stovel, Nora Foster, 1942- editor.
Series: Carleton library series ; 251.
Description: Series statement: Carleton library series ; 251 | Includes bibliographical
   references and index.
Identifiers: Canadiana (print) 20200235745 | Canadiana (ebook) 20200235842 | ISBN
   9780228003472 (paper) | ISBN 9780228003465 (cloth) | ISBN 9780228004752 (ePDF) |
   ISBN 9780228004769 (ePUB)
Classification: LCC PS8523.A86 A6 2020 | DDC C814/.54—dc23

For my children, Laura and Grant

Contents

Chronology / xi

Foreword *David Laurence* / xv

Acknowledgments / xvii

Introduction: "A Natural-Born Reformer" / xix

Notes on the Text / xliii

PART ONE

Essays about Laurence's Writing: "Gadgetry or Growing"

Sources (1970) / 3

Ten Years' Sentences (1969) / 8

Time and the Narrative Voice (1972) / 15

Half War – Half Peace: A Writer's Working Relationship
with Publishers (n.d.) / 20

Gadgetry or Growing: Form and Voice in the Novel (1980) / 28

On "The Loons" (1993) / 38

Eye on Books: The Writer as Performer (n.d.) / 40

A Tale of Typewriters (1984) / 45

Ivory Tower or Grassroots? The Novelist as Socio-political Being (1978) / 50

PART TWO

Personal and Creative Essays: "The River Flows Both Ways"

Where the World Began (1972) / 63

Love and Madness in the Steel Forest (1969) / 69

Upon a Midnight Clear (1974) / 74

Don't Whisper Sudden; I Scare Easy (1969) / 80

The River Flows Both Ways (1971) / 87

Salute of the Swallows (1971) / 92

The Shack (1974) / 97

A Fantasy Fulfilled (n.d.) / 101

The More Interesting Country (n.d.) / 104

Down East (1971) / 114

Journey from Lakefield (n.d.) / 119

PART THREE
Essays on Canada and Canadian Literature: "The Case for Canadian Literature"

Canadian Novels: Change in the Past Decade (1967) / 127

Canada Still Too Canada-Focused (1966) / 137

Voices from Future Places (1972) / 143

The Case for Canadian Literature (1977) / 150

Canadian Writers: From Neglect to Special Treatment (1970) / 154

When You Were Five and I Was Fourteen (1985) / 158

Books That Mattered to Me (1981) / 161

(a) Introductions to New Canadian Library Editions

Afterword to Sinclair Ross, *The Lamp at Noon and Other Stories* (1968) / 173

Introduction to Jack Ludwig, *Above Ground* (1973) / 178

Introduction to Percy Janes, *House of Hate* (1976) / 184

Introduction to Adele Wiseman, *Crackpot* (1978) / 189

(b) Unpublished Speeches and Tributes

W.L. Morton – A Tribute (1981) / 199

Tribute to Malcolm Ross (1982) / 201

Clara Thomas ... Biographer, Teacher, Critic ... and Pioneer (1984) / 203

Lois Wilson (1984) / 207

For Marian Passmore Engel (1986) / 210
Madeleine Wilkie Dumont (n.d.) / 212
YWCA Woman of the Year Award (1985) / 214

PART FOUR

Essays on Nuclear Disarmament: "The Most Pressing Practical, Moral, and Spiritual Issue of Our Times"

A Message to the Inheritors (n.d.) / 221
A Matter of Life or Death (1982) / 226
The Artist Then, Now, and Always (1984) / 231
A Statement of Faith (1982) / 234
"Peace": A Word's Meaning (1986) / 239
Operation Dismantle (1982) / 242
My Final Hour (1983) / 246

PART FIVE

Socio-political Essays: "Listen, Just Listen"

"Listen, Just Listen" (1977) / 259
Quebec's "Freedom" Is a Vital Concern, but Freedom Itself Is That
and More (1978) / 265
Open Letter to the Mother of Joe Bass (1968) / 268
The Greater Evil: Pornography or Censorship? (1984) / 272
Statement – PEN (1985) / 280
A Constant Hope: Women in the Now and Future High Tech
Age (1985) / 283

Afterword: Rediscovering Margaret Laurence *Aritha van Herk* / 291

Annotations / 297
Works Cited / 325
Index / 335

Chronology of Margaret Laurence's Life and Works

1926 Jean Margaret Wemyss born 18 July in Neepawa, Manitoba, to Robert Wemyss and Verna Simpson Wemyss.

1930 Verna Simpson Wemyss dies. Her sister, Margaret Campbell Simpson, returns to Neepawa to care for niece.

1931 Margaret Campbell Simpson marries Robert Wemyss.

1933 Robert Morrison Wemyss born.

1935 Robert Wemyss, the author's father, dies.

1938 Margaret Simpson Wemyss moves with children Margaret and Robert to home of her father, John Simpson.

1940–44 Attends the Viscount School, now Neepawa Collegiate, edits its newspaper, wins Governor General's Medal.

1944–47 BA in Honours English at United College, Winnipeg. Publishes poetry and stories in *Vox* and *Manitoban*.

1947–48 Works as a reporter on the *Westerner* and *Winnipeg Citizen* and as assistant registrar at Winnipeg YWCA.

1947 Marries Jack Laurence, born 1916 in Prince George, British Columbia, a war veteran and civil engineering student.

1949 Jack graduates from University of Manitoba. Laurences move to England.

1950 Laurences move to British Protectorate of Somaliland. Margaret Laurence collects material for *A Tree for Poverty*.

1952 Laurences move to the Gold Coast, now Ghana. Daughter Jocelyn born.

1954 *A Tree for Poverty: Somali Poetry and Prose* published in Nairobi.

1955 Son David born.

1957 Ghana achieves independence. Laurences move to Vancouver. Margaret Laurence's stepmother dies in Victoria.

1960 *This Side Jordan*, a novel set in Ghana, published.

1962 Margaret Laurence moves to Hampstead, London, with children. Jack Laurence takes up post in East Pakistan.

1963 Margaret Laurence moves to Elm Cottage in Penn, Buckinghamshire, and publishes *The Tomorrow-Tamer and Other Stories*, set in Ghana, and *The Prophet's Camel Bell*, based on her Somali journals.

1964 *The Stone Angel*, first Manawaka novel, published.

1966 *A Jest of God* published and awarded Governor General's Award for Fiction.

1968 *Long Drums and Cannons: Nigerian Dramatists and Novelists 1952–1966* published.

1969 *The Fire-Dwellers* published. Laurences divorced. Margaret returns to Canada as writer-in-residence at Massey College, University of Toronto. Purchases cabin on Otonabee River near Peterborough, Ontario.

1970 *A Bird in the House*, a collection of Canadian short stories, and *Jason's Quest*, children's novel, published.

1971 Companion of the Order of Canada.

1972 Honorary degrees conferred by Trent, Dalhousie, and University of Toronto. Over her lifetime, Laurence received fourteen honorary degrees.

1973 Writer-in-residence at University of Western Ontario. Sells Elm Cottage and buys house in Lakefield, Ontario.

1974 *The Diviners* published, winning Governor General's Award for Fiction. Writer-in-residence, Trent University.

1975 Awarded Molson Prize and D. Litt. by the universities of Brandon, Mount Allison, and Western Ontario.

1976 *Heart of a Stranger* published. Controversy over teaching *The Diviners* in Peterborough high schools begins.

1979 *Six Darn Cows* and *The Olden Days Coat*, children's fiction, published.

1980 *A Christmas Birthday Story*, a children's version of the Nativity, published.

1981–83 Chancellor, Trent University. Begins work with Probe, Project Ploughshares, Operation Dismantle. Censorship controversy regarding her books redevelops.

1987 Dies 5 January in Lakefield, Ontario.

1989 *Dance on the Earth: A Memoir* published posthumously, edited by daughter, Jocelyn Laurence.

Foreword

My mother always seemed to me, as I was growing up, to be both full-time writer and part-time activist, although, over time, as the urgency of the first began to recede, the other advanced more to the fore. Consequently, it would be entirely wrong to assume that after publication of *The Diviners* in 1974 she spent the next decade pacing the floor, her typewriter having fallen silent with writer's block. This was not the case.

By that year my mother had managed to achieve a certain amount of fame, if not fortune, in this country and arguably a status as closely akin to that of celebrity as could tastefully be allowed an author at that time in Canada. In other words, if she chose to speak up on a particular subject, the odds were fairly good that she'd be heard. Speak up she did, believing that, if you've been given a voice, the obligation is there to use it. She was now able to devote more of her time to causes that had always been close to her, that she felt increasingly passionate about, such as environmental protection, human rights, nuclear disarmament (I remember the London Campaign for Nuclear Disarmament marches of the early 1960s), and, of course, gender equality, not to forget Canadian literature itself. She continued to be almost as busy during those final years as she had been throughout all the rest of her too short life.

She talked a great deal, and she spoke out, but mostly she did what she always had done; she wrote. Had she lived long enough to encounter the Twitterverse, who knows, perhaps her tired old typewriter friend might ultimately have been forced into retirement in favour of a computer. Frankly though, it's hard to imagine her lightly tapping a computer keyboard (or heaven forbid, touch screen), since she could often be heard pounding harder and faster at the typewriter keys with increasing fury or joy, depending on the emotional content of the subject at hand, even to the point where typewriter letters broke and flew off through sheer metal fatigue. So, no word processor for her; she only typed directly onto paper.

But fast she was, and over the years she typed many, many letters, no doubt helping to keep Canada Post in the black: letters to people, both friends and not friends; to publications of all kinds; to companies; to government. She continued to write articles, essays, and reviews, and for other writers she would often type up TM's as she called them – tender messages, such as a positive quote for the back of the book jacket for an upcoming publication. She consistently went out of her way to help other writers, other people, as much as she was able. She had a true generosity of spirit, yes, but was also driven by an almost unshakable faith in humanity and by the deeply held belief that, if each of us tried our best, we would make our planet, our only home, a better place for all, or at least increase its chances of survival.

I am very grateful to Nora Foster Stovel for all the time and effort she has expended in carefully assembling this collection of essays, and I hope that together they may present the reader with a door through which to encounter and get to know better the complex person behind the fiction. And, certainly, it does seem to me, although it's now a little over thirty years since my mother died, that much of what she wrote here remains relevant today.

DAVID LAURENCE

Acknowledgments

I wish to acknowledge, first and foremost, the Margaret Laurence Estate, with special thanks to David Laurence and the late Jocelyn Laurence. I also wish to thank the Humanities and Social Sciences Research Council of Canada for the Strategic Grant that enabled me to research the Laurence Archives at York and McMaster universities, and the University of Alberta Faculty of Arts for the McCalla professorships that allowed me to compose *Divining Margaret Laurence: A Study of Her Complete Writings* (2008) and to edit this collection of her essays. I am grateful to Michael Muir, York University librarian, and his staff for their assistance in researching the Laurence Archives, and Carl Spadoni and the staff of McMaster University's Mills Memorial Library. My colleagues, the late Clara Thomas, John Lennox, Michael Peterman, David Staines, Carole Gerson, and Christl Verduyn provided generous advice and support for which I am grateful. I wish to thank my graduate research assistants who helped me digitize and annotate these essays – Mitchell Johnston, Nadine Adelaar, Cynthia Springs, and especially Laura Sydora, whose commitment and capabilities have helped bring this edition to completion – and Dean Irvine and the SSHRC for the Editing Modernism in Canada Graduate Research Assistant Grant that enabled me to hire the students named to help with this edition. I also wish to thank Dr Peter Midgley, former senior acquisitions editor with the University of Alberta Press, and Mark Abley of McGill-Queen's University Press for their valuable advice and guidance; Kate Merriman for her excellent copyediting; and Stephen Ullstrom for his excellent indexing.

Introduction:
"A Natural-Born Reformer"

Margaret Laurence (1926–1987) is one of Canada's most respected authors. She received federal designation as a National Historic Person in 2014, and Parks Canada installed a plaque in her honour at the Margaret Laurence House in Neepawa, Manitoba, in 2018. Most famous for her Manawaka Saga of five fictions set on the Canadian Prairies – *The Stone Angel* (1964), *A Jest of God* (1966), *The Fire-Dwellers* (1969), *A Bird in the House* (1970), and *The Diviners* (1974) – she also wrote many essays that reveal a very different view of this artist. Although she published a collection of her nineteen "travel articles" in *Heart of a Stranger*[1] in 1976, Laurence published many more works in various venues between 1960 and 1985, works that have never been collected, and wrote others that have never yet been published. This is the one remaining gap in Laurence's oeuvre – one that I hope *Recognition and Revelation*, an edition of fifty-one primarily uncollected essays and addresses, will fill. By contextualizing her nonfiction in her life and oeuvre, I hope this edition will assist students of her writings and inspire a long-overdue renaissance in Laurence studies, over thirty years after her death.

Laurence writes in *Dance on the Earth: A Memoir*, "I believe we have to live, as long as we live, in the expectation and hope of changing the world for the better" (221). She affirms, "I am not by nature a revolutionary but rather a natural-born reformer" (57). Nowhere is this reformist zeal more apparent than in her essays. It is unfortunate that these works are so little known simply because they have been largely unavailable. Because Laurence was in the habit of working out issues in nonfiction before dramatizing them in fiction, her essays illuminate her fiction,[2] revealing Laurence as a socially and politically committed artist. These articles bring to the surface the socio-political undercurrents of her creative writing and help us read her fiction in a new light.

Why, when Laurence was so admired as a writer of fiction, did she write so many essays, we might wonder. As a writer who lived by her pen, she needed the income, as her correspondence with Will Ready regarding the sale of her manuscripts to McMaster University reveals. But there are other more interesting reasons. She had to defend her innovative fictional techniques against the negative criticism of reviewers, especially male academics, regarding her early sister novels *A Jest of God* and *The Fire-Dwellers*. As a supporter of Canadian literature generally, she was often called on to discuss it. Most important, she was passionately interested in many issues, from the rights of women to those of Canada's Indigenous peoples, from pornography to censorship, and from ecology to nuclear disarmament.

Nonfiction offered Laurence a forum for addressing topical issues about which she cared deeply, but which she could not address directly in fiction. Christl Verduyn's observation regarding Carol Shields in "(Es)saying It Her Way: Carol Shields as Essayist" applies equally well to Laurence: "Her particular style of essay-writing represents a kind of symbiosis between the broad essay genre and her personal artistic vision" (60). In the twentieth century, beginning with Virginia Woolf, women writers adopted the traditionally masculine essay genre and adapted it for their own purposes. Laurence was particularly creative in adapting this form; her nonfiction work ranges from traditional essays through oral addresses to creative pieces and even epistolary structures. This flexible genre enabled Laurence to advocate for issues of critical importance to her in a polemical manner inappropriate, she believed, for fiction. Nevertheless, the two forms are inextricably interconnected and demand comparison. As Verduyn concludes, "Canadian women's essay-writing deserves as much critical attention as their texts of fiction and poetry" (67).

Laurence's earliest essays, collected in part 1, "Gadgetry or Growing," focus on her early fiction, as she defends her innovative techniques for conveying the inner dilemmas of her female protagonists against the negative criticism of reviewers. Several creative articles, published in the *Vancouver Sun* and collected in part 2, "The River Flows Both Ways," celebrate Canada's natural resources, while advocating for conservation in a personal mode. After winning the Governor General's Award for fiction in 1966, Laurence was frequently invited to comment on Canadian literature; some of these essays are collected in part 3, "The Case for Canadian Literature." She was invited to compose introductions to New Canadian Library editions and deliver eulogies honouring Canadian dignitaries, especially as chancellor of Trent University between 1981 and 1983.

During the last decade of her life, Laurence was unable to compose fiction, except children's books – *Six Darn Cows* (1979) and *The Christmas Birthday Story* (1980) – although she tried to write another novel, "Dance on the Earth," intended to conclude her Manawaka cycle. "The Controversy," as it became known – when citizens of Peterborough County agitated to have *The Diviners* removed from the grade 13 high-school curriculum in 1976 and 1985 for its alleged obscenity – distressed Laurence greatly and contributed to her inability to compose further fiction, as she explains in her memoir *Dance on the Earth* (213–17) and as the National Film Board's *First Lady of Manawaka* demonstrates. *The Stone Angel* was called "demeaning to human nature," and a letter to the *Peterborough Examiner* declared, "We know that Margaret Laurence's aim in life is to destroy the home and the family" (*Dance on the Earth*, 216). Ultimately, she composed *Dance on the Earth* as a memoir – a tribute to her mothers and a chronicle of her own life as a mother and writer – edited posthumously by her daughter, Jocelyn Laurence, in 1989.

Consequently, many later essays, collected in part 4, "The Most Pressing Practical, Moral, and Spiritual Issue of Our Times," focus on protecting the environment by advocating for nuclear disarmament. Others, collected in part five, "Listen, Just Listen," voice socio-political concerns regarding Canada and its francophone population, Indigenous peoples, and women. Thus, while *Heart of a Stranger* includes primarily "travel articles," *Recognition and Revelation* collects literary essays about Laurence's fiction and Canadian literature generally, and socio-political articles focusing on ecology and nuclear disarmament and social justice. A creative artist and critical thinker, Laurence was true to her family motto "Je pense" (*Heart of a Stranger*, 114).

Essays on Laurence's Novels: "Gadgetry or Growing"

Laurence published several essays about literature in response to negative criticism of her early novels. Her innovative narrative techniques had proved too avant-garde for some reviewers, and she therefore wrote to explain their purpose. These essays reveal her critical acumen and nascent feminism.

The earliest essays chronicle her transition from writing fiction about Africa to writing fiction about Canada. In "Ten Years' Sentences" (1969) she reviews her writing career, terming it, ironically, "a life sentence of sentences" that had commenced a decade earlier with *This Side Jordan* (1960), set in Ghana. One publisher's reader, who claimed he was "only reasonably nauseated" by the character's interior monologues, urged her to purge its passages of purple prose. She reviews the books she wrote during her "seven years' love affair with a continent": *This Side Jordan*, her Somali travel memoir *The Prophet's Camel Bell* (1963), and *The Tomorrow-Tamer and Other Stories* (1963), which, she says, were optimistic texts "written out of the milieu of a rapidly ending colonialism and the emerging independence of African countries." She also composed *A Tree for Poverty* (1954), the first translation and publication of Somali folk literature, and her critical study *Long Drums and Cannons: Nigerian Dramatists and Novelists, 1952–66*, chronicling a "renaissance" in Nigerian literature in the work of such authors as Wole Soyinka, Chinua Achebe, John Pepper Clark, Amos Tutuola, and Cyprian Ekwensi, among others. Eventually, she realized she could not continue to write about Africa, but now felt impelled to write about her own country, Canada, as she explains in "Sources" (1970). While she marvels that she dared to write from the viewpoint of an African man – Nathaniel Amegbe, her Ghanaian protagonist – she explains how Hagar Currie Shipley, protagonist/narrator of *The Stone Angel*, conveyed in her grandparents' Scots-Irish idiom, draws on her Canadian background. Her sympathy with the approaching independence of Somaliland and Ghana, the African countries where she lived from 1951 to 1957, inspired her to emphasize "the promised land of one's own inner freedom" in her subsequent Manawaka fiction.[3]

Laurence's narrative structure became increasingly postmodernist in her Manawaka novels, especially *The Fire-Dwellers* and *The Diviners*. In "Time and the Narrative Voice" (1972) she discusses the relationship between the narrative voice and the treatment of time in her fiction, specifically *A Bird in the House*, her 1970 collection of eight linked stories about the maturing of Vanessa MacLeod. Laurence identifies so strongly with her characters that she labels herself a "Method writer," invoking the Stanislavsky theory of method acting, in which the actor becomes the character. In "Sources" she affirms that the stories in *A Bird in the House* are "based upon my childhood and my childhood family, the only semi-autobiographical fiction I have ever written" (*Heart of a Stranger*, 8). "On 'The

Loons'" forms a fascinating commentary on the autobiographical origins of this story, where changing the name "Diamond Lake" to "the more tourist-appealing Lake Wapakata" (119) ironizes the Indian stereotypes that she critiques.

In "Gadgetry or Growing: Form and Voice in the Novel" (1980) she addresses structure and narrative method, as the writer attempts to create "the kind of vehicle or vessel capable of risking that peculiar voyage of exploration which constitutes a novel." Searching for the best ways to convey characters and their dilemmas, Laurence wonders if such innovative methods represent gimmickry or genuine development – that is, "gadgetry or growing." She reviews the narrative structure of her novels, from *This Side Jordan* to *The Stone Angel*, where she employs first-person narration with flashbacks triggered by present-day events and conveyed chronologically. Her husband, Jack Laurence, an engineer, believed she should employ third-person, chronological narration. In *Dance on the Earth*, she credits Hagar with ending her marriage: "Strange reason for breaking up a marriage: a novel. I had to go with the old lady, I really did, but at the same time I felt terrible about hurting him" (158). *A Jest of God*, which won the Governor General's Award in 1966, employs dual narrative method.[4] *The Fire-Dwellers* demonstrates Laurence's most experimental narrative structure, employing numerous typographical styles to convey Stacey MacAindra's frantic life as wife and mother – reflecting Laurence's own "impossible juggling act" (*Dance on the Earth*, 157).[5] *The Diviners*, which also won the Governor General's Award, is her most complex, heteroglossic novel.

"Half War – Half Peace" (1980) chronicles Laurence's relationships with publishers – usually a "diplomatic exchange," but sometimes "verging on war" – regarding battles over titles of novels. She affirms, "I've had more trouble with titles than a prospective peer. And I've defended my titles more often than a middleweight boxer" (*Heart of a Stranger*, 144). In fact, she and her publisher Jack McClelland crossed swords over the title of *Heart of a Stranger*: in a letter of 10 March 1976 she suggested titling it *Road to the Isles*, but McClelland called that title "horrible," adding, "The book deserves a good title" (Davis and Morra, *Letters*, 376). When she suggested *Heart of a Stranger*, however, he acquiesced.

"A Tale of Typewriters" (1984), written in the form of a letter to her lifelong friend and fellow novelist Adele Wiseman and her family, and Laurence's own children, chronicles her commitment to her writing career, with jokes about a "space bar" being where the beer is kept on a spaceship. Laurence, who

distrusted machinery, anthropomorphized her "tripewriter" by applying female names, from "Felicity" to "Monica Olympia," with her electric typewriter
dubbed "Pearl Cavedweller" – a translation of her name, since "Margaret"
means "pearl" and "Wemyss," her Scottish paternal grandfather believed, sig-
nifies a Pictish cavedweller.

"Eye on Books: The Writer as Performer" (n.d.) focuses on her embarrassment over television interviews and book-promotion tours that were agony for
such a shy author. Here she explains the reasons that writers must engage with
"the Dreaded Media," or "DM" for short, including the need to earn income, promote new publications, and educate students about "Canlit." Responding to a
question about the "Controversy" in an interview, Laurence, chain-smoking in
her nervousness, set fire to the tablecloth.

"Ivory Tower or Grassroots? The Novelist as Socio-political Being" is Laurence's manifesto. Here she states her central tenets regarding fiction, including
the importance of creating characters true to their environment; the inextri-
cable interrelationship of history and fiction, a theme she dramatizes in *The
Diviners*; and the value of "social commentary" that is "both religious and political" at the "grassroots level." "Third-world" writers, a category in which she
includes herself and Chinua Achebe, must overcome the "cultural imperialism"
of America and Britain to discover their own voices. She relates colonialism to
the subservient role of women under patriarchy, a role she resists through her
Manawaka heroines.

Creative Articles: "The River Flows Both Ways"

Laurence was pre-eminently a fiction writer, and many early essays, including
several published in the *Vancouver Sun* while she lived in Vancouver from 1957
to 1962, resemble fiction in their creativity, while predicting her passionate
concern for the environment. "Where the World Began" acknowledges the significance of her hometown of Neepawa, Manitoba in creating the vision that
informs her fiction. She expresses her love of Canada and concern at the pollution of its lakes and rivers, evoking the river she lived beside and loved while
composing *The Diviners*.

"Love and Madness in the Steel Forest" (1969) is a dystopic portrayal of Toronto, the metropolis in which she lived while she was writer-in-residence at

Massey College in 1969–70, the first woman to hold an office in that "male stronghold" (*Dance on the Earth*, 190), when Robertson Davies was master. Having grown up in a small prairie town, she had a "lifelong fear and mistrust of cities" (*Heart of a Stranger*, 173) and was appalled by Toronto, dubbed "the Vile Metropolis," or "vm," where skyscrapers create a "steel forest." She paints a vivid picture of York University's lunar landscape, where her archives are now housed. "Don't Whisper Sudden; I Scare Easy" (1969) chronicles her visit to the New York offices of Alfred Knopf, who published three of her books on one day in 1964 – *This Side Jordan*, *The Tomorrow-Tamer and Other Stories*, and *The Stone Angel* – a visit that made Toronto seem almost palatable. Comic actor Peter Ustinov quipped that Toronto is like New York run by the Swiss. After living for several years in the English village of Penn, Buckinghamshire, Laurence found Manhattan overwhelming. The "hoopla" involved in book promotion appalled her: "I was a babe in the literary woods" (*Dance on the Earth*, 178, 180), she confesses.

The shock of the metropolis inspired her to buy her cabin on the Otonabee River near Peterborough, her "foothold in Canada" (*Dance on the Earth*, 196–7), which she writes about in "The Shack" (*Heart of a Stranger*, 147–50) and where she composed *The Diviners*. "Salute of the Swallows" (1971) also relates to *The Diviners*, whose protagonist, Morag Gunn, observes river birds, and it too reflects Laurence's interest in Canadian history. Her neighbour, fisherman Jack Villerup, inspired the water diviner Royland. "A Fantasy Fulfilled" recounts Laurence's delight in fulfilling a Depression-era childhood dream of ordering anything she wanted from Eaton's catalogue to furnish her cabin – a measure of her self-empowerment. "The River Flows Both Ways" (1971) offers insights into *The Diviners*, as the river is the current of inspiration that flows through "The River of Now and Then," symbolizing the mind's oscillation between past and future as time flows forward and backward. Laurence concludes *The Diviners* with the injunction, "Look ahead into the past, and back into the future, until the silence" (477).

Her riverside cabin, which inspired her love of Canada's waterways, flora, and fauna, also transformed her view of Eastern Canada, as she chronicles in "Down East." Despite her enthusiasm for her newfound homes in Ontario, however, Laurence retained a lifelong love for the Prairies. In "The More Interesting Country" Laurence expresses her love of the railway, as she remembers her last trip along "Nostalgia Road" through her "heartland" of southern Manitoba in 1983 to visit her half-brother, Bob (Robert Wemyss), who was dying of cancer near

Calgary. "Via Rail and Via Memory" concludes with the words "for me/ this is the more interesting country" (*Dance on the Earth*, 275, 277), the phrase that provides the title of the essay included here.

Laurence bought a house on Regent Street in Lakefield, Ontario, near Peterborough, represented as "Jordan's Landing" in *The Diviners*, that had been a funeral home – like the Brick House in Neepawa. There she continued her family Christmas traditions, including the "agreeable anarchy" of Elm Cottage, as she recalls in "Upon a Midnight Clear" (1974). Because she did not drive, she relied on taxis and buses to transport her between Lakefield and Toronto. She often encounters interesting people, including the taxi drivers, as she records in "I Am a Taxi" in *Heart of a Stranger* (135–40). Laurence avoids conversation on public transport, preferring to read, but overhears conversations that she, with her genius for dialogue, renders in both direct and indirect speech. The dramatic vignette "Journey from Lakefield" (n.d.) records an occasion when she was not successful in avoiding a conversation with another, antipathetic, passenger.

Essays on Canadian Literature: "Books That Mattered to Me"

Given Laurence's passionate interest in Canadian literature, it is natural that she wrote several essays chronicling its development. As interim chair of the Writers' Union of Canada, she became den mother to her "tribe" of Canadian authors. Graeme Gibson records, "Margaret Laurence was unanimously elected interim chair – albeit against her better judgment" (Gibson, "Margaret Laurence Lecture," 390). Laurence composed innumerable letters supporting her fellow authors' applications for grants, writing numerous book reviews and essays in support of Canadian literature, and sending many "TMS" – tender messages of support. In "Listen, Just Listen" she affirms, "I feel such a sense of connection with my tribal sisters and brothers, the writers all across this land who are writing in my language." Aritha van Herk recalls how warmly Laurence welcomed her to the Writers' Union of Canada.

Laurence's relationships with other writers were, however, complex. In her 2007 "Margaret Laurence Lecture" Margaret Atwood addresses the aging Laurence's increasing dependence on alcohol, following the "Controversy," and concludes, "Thus there were two Margarets – the warm, kindly, generous woman who helped young writers and spoke of other writers as 'the tribe'; and the sad and angry and jealous one who came out at dusk, and then, as time passed, arrived earlier and earlier in the day, and railed and cursed and savaged people, and put their names on her official Shit List." Atwood asks, "Which one was real?" and answers, "Both were real" (Atwood, "Margaret Laurence Lecture," 319–20).

Atwood writes about "Margaret One and Margaret Two," explaining, "Margaret One is of course Margaret Laurence herself" (315), whom she identifies as her "role model" (326). She lauds Laurence: "At her best as a writer Margaret Laurence was amazing; as a participant in the emerging Canadian literary life of the 60s and 70s, she was crucial" (320). Atwood describes the epiphanic experience of reading Laurence's first Canadian novel, *The Stone Angel*, which was published in 1964, winning the Governor General's Award for fiction: "*The Stone Angel* was one of those moments ... that were like beacons to young writers such as myself. It could be done, then. The impossible, dreamed-of thing could be done ... You could write a novel about Canada that was real, and strong, and authentic, and smart, and moving. It was like watching an albatross take off from a cliff top for the first time, and spread its wings, and soar – yes! Flight is possible!" (316).

Laurence became an advocate for Canadian literature decades before it was recognized, when her stepmother, Margaret Simpson Wemyss, an "early evangelist for Canadian writing" and unofficial librarian of Neepawa's public library, invited Peggy to select books for the library from *Quill & Quire*. "Canadian books then? You bet," Laurence recalls in "When You Were Five and I Was Fourteen." She admired her predecessors Sinclair Ross, Ethel Wilson, Morley Callaghan, Hugh MacLennan, and Gabrielle Roy. In "The Case for Canadian Literature" she affirms the value of Canadian literature: "it speaks to us, through its many and varied voices, of things which are close to our hearts; it links us with our ancestors and with one another."

Laurence was invited to write introductions to McClelland and Stewart's New Canadian Library series, edited by her former professor Malcolm Ross – "the general editor, whose idea the NCL had been and to whom so many of us owe so much" (*Dance on the Earth*, 187). *Recognition and Revelation* collects Laurence's contributions to the NCL.

Her afterword to Sinclair Ross's *The Lamp at Noon and Other* Stories gave Laurence the opportunity to express her admiration for this author who proved that one could write about one's place of origin, even a prairie town, with realism and compassion. His books, especially *As for Me and My House* (1941), she acknowledges, influenced her Manawaka fiction. She credits Ross, like W.O.

Mitchell, with inspiring her "to write out of my own place, my own time, my own people" (*Dance on the Earth*, 187). The ability of Ross's characters, male and female, to not merely survive, but "survive with some remaining dignity," reflects her emphasis on "not just physical survival, but the preservation of some human dignity and in the end some human warmth and ability to reach out and touch others" ("Sources").

In her introduction to Jack Ludwig's *Above Ground*, Laurence highlights Ludwig's ability to portray character, especially women's characters – an important aspect of her fiction, which empowers female protagonists – and his narrative method, which employs the protagonist's "double consciousness" – another feature shared by her Manawaka texts.

In her introduction to Percy Janes's *House of Hate* she comments on his portrayal of patriarchal personalities who resemble Old Testament prophets and whose families maintain "survival humour." These qualities relate to her own characters, including Vanessa MacLeod's wise-cracking Aunt Edna, who employs humour to cope with her father, pioneer Timothy Connor, modeled on Laurence's Grandfather Simpson, in *A Bird in the House*.

Her introduction to Adele Wiseman's *Crackpot* gave her the opportunity to praise her university friend, whose 1956 novel, *The Sacrifice*, won the Governor General's Award. Laurence analyzes the metaphorical and mythic aspects of the crackpot/creation theme, the characterization of Hoda as flawed heroine, and Wiseman's tragi-comic vision.

In "Canadian Writing," Carol Shields declares, "We can … take the year 1960 as the real beginning of our literature" (138). Margaret Atwood corroborates that opinion in *The Burgess Shale: The Canadian Writing Landscape of the 1960s*, where she defines the sixties as "that decade in which the current writing landscape of Canada and the various infrastructures we now take for granted was formed" (3). Laurence observes enormous change in Canadian fiction in the sixties as nationalism gives way to literary merit. While previous Canadian authors are overshadowed by "Uncle Sam and Britannia" (*Heart of a Stranger*, 172), sixties writers abandon "the god's eye view" in favour of the character's "inner geography," developing their individual vision of universal, rather than strictly national, concerns.

In "Canadian Novels: Change in the Past Decade" (1967), Laurence reviews nineteen novels, outlining developments in Canadian fiction through the twentieth century. Texts considered worthy because they extol the "puritan virtues of plain living and high thinking" give way to genuinely good fiction. She praises novelists of the thirties and forties – especially Morley Callaghan, Gabrielle Roy, and Hugh MacLennan – who defied "the confines of provincialism" by employing social realism that frequently offended readers, as did her own novels. She notes the movement from "the 'land' novel," where the hero is "wrestling with the recalcitrant soil or the demon Rum [or] the grizzly bear," to urban novels set in Canada's metropolises. Although Laurence primarily addresses English-language novels, she also considers novels by francophone writers Marie-Claire Blais and Roger Lemelin. Her four dozen published book reviews, primarily of Canadian novels, demonstrate her expertise regarding Canadian fiction.[6]

As a fervent anti-colonialist who believed Canadian writers were writing "a truly non-colonialist literature" (*Dance on the Earth*, 185), Laurence abjured the domination of British and American literature over Canada's homegrown authors. At the same time, she observes change in Canadian fiction as national considerations become secondary to literary merit and Canadian authors are less "spiritually intimidated by England and America." Living in England through the sixties, Laurence was distanced from Canadian nationalist fervour. While she advocated passionately for support for Canadian literature through school curricula and the like, she believed Canadian literature should be valued for its merit, not its nationality. In "Canada Still Too Canada-Focused" (1966), she finds Canadian critics too engrossed with their national literature because insufficiently aware of postcolonial literature. After living in Africa for seven years and publishing five books inspired by that experience, Laurence knew this body of literature well. Nevertheless, she reviews many writers positively while on a cross-Canada book promotion tour for *A Jest of God* (*Heart of a Stranger*, 131).

Similarly, in "Canadian Writers: From Neglect to Special Treatment" (1970), Laurence balances the just and overdue recognition that Canadian writers are receiving with the principle that literature should be lauded for intrinsic value, not simply for nationalistic reasons. While she laments that earlier Canadian writers, including Sinclair Ross and Ethel Wilson, remained unrecognized in their own day, she suspects the pendulum has swung too far and cautions reviewers against parochialism.

In "Books That Mattered to Me" (1981), Laurence discusses novels that influenced her. She asks, "Were there no women writers who spoke to my childhood?" and replies, "Not many." She found role models in L.M. Montgomery's and Emily Murphy's novels, however, although it was years before she realized how much Murphy and McClung contributed to having women designated "persons" in Manitoba in 1929 or how Montgomery and McClung helped Manitoba women win the vote. Their heroines contributed to Laurence's conviction that a woman could be "an intelligent, independent-minded person who was determined to pursue her own vocation as well as being a wife and mother," ultimately inspiring the strong heroines of her Manawaka fiction.

Laurence championed many promising writers during her tenure as writer-in-residence at Canadian universities, including the University of Toronto in 1969–70, the University of Western Ontario in 1971, and Trent University in 1972. "Voices from Future Places," about her residence at Massey College, confirms her generosity in fostering blossoming talent and her belief that "the act of writing is in itself some kind of act of hope." Her reasons for why students write may suggest her own motives – "Therapy. Loneliness. Exhibitionism. Money. The desperate need to communicate." Although Jack Ludwig advised her against "acting as confessor-figure, headshrinker, parent-substitute, money-lender, marriage-broker, etcetera," she became "a knockdownable parent-figure, a financial consultant, an amateur friend," calling herself the "Ann Landers of Massey College" offering advice to the lovelorn (*Dance on the Earth*, 195).

Fourteen universities conferred honorary degrees on Margaret Laurence, and on such occasions she was invited to address convocation. She took these invitations as opportunities to advocate for CanLit. "The Case for Canadian Literature" was delivered at Simon Fraser University's convocation in 1977. She encourages graduands to support Canadian literature in their futures as parents and teachers. She was also invited to deliver encomiums on the retirement or honouring of literary celebrities, including W.L. Morton, Malcolm Ross, Clara Thomas, Lois Wilson, and Marian Engel. Her role as chancellor of Trent University, 1981–83, gave her ample opportunities to celebrate her literary heroes. These unpublished tributes are included in this collection.[7]

"The Artist Then, Now, and Always"

Laurence's interests extended beyond literature, however. She embraced many causes, including social-political, cultural, and ecological. They inspired her to write essays aiming to energize community engagement at regional and international levels on not only Canadian unity, literature, and the arts, but also on ethical issues, including nuclear disarmament, pornography and censorship, pro-choice legislation, the environment, and government treatment of Canada's Indigenous peoples. While her earlier essays address literature, including her own fiction and Canadian literature generally, her later essays and speeches addressing environmental concerns are more urgent in tone, as she attempts to persuade her audience to nonviolent action.

Laurence believed that the writer has a responsibility to the community, as she affirms in "The Artist Then, Now, and Always" (1984). Here she emphasizes the artist's moral responsibility to honour the past, protect the present, safeguard the future, and celebrate life, for art is "an act of faith, an acknowledgment of the profound mystery at the core of life." She revered all life on earth, both human and animal, citing our responsibility as guardians of our planet because "we, humankind, are the custodians of that earth." In "'Peace': A Word's Meaning" she seeks the "means of ensuring the survival of our only home, Earth." She affirms in *Dance on the Earth*, "I continue to believe, all evidence to the contrary, that it is not too late to save our only home, the planet earth, and that it is not too late, even at this very late date, to learn to live on and with the earth, in harmony with all creatures. Part of that belief is social belief, part of it is religious faith" (98). In "Sources" she affirms that the most important elements in her writing are "people and places," emphasizing her sense of "my place, the prairies, and of my people." She often quotes the blessing "Peace on earth, good will to men," representing her two causes, environmentalism and humanitarianism.

Conservation of the Environment: "The Rape of the Planet"

Laurence's major interventions regarding stewardship of the planet involve ecology and nuclear disarmament. She advocated for conservation in her creative articles, as previously noted, before ecology became a widespread concern. In "A Matter of Life or Death" she writes, "We had taken it for granted that through wars, through disasters, yet would the earth endure forever. It was clear to many of us in 1945 that this was no longer to be taken for granted." But she urges readers still to hope: "Even after all the failures – the wars, the pollution, the radioactive waste, the real possibility of nuclear reactors melting down, the slaughter of whales and dolphins – even after all these atrocities, I believe that we cannot and must not give up" (*Dance on the Earth*, 98–9).

Laurence loved Canadian landscapes: "The land still draws me more than other lands," she affirms in *Heart of a Stranger* (173). Her love for this land led her to value the environment – both land and water. She subscribes to the Aboriginal belief that the land belongs not to humanity, but to God. In "Listen, Just Listen" she refers to "the taking away of the land from the native peoples by colonialists who believed men could actually own the land, whereas the original inhabitants believed that the land belonged to God, the Great Spirit, and was for mankind's shared use." She agrees with George Woodcock's distinction, in *The Métis Chief and His Lost World*, between those who "'lived in and on and with the environment – whether they were Indians or Métis – and those who wished to live off it, to dominate and exploit it" (*Heart of a Stranger*, 163).

While she laments people-slaying, she considers river-slaying a more heinous crime. In "Where the World Began," she laments, "When I see the killing of our lakes and rivers with industrial wastes, I feel rage and despair" (*Heart of a Stranger*, 172). In "Don't Whisper Sudden; I Scare Easy" she deplores "the rape of the planet, the poisoning of lakes and air." In "Man of Our People" she exhorts, "witness the killing of rivers and lakes; the killing of the whales; the proliferation of apartment blocks on irreplaceable farmlands" (*Heart of a Stranger*, 167).

In "Down East" she sheds her "prairie chip" to marvel at the maples, the "scarlet flames of trees" that defeat even the skilful "wordsmith" (*Diviners*, 33). They help her understand the Group of Seven's obsession with Ontario landscapes and why "Canadian writers couldn't see the people for the trees." "Scratch a Canadian, and you find a phony pioneer," she quips.

Never a city-lover, Laurence preferred small towns, like Neepawa. Her admiration for Ontario landscapes, however, inspired her to purchase her cedar cabin on the Otonabee River, her "personal talisman." Jack McClelland, her "Boss" at "McStew," as she labelled McClelland and Stewart, had a sign made for the Shack declaring, under a parody of Ontario's coat-of-arms, "No Visitors Allowed: By Order of the Government of Ontario. By Authority of J.G. McClelland, Servant & Publisher" (*Heart of a Stranger*, 147).

Laurence equates pollution with imperialism. Always opposed to colonialism, she laments, "When I see our industries and natural resources increasingly taken over by America, I feel an overwhelming discouragement" (*Heart of a Stranger*, 172). She acknowledges Canada's complicity in this invasion, however, admitting, "it is we ourselves who have sold such a large amount of our birthright for a mess of plastic Progress" (*Heart of a Stranger*, 172). She chastises Imperial Oil for resource extraction that diminishes the prairie water table. In 1974 she refused to write a script for *A New Land*, a television series about Canadian settlers made by the independent production company Nielsen-Ferns, because it was to be funded by Imperial Oil. As Laura Davis observes, "Laurence's rejection of Nielsen-Ferns' and Imperial Oil's offer is an extension of her broader condemnation of imperialism, the nuclear arms race, and indeed war itself" (Davis, "Margaret Laurence's Correspondence with Imperial Oil," 61).

Nuclear Disarmament: "Peace on Earth"

In "'Peace': A Word's Meaning" Laurence pleads for "peace on earth" through de-escalation of nuclear munitions by the superpowers. She sees the nuclear arms race as the greatest threat to world peace. In "Operation Dismantle" she declares, "As a writer, I believe that artists have a moral responsibility to work against the nuclear arms race." She pleads for nuclear disarmament in several 1980s essays and addresses. Indeed, her repetitiveness in these essays, necessitating discreet selection, is a testament to her passionate, almost obsessive, attitude to the cause. In "A Matter of Life or Death" (1983) she calls nuclear disarmament "the most pressing practical, moral, and spiritual issue of our times," on the grounds that nuclear war could destroy humanity and the earth itself.

Her convocation addresses are no longer filled with the encouraging, optimistic rhetoric we expect on such celebratory occasions. Instead, she laments the heritage of violence that her generation has passed on: "You, my generation's inheritors, inherit a deeply troubled world." She explains how her generation, graduating in 1947, comprehended "the insanity of wars": "on September 5, 1939, my world changed out of all recognition, forever" (*Dance on the Earth*, 72). The insanity of war came home to her following Dieppe, a 1942 battle where many Canadians, especially prairie men, lost their lives. She writes about Dieppe in *The Diviners*, as Jules Tonnerre recalls the carnage to Morag Gunn. There were no boys in Peggy's grade 12 class because they were all fighting overseas (*Dance on the Earth*, 83–4). One boy she knew died in a burning tank. In "My Final Hour," her 1983 Trent University address, she appeals to students to advocate for disarmament.

In "'Peace': A Word's Meaning," Laurence, a writer who respects language, focuses on its abuse by advertisers, politicians, and, especially, militarists, whose jargon terms, including "overkill" and "megadeaths," distort language, using it to disguise the potential human suffering caused by nuclear weapons, as language becomes a vehicle of deception – as George Orwell argues in "Politics and the English Language."

Laurence was horrified by the bombing of Hiroshima and Nagasaki by the American military on 6 and 9 August 1945 that killed tens of thousands, "etching their shadows on the stones." Joy Kogawa recalls this horror in her 1981 novel *Obasan*. Laurence extends that horror to a condemnation of nuclear weapons, whose damage would be far more devastating. She recalls, "We were the first generation in the whole world to know that humankind had the power to destroy itself, all other creatures, and the planet on which we lived" (*Dance on the Earth*, 100). Her lament encompasses subsequent hostilities in Vietnam and racial "cleansing" in Argentina and the Soviet Union. Finally, she exhorts graduands to refuse to give way to despair, to believe in faith, hope, and love, and to honour, protect, and celebrate life.

"Operation Dismantle" (1982) states her objections to the theory that escalation of weaponry prevents nuclear war, labelling it "the Precipice Theory" and "a deadly fantasy." She claims nuclear build-up makes nuclear war more, not less, likely. She advocates for reallocating the billions of dollars spent on munitions to resolving social and environmental ills, including poverty and pollution. In "A Matter of Life or Death" she argues that nuclear arms have ceased to be a deterrent as the Cold War escalates. She fears our leaders may "succeed in destroying all life on earth, not only humankind, but all creatures who share this planet with us" (*Dance on the Earth*, 221).

In "Canadian Third Track," where she condemns the escalation of nuclear weapons by the superpowers, she notes American militarists' announcement that "only 500 million people would be killed" in a nuclear attack, as reported in George Kennan's *The Nuclear Delusion*.[8] In several essays she laments the "psychic numbing" identified by Dr Helen Caldicott, equating it with despair, which, as the Christian Church Fathers taught, is a deadly sin.

Is Canada immune from blame? In "'Peace': A Word's Meaning," she acknowledges "Canada's complicity in the nuclear arms race" by allowing the American government to test Cruise missiles, designed as a "first-strike weapon," over Canadian skies, and by supplying guidance systems for those missiles at Ontario's Litton Plant with Canadian taxpayers' dollars. She also condemns Canada's selling nuclear reactors to Argentina and supplying fuel for those reactors, since

Argentina was a repressive regime and was, she believed, attempting to develop nuclear weapons of its own.

Laurence's patriotism is manifest in her anti-war articles. She advocates for an international role for Canada as a peacemaker and mediator between the United States and the Soviet Union in de-escalating the arms race, thus increasing Canada's credibility on the world stage. She encourages her audience to work nonviolently for peace, urging them to join Operation Dismantle and Project Ploughshares, as she did, claiming, "Our ultimate aim must be no less than the abolition of wars of any kind." "This is my personal credo."

"Many of us," she asserts, have struggled against the awful, the unconscionable, nuclear arms race" (*Dance on the Earth*, 100), as she herself did by participating in Terri Nash and Bonnie Klein's film *Speaking Our Peace* and by serving on the board of Energy Probe, founded in 1969 to research nuclear power and radiation concerns and address energy policy in Canada. "I have taken as active a part as I could in the entire peace movement," adding, "I have often felt, in fact, that as one grows older, one should take not fewer risks, but more" (*Dance on the Earth*, 219).

Laurence commends the United Nations for declaring 1986 the International Year of Peace. She commends peacemakers and hopes for "peace on earth," citing Jesus's sermon on the mount: "Blessed are the peacemakers, for they shall be called the children of God." She recalls the injunction in Deuteronomy: "I have set before you life and death, blessing and cursing; therefore choose life, that both thou and thy seed may live." She concludes, not with optimism, but with hope – hope for the survival of the planet and humanity, praying, "May our hearts be touched, our minds opened, our voices raised."

Equality in Diversity: "Good Will toward Men"

In discussing the importance of "people and places" in "Sources," Laurence concludes that, crucial as the environment is, "nevertheless, the people [are] more important than the place." Well versed in the United Church hymnal, she often recalls the "Old Hundredth," "All people that on earth do dwell," the hymn that catalyzes Hagar's epiphany in *The Stone Angel* (291–2). Laurence believed passionately in the value of the individual, regardless of nationality, race, or ethnicity: "one of my main concerns has been to show the uniqueness, the value, and the reality of the human individual" (*Dance on the Earth*, 99). She advocates for re-spect for all people who dwell on earth: "Within our diversity lies our strength ... Differences are to be honoured, recognized, and understood on both sides" ("Listen, Just Listen"). In her 1981 "Reply to the Toast to Canada," she says, "My prayer for Canada is that we may learn to value more greatly the multi-faceted nature of our land and our heritage, and to respect more greatly our differences," exhorting her audience to, "Try to feel, in your heart's core, the reality of others."[9]

In her memoir, Laurence professes, "I am a Christian, or at least aspire to be, although perhaps not an orthodox one" (*Dance on the Earth*, 13), and she draws a close connection between her faith and her fiction. "I believe that two of the major threads running throughout all my work have been, in some form or another, religious and socio-political themes" (*Dance on the Earth*, 99). She re-iterates that claim, that religious and political beliefs underpin her fiction, in "Ivory Tower or Grassroots?"

Two ideologies influenced young Peggy Wemyss. First was the social gospel, founded on the summary of the law. When a lawyer asks Jesus which is the great commandment in the law, Jesus replies, "Thou shalt love the Lord thy God with all thy heart and with all thy soul and with all thy mind. This is the first and great commandment. And the second is like unto it, Thou shalt love thy neighbour as thyself" (Matthew 22:37–39 KJV).[10] In "My Final Hour" she declares, "I want to proclaim my belief in the social gospel, as a Christian, a woman, a writer, a mother, and a member of humanity, a sharer in a life that I believe in some way to be informed by the Holy Spirit." The second ideology derives from North Winnipeg's Old Left, which she encountered while a student at United College and an employee at the *Winnipeg Citizen* and the YWCA. "North Winnipeg in the 1940s decided a lot of my life" (*Dance on the Earth*, 108).[11] The Old Left involved a socialist approach exemplified by the Co-operative Commonwealth Feder-ation, precursor of the New Democratic Party. With its support of "the struggles for justice, the necessity to proclaim – in the words of St Paul – the qualities of faith, hope, and love," in Laurence's words, it appealed to the idealistic young au-thor. "I was then, and have remained, a Christian Social Democrat" (*Dance on the Earth*, 107) who espouses the "liberal conscience and the Christian outlook" of that movement (*Dance on the Earth*, 171). She upholds "faith, hope, and love" and opposes "racism, violence, oppression, violations of civil liberties" through-out her essays, including her "Message to the Inheritors," convinced that we should "express our beliefs in social justice, in human relationships of love and

value, and in the possibility and necessity of peoples of different cultures communicating with one another and trying to understand one another." "Despite
my Presbyterian background," she wryly admits, "there has always been a faint
streak of the wild-eyed evangelist in me" (*Heart of a Stranger*, 112).

Laurence champions Indigenous peoples everywhere – from the Scots of the
Highland Clearances to the Ghanaians of colonial Britain to the Aboriginal
peoples of Canada. In "Ten Years' Sentences" she laments "the appalling grip on
the human heart of tribalism in its hate aspect." She sympathizes with the dis-
advantaged, be they Scottish crofters, Manitoba francophones, or Prairie Métis.
In "The Artist Then, Now, and Always" she asserts, "Our aim must be no less than
human and caring justice, and peace … for all people that on earth do dwell."

Laurence's own ancestors were dispossessed. Her paternal family were Scots
who hailed from the Lowlands of Fifeshire, and her Irish maternal forebears emigrated from County Tyrone around 1850. She lamented the Irish driven out of
their land by the potato famine; she was haunted by the shattering of the Scottish
clans by English cannon at Culloden in 1746[12] and the Scots driven out of their
crofts by the English. The dispossession of Scottish crofters appears in *The Diviners* where "The Dispossessed," a painting by Dan McRaith, Morag's Scottish
lover, is inspired by that event (402).

Laurence's sympathies lie with the "Other," especially those defeated and
subjugated by colonialist powers equipped with technologically superior weaponry. Her 1964 essay "The Poem and the Spear" (*Heart of a Stranger*, 31–58)
celebrates Somali leader Mahammed 'Abdille Hasan, known to the Somalis as
the Sayyid, or Lord, and to the British as "The Mad Mullah" (*Heart of a
Stranger*, 32). He led the Dervishes in their revolt against the English using
what she calls "the strangest of all military weapons – poetry" (31). She admires
this early nationalist leader for the brilliance of his poetry and his idealism,
demonstrating her partisanship with the valiant but vanquished underdog.
The seven years she spent in Somalia and Ghana informed her sympathy for
all African countries colonized by Europe, and she extended that attitude to
Canada as a postcolonial nation.

Her empathy with Canada's Aboriginal peoples, especially the Canadian
Prairie Métis and their leaders Louis Riel and Gabriel Dumont, is manifested in
"Man of Our People" (*Heart of a Stranger*, 161–7), which celebrates Dumont as
"chief of the Saskatchewan Métis" (164). "The tragic story of the last stand of the
Métis has haunted me" (162), she reports, for she believes the Métis, like Scottish

Highlanders and nomadic Somalis, were victims of "the colonialist-imperialist wars of Britain" (163). "Man of Our People" is a particularly clear example of how Laurence's essays illuminate her fiction, because it relates to her compassionate portrayal of the Tonnerres, her fictional Métis family, in her Manawaka Cycle, especially *The Diviners*, where Jules's "Tale of Rider Tonnerre" celebrates his ancestor, the Chevalier, "Prince of the Braves," leader of the Métis, or Bois-brûlés. Rudy Wiebe, author of *The Temptations of Big Bear* (1973), advised Laurence, before her pilgrimage to Batoche, "When you get there, listen. Just listen," referring to the voices of spirits of Métis killed on that battlefield by Canadian forces under General Middleton in 1885. Significantly, her final, unfinished novel, "Dance on the Earth," which she attempted to compose in 1983, began in 1885.[13]

Laurence empathized not only with African peoples but also with African-Americans. She wrote an "Open Letter to the Mother of Joe Bass," a twelve-year-old boy shot by police in Detroit in 1968, in which she skilfully describes the anguish of the mother by drawing parallels with her relationship to her own son, and at the same time pointedly comments on the differences that racism creates. She addresses his mother: "I cannot say them. It is forced upon me to say us" – a view reflected in "Tribalism as Us Versus Them."[14]

Laurence was horrified by the Holocaust, in which six million Jews were exterminated in Europe during the Third Reich. The realization that human beings are capable of such evil marked the end of Eden for her generation. Adele Wiseman, whose Winnipeg family Peggy came to love, brought home for Laurence the suffering of the Jewish people during the Shoah. Adele and the Wisemans became the models for Ella and the Gerson family in *The Diviners*. The two life-long friends frequently concluded their correspondence with the encouraging injunction, "*Coraggio. Avanti!*"

Canada is not immune from blame, however. Laurence laments its government's treatment of Canadian citizens of Japanese ancestry who were interned and stripped of their property in British Columbia during the Second World War and who never received proper reparation. In a 1985 letter to the *Toronto Star*, she asks, rhetorically, "Are Holocaust victims expected to die again and again?" She declares, "I am proud to be a Canadian, but I am not proud of the way the Japanese Canadians were treated in World War II, nor do I claim that this disgraceful episode in our history never happened." She asks, "O Canada, where are the cries of public outrage and the concern for justice and humanity?"[15]

Margaret Laurence felt enormous anger on behalf of the underdog, whether Japanese Canadians, Europe's Jews, or Canada's Indigenous peoples. In her 2007 "Margaret Laurence Lecture," Margaret Atwood summarizes the origins of Laurence's outrage: "Here comes Margaret Laurence, then – determined to be a writer. This is the world she stepped into. A Depression childhood, a dead mother, then a dead father, then a war that wiped out a lot of the young men she knew; then a literary world in which it was commonplace to say that women couldn't write, and neither could Canadians, and any woman or any Canadian who tried was likely to meet more than one big slap-down. It's hard to imagine the sheer guts or perhaps obsessiveness that it must have taken to persevere in what must have seemed a futile and indeed a loony endeavour." Atwood adds, "Writing – for Margaret Laurence – was not a hobby. Writing was not a hockey book on which you might spend fifteen minutes a day. Writing was a life-and-death struggle. The metaphor she most often used about it was Jacob wrestling with the angel" (319).

In a 1986 broadcast on CBC radio's *As It Happens*, Laurence's feminism is manifest in her desire to valorize "our bravest foremothers," those heroic women whose stories have remained unrecorded. Laurence considers Madeleine Wilkie Dumont, Gabriel Dumont's Métis wife, a hero. She tended the wounded in her home after the battle of Batoche; she risked imprisonment by taking supplies to her husband hiding in the woods following the defeat of Riel's "rebels" by General Middleton's army; and she followed Dumont into exile in the United States, dying far from her Saskatchewan home two decades before him.

Some people, including her Métis friend, artist Alice Williams, speculate that Laurence herself had Anishnaabe ancestry. Laurence envied her friend, historian Jean Murray Cole, for having an Aboriginal ancestor about whom she published *Exile in the Wilderness: The Biography of Chief Factor Archibald McDonald 1790–1853*, and often claimed that, if she had an Aboriginal ancestor herself, she would be proud to proclaim it. There is no evidence to support such a claim, however, despite her appearance, which led cruel Neepawa adolescents to call her "the Squaw" – an indication of the attitude of some residents to both Laurence and Indigenous citizens. Laurence's desire to possess the courage of Madeleine Wilkie Dumont and that heritage is reflected in Morag Gunn of *The Diviners*, who imagines a foremother who shares her name and strengthens and inspires her. In "Man of Our People," Laurence asks, "Will we ever reach a point when it is no longer necessary to say Them and Us? I believe we must reach that point or perish. Canadians who, like myself, are the descendants of various settlers, many of whom came to this country as oppressed or dispossessed peoples, must hear native peoples' voices and ultimately become part of them, for they speak not only of the soul-searing injustices done to them but also of their rediscovered sense of self-worth and their ability to tell and teach the things needed to be known" (*Heart of a Stranger*, 166).

Within contemporary Canada, Laurence also empathizes with the Québécois. In "Listen, Just Listen" she affirms, "The oppression ... of the Québécois is part of an entire system of colonialism and oppression." In "Quebec's 'Freedom' Is a Vital Concern, but Freedom Itself Is That and More,"[16] Laurence, as a fervent nationalist, hopes to see Canada remain unified. As a person who sympathizes with the oppressed, however, she wants to see Quebec recognized as a cultural and linguistic entity within the dominion of Canada. She feels comradeship with other "non-colonial" (*Dance on the Earth*, 185) writers, including Canadian authors Gabrielle Roy, a francophone author, and Rudy Wiebe, a Mennonite, and Nigerian authors Chinua Achebe and Wole Soyinka.

Laurence's sympathy with Quebec is countered by her belief in the Confederation of Canada, demonstrated in her article on Quebec's freedom mentioned above, where she argues, "Any new constitution will have to recognize the fact that the Québécois are a nation, bound together by ancestral roots, culture, language, religion." She adds, however, that, if a new constitution recognizes the sovereignty of Quebec, it will be obliged to address the grievances of other regions, including "the West Coast, the Prairies, the Atlantic Provinces, and above all, the grievances, needs, and rights of the native peoples, who have suffered more injustice than any other people in this land."[17] She argues that, without Quebec, Canada would be "poorer in spirit and in culture," but would not "disintegrate and fall prey to the United States." She fears that Quebec anglophones might be deprived of their civil rights by Quebec's separatist movement. She wishes she could repeat to Quebec citizens Rudy Wiebe's words, "Listen. Just listen."

Laurence's feminism is a strong theme in her later essays. In her 1985 speech for the "YWCA Woman of the Year Award" she pays tribute to "the true heroines, our mothers, our grandmothers, our great-grandmothers," whose achievements have gone unrecorded, and recommends "a steadfast recognition of women's rights and needs, of women's immeasurable contribution to all societies, and our ongoing struggle for equality." In "A Constant Hope: Women in the Now and Future High Tech Age," she challenges the notion that women have not played a role in the practical, material, technological, and manufacturing side of a culture, arguing that women have always operated machinery "when it was to the advantage of society for them to do so, but always for poorer wages than their male counterparts." She focuses on women writers, especially single mothers, who must keep house, raise children, and work as freelance journalists to make a living. She is happy if computers save them work by making editing easier. She recalls a distinguished woman writer who used her modest Canada Council grant to buy a washing machine, saving herself precious hours for writing. Carol Shields used her $600 Canada Council Grant to send her husband's shirts to the laundry and hire housecleaners. Laurence hopes greater equality will reign between men and women. She concludes by quoting the motto on the Scots plaid pin that she describes in *The Diviners*: "My Hope Is Constant in Thee," thus explaining the title of her essay.

In "The Greater Evil," Laurence debates which is the greater evil: pornography or censorship. Although opposed to censorship, she detests pornography, especially "kiddie porn" and pornography involving the torturing and demeaning of real women in the proliferating market of videos and magazines. She clarifies her conflicting attitudes: "I absolutely hate, despise, and loathe real pornography, films or porn magazines that make use of actual women and children in situations that are horribly degrading and demeaning. I cannot really believe, though, that the printed word should ever be censored, however terrible it may be" (*Dance on the Earth*, 216). She distinguishes between erotic and pornographic literature. As a self-styled "feminist and strong supporter of civil liberties and free speech," she defends our federal obscenity laws, while acknowledging the difficulty of determining "public good." Laurence dislikes censorship and promotes free speech, but urges citizens to protest "the brutalities and callousness of pornography."

In "Ivory Tower or Grassroots? The Novelist as Socio-political Being," Laurence explains how living in Somalia and Ghana in the 1950s, when both were emerging from colonial domination, inspired her belief in independence for Canada: "I had come back home to Canada via Africa, both physically and spiritually."[18] She extends her theme of independence from postcolonial Africa to Canada and the position of women: "[Canada's] situation at the time, like that of all peoples with colonial mentalities, was not unlike that of women in our society." These parallels encouraged her growing awareness of "the dilemma and powerlessness of women" and inspired her emphasis on the "quest for physical and spiritual freedom, the quest for relationships of equality and communication." Realizing how women have been colonized under patriarchy, she applauds the suffragette movement of the 1910s and the women's liberation movement of the 1960s. Her experience in African countries – Ghana and Somalia – preparing for independence led her to emphasize "the promised land of one's own inner freedom" in the self-empowerment of the Canadian female protagonists in her Manawaka cycle – Hagar Shipley of *The Stone Angel*, Rachel Cameron of *A Jest of God*, Stacey Cameron MacAindra of *The Fire-Dwellers*, Vanessa MacLeod of *A Bird in the House*, and Morag Gunn of *The Diviners*.

Laurence's essays, the most neglected element of her oeuvre, constitute the missing link that connects her beliefs with her fiction. They reveal her commitment to literature, particularly Canadian literature, and to Canada itself. They also reveal her passionate concerns regarding ecology and nuclear disarmament and equality, especially of Indigenous peoples and women, and they illuminate the socio-political undercurrents of her fiction, inviting us to read her fiction with fresh eyes. Indeed, the issues she addresses, especially nuclear disarmament and the environment, are more pressing now than ever before in this time of drastic pollution, climate change, and nuclear buildups.

NORA FOSTER STOVEL

Notes on the Text

Laurence's essays have been reproduced as exactly as possible, with only the occasional strategic comma inserted for clarification. Where necessary, typographical and other errors have been silently corrected, but such errors in Laurence's writings are rare indeed. The spelling has been altered in a few places for the sake of consistency.

Unless otherwise stated, words of Laurence quoted in the introduction to each essay are drawn from the essay in question. All references to Laurence's 1976 collection of travel essays, *Heart of a Stranger*, are to the University of Alberta Press 2003 edition.

PART ONE

Essays about Laurence's Writing: "Gadgetry or Growing"

Sources

"Sources" was first published in Mosaic *in 1970, and later collected under the title "A Place to Stand On" in* Heart of a Stranger *in 1976. Laurence agrees with Greene's statement in "The Young Dickens," an essay in* The Lost Childhood and Other Essays *(1952), with which she prefaces her article, that authors attempt to communicate their private world, inspired by their personal past, through their writing. She finds the same view about writing expressed by contemporary African writers. Manawaka, her "town of the mind," was inspired by her hometown of Neepawa, Manitoba. Laurence introduced this opening essay in* Heart of a Stranger *with the following commentary: "Written in 1970, this article deals both with my debt to African writers and with my concepts of a writer's sources. I had not yet begun writing* The Diviners, *but it was very much in my mind and I was soon to begin it. The lines quoted here from one of Al Purdy's poems were the same lines I later quoted at the beginning of the novel. A rather curious aspect of this article is that it deals with the theme of survival. At that time, Margaret Atwood's* Survival *had not yet been written, and when she was writing her thematic study of Canadian literature, she had not read this article."[1]*

> The creative writer perceives his world once and for all in childhood and
> adolescence, and his whole career is an effort to illustrate his private world
> in terms of the great public world we all share.
> Graham Greene, *Collected Essays*

I believe that Graham Greene is right in this statement. It does not mean that the individual does not change after adolescence. On the contrary, it underlines the necessity for change. For the writer, one way of discovering oneself, of changing from the patterns of childhood and adolescence to those of adulthood, is through the explorations inherent in the writing itself. In the case of a great many writers, this exploration at some point – and perhaps at all points – involves an attempt to understand one's background and one's past, sometimes even a more distant past which one has not personally experienced.

This sort of exploration can be clearly seen in the works of contemporary African writers, many of whom re-create their people's past in novels and plays in order to recover a sense of themselves, an identity and a feeling of value from which they were separated by two or three generations of colonialism and missionizing. They have found it necessary, in other words, to come to terms with their ancestors and their gods in order to be able to accept the past and be at peace with the dead, without being stifled or threatened by that past.

Oddly enough, it was only several years ago, when I began doing some research into contemporary Nigerian writing and its background, that I began to see how much my own writing had followed the same pattern – the attempt to assimilate the past, partly in order to be freed from it, partly in order to try to understand myself and perhaps others of my generation, through seeing where we had come from.[2]

I was fortunate in going to Africa when I did – in my early twenties – because for some years I was so fascinated by the African scene that I was prevented from writing an autobiographical first novel. I don't say there is anything wrong in autobiographical novels, but it would not have been the right thing for me – my view of the prairie town from which I had come was still too prejudiced and distorted by closeness. I had to get farther away from it before I could begin to see it. Also, as it turned out ultimately, the kind of novel which I can best handle is one in which the fictional characters are very definitely themselves, not me, the kind of novel in which I can feel a deep sense of connection with the main character without a total identification, which for me would prevent a necessary distancing.

I always knew that one day I would have to stop writing about Africa and go back to my own people, my own place of belonging, but when I began to do this, I was extremely nervous about the outcome. I did not consciously choose any particular time in history, or any particular characters. The reverse seemed to be true. The character of Hagar in *The Stone Angel* seemed almost to choose me. Later, though, I recognized that in some way not at all consciously understood by me at the time I had had to begin approaching my background and my past through my grandparents' generation, the generation of pioneers of Scots-Presbyterian origin, who had been among the first to people the town I called Manawaka. This was where my own roots began. Other past generations of my father's family had lived in Scotland, but for me, my people's real past – my own real past – was not connected except distantly with Scotland; indeed, this was true for Hagar as well, for she was born in Manawaka.

The name Manawaka is an invented one, but it had been in my mind since I was about seventeen or eighteen, when I first began to think about writing something set in a prairie town. Manawaka is not my hometown of Neepawa – it has elements of Neepawa, especially in some of the descriptions of places, such as the cemetery on the hill or the Wachakwa valley through which ran the small brown river which was the river of my childhood.[3] In almost every way, however, Manawaka is not so much any one prairie town as an amalgam of many prairie towns. Most of all, I like to think, it is simply itself, a town of the mind, my own private world, as Graham Greene says, which one hopes will ultimately relate to the outer world which we all share.[4]

When one thinks of the influence of a place on one's writing, two aspects come to mind. First, the physical presence of the place itself – its geography, its appearance. Second, the people. For me, the second aspect of environment is the most important, although in everything I have written which is set in Canada, whether or not actually set in Manitoba, somewhere some of my memories of the physical appearance of the prairies come in. I had, as a child and as an adolescent, ambivalent feelings about the prairies. I still have them, although they no longer bother me. I wanted then to get out of the small town and go far away, and yet I felt the protectiveness of that atmosphere, too.[5] I felt the loneliness and the isolation of the land itself, and yet I always considered southern Manitoba to be very beautiful, and I still do. I doubt if I will ever live there again, but those poplar bluffs and the blackness of that soil and the way in which the sky is open from one side of the horizon to the other – these are things I will carry inside my skull for as long as I live, with the vividness of recall that only our first home can have for us.

Nevertheless, the people were more important than the place. Hagar in *The Stone Angel* was not drawn from life, but she incorporates many of the qualities of my grandparents' generation. Her speech is their speech, and her gods their gods. I think I never recognized until I wrote that novel just how mixed my own feelings were toward that whole generation of pioneers – how difficult they were to live with, how authoritarian, how unbending, how afraid to show love, many of them, and how willing to show anger. And yet, they had inhabited a wilderness and made it fruitful. They were, in the end, great survivors, and for that I love and value them.

The final exploration of this aspect of my background came when I wrote – over the past six or seven years – *A Bird in the House*, a number of short stories set in Manawaka and based upon my childhood and my childhood family, the only semi-autobiographical fiction I have ever written.[6] I did not realize until I had finished the final story in the series how much all these stories are dominated by the figure of my maternal grandfather, who came of Irish Protestant stock. Perhaps it was through writing these stories that I finally came to see my grandfather not only as the repressive authoritarian figure from my childhood, but also as a boy who had to leave school in Ontario when he was about twelve, after his father's death, and who as a young man went to Manitoba by sternwheeler and walked the fifty miles from Winnipeg to Portage la Prairie, where he settled for some years before moving to Neepawa. He was a very hard man in many ways, but he had had a very hard life. I don't think I knew any of this, really knew it, until I had finished those stories. I don't think I ever knew, either, until that moment how much I owed to him. One sentence, near the end of the final story, may show what I mean: "I had feared and fought the old man, yet he proclaimed himself in my veins."

My writing, then, has been my own attempt to come to terms with the past. I see this process as the gradual one of freeing oneself from the stultifying aspect of the past, while at the same time beginning to see its true value – which, in the case of my own people (by which I mean the total community, not just my particular family), was a determination to survive against whatever odds.

The theme of survival – not just physical survival, but the preservation of some human dignity and in the end some human warmth and ability to reach out and touch others – this is, I have come to think, an almost inevitable theme for a writer such as I, who came from a Scots-Irish background of stern values and hard work and puritanism, and who grew up during the drought and Depression of the thirties and then the war.

This theme runs through two of my novels other than *The Stone Angel* (in which it is, of course, the dominant theme). In *A Jest of God* and *The Fire-Dwellers*, both Rachel and Stacey are in their very different ways threatened by the past and by the various inadequacies each feels in herself. In the end, and again in their very different ways and out of their very different dilemmas, each finds within herself an ability to survive – not just to go on living, but to change and to move into new areas of life. Neither book is optimistic. Optimism in this world seems impossible to me. But in each novel there is some hope, and that is a different thing entirely.

If Graham Greene is right – as I think he is – in his belief that a writer's career is "an effort to illustrate his private world in terms of the great public world we all share," then I think it is understandable that so much of my writing relates to the kind of prairie town in which I was born and in which I first began to be aware of myself. Writing, for me, has to be set firmly in some soil, some place, some outer and inner territory which might be described in anthropological terms as "cultural background." But I do not believe that this kind of writing needs therefore to be parochial. If Hagar in *The Stone Angel* has any meaning, it is the same as that of an old woman anywhere, having to deal with the reality of dying. On the other hand, she is not an old woman anywhere. She is very much a person who belongs in the same kind of prairie Scots-Presbyterian background as I do, and it was, of course, people like Hagar who created that background, with all its flaws and its strengths. In a poem entitled "Roblin's Mills, Circa 1842," Al Purdy said,

> They had their being once
> and left a place to stand on[7]

They did indeed, and this is the place we are standing on, for better and for worse.

I remember saying once, three or four years ago, that I felt I had written myself out of that prairie town. I know better now. My future writing may not be set in that town – and indeed, my novel *The Fire-Dwellers* was set in Vancouver. I may not always write fiction set in Canada. But somewhere, perhaps in the memories of some characters, Manawaka will probably always be there, simply because whatever I am was shaped and formed in that sort of place, and my way of seeing, however much it may have changed over the years, remains in some enduring way that of a small-town prairie person.

Ten Years' Sentences

"Ten Years' Sentences," an ironic reference to Laurence's career as a writer – "a life sentence of sentences" – was first published in Canadian Literature *(1969) and republished in Woodcock,* A Place to Stand On. *Recollecting the five optimistic fiction and nonfiction texts that emerged from her "seven years' love affair with a continent," she chronicles her transition from writing about Africa to writing about her native land of Canada in her Manawaka Saga.*

Almost exactly ten years ago I was sitting in the study of our house in Vancouver, filled with the black Celtic gloom which sometimes strikes. I had just received a letter from an American publisher[1] which said, among other things, that their chief reader reported himself to be "only reasonably nauseated" by the lengthy interior monologues of the main character of my first novel, *This Side Jordan*. If I could see my way clear to reconsidering parts of the novel, they would be willing to look at it again. More revision, I thought, was out of the question. I had already rewritten half the book from scratch when I decided, after leaving Africa and getting a fresh perspective on colonial society, that I'd been unfair to the European characters. More work I couldn't face. A quick cup of hemlock would be easier. However, as we were a little short on hemlock just then, I got out the manuscript instead. I hadn't looked at it for months, and I saw to my consternation that the gent with the upset stomach was undeniably right in some ways. I managed to cut some of the more emotive prose (although not enough) and lived to bless him for his brutal criticism.

Ten years ago I was thirty-two years old and incredibly naive about writing and publishing. I had never talked with any publisher face-to-face. I knew only one other writer as a close friend – Adele Wiseman, whose letters throughout the years had heartened me.[2] I had had one short story published in *Queen's*

Quarterly[3] a few years earlier, and had been encouraged by Malcolm Ross,[4] the then-editor. I had also recently had a story published in *Prism*,[5] and Ethel Wilson[6] had graciously written to say she liked it – that meant more to me than I can ever express and began a friendship which has been one of the most valued in my life.

Can it only have been ten years ago? What has changed? Everything. The world and myself. In some ways it's been the most difficult and most interesting decade of my life, for almost everything I've written which has been publishable has been written in these years. I've mysteriously managed to survive the writing of six more books, after that first novel. It's been said that for some writers the only thing worse than writing is not writing, and for me this is nearly true, for I don't write any more easily now than I did ten years ago. In fact, I write less easily, perhaps because, as well as the attempt to connect directly with the character's wavelength, there is now also a kind of subconscious monitor which seeks to cut out the garbage (the totally irrelevant, and the "fine" oratorical writing, which I have come to dislike more and more) before it is written rather than after, and the two selves sometimes work in uneasy harness. Simultaneously, of course, it's had its exhilaration, the feeling that comes when the writing is moving well, setting its own pace, finding its own form. I've learned a few things I needed to know – for example, that the best and worst time is when the writing is going on, not when the book is published, for by that point one is disconnected from that particular thing. I've learned that my anxieties and difficulties with writing aren't peculiar to myself – most writers have the same kind of demons and go on having them, as I do. (This seems so obvious as to be hardly worth stating, but I didn't really know it ten years ago.) I've lived for the past six years in England, and, although I've picked up a lot of peripherally useful information about the publishing aspect of books and a sense of the writing going on in many countries, I don't really believe my being here has influenced my writing one way or another, certainly not to anything like the same extent as Africa once did.

This Side Jordan and the two other books I wrote which were set in Africa, *The Prophet's Camel Bell* and *The Tomorrow-Tamer*, were written out of the milieu of a rapidly ending colonialism and the emerging independence of African countries. They are not entirely hopeful books, nor do they, I think, ignore some of the inevitable casualties of social change, both African and European, but they do reflect the predominantly optimistic outlook of many Africans and many Western liberals in the late 1950s and early 1960s. They were written by an outsider who experienced a seven years' love affair with a continent but who in the end had to remain in precisely that relationship, for it could never become the close involvement of family. The affair could be terminated – it was not basically for me a lifetime commitment, as it has been for some Europeans. On Africa's side, in its people's feelings toward me, it was, not unnaturally, little more than polite tolerance, for white liberals were not much more loved then than they are now, and with considerable justification, as I discovered partly from listening to myself talking and partly in writing *This Side Jordan*. Another thing all my African writing had in common was that the three books were written by a person who had lived in Africa in her late twenties and early thirties, and it all therefore bears the unmistakable mark of someone who is young and full of faith. In *This Side Jordan* (which I now find outdated and superficial and yet somehow retrospectively touching) victory for the side of the angels is all but assured. Nathaniel holds up his newborn son, at the end, and says, "Cross Jordan, Joshua."[7] Jordan the mythical could be crossed; the dream-goal of the promised land could be achieved, if not in Nathaniel's lifetime, then in his son's. This was the prevailing spirit, not only of myself but of Africa at that time. Things have shifted considerably since then.

After I came to England, in 1962, I picked up some of the threads of a relationship with Africa, although this time only as an observer and amateur friend, for I had had to abandon every ism except individualism and even that seemed a little creaky until the last syllable finally vanished of itself, leaving me ismless, which was just as well. I became extremely interested in contemporary African writing in English. It had seemed to me, a few years before, that if anything was now going to be written about Africa, it would have to be done from the inside by Africans themselves, and this was one reason I stopped writing anything with that setting. In fact, although I did not realize it then, already many young African writers were exploring their own backgrounds, their own societies and people. In a period of hiatus after finishing *A Jest of God*, I read a great deal of contemporary Nigerian writing and even rashly went so far as to write a book of commentary on it. This book, called *Long Drums and Cannons* (the title is taken from a poem by Christopher Okigbo[8]) I now feel refers to a period of history which is over – the fifteen years in which Nigerian writers created a kind of renaissance, drawing upon their cultural past and relating it to the present, seeking links with the ancestors and the old gods in order to discover who they themselves were. This exploration and discovery ended abruptly with the first massacre of the Ibo in the north, some two years ago.[9] When Nigeria finally emerges from its present agony, it will be in some very different and as yet un-predictable form, and its writers may well find themselves having to enquire into themes they have so far hardly touched, such as the appalling grip on the human heart of tribalism in its hate aspect.

In London, in 1965, I got to know a few Nigerian writers when they visited this country. I remember especially the times I met Christopher Okigbo, and how surprised I was at his external ebullience, his jazziness, so much in contrast to his deeply introverted poetry. And I remember, after having read Wole Soyinka's[10] plays and seeing *The Road* performed here, having lunch with Wole and hearing him talk about the travelling theatre company he hoped to get going (he had al-ready set up two theatres in Nigeria, the first contemporary theatres there). How much everything can change in a couple of years! Chris Okigbo is dead, fighting for Biafra.[11] Wole Soyinka, undoubtedly the best writer that English-writing Af-rica has yet produced, and one of the best anywhere, has been in a federal jail in Kaduna for more than a year. Chinua Achebe,[12] that excellent and wise novelist, isn't writing for himself these days – he's doing journalism for Biafra, and all one can hope at the moment is that he manages to survive.

I guess I will always care about Africa. But the feeling I had, in everything I wrote about it, isn't the feeling I have now. It would be easy to convey the im-pression that I've become disillusioned with the entire continent, but this would be a distortion. What has happened, with Africa's upheavals, has been happening all over the world. Just as I feel that Canadians can't say "them" when we talk of America's disastrous and terrifying war in Vietnam, so I feel we can't say "them" of Africans. What one has come to see, in the last decade, is that tribalism is an inheritance of us all. Tribalism is not such a bad thing, if seen as the bond which an individual feels with his roots, his ancestors, his background. It may or may not be stultifying in a personal sense, but that is a problem each of us has to solve or not solve. Where tribalism becomes, to my mind, frighteningly dangerous is where the tribe – whatever it is, the Hausa,[13] the Ibo, the Scots Presbyterians, the Daughters of the American Revolution, the in-group – is seen as "the people," the human beings, and the others, the un-tribe, are seen as sub-human. This is not Africa's problem alone; it is everyone's.

When I stopped writing about Africa and turned to the area of writing where I most wanted to be, my own people and background, I felt very hesitant. The character of Hagar had been in my mind for quite a while before I summoned enough nerve to begin the novel. Strangely enough, however, once I began *The*

Stone Angel, it wrote itself more easily than anything I have ever done. I experienced the enormous pleasure of coming home in terms of idiom. With the African characters, I had to rely upon a not-too-bad ear for human speech, but in conceptual terms, where thoughts were concerned, I had no means of knowing whether I'd come within a mile of them or not. With Hagar, I had an upsurge of certainty. I wouldn't go to great lengths to defend the form of the novel, at this distance, for I know its flaws. The flashback method is, I think, a little overworked in it, and I am not at all sure that flashbacks ought to be in chronological order, as I placed them in order to make it easier for the reader to follow Hagar's life. But where Hagar herself is concerned, I still believe she speaks and feels as she would have done. She speaks in the voice of someone of my grandparents' generation, but it is a voice I know and have always known. I feel ambivalent toward her, because I resent her authoritarian outlook, and yet I love her, too, for her battling.

I didn't know I was changing so much when I wrote *The Stone Angel*. I haven't ever decided beforehand on a theme for a novel (I know that where *This Side Jordan* is concerned, this statement sounds untrue, but it isn't). The individual characters come first, and I have often been halfway through something before I realized what the theme was. *The Stone Angel* fooled me even when I had finished writing it, for I imagined the theme was probably the same as in much of my African writing – the nature of freedom. This is partly true, but I see now that the emphasis by that time had altered. The world had changed; I had grown older. Perhaps I no longer believed so much in the promised land, even the promised land of one's own inner freedom. Perhaps an obsession with freedom is the persistent (thank God) dance of the young. With *The Stone Angel*, without my recognizing it at the time, the theme had changed to that of survival, the attempt of the personality to survive with some dignity, toting the load of excess mental baggage that everyone carries, until the moment of death.

I think (although I could be wrong) that this is more or less the theme of my last two novels as well. *A Jest of God*, as some critics have pointed out disapprovingly, is a very inturned novel. I recognize the limitations of a novel told in the first person and the present tense, from one viewpoint only, but it couldn't have been done any other way, for Rachel herself is a very inturned person. She tries to break the handcuffs of her own past, but she is self-perceptive enough to recognize that for her no freedom from the shackledom of the ancestors can be total. Her emergence from the tomb-like atmosphere of her extended childhood is a partial defeat – or, looked at in another way, a partial victory. She is no longer so much afraid of herself as she was. She is beginning to learn the rules of survival.

In *The Fire-Dwellers*, Stacey is Rachel's sister (don't ask me why; I don't know; she just is). Her boundaries are wider than Rachel's, for she is married and has four kids, so in everything she does she has to think of five other people. Who on earth, I asked myself when I began writing this novel, is going to be interested in reading about a middle-aged housewife, mother of four? Then I thought, the hell with it – some of my best friends are middle-aged housewives; I'm one myself, but I deplore labels, so let's just call one another by our proper names. I was fed up with the current fictional portraits of women of my generation – middle-aged mums either being presented as glossy magazine types, perfect, everloving and incontestably contented, or else as sinister and spiritually cannibalistic monsters determined only to destroy their men and kids by hypnotic means. I guess there are some women like the latter, but I don't happen to know any of them. There are no women like the former; they don't exist. Stacey had been in my mind for a long time – longer than Rachel, as a matter of fact. She's not particularly valiant (maybe she's an anti-heroine), but she's got some guts and some humour. In various ways she's Hagar's spiritual granddaughter. When I finally got going at the novel, I experienced the same feeling I had had with *The Stone Angel*, only perhaps more so, because this time it was a question of writing really in my own idiom, the ways of speech and memory of my generation, those who were born in the 20s, were children in the dusty 30s, grew up during the last war. Stacey isn't in any sense myself or any other person except herself, but we know one another awfully well. She is concerned with survival, like Hagar and like Rachel, but in her case it involves living in an external world which she perceives as increasingly violent and indeed lunatic, and trying simultaneously within herself to accept middle age with its tricky ramifications, including the suspicion, not uncommon among her age-peers, that one was nicer, less corrupt, and possibly even less stupid twenty years ago, this being, of course, not only a comprehension of reality but also a mirage induced by the point-of-no-return situation.

With this last novel (which interests me more than the others, because I've just finished it and am not yet disconnected) the writing is more pared-down than anything I've written yet, but the form itself is (or so I believe) wider, including as it does a certain amount of third-person narration, as well as Stacey's idiomatic inner running commentary and her somewhat less idiomatic fantasies, dreams, memories.

A strange aspect of my so-called Canadian writing is that I haven't been much aware of its being Canadian, and this seems a good thing to me, for it suggests that one has been writing out of a background so closely known that no explanatory tags are necessary. I was always conscious that the novel and stories set in Ghana were about Africa. My last three novels just seem like novels.

Over ten years, trying to sum up the changes, I suppose I have become more involved with novels of character and with trying to feel how it would be to be that particular person. My viewpoint has altered from modified optimism to modified pessimism. I have become more concerned with form in writing than I used to be. I have moved closer (admittedly, in typically cautious stages) to an expression of my own idiom and way of thought. These are not qualitative statements, of course. I don't know whether my writing has become better or worse. I only know the ways in which it has changed. Sometimes it seems a peculiar way to be spending one's life – a life sentence of sentences, as it were. Or maybe not a life sentence, because one day I won't have any more to say, and I hope I'll know when that time comes and have the will power to break a longstanding addiction. (How is that for mixed metaphors?)

I've listened to the speech of three generations – my grandparents, my parents, and my own, and maybe I've even heard what some of it means. I can listen with great interest to the speech of a generation younger than mine, but I can't hear it accurately enough to set it down and I have no desire to try. That is specifically their business, not mine, and, while envying them meanly, I also wish them godspeed.

At the moment, I have the same feeling as I did when I knew I had finished writing about Africa. I've gone as far as I personally can go, in the area in which I've lived for the past three novels. A change of direction would appear to be indicated. I have a halfway hunch where I want to go, but I don't know how to get there or what will be there if I do. Maybe I'll strike it lucky and find the right compass, or maybe I won't.

Time and the Narrative Voice

"Time and the Narrative Voice" was first published in 1972 in Narrative Voice: Short Stories and Reflections by Canadian Writers, *edited by John Metcalf, with two stories from* A Bird in the House – *"To Set Our House in Order" and "The Loons" – which illustrate through their dual narrative method Laurence's belief in the interrelationship of the narrative voice and the chosen time scheme.*

The treatment of time and the handling of the narrative voice – these two things are of paramount importance to me in the writing of fiction. Oddly enough, although they might seem to be two quite separate aspects of technique, in fact they are inextricably bound together. When I say "time," I don't mean clock-time, in this context, nor do I mean any kind of absolute time – which I don't believe to exist, in any event. I mean historical time, variable and fluctuating.

In any work of fiction, the span of time present in the story is not only as long as the time-span of every character's life and memory; it also represents everything acquired and passed on in a kind of memory-heritage from one generation to another. The time which is present in any story, therefore, must – by implication at least – include not only the totality of the characters' lives but also the inherited time of perhaps two or even three past generations, in terms of parents' and grandparents' recollections, and the much longer past which has become legend, the past of a collective cultural memory. Obviously, not all of this can be conveyed in a single piece of prose. Some of it can only be hinted at; some of it may not be touched on at all. Nevertheless, it is *there* because it exists in the minds of the characters. How can one even begin to convey this sense of time? What parts of the time span should be conveyed? These are questions which I always find enormously troubling, and before beginning any piece of writing, I tend to brood for quite a long time (clockwise) on these things.

Not that the brooding does very much good, usually, or perhaps it bears fruit at some unrecognized subconscious level, because when the writing begins, a process of selection takes place in a way not consciously chosen, and this is where the long-time-span implicit in every story or novel is directly and intimately related to the narrative voice.

Most fiction I have written in recent years has been written in the first person, with the main character assuming the narrative voice. Even when I have written in the third person, as I did in part of my novel *The Fire-Dwellers*, it is really a first-person narrative which happens to be written in the third person, for the narrative voice even here is essentially that of the main character, and the writer does not enter in as commentator. Some people hold the erroneous belief that this kind of fiction is an evasion – the writer is hiding behind a mask, namely one of the characters. Untrue. The writer is every bit as vulnerable here as in directly autobiographical fiction. The character is not a mask but an individual, separate from the writer. At the same time, the character is one of the writer's voices and selves, and fiction writers tend to have a mental trunk full of these – in writers, this quality is known as richness of imagination; in certain inmates of mental hospitals this method has other names, the only significant difference being that writers are creating their private worlds with the ultimate hope of throwing open the doors to other humans. This means of writing fiction, oriented almost totally toward an individual character, is obviously not the only way, but it appears to be the only way I can write.

Once the narrative voice is truly established – that is, once the writer has listened, really listened, to the speech and idiom and outlook of the character – it is then not the writer but the character who, by some process of transferral, bears the responsibility for the treatment of time within the work. It is the character who chooses which parts of the personal past, the family past, and the ancestral past have to be revealed in order for the present to be realized and the future to happen. This is not a morbid dwelling on the past on the part of the writer or the character. It is, rather, an expression of the feeling which I strongly hold about time – that the past and the future are both always present, *present* in both senses of the word, always now and always here with us. It is only through the individual presence of the characters that the writer can hope to convey even a fragment of this sense of time, and this is one reason, among others, why it is so desperately important to discover the true narrative voice – which really means knowing the characters so well that one can take on their past, their thoughts, their responses, can in effect for awhile *become* them. It has sometimes occurred to me that I must be a kind of Method writer,[1] in the same way that some actors become the characters they play for the moments when they are portraying these characters. I didn't plan it this way, and possibly it sounds like gibberish, but this is how it appears to take place.

Theorizing, by itself, is meaningless in connection with fiction, just as any concept of form is meaningless in isolation from the flesh and blood of content and personality, just as a skeleton is only dry bone by itself, but when it exists inside a living being it provides the support for the whole creature. I'll try to show something of what I mean about time and voice by reference to the two stories of mine which appear in this book.

These stories are part of a collection called *A Bird in the House*, eight in all, published separately before they were collected in a single volume, but conceived from the beginning as a related group. Each story is self-contained in the sense that it is definitely a short story and not a chapter from a novel, but the net effect is not unlike that of a novel. Structurally, however, these stories as a group are totally unlike a novel. I think the outlines of a novel (mine, anyway) and those of a group of stories such as these interrelated ones may be approximately represented in visual terms. In a novel, one might perhaps imagine the various themes and experiences and the interaction of characters with one another and with themselves as a series of wavy lines, converging, separating, touching, drawing apart, but moving in a *horizontal* direction. The short stories have flow-lines which are different. They move very close together but parallel and in a *vertical* direction. Each story takes the girl Vanessa along some specific course of her life, and each follows that particular thread closely, but the threads are presented separately and not simultaneously. To this extent, the structure of these stories is a good deal simpler than that of a novel. Nevertheless, the relationship of time and the narrative voice can be seen just as plainly in the stories as in a novel.

"To Set Our House in Order" takes place when Vanessa is ten years old. Her age remains constant throughout the story. The actual time span of the story itself is short, a few days in her life, immediately before, during, and after the birth of her brother. The things which happen on the surface are simple, but the things that happen inside Vanessa's head are more complex.

The narrative voice is, of course, that of Vanessa herself, but an older Vanessa, herself grown up, remembering how it was when she was ten. When I was trying to write this story, I felt as I did with all the stories in *A Bird in the House*, that this particular narrative device was a tricky one, and I cannot even now personally judge how well it succeeds. What I tried to do was definitely *not* to tell the story as though it were being narrated by a child. This would have been impossible for me and also would have meant denying the story one of its dimensions, a time-dimension, the viewing from a distance of events which had happened in childhood. The narrative voice had to be that of an older Vanessa, but at the same time the narration had to be done in such a way that the ten-year-old would be conveyed. The narrative voice, therefore, had to speak as though from two points in time, simultaneously.[2]

Given this double sense of time-present, Vanessa herself had to recollect those things which were most meaningful to her, and in doing so, she reveals (at least I hope she does to the reader as she does to me) what the story is really about. It is actually a story about the generations, about the pain and bewilderment of one's knowledge of other people, about the reality of other people, which is one way of realizing one's own reality, about the fluctuating and accidental quality of life (God really doesn't love Order), and perhaps more than anything, about the strangeness and mystery of the very concepts of *past, present,* and *future.* Who is Vanessa's father? The doctor who is struggling to support his family during the Depression and who seems a pillar of strength to the little girl? Or the man who has collected dozens of travel books because once he passionately wanted to go far beyond Manawaka and now knows he won't? Or the boy who long ago half-blinded his brother accidentally with an air rifle? Or the nineteen-year-old soldier who watched his brother die in the First World War? Ewen is all of these, and many, many more, and in the story Vanessa has the sudden painful knowledge of his reality and his intricacy as a person, bearing with him the mental baggage of a lifetime, as all people do, and as she will have to do. The events of the story will become (and have become, to the older Vanessa) part of her mental baggage, part of her own spiritual fabric. Similarly, her father passes on to her some actual sense of her grandparents, his parents – the adamant Grandmother MacLeod, whose need it has been to appear a lady in her own image of herself; the dead Grandfather MacLeod, who momentarily lives for his granddaughter when she sees for the first time the loneliness of a man who could read the Greek tragedies in their original language and who never knew anyone in the small prairie town with whom he could communicate.

In "The Loons," the narrative voice is also that of the older Vanessa, but in her portrayal of herself in past years, she ranges in age from eleven to eighteen. This meant, of course, that the tone of the narration had to change as Vanessa recalled herself at different ages, and this meant, for me, trying to feel my way into her mind at each age. Here again, the narrative voice chooses what will be recalled, and here again, the element of time is of great importance in the story. The eleven-year-old Vanessa sees the Métis[3] girl, Piquette Tonnerre, in terms of romanticized notions of Indians, and is hurt when Piquette does not respond in the expected way. That summer lies submerged in Vanessa's mind until she encounters Piquette at a later time, but even then her reaction is one mainly of embarrassment and pity, not any real touching, and Piquette's long experience of hurt precludes anything except self-protectiveness on her part. It is only when Vanessa hears of Piquette's death that she realizes that she, too, like the entire town, is in part responsible. But the harm and alienation started a long way back, longer even than the semi-mythical figure of Piquette's grandfather Jules Tonnerre, who fought with Riel[4] at Batoche.[5] The loons, recurring in the story both in their presence and in their absence, are connected to an ancestral past which belongs to Piquette, and the older Vanessa can see the irony of the only way in which Piquette's people are recognized by the community, in the changing of the name Diamond Lake to the more tourist-appealing Lake Wapakata.

What I said earlier may perhaps be more clearly seen now to show a little of the relationship between the narrative voice and the treatment of time – it is the character who chooses which parts of the personal past, the family past, and the ancestral past have to be revealed in order for the present to be realized and the future to happen.

Half War – Half Peace: A Writer's Working Relationship with Publishers

"Half War – Half Peace" is a previously unpublished typescript in the York University Archives and Special Collections, Margaret Laurence Fonds 1980–001 1023. It addresses Laurence's relationship with her American, British, and Canadian publishers, including her editors Judith Jones of Knopf, Alan Maclean of Macmillan, and Jack McClelland of McClelland and Stewart. It partially parallels the section of her essay "Living Dangerously … by Mail" in Heart of a Stranger, *where she defends the titles of her texts, especially* The Stone Angel.

I'd like to talk a little about the relationship between writer and publisher – the working editorial relationship, which every writer must ultimately establish in his or her own way with the publisher.

How much does a writer accept of a publisher's criticisms and suggestions? Beginning writers – myself included, at one point – do, I think, tend to believe that, once a novel has been completed, the last word typed on the last page, that it is *done*, finished, out of one's hands. But this isn't necessarily so – in fact, it is very seldom so. Every reputable publisher wants to produce as good a book as possible, and naturally every publisher's editor has his own opinion about what makes a good book. Some of these criticisms and suggestions are worthwhile – they really do relate to the manuscript, and the writer would be extremely foolish, in my opinion, not to consider them with great care. Other criticisms and suggestions seem to the writer to be untrue assessments, misinterpretations.

I think one is very lucky to have a good publisher and a good editor, as I have had, with three publishing firms – McClelland & Stewart in Canada, Macmillan in England, and Knopf in America. None of these publishers have ever held their suggestions like a stick over my head, I may say. I have always felt myself free to refuse their suggestions about altering a manuscript, provided I could show good reason why I felt my way was right. It has been, with every book, a strange kind of diplomatic exchange, sometimes verging on war but never quite – so far – getting to that point, thank God.

Like most writers, I have at times argued passionately with my publishers, and they with me, and I have the conviction that every book I have written has been in some way improved by this exchange of views.

I am not good at speaking theoretically. I don't have an abstract mind, and I also believe Norman Mailer's statement that "the truth is in the detail." I don't know whether my relationships with publishers through the last ten years will have any interest or value, but some of these experiences may possibly relate to what younger writers have either gone through or will go through, and that is why I am going to tell some of it to you now. To tell you the truth, I feel some slight reticence about it, as I have never talked about this aspect of my work before. Also, I hope that if my publishers get to hear about what I've said, they won't hate me. But – let us live dangerously.

American publishers' editors, in my experience, are almost always more detailed and demanding in their criticisms than either English or Canadian publishers. English and Canadian editors both tend to give general and usually helpful criticisms, but American editors go through the manuscript with a fine-toothed comb. Nothing is too small a detail for their attention. I have had an American editor say, "Is this particular word in common idiomatic usage in Canada? It is unfamiliar to me, as an American." When I first met with this scrupulous editorship, I was unnerved and irritated. How could they be bothered to concern themselves with such trivial details? It frightened me that they *did* – where was I going to be found out? I felt like a person going through Customs inspections at an airport, not knowing whether one's suitcase contained contraband or not.

I do not feel this way now. I don't know how the change has happened. All I know is that now I appreciate my American editor at Knopf very much indeed. She happens to be a first-rate editor, and I have established some kind of deep rapport with her.[1] I value her meticulous professionalism, which is always combined with a liberality of thought. She, too, is open to suggestion. We can argue and discuss, and I think both of us are willing to be convinced, over any point in dispute, if the other's arguments are good enough.

But, although I have accepted many suggestions from editors connected with publishers in Canada, England, and America, I do *not* go along with the school of thought which believed that an editor should practically write – or rewrite – a book for an author. The novel is the novelist's work. An editor can make criticisms and suggestions, and, if these are true and helpful, a writer would be daft to reject them. But an editor of real integrity will never, in my opinion, insist on changes with which the writer cannot finally agree. If they don't think enough of it to publish it with some of its flaws still there, they will reject it, and that is that. It is after they have accepted a manuscript that the exchange of opinions begins.

This verbal exchange, through letters, can be nearly killing for a writer. My first novel, *This Side Jordan* (1960), was at last accepted by an American publisher (St Martin's Press, in this case, not Knopf, although Knopf has published all my books after the first one).[2] I received from the American publisher one day a letter containing extracts from a publishers' reader's report. This, they said, they hardly ever did, but in this case they thought I should see what their principal reader had said. What he had said was that he was "only reasonably nauseated" by the oratorical nature of much of the inner monologue in the novel, and, while he liked the book basically, he thought it would be much improved by cutting out a hell of a lot of the purple prose.

For several days I debated whether to kill myself now or later. Then I got out the manuscript, which I had not looked at for some months, and with fury and sullen rage I realized that the reader had been right. I went back and weeded out a very great deal, although I see now that I did not weed out enough, and I lived to bless him for his cruelly outspoken opinion.

I did not accept all his criticisms, however. The novel is set in Ghana,[3] just before Independence, and one thing he said was that Miranda, one of the main European characters, talked too much like a white liberal. Ye gods, I wrote back, she *is* a white liberal – that's what's wrong with her – she does not see how patronizing she is being.

When I had completed my second book, *The Prophet's Camel Bell* (1963), an account of my life in Somaliland, Jack McClelland wrote to me and said, "My God, Margaret, what's the matter with you? You make yourself sound like the white man's burden in Africa. Can't you cut out all these apologetic passages?" I mulled that one over for a while, smarting to some extent and cursing Jack McClelland every hour on the hour. In these circumstances, I have to admit, I tend to overreact and to fire off intense ten-page letters in my own defence, before really thinking about the matter. I explained to Jack McClelland that I had been trying to analyze *why* I had reacted the way I had, all those years before. I no longer felt remorse over my long-lost white liberalism, being interested now only in relating to individual people of whatever race, people who wanted to relate to me, and that my explication of my flaws was not intended to be a kind of breast-beating. This was all true. But McClelland was right, as well. I took another long look at the manuscript, and it came across as a kind of apology for breathing, which I then – and maybe only then – perceived as another trap, the last final trap of the poor benighted white liberal. The hell with apologies, I thought, I am what I am. And yet I wanted still to show the process – the long gradual process of self-knowledge, a process which never ends and which for me began in Africa, for it really was Africa which taught me to look at myself. So I rewrote and tried to think my way back into the book. I cut a fair amount, and finally I had to say, "This is it. It isn't really what I want, but it is all I can do." All three publishers accepted this, and an irony of my life is that this book of nonfiction sold better, at least when it was first published, than any other of my books, although in the deepest sense it is the least true, because for me it is not possible to speak as truthfully in factual writing as it is in fiction.

With my three Canadian novels, *The Stone Angel* (1964), *A Jest of God* (1966), and *The Fire-Dwellers* (1969), I have had relatively few problems with publishers over the actual novel itself, although in all cases I have received critical suggestions, some of which I have accepted and some not. When I finished *A Jest of God*, Alan Maclean of Macmillan's in London phoned me as soon as he had read the manuscript. Over the years he has been truly considerate to me in this way, knowing how neurotic I am about the submission of a manuscript – I never stop pacing the floor until I hear what at least one publisher thinks of it. As far as *A Jest of God* was concerned, they liked the novel and there was no question about their publishing it. Whew! Massive relief. But he and about six others were agreed that it got off to a very slow start, and that something should be done about this. I knew perfectly well that the novel *did* get off to a slow start, so I finally managed to make three chapters into two, by the ruthless cutting of every inessential word, phrase, and paragraph.

With *The Fire-Dwellers*, most of the critical suggestions came from my American editor, and almost all of these concerned scenes which she felt were too abrupt and inadequately led into. I had tried to pare everything down to the bone with this novel, and the result was the absolute opposite of what I had experienced with my first novel. Far from having to cut out the emotive prose, I now had to give thought to filling in places which might be too sparse, too abbreviated. There were a number of places where I could instantly see that my editor was right – a few months' distance from a novel gives you a better perspective. So I did try, in these cases, to make the transitions from one scene to another a little less stark, while still trying to stick to my original concept that nothing must be explained – it must all be self-evident, happening right now, by itself.

The most nerve-wrecking exchange I have had recently was over a volume of short stories of mine, *A Bird in the House* (1970), published recently.[4] All three publishers originally felt that, as the stories were interconnected and made use of the same characters, there might be some way of making a continuous narrative of them, not exactly a novel but something closer to a novel than a series of stories. I could see the logic of this point of view. The only trouble was that I could not go along with it. They had been written as stories; they were self-contained, and, even though they were in a very real sense interwoven and had been conceived as a set of stories nearly from the beginning, I knew I could not alter them, and I had to try to explain why. One reason was that they had mostly been previously published, some in anthologies, and it did not seem ethical to me to change them. Also, I did not want to end up doing a mock-up of a novel. If they had been intended to be a novel, that is how they would have been written. At last, after an interchange of some dozens of letters, I managed to convince all three publishers that it was either a set of interconnected short stories or nothing – and I am glad to say they gave in gracefully. The trouble with this sort of difficulty – which concerns the very construction of the work itself – is that I could see the publishers' viewpoint, and they could see mine, but it amounted to an impasse for quite a while, during which time I thought I would probably have a nervous breakdown. Books of short stories, as is well known, are not considered to be a publisher's dream, from the point of view of saleability. I knew this as well as anyone. But I also knew I could not change the stories from their original form – it would have been some kind of violence done to them, and it would not have succeeded.

The worst – or perhaps the most entertaining – battles I've ever had with publishers have been over the matter of titles. I have had more trouble with titles than a prospective peer. And I have defended my titles more often than a middleweight boxer.[5]

I should explain, perhaps, that I am quite capable of seeing almost any particular phrase, paragraph, or page of prose as expendable – I do not regard what I have written as deathless or untouchable. I am principally interested in making as strong a book as possible, and for this reason, any of the parts are always subservient to the whole. A paragraph here or there is not going to break my heart, unless it happens to be an *essential* paragraph, in which case I'll fight for it.

I do *not* have the same feeling about titles.

I become, I'm afraid, embattled very easily over my titles. They are not ever chosen accidentally or lightly. I think a title should, if possible, be like a line of poetry – capable of saying a great deal with hardly any words at all. The title of a novel should, in my view, express the whole novel, its themes and even something of its outcome. It should all be there, in a phrase. I do not pretend that my titles are absolutely right for the books to which they relate, but I have a deep belief that they are the best titles that could have been found.

No one disputed the title for my first novel, *This Side Jordan*, which was in fact taken from the Bible.[6] Now I come to think of it, I am astonished that no one objected to it. The title difficulty began when Knopf in America decided to publish three of my books all at once.[7] The trouble was that they did not like the title of my travel book, *The Prophet's Camel Bell*, which was already published in England and Canada. Nor did they like the title of my Canadian novel, which at that point still was unpublished anywhere and which I had originally called *Hagar*. I was determined that, whatever happened, no one else would choose the title of a novel of mine, so I gave in on the travel book, in the hope that this would give me greater bargaining power in regard to the novel. The American title of the Somaliland book, therefore, is *New Wind in a Dry Land*, which I consider to be an indifferent title, at best, and it was not one I had chosen. I simply felt at the time that I could not fight on two fronts at the same time. I think now I was probably wrong – and I should have stood my ground.

The story of the title of the novel which ultimately became *The Stone Angel* is slightly ludicrous. I kept receiving fantastic letters from my American publishers, saying things like "What about calling it *Old Lady Shipley*?" I would then hurl myself at my typewriter and yell loudly in print, "No, No, a Million Times NO!"

I also received in every other post a letter from my editor at Macmillan's in London, saying things like, "Dear Margaret – I am very interested to hear you have been rereading the Psalms in an effort to find a title for *Hagar*. I think I have just the right title, also from the Psalms. What about *Bottle in the Smoke*? You know, from that verse that says 'And I am become as a bottle in the smoke.'"[8]

Once more, my rueful nonacceptance flooded the mails. I sat up night after night, convinced that somewhere in the Psalms was the answer to the theme of Hagar. Once I really thought I had it. The verse was "As with a sword in my bones, so do mine enemies reproach me, while they say daily unto me, Where is thy God?" I bashed off a letter to the publishers, saying, "What about *Sword in My Bones*?"[9] An hour later, I was again at the typewriter, saying, "*Sword in My Bones* is *obviously* no good – it sounds like a tale of pirates and buried treasure."

My Canadian publishers, all credit to them, stayed out of this particular battle. Their feeling was that I would in due course find the right title and when I did, I would let them know. For this I was grateful. But I found myself in a state of depression over the whole question. The right title existed somewhere, I was certain, but I could not seem to find it. Then one evening I picked up the manuscript, by now having almost given up hope of finding even a passable title. I read the first sentence of the novel. It was this. "Above the town, on the hill brow, the stone angel used to stand." The stone angel that had recurred again and again throughout the novel, the marble figure, the woman held in stone, wanting always to be released but never able to release herself – Hagar. The title, the real and true and only possible title had been there all the time, in the first sentence of the book. I simply wrote to all three publishers and told them I had found the right title, and they all saw it at once. It was like the calm after the storm.

With *The Fire-Dwellers*, I had another set-to. My American editor, Judith Jones, had written with enormous understanding about what she called "the orchestration" of the novel – that is, the form in which it was set, and the fact that the typesetting of the book would have to be done with great care in order to convey this form properly. But she originally thought that *The Fire-Dwellers* was not the right kind of title. As usual, I overreacted. I instantly wrote her a five-page single-spaced letter, explaining why this was the only possible title. I explained that it had connotations, to me, anyway, of things like Cave-dwellers[10] and Apartment-dwellers, the two most separate poles of our existence on earth, and that it also related to the verse from Sandburg's *Losers*, used at the beginning of the novel – "I who have fiddled in a world on fire."[11] It related as well, to Stacey's recurring thought about the nursery rhyme – "Ladybird, ladybird, fly away home / Your house is on fire, your children are gone" (5). The fire theme threads through the whole novel, because the fires are both inner and outer, and if we are to live in the present world, we must learn to be fire-dwellers, to live within the fires and still survive until we die. All this I expressed in what at the time I thought was cool rational prose, but later saw was an intense defence of something I utterly believed in.

I got a letter back from my American editor not long after, saying, in effect, "Okay, relax, we get the message."

This, then, is more or less the history of my relationships with publishers. If one can draw any conclusions, maybe they are personal ones only. Maybe they do not apply to anyone else. I don't know. But I know that, for myself, it would have been a great mistake to feel that the publishers were totally on the other side of the fence. They aren't. And yet they are never quite on the same side of the fence as a writer. I think I have gained a lot from some of the critical suggestions of publishers' editors, and at other times I have had to do battle with them, because there are some things in one's writing that any writer has to be prepared to do battle for, if necessary.

No one is ever totally right or totally wrong in these matters. Personally, I feel that if a writer rejects, out of hand, all of a publisher's suggestions, he is being pretty foolish. If, on the other hand, he is too agreeable only in order to please the publisher and get the book published, he is really throwing away his own life. I think one has to play it by ear, and one is sometimes not certain that the decisions taken have been the right ones. But publishers and writers, although they may disagree often and intensely, cannot really live without one another, so both sides must try to work out a reasonable way of getting on together, with mutual respect and with a mutual agreement to be able to argue.

Gadgetry or Growing: Form and Voice in the Novel

"Gadgetry or Growing: Form and Voice in the Novel" was first presented as an address at the University of Toronto in 1969 and first published in the Journal of Canadian Fiction *27 (1980); it was reprinted in 1983 in* A Place to Stand On: Essays in Honour of Margaret Laurence, *edited by George Woodcock. Laurence addresses her changing narrative methods from her African to her Canadian novels, wondering if her innovative techniques constitute gimmicks or genuine development – "gadgetry or growing."*

Graham Greene,[1] in an essay, once advanced the idea that at some point every serious writer discovers something which he knows he cannot do, and that out of this knowledge he evolves a technique in order to cover this impossibility – in other words to try to convey at least something of what he perceives to be un-conveyable. With the occasional rare genius – and let us never forget that great writers are exceedingly rare – the old forms are broken; truly new forms are evolved, and – as was the case, I believe, with James Joyce – the face of the language is changed. With the rest of us, the evolution of form is never totally new and is usually much less experimental or original than we might like to imagine, but it is an attempt at something new to us, an effort to discover a means – a ve-hicle, if you like – which is capable of getting across some of the things we feel compelled to try to communicate.

I am not – you will be glad to hear – going to attempt a survey of the many ways in which the contemporary novel is changing. I am not even certain that anything I have to say will be of any value or interest. But I propose to speak mainly of changing forms in my own work, simply because I know it from the in-side better than I know anyone else's work, and I know the reasons for the changes and – as I like to think – the developments within it. I also know the many problems I've had in trying to find the form which would allow the characters to come through.

How much is any writer influenced by other writers? One is always very interested in what others are doing, but personally I believe that most writers are influenced very little by what their contemporaries are doing. "Schools" of writing seldom, upon examination, turn out to be actual groups. The so-called Angry Young Men of the 50s, in England,[2] really only expressed the tone and feelings of their generation. Each was working out of his own necessity, not in any conscious sense in relation to one another.

Generally speaking, I believe that most writers work out their own forms and means of expression through a strong compulsion to get closer to their material, to express it more fully, to speak as much of their own truth as they can, according to the sight of their own eyes.

I have never thought of forms and means of expression (I refuse to use that odious word *style*) as having any meaning in themselves. I am not concerned at all about trying forms and means of expression which are new – or at least new to me – simply for their own sake or for the sake of doing something different. Form for its own sake is an abstraction which carries no allure for me. I do not make this as a qualitative statement – I only say that it happens to be true for myself. I am concerned mainly, I think, with finding a form which will enable a novel to reveal itself, a form through which the characters can breathe. When I try to think of form by itself, I have to put it in visual terms – I see it not like a house or a cathedral or any enclosing edifice, but rather as a forest, through which one can see outward, in which the shapes of trees do not prevent air and sun, and in which the trees themselves are growing structures, something alive. That is, of course, an ideal, not something that can ever be achieved.

When I wrote my first novel, *This Side Jordan*, I had very little consciousness of form. The novel is cast in a traditional mould, with a straightforward third-person narration, and the chapters alternate between the viewpoints of the African teacher, Nathaniel Amegbe, and the Englishman, Johnnie Kestoe. I wrote the novel episodically, in no particular order, and in fact it did not even assume any kind of shape in my mind until I had more than a hundred pages written. I wrote the last few pages first. When I had a lot of episodes, I spread them out on the dining room table of our house in Ghana, and thought, "What a mess."

Which was certainly true. I began to see that what I had was a whole lot of fictional flesh, so to speak, and no skeleton, no underlying bones which would hold the whole structure up.

I began to see the need to sort out this amorphous mass, but I did not want to superimpose a false order and shape on it. Then I finally realized there was a natural order to the story, and I had simply missed seeing the connecting points. In the end, I cut out a great deal of what I had originally written with such exuberance, because a lot of it was repetitive and over-written. The device of using alternating chapters to convey the African and the European points of view does not seem to me to be entirely satisfactory, but I don't know how else it could have been done. Even at that time, I had rejected the idea of the narrator's being able to whip in and out of the mind of more than one character at a time – that particular method always seemed unworkable for me. The chapters, I think, did need to be alternating, especially since the African viewpoint and the European were so different.

As far as voice is concerned, I think now that the novel contains too much of Nathaniel's inner monologues. I actually wonder how I ever had the nerve to attempt to go into the mind of an African man, and I suppose if I'd really known how difficult was the job I was attempting, I would never have tried it. I am not at all sorry I tried it, and in fact I believe from various comments made by African reviewers that at least some parts of the African chapters have a certain authenticity. But not, perhaps, as much as I once believed.

I really hardly ever look at a book again once it is published, but in thinking about this talk, I re-read parts of *This Side Jordan*. I was astonished to find that it was actually not the African chapters (which I had liked best when I wrote it) which stood up best at this distance, but the European ones. In the end, I was able to understand the Europeans best, I think, even though my sympathy with colonial Europeans was certainly minimal or even nonexistent.

My novel *The Stone Angel* presented a great many problems of form and voice. I had decided I could never get deeply enough inside the minds of African people – or, at least, I'd gone as far as I personally could as a non-African – and had a very strong desire to go back and write about people from my own background, people whose idiom I knew and whose concepts were familiar to me. Hagar was a woman of ninety, and it seemed to me impossible to convey sufficiently her unvoiced thoughts, her rage against her fate, except by writing the novel in the first person. I suppose it might be thought just as difficult to write a novel from the point of view of a ninety-year-old woman as from that of an African school-teacher, but I did not see it that way. Hagar was my grandparents' generation – I felt I knew her extremely well, although she was certainly not based on any actual person. Indeed, none of the characters in any of my novels are based on actual persons. I felt when I was writing *The Stone Angel* an enormous conviction of the authenticity of Hagar's voice, and I experienced a strange pleasure in re-discovering an idiom I hardly knew I knew, as phrases from my grandparents kept coming back to me. A first-person narrative can be limiting, of course, but in this case it provided an opportunity to reveal to the reader more of Hagar than she knew about herself, as her judgments about everything are so plainly and strongly biased.

The form of the novel gave me more trouble than the voice. I decided I would have to write it in the present tense, with flashbacks in the past tense. This method seems a little rigid, but I was dealing with a very rigid character. I did not really like the flashback method much, and God knows it has been over-worked – which is probably why fewer and fewer writers use it now. But I could not discover any alternative which would convey the quality and events of Hagar's long past. In a sense, I think this method works not too badly in *The Stone Angel* simply because Hagar is so old, is living largely in her past, does – like many old people – remember the distant past better than more recent events.

But should episodes from the past, in novels, be in any kind of chronological order? That is not, after all, the way people actually remember. In some ways I would have liked Hagar's memories to be haphazard. But I felt that, considering the great number of years those memories spanned, the result of such a method would be to make the novel too confusing for the reader. I am still not sure that I decided the right way when I decided to place Hagar's memories in chrono-logical order. This is a very tricky point. One can say that the method I chose diminishes the novel's resemblance to life, but on the other hand, writing – however consciously unordered its method – is never as disorderly as life. Art, in fact, is never life. It is never as paradoxical, chaotic, complex, or as alive as life.

All Hagar's memories are touched off by something which occurs in her present, and I think this is legitimate and the way it really happens. However, the coincidence of present happenings touching off – conveniently – memories in sequence is probably straining credulity. I feel now that the novel is probably too orderly. But it seemed the only means of writing it at all. One grapples with the flaws but cannot always do anything about them. On the other hand, the inter-linking of Hagar's past and present perhaps does give a needed unity to the whole and may – hopefully – communicate at least something about the immediacy of her past in her own mind.

Another problem I encountered in *The Stone Angel* was the question of how far a woman such as Hagar would have thoughts in which places and events are described partly in terms of poetic imagery. Were the descriptions of the forest, for example, or the prairie in the drought – all the descriptions which came nat-urally when I was writing the book – were these in fact Hagar or were they me? I worried about this quite a lot, because I did not want Hagar to think out of character, and I recognize this as one difficulty of first-person narration – the lack of external viewpoint, in fact the abolishing of the narrator. On the other hand, I could not really believe those descriptions were out of character. I don't know why I felt this, but I simply felt they were right when I was actually doing them. They seemed like Hagar. Truthfully, I did not even think about this whole question when I was writing the novel. It was only afterwards, in the re-writing, that I worried. I finally came to the conclusion that even people who are relatively inarticulate, in their relationships with other people, are perfectly capable within themselves of perceiving the world in more poetic terms (although I mistrust that expression) than their outer voices might indicate. Maybe this was only a rationalization, but I don't believe so. It seemed to me that for me to cut out de-scriptions which appeared so plainly to have come from Hagar herself, during the writing, would be a kind of insult to her. And that, I wasn't willing to risk – indeed, I did not dare. So I let her have her way, and perhaps this is all one can do with one's characters – try to set them free as much as possible, or rather, to accept the simple fact of their freedom. If one is writing, as we all partly must do, out of the subconscious, then the voices of the characters must be trusted. Not that this means one should not attempt any re-writing – that isn't part of the bargain. Not even one's characters have the right to demand that the writer shouldn't go through a novel after the first draft is written and weed out repeti-tions or tear out mercilessly any purple prose which may inadvertently have sprouted like a kind of poisonous toadstool growth.

When my third novel, *A Jest of God*, was published, some reviewers criticized it for being, once again, in the first person and present tense, but this time with-out the balancing of past events which the flashbacks provided in *The Stone*

Angel. Well, I could certainly sympathize with those critics' point of view – I really wished I could tell them that I understood their criticism very well, and half agreed with it, and if I could have written the novel in any other way, I would have done so.[3]

I did not want to write another novel in the first person, or at least I thought I didn't want to. I tried again and again to begin the novel in the third person, and it simply would not write itself that way. Everything about those first drafts of the first pages was wrong. They were too stilted; the character of Rachel would not reveal herself. So finally I gave up and stopped struggling. I began to write the novel as I really must have very intensely wanted to write it – in the first person, through Rachel's eyes. I knew that this meant the focus of the book was narrow – but so was Rachel's life. I knew I had to be very careful, for Rachel is a potential hysteric who does not for quite a while realize this about herself, but the prose must not be hysterical or it would lose its ability to convey her. I knew that the other characters, viewed only by Rachel, might not emerge as clearly as I wanted them to – Nick, her brief lover, in particular had to communicate more to the reader than Rachel herself really understood about him until nearly the end.

On the positive side, however, was the fact that Rachel was self-perceptive, indeed a compulsive pulse-taker. She saw things about herself which Hagar did not see about herself, although Rachel tended to exaggerate vastly her own inadequacies and shortcomings. I hoped that this exaggeration would be plain, not only through Rachel's own obviously loaded assessments of herself, but also through Nick's reaction to her. To Nick, Rachel does not at first seem anything except a fairly attractive and intelligent woman, and it is only when Rachel reveals her deep uncertainties to him that he perceives how desperate is her need and how little he can fulfill it. No one could fulfill it – she needs too much, and Nick recognizes that he is not God, not all-powerful, not able to save anyone else.

The present tense of the novel naturally presented problems in terms of the narrative continuation – getting from point A to point B, as it were – and I think there are places in the novel where this becomes a serious flaw. On the other hand, I felt that the present tense was essential in order to convey a sense of immediacy, of everything happening right that moment, and I felt that this sense of immediacy was necessary in order to get across the quality of Rachel's pain and her determined efforts to survive.

Her fantasies were necessary, partly just because they were there, an integral part of herself, and partly to convey the sort of yearning she had, for a man, for her own children. (Incidentally, when the film was being made of this novel, most of the extras were hired in Danbury, Connecticut. Stewart Stern, who wrote the film script, told me about one scene which ultimately wasn't used in the film but which one young man in Danbury will probably never forget. This good-looking young man kept wandering around the set for several days, mournfully enquiring what was his role to be? He finally got an answer. "Oh, not to worry," someone told him, "You're just a masturbation fantasy.")

Which brings us to the question of how writers feel when a film is made from one of their books. I don't quite know why, but this is a question which I am asked several dozen times a week, so now I will answer it en masse, as it were, and hopefully it may not crop up again. I liked the film very much; I was glad it was made; I approved in general of what was done with it. But in a sense it didn't have anything to do with me – it wasn't my work. Once, at a party in England, a terribly well meaning lady introduced me like this – "This is Margaret Laurence – she wrote the book of *Rachel, Rachel*, and just think – I knew it when it was only a novel!" Like, how to kill writers with one easy stab. Well, much as I was interested in the film and glad to see it, to me it is still only a novel.

Although nothing in my fourth novel, *The Fire-Dwellers*,[4] is really new in terms of general form in the contemporary novel, the shape of this novel worried me very much before I began writing it, and I looked at and discarded many methods before I finally worked out the one in which the novel is written.

The main need was for some kind of form which would convey the sense of everything happening all at once, simultaneously. Obviously, if you are trying to get across the vast number of things which impinge upon the individual consciousness every minute of the day, you must be very selective and hope to convey quite a lot by implication rather than quantitative description. Either that, or write a novel of fifty thousand pages, which was very far from being my aim. In fact, I wanted to write something in a kind of prose which would be much more spare and pared down than anything I had ever done before. I had moved a long way, at least in my own mind, from the ornate and rather oratorical quality of Nathaniel's inner thoughts in *This Side Jordan*. I did not want any lengthy narration, nor indeed any lengthy passages of any kind. Narration, dreams, memories, inner running commentary – all had to be brief, even fragmented, to convey the jangled quality of Stacey's life.

I did not want to write a novel entirely in the first person, but I did not want to write one entirely in the third person, either. The inner and outer aspects of

Stacey's life were so much at variance that it was essential to have her inner commentary in order to point up the frequent contrast between what she was thinking and what she was saying.

Stacey had been in my mind for a number of years. I almost knew too much about her and her family. I was often overcome with the absolute impossibility of getting enough of it into a novel, while at the same time leaving out much of the strictly domestic detail, such as cleaning the house, which in fact occupied most of her time but was not likely to make very thrilling reading. Maybe I did not put enough of this sort of detail in – one reviewer made the comment that Stacey never does anything except sit around drinking gin and reading women's magazines. One wanted to ask him who the hell he thought got the meals and washed the dishes in the MacAindra house.

In any event, the novel gave me much trouble in the beginning. I had begun it several times, and each time discarded it because the form did not seem to be conveying the characters and the real dilemmas. I even once burned, dramatically, nearly a hundred pages of a second draft, and then sat down at my typewriter and wrote a deeply gloomy letter to a friend, which began, "I am a firebug."

I then thought the novel should be written in three or four columns, newspaper style, with three or four things happening simultaneously. Luckily, it occurred to me in time that few readers were likely to have three or four pairs of eyes.

I had, or felt I had, perhaps rather too many interlocking themes to deal with, but these were all inherent in Stacey and her situation, so no one thread could be abandoned without weakening the total structure, and yet, I was appalled at the number of threads. They may not seem too many to you, but to me at the time they seemed multitudinous – the relationship between a man and woman who have been married many years, when the woman does not have any real area of her life which is her own; the frustration of Stacey in trying to communicate with Mac and her ultimate realization of his bravery and his terrible hangups in having to deal with his problems totally alone; the relationship between generations – Stacey and Mac in relation to their children, as parents, and to their own parents as children; the sense of anguish and fear which Stacey feels in bringing up her kids in a world on fire; and also the question of a middle-aged woman having to accept middle age and learn how to cope with the essential fact of life, which is that the process of life is irreversible. So – these themes. But how to express these things in Stacey's dilemma without saying them in so many words, without actually ever stating them?

Finally the form and material sorted themselves out. I was, I think, considerably influenced, although subconsciously, by years of TV watching. I kept thinking, "What I want to get is the effect of voices and pictures – just voices and pictures." I became obsessed with this notion, as it seemed to convey the quality of the lives I wanted to try to get across. It was only much later that I realized that "voices and pictures" is only another – and to my mind, better – way of saying "audio-visual." Except, of course, that both voices and pictures in a novel have to be conveyed only through the printed word – although in the future this may change, and some day I would dearly love to write a novel which was illustrated in some kind of bizarre way by a really good artist. In any event, I wanted the pictures – that is, the descriptions – whether in outer life or dreams or memories, to be as sharp and instantaneous as possible, and always brief, because it seemed to me that this is the way – or at least one way – life is perceived, in short sharp visual images which leap away from us even as we look at them.

I decided that a certain amount of external narration was necessary, partly to avoid the awkwardness of forward-moving which had plagued *A Jest of God*, and partly to give some distance to the reader's view of Stacey, for she was not the shut-in and withdrawn person that Rachel was.

The inner monologue, of course, is strictly in Stacey's voice, and it was through this, largely, that I hoped to convey her basic toughness of character, her ability to laugh at herself, her strong survival instincts.

Her memories were set to one side on the page in an attempt to clarify the fact that these are flashing in and out of her mind while she is doing other things. Incidentally, when I complained to one of Macmillan's sales' staff in England about the high price of *The Fire-Dwellers*, he said, "Well, Margaret, if you insist on wasting all that space on every page, what can you expect?"

Stacey's memories are not flashbacks, nor do they occur in any chronological order. They are snatches, fragments from the past, because this seemed to me to be the way my own memories returned, and it appeared to me that the same would be true of Stacey, whose life is busy, and indeed often frantic.

The dreams and fantasies were put in italics only in order to identify them as dreams and fantasies, and also, perhaps, to provide a kind of visual variety on the page – something I have myself felt a need for, sometimes, in reading novels – that no one tone should go on too long, that there should be some visual break – and I think that probably our need for this kind of variety has been conditioned by films and TV. I do not think this is either a good or a bad thing. I simply think it is a fact. But if pressed for an opinion, I would say it was probably more a good thing than a bad, because as long as the novel continues to be able to change – not for gimmicky reasons, but for reasons of inner necessity – there is a good chance it may remain alive.

The reason that I did not use any quotation marks in *The Fire-Dwellers* for characters' speech to one another was that I wanted to get, once again, the sense of everything happening all at once, the way in which talk flows in and out of people's lives and is not cut off or separate from events. The reason that some sentences in Stacey and Mac's talk are unfinished or simply trail off is because that is the way they talked and, in fact, the way many people talk. I did not use "he said" or "she said" because I hoped that the tone of voice and what was being said would be enough to identify each speaker, although I do identify the speaker fairly often before the conversation begins, and also sometimes characters happen to call each other by their names, but I had to check this particular identity method very carefully when I was re-writing the novel, to try to make sure that it wasn't being used as a method, but only when they really would speak each other's names.

Well, I've tried to explain some of my reasoning when the forms and voices of novels were working themselves out. No form, of course, really ever succeeds as one would like it to; the finished novel is never as good as the one which existed in the mind. But that is a condition of this profession, and one must accept it.

Form, in writing, concerns me more than it once did, but only as a means of conveying the characters and their particular dilemmas, because this matter of dealing with individual dilemmas seems to be my fate in writing. Where my writing will go next, and whether or not I will be able to evolve some kind of form which can at least partly convey what I want to convey – what is at the moment, there to be written, as it were – I honestly cannot say. But – hopefully – I may discover what I'm looking for, which – as far as form in writing is concerned – is the kind of vehicle or vessel capable of risking that peculiar voyage of exploration which constitutes a novel.

On "The Loons"

"On 'The Loons'" was first published in Transitions II: Short Fiction *(Comm-cept) and reprinted in* The Art of Short Fiction: An International Anthology *(1993), edited by Gary Geddes. "The Loons" was broadcast on the Canadian Broadcasting Corporation, then published in* The Atlantic Advocate *in 1966 as "The Crying of the Loons" and later included in* A Bird in the House *(1970), Laurence's Canadian collection of short stories, which she terms "the only semi-autobiographical fiction I have ever written" (*Heart of a Stranger, *8). Here Laurence addresses the mysterious relationship of life and fiction in "The Loons."*

This story was first published in *The Atlantic Advocate*, in 1966. The roots of it go back a very long way into my childhood. The ways in which memories and "created" events intertwine in this story probably illustrate a few things about the nature of fiction. When I was about eleven or twelve, I got to know a young Métis girl who was several years younger than I. The Matron of the Neepawa Hospital was a close friend of our family, and the Métis child was in her care be-cause the girl had tuberculosis of the bone in one leg. When the girl was well enough to walk (first with a cast, then with an awkward leg brace), she used to visit our house often. She was, not surprisingly, very shy and withdrawn, and I was puzzled by her at the time. Only many years later did I realize how unhappy she must have been. I learned something about her when we were both grown up – she did indeed marry an English-Canadian, and the marriage turned out badly. I never heard anything more. She became the basis of the character of Piquette Tonnerre.

The character of Vanessa is based on myself as a child, and the MacLeod family is based on my own childhood family, but here is where the process of fic-tion becomes interesting. When I knew the Métis girl, my father had died several years previously. He was in fact a lawyer, not a doctor. We did indeed have a cottage at Clear Lake, Riding Mountain, and this is the very beloved place I am describing in the fictional Diamond Lake, Galloping Mountain. The loons used to be there, nesting on the shore, when I was a child, and we used to hear their eerie unforgettable cry. The loons did move away when the cottages increased in number and more and more people came in. All these things somehow wove themselves into the story. Other things surfaced, part of the mental baggage which one carries inside one's head always. When I was young, fires in winter among the collection of destitute shacks at the foot of the hill, in the valley below town, were tragically common. Years later, when I lived in Vancouver, I used to read in the newspapers about fires destroying the flimsy shanties of native peoples. All these various things combined in my mind with a sense of outrage at the treatment of Indian and Métis people in this country throughout our history. History for me, as with social issues, is personalized – these events happen to real people; people with names, families, and places of belonging. The loons seemed to symbolize in some way the despair, the uprootedness, the loss of the land that many Indians and Métis must feel. And so, by some mysterious process which I don't claim to understand, the story gradually grew in my mind until it found its own shape and form.

I never knew a family exactly like the Tonnerre family, but the fictional family first appeared in my writing in The Stone Angel [1964]. Next came the writing of the short story, "The Loons." Something about that fire, and the terrible and unnecessary waste of lives, must have obsessed me, for that event came into my fiction twice more after the short story – a relatively brief reference in my novel The Fire-Dwellers [1969], and a long scene and many other references in my novel The Diviners [1974].

Although certain details are taken from one's own life, and from memories of places and people, I think that the fiction comes to have its own special reality. In fact, the fictional town of Manawaka often seems as real to me as my own town of Neepawa, and its people seem very real in my mind. Of course, the odd thing about fiction is that even when the characters are based to some extent on actual people, they cease to be those people and become themselves. Ultimately, Vanessa is herself and not me at all, just as Piquette is herself.

And the process of fiction remains, thank God, mysterious.

Eye on Books: The Writer as Performer

"Eye on Books: The Writer as Performer" is an unpublished typescript with no citation information in the Clara Thomas Archives, York University. The Peterborough Committee for Citizens on Decency petitioned to ban The Diviners *from the grade 13 curriculum in 1976. The Reverend Sam Buick opened his Dublin Street Pentecostal Church for people to sign the petition. Laurence's reference to "the Controversy" suggests this essay was written after 1976.*

My feelings about the writer as performer are strong, but ambivalent. I don't think of it as either A Good Thing or A Bad Thing. I don't enjoy taking on the role of performer, quite frankly, because, like most writers, I am a private person, and I do my work alone, sweating over a hot or (much worse) stone-cold typewriter. It is not committee work. It is not done in the public eye. Nor do I believe that, because I happen to be a writer, my personal life is public property. It isn't. It's mine, and it isn't about to appear on colour television. Nevertheless, I've done my fair share of being a performing writer, and I've done it for a variety of reasons. Some of it has been excruciatingly difficult for me, and some of it has been fun.

There are different areas of performing, if you are a writer. These can be grouped roughly as: (a) the delivering of entertaining (you hope) talks to various clubs and groups; (b) the media; (c) sessions with high school or university students. Your reasons for doing these quite different types of performances are, quite naturally, quite different.

To begin with (a). In 1969–70, when I was a writer-in-residence at the University of Toronto, I must have given literally dozens of talks to various groups, mostly women's groups. I did it mainly for a very legitimate reason – money. Don't mistake me – I am not knocking these groups. They were reading and even buying my books, and for that I was, and am, grateful. But, considering how nervous I get under these circumstances, I don't think I could have done it unless I had had an overwhelming desire to buy a piece of land in this country (I was then based in England) and, if possible, a small cottage on a river. I went through the stint, and I bought the cottage, where I'm now writing this piece. This is my sixth summer here, and I now have a permanent house twenty miles away, and I'm back for good. Was it worth the agony of these talks to gain this first foothold, this first place of my own in my own country? You bet it was.

The hospitality at these events was always great. People were genuinely friendly, and I appreciated that. But the setup was usually another thing. There would be a session of pre-dinner drinks, and I would be sipping at my boring ginger ale, unable to risk a noggin before going onstage. Then dinner. I would pick at my steak and roast potatoes and end up eating perhaps a forkful of peas and half a bread-roll, too nervous to get anything else down. After dinner, my performance.

I do not, I proudly affirm, faint onstage. Nor does my voice shake. My entire physical structure, though, tends to shake uncontrollably. I ultimately found that if I can give a talk sitting down, or leaning heavily on a very solid lectern, so solid as to resemble a pulpit, I don't shake so much. I would get through my act, and invariably a few people would tell me how lucky I was that I didn't get nervous. All I would want was three double Scotches and a large steak, but of course at that point all the food and drink had disappeared. It's a hard way to earn a few bucks.

The media (or the Dreaded Media, as some put it) are another cup of tea, or perhaps hemlock. The only reason for any writer to go on television or radio (unless they're going on to promote some very good cause) is to publicize a recent book. This is understood among writers, publishers, and the DM, and is, of course, the reason why only the most confident and best-selling and least financially needful writers get paid for their performances. I seldom have been paid, but I am getting tougher and smarter. The deal is (although it is never expressed in so many words) that *they* get free material for their talk shows, etc., and *you* get free publicity for your book. Fair enough, I have always thought. I don't think any longer that a writer has to jump up obediently whenever the media snap their collective fingers, but I do think that (to be realistic) a writer should be prepared for a certain amount of radio and television work when a book comes out, if the publisher can persuade the DM to take you on. The presence of the cameras, of course, is traumatic, and if you are so idiotic as to look at the monitor, where you can watch yourself on-screen, the temptation is to stop talking and just watch – to see what you'll say next. It's all happening on television, and you aren't real. However, it's still a fair exchange and a mutually useful one, and I respect most of the television and radio people who have interviewed me. One is not always lucky enough to get someone like Helen Hutchinson, Carol Taylor, or Adrienne Clarkson,[1] with whom I've done interviews, and all of whom do their homework, have read your work and ask intelligent questions. Sometimes you get the kind of interviewer who asks you if you write on the typewriter or with a ballpoint pen. Sometimes (and this goes for magazine and newspaper interviews as well) you get someone who asks you how you feel about your divorce, and do you think you've been a good or a rotten parent. As in one's real profession, in the role of performer you learn by doing. You learn that you don't have to answer that kind of question. You learn to turn it off, tactfully or wittily if possible, and if not possible, a snarled NO will do.

You also learn to admire the television crews who can move into your house, shift all the furniture, bring in a thousand tons of equipment, and leave the place looking as it did when they moved in, exactly. The stories I have about the encounters I've had with the media would probably fill a book. Suffice it to tell about a television crew from Winnipeg who came out to my cottage one summer to do an interview. In one shot, they wanted me to do something kind of natural, see, like strolling out and picking a wild flower. The one I chose happened, as I later learned, to be a Greater Mullein of the Figwort Family[2] (how about that for genealogy?), and when I picked it, it didn't agree to be picked. I wrestled with the damn plant until I realized that the cameras were off and the whole crew was in stitches of laughter.

The third category of writer as performer is going out to high school and university classes in "Canlit," to do readings or to talk in a seminar-type situation with the kids. This is the situation I have found the most rewarding. They are interested, mostly, and they ask bright questions. I enjoy this kind of encounter, and I also think that it is worthwhile. For a very long time, Canadians never suspected that some of their own writers might be worth reading. Now, with the enthusiasm of some high school and university teachers, and the enthusiasm of many of the kids themselves, Canadian writing is at last beginning to reach our schools.

Thus, there are, I think, three valid reasons for a writer to become temporarily a performer. One is, of course, money. Another is to publicize a book. The third is to try to encourage schools and universities to teach some of the literature of this country. The Writers' Union of Canada[3] has a program which consists of writers going hither and thither, doing readings and meeting students. I think this is a good thing because it combines the need of many of us to whomp up a few extra dollars with the need we have now in this country to push the teaching of "Canlit." Can you imagine any other country which doesn't have at least one high school course, in every school, in the literature of its own people?

My reservations about the writer as performer, of course, are related to the writer as writer. I think one has to watch it. One could easily turn into a performer and cease to be a writer. I don't think that any writer, when working on a book, should have to accept any performer role at all. Unfortunately, this is still frequently necessary, simply as a matter of financial survival. A wealthy Rosedale lady once asked me, years ago, at a Toronto literary party, how it felt to be a "successful writer." I shuffled off a reply, but what I wanted to say to her, and should have said, was "Lady, it feels this way – you sit up nights with the checkbook, wondering how in hell you're going to pay the next month's rent."

You hear the horror stories, and you sometimes live them, as writer/performer. But you can also receive the gift of something harmlessly bizarre. Not so long ago, I agreed to speak in a panel situation to a local women's group, who, apparently, were much concerned about the four-letter words I'd used in *The Diviners*. I was delighted to have the opportunity of fielding that question – "Why did you use those words?" The meeting was in a church hall. I was, as I later realized, the only person there who was smoking. One of the panel members dutifully asked me the dire question. I gathered my strength and my dignity. I explained that I felt very strongly that words were only obscene if they were used to hurt another person. Also, I went on, in fiction one had to be careful not to betray one's characters. One had to try, always, to have them speaking in their own idiom. If, I said, I had had Christie Logan speaking in the same polite phraseology with which I was addressing this meeting, it would have been a total betrayal of him. The audience nodded, and I felt I'd handled that one pretty well. I fumbled for another cigarette, in relief, and then suddenly looked down. There, in front of me, the fringe of the tablecloth was burning merrily away. In my shock and horror (newspaper headlines in my imagination – MARGARET LAURENCE

BURNS DOWN CHURCH HALL), I heard a very loud voice, mine, proclaiming over the efficient loudspeaker system, *"My God, I've set fire to the bloody tablecloth!"* I beat out the fire with my bare hands, and there was a short silence, followed, mercifully, by an outburst of laughter.

Roderick Haig-Brown[4] once said, "A writer should write, not talk." In general, I agree, but I believe there are certain times when a writer should talk. I also believe that these times should be clearly limited. Basically, we are not performers. If we'd really wanted that role, there wouldn't be any writers in the country – just a lot of unemployed actors.

A Tale of Typewriters

"A Tale of Typewriters," in the Clara Thomas Archives, York University, No. 1986–006/001 (43), was first published in John Lennox and Ruth Panofsky's Selected Letters of Margaret Laurence and Adele Wiseman, 398–402. *Written as a letter to Wiseman and her family and to Laurence's own family on 22 March 1984 from her home at 8 Regent Street, Lakefield, Ontario, it chronicles her typewriters, to which she gave female names in a form of feminist anthropomorphism. The latest was named "Pearl Cavewoman," a translation of her name, "Margaret Wemyss," as "Margaret" means "pearl" and "Wemyss" signified "cave dweller" in Pictish.*

Once upon a time, long ago in 1940, there was a prairie flower named Peggy Wemyss.[1] She was 14 years old and she had just acquired two things – her first boyfriend and a knowledge of touch-typing at the Neepawa Collegiate Institute. The first proved not to be of lasting value in her young life. The second proved to be one of the smartest things she ever did. Why? Because she was a writer. No one else, except maybe her Mum[2] and Miss Mildred Musgrove, English teacher,[3] knew that young Peg was a writer, but she herself, knowing this interesting fact, thought it prudent to learn how to type. Which she did, taking Typing in grades 9 & 10 as an extra subject, from the aforementioned Miss M.M. Her first typewriter, a small Remington portable, was obtained for her by her dear Aunt Ruby, second-hand, in the city of Regina. It cost $14, and in those far-off days, fourteen bucks wasn't peanuts. Peggy saved half from her Saturday afternoon job at Leckie's Ladies' Wear,[4] and her mum put up the other half. The aspiring kid named the typewriter Victoria, which, as she later liked to think, had more to do with her aspirations than with a starchy monarch of the same name.

The years passed, as they are wont to do. Since that long-ago time, she has had, she estimates, five typewriters. All but one had names. To her eternal shame, Margaret (as she is now called, resuming her true name upon publication of her first book)[5] cannot remember all their names. She recalls, however, the faithful Felicity, upon whose hard-worked keyboard most of M's books were typed ... the final version in triplicate ... what a horrible job that was! She also recalls Monica, the one before the last, because the make of the typewriter was Monica Olympia. The last one, alas, was (in parlance of yore) kind of like a horse unbroken and unruly ... M.L. never did get on so swell with that beast, which kept breaking down and doing other obnoxious things, such as demanding a touch that was heavier by far even than Margaret's considerably heavy touch on the keys.

Now, Margaret always considered herself a progressive thinker – a small 'l' liberal, a social democrat,[6] you name it. Underneath all this, however, in strictly personal/business ways, lurked a – oh woe – conservative heart. She resisted CHANGE in some areas. She continued with manual typewriters until that species was damn near extinct.

... see p. 2 for next thrilling episode[7]

Then, nearly 44 years after learning how to type, M.L. took the plunge. Unbelievable! She bought an electric typewriter at the very moment in history when these, too, looked to be doomed to extinction and everyone was going in for Word Processors. She lmade[8] this incredible leap into the age of High Tech for 2 reasons – (a) she figured that in a few years no parts or repairs for manual typewriters would be available; (b) she developed arthritis in her hands and thought – correctly – that if she could develop a light touch, l (that extra l will be explained soon), typing would not be such a physical strain on her hands and wrists as it had become. She thought she would take weeks if not months to get used to the new typewriter.

NO: Within four days, she could work it almost without flaw.!!!! Some of the things were in different places on the keyboard. The light touch did not prove a problem, but lthe fact that there was no space bar (an antiquated term referring to manual typewriters, not to the place where the beer is in a space ship) was a mite tricky, as the left hand, after 44 years of typing, automatically reached up to move the lcarriage and space. On her new electric model, simplest on the market, there is a dinky little button marked RETURN, which one touches with the pinky finger. After several days, Margaret thought, "Hey, this is neat! No more need to swing up the old left arm … a simple touch with the tiny finger does it." She found she could do super things …

A little extra pressure on some keys produces a continuous line of:

_____ or ——————————————————————————— whee! Or

xxxxxxxxxxxxxxxxxxxxxxxxxxxxxxxxxx whee!

The asterisk turned out to look like a daisy *************

The ribbon is the cartridge type and can be slid in and out and replaced with a flick … no problem. No more cursing and swearing while getting inky fingers changing a ribbon. The correction cartridge, white, can be slipped in and errors whited out in no time at all! Wow!! Terrific! (There still is, however, no way of correcting carbon copies, but probably one is meant to do only one copy and get xeroxes, which is swell if you work in an office with a xerox machine but not too swell if you have to march down to Millages Plumbing & Heating to get same, so carbons, as now, will continue to have errors x-d out, rather than classily corrected.

… more …

M.L.'s dear friend Adele, also a prairie flower and a writer[9] (although, like M, not necessarily in that order) had gone electric some time ago, with notable success. She had told M that the only thing she didn't like about the electric typewriter was that it buzzed while she was not typing and was trying to think and dream up marvellous things. M did not find this too much of a problem. Her model has a subdued buzz but also a button marked OFF, that can switch the little charmer off without having to unplug it. Do I sound naive and as though I'm not great at understanding THE MACHINE PER SE WHATEVER THE MACHINE MAY BE? You're right. But I can work this tripewriter and am even getting (after only 4 days) so that I can type while looking out the window as I am doing now at the swirling flakes of YET ANOTHER snowstorm oh hell. I still have to glance down from time to time because some of the punctuation isn't where I expect it to be, but shoot, that's nothing.

As in any garden of roses, there is a THORN. An ironic thorn.

M.L. got this electric job, as you will recall, partly because of her arthritis. The touch, light, is really a help to the hands and wrists, and I find I can do it really without any trouble because the fingers and wrists really don't want to pound the keys any longer. But … ah irony! The third finger of my right hand is now slightly crooked, bent down and won't straighten up. I found it puzzling why I was striking the letter 'l' so often without meaning to. The answer is so obvious

I am amazed I didn't see it right away. The bent finger is positioned at starting point, so to speak, over the letter 'l'. When the finger moves either up or down to hit other keys, it tends to brush the 'l', thus causing the damn letter to print. However, now that I know this, I think I can overcome it. It is just that that finger is at a different angle from all my other fingers, but I'm doing better today than yesterday, so we may yet overcome this slight problem. Ironic, though: I buy the typewriter because of arthritis, and arthritis makes it difficult to type accurately.

Well, what a boring account. But this event is important in my fairly staid life. I have, however, named this lady. She has the most sensational name of all my typewriters.

PEARL CAVEWOMAN

... see p. 4 for explanation

I thought of calling her something really CONTEMPORARY. I abandoned the idea instantly. She must be called something relevant to the fact that I recognize that she and I are going to get on well ... I can feel the rapport already. I also felt that the name should reflect a sense of the past and what could be more past than CAVEWOMAN, I ask you. And yet, Adele, I was recalling with some amusement Mary Warshaw's friend who changed her name, legally, her surname, to River-woman and I thought, "Oh shucks, what an embarrassment to her son!" But the name PEARL CAVEWOMAN is a different version of my own name, you see! Wow! How about that? "Margaret" means "a pearl" and my family name "Wemyss," as I was told when a child, according to my paternal grandfather John Wemyss,[10] means "a cave dweller," because it refers to the Picts from whom he always (apparently) said we were descended, and indeed, in my trusty book that I've referred to so often throughout the years, *The Clans and Tartans of Scotland*,[11] the word in Gaelic, "weem," means "a Pictish[12] earth house"... they did live in caves and in quite complex earth dwellings dug into hillsides ... that was in the time of Roman Britain. So PEARL CAVEWOMAN is this one's name ... the latter word a laugh at High Tech, too, of course. The Pict connection is also a tribute to Chaika.[13]

As you can all see, I have been having enormous fun learning how to use this machine, and if it were not for the fact that I am doing 2 carbons I would demonstrate how the correction cassette does indeed make correction of errors easy and simple.

This letter is for Jocelyn, for David and Sonia, and for Adele, Dmitry, and Tamara.[14]

The manual, which I have been studying as though it were Holy Writ, says a bunch of stuff about Safe Operation of this machine, making it sound like a potentially lethal weapon. Don't get it wet! Make sure it is plugged into a 3-point plug, etc. Well, heck, it would be the same for any electrical thing. I got my electrician, Karl Maskos, to come on Tuesday and install 3-point plugs in my study.

Love to all from the person who now has a SOUND SYSTEM (not a record player) and an ELECTRONIC TYPEWRITER WITH A NAME AND A PERSONALITY.

Ivory Tower or Grassroots? The Novelist as Socio-political Being

"Ivory Tower or Grassroots? The Novelist as Socio-political Being," in the Clara Thomas Archives, York University, No. 1980–001/022 (154), was first published in A Political Art: Essays and Images in Honour of George Woodcock, *edited by William H. New, in 1978. In this manifesto essay Laurence affirms the importance of politics and religion to fiction, a view held by both African and Canadian writers, specifically "two Third World novelists" – Laurence herself and her colleague, Nigerian novelist Chinua Achebe – because both African and Canadian writers suffered under the cultural imperialism of "Uncle Sam and Britannia"* (Heart of a Stranger, *172). Her experience of living in Somaliland and Gold Coast, which she described as her "seven-year love affair with a continent," and editing* Long Drums and Cannons: Nigerian Dramatists and Novelists 1952–1966 *(1968), the first full-length study of Nigerian literature in English – in which she discusses the works of Wole Soyinka, Chinua Achebe, J.P. Clark, T.M. Aluko, Elechi Amadi, Flora Nwapa, and Gabriel Okara – familiarized her with the struggle of African writers to deal with their colonial past. She applied this struggle for spiritual freedom to her Manawaka heroines.*

I do not have a great deal of affinity with the ivory tower writer whose work bears no reflection of the concerns of everyday life. In fact, I don't believe the ivory tower breed has ever been all that numerous. Writers of serious fiction are almost always, in some way or other, consciously or unconsciously, expressing their own times. This is true of historical fiction just as it is true of the writing of history itself, for our perceptions and therefore our interpretations are formed by the communities in which we grow up. This is not to say that we always agree with the prevailing views in our communities; for many writers the reverse is often true. But we are products of our own era all the same.

For me, fiction is primarily a matter of portraying individual characters as faithfully as I am able to do. These characters, however, do not live in a vacuum. They live in specific places, and any writing about them must of necessity include social commentary.

In one way, fiction may be viewed as history, just as recorded history may be viewed as fiction. They are twin disciplines, and they include biography and autobiography, for the perceptions, interpretations, and choices of material of particular writers give form to our past and relate it to our present and our future. All fiction is written about the past. Even if we write about this day, now, this hour, this moment, as we set down the words the moment becomes the past. Science fiction may be the one exception, but I don't think so. Our projections about the future arise out of our view of our own times, and the themes which occupied the SF writers in the forties are not the same themes which occupy them thirty years later.

Fiction also may be viewed as belief, and by *belief* I mean something that has connotations both of faith and of politics. Humans are social and spiritual animals; we are, in the broadest sense of the words, both religious and political, although many people may be neither in any conscious way. We stand in need of our gods, and we need links with our ancestors, partly in order to determine who and what we are, to decide what we hope to become, and to know what sort of society we will try to form. Fiction, in the political sense, both binds us to and frees us from our ancestors; it acknowledges our dilemmas; it mourns and rages at our inhumanity to one another; and sometimes it expresses our faith in growth and change, and honours our children and our trust in them.

What do I mean by "politics" in this context? The *Concise Oxford Dictionary* defines politics in this way: "n. pl. Science and art of government, political affairs or life; political principles ... " Exactly what I mean. I am, of course, not talking here about so-called party politics. One says "Liberal with a small 'l,'" which means something vastly different and importantly more vast than the group of persons who at this moment in our history are attempting to run what we call our government. In the same way, I say "Political with a small 'p,'" meaning something wider than the often-moronic exchanges in our (or any other) parliament, meaning a social commentary at a grassroots level. A novel can scarcely avoid being this kind of commentary. It may not be a helpful commentary, or even a particularly relevant one, but a social commentary it most certainly is.

In this commentary, in the re-creation on the printed page of a community
of human individuals, the novelist usually does not and should not write in any
polemical way. We are not dealing in propaganda. We do not presume to tell the
reader how to think, nor can we offer any easy solutions. Nonetheless, no novelist
writes in an objective way, if indeed there is anywhere such a mode of writing.
The novelist takes a stand, and this is what makes us so vulnerable. The novelist
asks that the reader should see these characters, these humans, both in their own
minds and spirits and in their relationship with other humans. The novelist attempts (and it is always an uncertain attempt, for this is a humbling profession)
to communicate to the reader, or at least some readers, the pain and struggle,
the joy and anguish of characters who – although they are fictional – are felt by
writers to be as real as anyone we know. The writer's life view, the way in which
people and their dilemmas and their society are seen, permeate any work of fiction. Fiction, for me at least, then becomes a matter of the individual characters
moving within a history which includes past, present, and future, and the emergence through these characters of beliefs which cannot be didactic but which in
the most profound way are both religious and political.

To illustrate my views, I would like to look briefly at the work of two Third
World novelists. One of them is Chinua Achebe of Nigeria. The other is a Canadian writer, namely myself.

Yes, *Third World* novelists is what I said. Are Canadian writers Third World
writers? In a cultural sense, very definitely yes. Canadian artists in general can
be said to be of the Third World. I was pleased to see in the *Canadian Forum*
(December-January 1976/77) an article by Peter Such on the Canadian League
of Composers, in which he said, "'International art' ... means the cultural forms
of the dominant imperial cultures of the times. And it is only as that dominance
wavers or becomes suspect that independent artists of Third World countries
like ours can assert their true voices even in their own society, let alone the
world at large." That is a statement with which I wholeheartedly agree. Canadian
writers, like African writers, have had to find our own voices and write out of
what is truly ours, in the face of an overwhelming cultural imperialism.

In Nigeria, as in many parts of Africa, people lost their own self-value, their
own distinctive voices, throughout three generations of colonialism. They were
taught as children to despise their ancestors and the old gods, and the result was,
of course, that they learned to despise themselves. Chinua Achebe's generation

of writers (which includes very many writers of distinction, such as Wole Soyinka, John Pepper Clark, Cyprian Ekwensi, T.M. Aluko, Elechi Amadi, Flora Nwapa, and Gabriel Okara)[1] has drawn on their relatively newfound sense of self-worth and on their people's past and has tried consciously to impart these values to their own people, to combat the psychic damage done during the years of domination by British imperialism. Their novels and plays have been published mainly in Britain, ironically enough, because of the lack of indigenous publishing houses (the same has been true for West Indian writers). At first, of course, English critics reviewed Nigerian writers because they were a curiosity; these same critics have often been surprised, or, at the opposite pole, indifferent, when a Canadian novel appeared in England and made use of themes other than those involving Mounties and mad trappers. As the years have gone on, some of the English critics have conceded that maybe some of these writers do have something to say after all. The view of the English critics, however, is not what has mattered. Writers like Achebe found that they had an audience among their own people, and not just among upper-middle-class academics, either, but among a very wide range of people. I recall once reading an interview with Cyprian Ekwensi, who said that among the people who bought and read his books the Lagos taxi drivers ranked high.

In Canada, our dilemma was perhaps more subtle. We ostensibly gained our independence in 1867, and yet we remained colonial in outlook for many years. In literary terms, our models remained those of Britain and more recently of America. We did have indigenous publishing houses, and that has been a great advantage for Canadian writers, although it has to be said that when Ernest Buckler's novel *The Mountain and the Valley*, probably one of the best novels in English in this century, first came out in 1952, it was published by an American firm, and only in 1961, when McClelland and Stewart brought out the novel in their New Canadian Library paperback series, was this book published at home. The case was not untypical. The Canadian writers just before my generation – Ernest Buckler, Sinclair Ross, Morley Callaghan, Hugh MacLennan, Ethel Wilson, W.O. Mitchell, Howard O'Hagan, Hubert Evans, and others – all laboured for many years with hardly any response from their own people and hardly any recognition unless it were first accorded in either England or America. The writers of that generation are our literary heroes. All of them would laugh at the mere mention of the word. All the same, they are, and we owe them more than we can possibly ever express. They kept on, alone and unaided, and they wrote out of what they truly knew, the things that were genuinely theirs and ours. They were the first generation of noncolonial Canadian writers.

My generation of novelists was probably the first – thanks chiefly to the previous sod-busters – who found we could not only write out of our own backgrounds and culture but also had a considerable audience among our own people. Times had changed by the time that Mordecai Richler, Adele Wiseman, myself, Alice Munro, Robert Kroetsch, Rudy Wiebe, Marian Engel, and all the rest came along. Younger writers such as Margaret Atwood, Dave Godfrey, Graeme Gibson, and many others have been from the start very much aware of these changing patterns in our culture.

There are still those in our country who talk about the uselessness of teaching "CanLit" because "there is no such thing," or "it doesn't accord with international standards," by which they mean that Canadian writing isn't the same as British or American. No, it isn't. Rudy Wiebe once told me that someone had asked him, "But, if you don't constantly apply international standards, how can you develop any standards at all?" (For "international" here, read "British.") Rudy replied, "I think we just make them up as we go along." Exactly. How else did Chaucer write? How else the writers of any culture? They simply wrote what they were compelled to write, as best they could, and those of their writings that struck deep chords among their own people and sometimes beyond their own people, endured. This is not to say that we remain untouched by literature elsewhere, or that we reject the great writings of the past, from whichever culture they have come. Anyone who writes in the English language is in some way an inheritor of Shakespeare and Milton, of Fielding and Jane Austen, of Dickens and Thackeray. Our task is not to reject the past but to assimilate it, to take the language and make it truly ours, to write out of our own familiar idiom and out of our deepest observations of our people and our place of belonging on this planet. I really do not think that as Canadian writers we have a great deal to learn from recent British fiction, in which I sense a widespread weariness, repetition, and even triviality. We would do better to go our own ways now and to make our discoveries, just as African writers are making theirs.

Chinua Achebe, for example, writes out of his own experience and out of the memories of his people. He grew up in the village of Ogidi, a few miles from the Niger River. He was born in 1930, and belongs to the Ibo, the largest group in southeast Nigeria. His family was a Christian one, his father being one of the first Ibo to be a mission teacher. His grandfather, however, was a grown man when the British administration first took over that part of Africa. In his novels, Achebe writes of precolonial times, when the old Ibo society was still firm. He writes of the mission-oriented era of his parents, and of the emancipated and troubled era of his own generation. During the civil war in the late 1960s, Achebe worked for Biafra, the Ibo heartland, which wanted to secede, and, although a majority of Ibo felt united on that issue, Biafra is not now a country. It was defeated in a civil war of terrifying proportions, a war which should never have taken place.

Achebe now lives in exile in America, teaching at a university. Perhaps some day he will be able to go home.

In his writing, the hatred of imperialism emerges, along with his sense of mourning and rage at the way the old Ibo society was broken by the colonialists. Achebe never writes simply or polemically. He has a sense of the reality of all people, and even his imperialist characters are complex and believable.

In *Things Fall Apart*, his first novel, he recreates the first impact of European invasion upon the old Ibo society in the late 1800s and shows how Okonkwo, the protagonist, changes. He moves from being a self-driving, proud, and respected man to committing suicide, which was a crime against Earth and therefore a complete alienation from his people. His fate is to be buried impersonally by strangers and never to be united with the spirits of his ancestors. Okonkwo, however, is portrayed as a man who suffers both from his own flaws (unbending pride, ambition) and from the terrible damage done to him by the external situation, the takeover of his land and the demoralization of his people.

In *Arrow of God*, Achebe's third novel and in my opinion one of the finest to have appeared anywhere in the past half century, we see Ezeulu, the priest of Ulu, and we feel his anguish at his responsibility for his people, his bewilderment at the influx of the missions, his attempts to meet the newcomers on their own ground (he sends one of his sons to be educated at the mission, in order to know what the white men are about). Achebe portrays here the life of an Ibo village in the 1920s, with love, authenticity, and fairness. The old gods are respected and are presented as real and true. At the same time, Achebe acknowledges the faith which the missionaries feel in their god. The Ibo villagers are shown as highly individualistic, and the British are portrayed as men caught up in a historical process which they do not understand, just as they do not understand their own very mixed motives for being in Africa at all.

My feelings about Ezeulu, and about Achebe's writings, are summed up in my book *Long Drums and Cannons*, essays on contemporary Nigerian literature:

> Underneath the restraint of the novel, there is an almost choking sense of rage and sorrow. Not that Achebe would have wanted the old Ibo society to go on unchanged, for he sees plainly the weaknesses within it. But the rage is because it broke the way it did, by the hands of strangers who had convinced themselves that they were bringing light to a dark place, and whose self-knowledge was so slight that they did not recognize the existence of darkness within themselves. The sorrow is for such a man as Ezeulu, broken by the violence of both the inner and the outer forces. Yet Achebe never allows his own emotions to sway the novel from its natural course. It is always the emotions of the characters that come across the most strongly, and because of this, the novel succeeds as few novels do.
>
> Ezeulu, man and priest, god's man, like Oedipus and like Lear, has the power to reveal not only moving and terrifying aspects of himself, but moving and terrifying aspects of ourselves as well. (116–17)

In *No Longer at Ease*, his second novel, Achebe deals with the story of Obi Okonkwo, grandson of Okonkwo in *Things Fall Apart*, and with Obi's inner conflicts between the contemporary world and the world of his Christian parents, and also between these two worlds and the further one of his ancestors, whom he has been taught to despise. In *A Man of the People*, the publication of which shortly preceded the first military coup in Nigeria, Achebe is perhaps more narrowly political, although Chief Nanga will remain for a very long time in our consciousness, as the seemingly simple and corrupt politician who is really a prey to his own fears.

Undoubtedly at some time it will become necessary for Achebe to write a novel out of the civil war, which will deal fictionally with the events of the Biafran holocaust. It will, I believe, be the most anguished work for him in his entire writing life. I also feel that, if any novelist can write such a novel, with truth, strength, and integrity, that novelist is Achebe. He sees history in terms of people with names and conflicts and places of belonging. His sense of social injustice is like a white-hot sword wielded through his powerful irony. Yet he knows one of the most frightening facts of life, the thing every novelist must come to know – the enemy is also within, and the external enemy is also human and feels pain as real as anyone's.

At the heart of Achebe's writing there is also, I sense, a profound belief that the whole order of things could be different. Mankind need not forever inhabit a world where, in the words of Matthew Arnold, "ignorant armies clash by night."[2] Understanding, respect, communication – these are possible among individuals as among nations, although a novelist frequently must define these possibilities by their absence. My own first two books of fiction [*This Side Jordan* (1960) and *The Tomorrow-Tamer and Other Stories* (1963)] were set in West Africa, although of course I could never write about Africa from the inside, but only as a concerned and involved outsider. Only about one's own people may one really write from the inside. Incidentally, I never read Achebe when I lived in West Africa. I returned to Canada in 1957. His first novel was published in 1958, and I read it about 1961, when I had completed the first draft of *The Stone Angel*, although that novel was not published until 1964.[3] The rest of Achebe's writing I have read as it has come out, feeling about it the kind of kinship that one does feel with another writer who is working within some of the same broad human territories that one is attempting to work in, and with a similar sense of specific place and particular people that I discovered when I began at last to write out of my own cultural background.

I had come back home to Canada via Africa, both physically and spiritually. In writing my first novel, *This Side Jordan*, set in Ghana, it had finally become clear to me why I had chosen the theme of an independence which was both political and inner. I was from a land that had been a colony, a land which in some ways was still colonial. My people's standards of correctness and validity and excellence were still at that time largely derived from external and imposed values; our view of ourselves was still struggling against two other cultures' definitions of us. A joke when I was at college had been: "Ask a Swede what's the best country in the world, and he'll say Sweden; ask an Englishman and he'll say England; ask an American and he'll say America; ask a Canadian and he'll say – any damn country in the world except Canada."

Who on earth taught us to think of ourselves that way? A whole history of imperialism, of being defined in others' terms, not our own. The ironic thing is that, while we went on knocking ourselves down and speaking in self-deprecating voices, we knew it wasn't true. Somewhere inside ourselves we knew our own value, and it was not low. Somewhere inside there was a deep anger and resentment at our betrayal and self-betrayal.

Our situation at the time, like that of all peoples with colonial mentalities, was not unlike that of women in our society.

Perhaps I interpret it in this way simply because I am a woman, but to me the parallels seem undeniable. These parallels, in my own mind, I may say, predated the contemporary women's movement, although of course I was aware of the earlier women's suffragette movement in Canada and elsewhere. The upsurge of the new women's movement in the 1960s, however, served to confirm my own perceptions and gave me a much-needed sense of community, of not being isolated. I have not taken an active or direct part in the women's movement, just as I have not taken an active or direct part in any party politics, simply because my work resides in my fiction, which must always feel easy with paradox and accommodate contradictions, and which must, if anything, proclaim the human individual, unique and irreplaceable, and the human spirit, amazingly strong and yet in need of strength and grace. But in making this statement of my own belief, I do not mean that I have been unaware or unsupportive of the women's movement. I have been aware and, I hope, supportive in my own way, and I have felt the warmth and support of many of my sisters, both those who are my contemporaries and those who are very much younger than my half century.

The growth of some of the themes in my writing – those themes which in the broadest sense I may define as political – took place in my mind in an intertwined and simultaneous way. My sense of social awareness, my feelings of anti-imperialism, anti-colonialism, anti-authoritarianism, had begun, probably, in embryo form in my own childhood; they had been nurtured during my college years and immediately afterwards, in the North Winnipeg of the Old Left; they had developed considerably through my African experience. It was not very difficult to relate this experience to my own land, which had been under the colonial sway of Britain once and was now under the colonial sway of America. But these developing feelings also related very importantly to my growing awareness of the dilemma and powerlessness of women, the tendency of women to accept male definition of ourselves, to be self-deprecating and uncertain, and to rage inwardly. The quest for physical and spiritual freedom, the quest for relationships of equality and communication – these themes run through my fiction and are connected with the theme of survival, not mere physical survival, but a survival of the spirit, with human dignity and the ability to give and receive love. It will be obvious that these themes relate to Hagar, in *The Stone Angel*, who finally even in extreme old age can find something of that inner freedom; to Rachel in *A Jest of God*, who will remain nervous and neurotic to some extent but who does succeed in freeing herself from her mother's tyranny and from her own self-doubt and self-hatred; to Stacey in *The Fire-Dwellers*, who comes to terms with her life and recognizes herself as a survivor; to Vanessa in *A Bird in the House*, who escapes from the authoritarian regime of her grandfather and who is ultimately able to be released from her hatred and fear of the old man; and finally, to Morag in *The Diviners*, who, more than any of the others, is able to assimilate her past and to accept herself as a strong and independent woman, able to love and to create. The themes of freedom and survival relate both to the social/external world and to the spiritual/inner one, and they are themes which I see as both political and religious. If freedom is, in part, the ability to act out of one's own self-definition, with some confidence and with compassion, uncompelled by fear or by the authority of others, it is also a celebration of life and of the mystery at life's core. In their varying ways, all these characters experience a form of grace.

In a good deal of my fiction, and especially in *The Diviners*, the theme of dispossession is an important one. It is shown in Christie's tales of the Highland Scots, turned off their lands during the Clearances,[4] and in the recurrence throughout my Canadian fiction of the Tonnerre family, descendants of the Métis, who were once the prairie horselords and who gradually were dispossessed of the lands which they and their Indian brothers had lived on and from and with, although not owned, for no man could own the land – the land was God's. Little did they know the concepts of the incoming European culture. They learned, however, in sorrow and pain.

Like love, like communication, like freedom, social justice must sometimes be defined in fiction by the lack of it. I believe this to be so in many instances throughout my fiction – the plight of the Métis; the town's scorn of such people as Lazarus Tonnerre, Christie Logan, Bram Shipley, Lottie Dreiser,[5] to name only a few; the depression years of the thirties; the way in which the true meaning of war comes to some of the town's men in the trenches of World War I, and again later to many of the townsfolk with the tragedy of Dieppe in World War II.[6]

Fiction has many facets, and I have mentioned only a few. For myself, it encompasses both history and belief, both social and spiritual themes. It speaks first and foremost of individual characters, and through them it speaks of our dilemmas and our aspirations, which are always in some way or other those both of politics and of faith.

PART TWO

Personal and Creative Essays:
"The River Flows Both Ways"

Where the World Began

"Where the World Began" was first published in Maclean's *in 1972, with the sub-title "A Small Prairie Town as an Aspect of Myself." In a cancelled introductory paragraph Laurence says it was "an article which would try to explain my self to my self." It was reprinted as the final essay in* Heart of a Stranger *in 1976, where Laurence introduced it thus: "I wrote this article in 1971, when I was beginning my novel* The Diviners. *I see now that I used it as one more means of working out a theme that appears in the novel, that is, the question of where one belongs and why, and the meaning to oneself of the ancestors, but the long-ago ones and those in remembered history. Until I re-read these articles, I didn't realize I had written so much on this theme before I ever dealt with it fictionally. I didn't realize, either, how compulsively I'd written about the river, the same river that appears in the novel."*[1]

A strange place it was, that place where the world began. A place of incredible happenings, splendours, and revelations, despairs like multitudinous pits of isolated hells. A place of shadow-spookiness, inhabited by the unknowable dead. A place of jubilation and of mourning, horrible and beautiful.

It was, in fact, a small prairie town.

Because that settlement and that land were my first and for many years my only real knowledge of this planet, in some profound way they remain my world, my way of viewing. My eyes were formed there. Towns like ours, set in a sea of land, have been described thousands of times as dull, bleak, flat, uninteresting. I have had it said to me that the railway trip across Canada is spectacular, except for the Prairies, when it would be desirable to go to sleep for several days, until the ordeal is over. I am always unable to argue this point effectively. All I can say

is – well, you really have to live there to know that country. The town of my childhood could be called bizarre, agonizingly repressive, or cruel at times, and the
land in which it grew could be called harsh in the violence of its seasonal changes.
But never merely flat or uninteresting. Never dull.

In winter, we used to hitch rides on the back of the milk sleigh, our moccasins
squeaking and slithering on the hard rutted snow of the roads, our hands in
ice-bubbled mitts hanging onto the box edge of the sleigh for dear life, while
Bert grinned at us through his great frosted moustache and shouted the horse
into speed, daring us to stay put. Those mornings, rising, there would be the
perpetual fascination of the frost feathers on windows, the ferns and flowers
and eerie faces traced there during the night by unseen artists of the wind.
Evenings, coming back from skating, the sky would be black but not dark, for
you could see a cold glitter of stars from one side of the earth's rim to the other.
And then the sometime astonishment when you saw the Northern Lights flar-
ing across the sky, like the scrawled signature of God. After a blizzard, when
the snowploughs hadn't yet got through, school would be closed for the day, the
assumption being that the town's young could not possibly flounder through
five feet of snow in the pursuit of education. We would then gaily don snowshoes and flounder for miles out into the white dazzling deserts, in pursuit of
a different kind of knowing. If you came back too close to night, through the
woods at the foot of the town hill, the thin black branches of poplar and choke-
cherry now meringued with frost, sometimes you heard coyotes. Or maybe the
banshee wolf-voices were really only inside your head.

Summers were scorching, and when no rain came and the wheat became
bleached and dried before it headed, the faces of farmers and townsfolk would
not smile much, and you took for granted, because it never seemed to have been
any different, the frequent knocking at the back door and the young men standing there, mumbling or thrusting defiantly their requests for a drink of water
and a sandwich if you could spare it. They were riding the freights, and you never
knew where they had come from, or where they might end up, if anywhere. The
Drought and Depression were like evil deities which had been there always. You
understood and did not understand.

Yet the outside world had its continuing marvels. The poplar bluffs and the
small river were filled and surrounded with a zillion different grasses, stones, and
weed flowers. The meadowlarks sang undaunted from the twanging telephone
wires along the gravel highway. Once we found an old flat-bottomed scow, and

launched her, poling along the shallow brown waters, mending her with wodges of hastily chewed Spearmint, grounding her among the tangles of yellow marsh marigolds that grew succulently along the banks of the shrunken river, while the sun made our skins smell dusty-warm.

My best friend lived in an apartment above some stores on Main Street (its real name was Mountain Avenue, goodness knows why), an elegant apartment with royal-blue velvet curtains. The back roof, scarcely sloping at all, was corrugated tin, of a furnace-like warmth on a July afternoon, and we would sit there drinking lemonade and looking across the back lane at the Fire Hall. Sometimes our vigil would be rewarded. Oh joy! Somebody's house burning down! We had an almost-perfect callousness in some ways. Then the wooden tower's bronze bell would clonk and toll like a thousand speeded funerals in a time of plague, and in a few minutes the team of giant black horses would cannon forth, pulling the fire wagon like some scarlet chariot of the Goths, while the firemen clung with one hand, adjusting their helmets as they went.

The oddities of the place were endless. An elderly lady used to serve, as her afternoon tea offering to other ladies, soda biscuits spread with peanut butter and topped with a whole marshmallow. Some considered this slightly eccentric, when compared with chopped egg sandwiches, and admittedly talked about her behind her back, but no one ever refused these delicacies or indicated to her that they thought she had slipped a cog. Another lady dyed her hair a bright and cheery orange, by strangers often mistaken at twenty paces for a feather hat. My own beloved stepmother wore a silver fox neckpiece, a whole pelt, *with the embalmed (?) head still on*. My Ontario Irish grandfather said "sparrow grass," a more interesting term than asparagus. The town dump was known as "the nuisance grounds," a phrase fraught with weird connotations, as though the effluvia of our lives was beneath contempt but at the same time was subtly threatening to the determined and sometimes hysterical propriety of our ways.

Some oddities were, as idiom had it, "funny ha ha"; others were "funny peculiar." Some were not so very funny at all. An old man lived, deranged, in a shack in the valley. Perhaps he wasn't even all that old, but to us he seemed a wild Methuselah figure, shambling among the underbrush and the tall couch grass, muttering indecipherable curses or blessings, a prophet who had forgotten his prophecies. Everyone in town knew him, but no one knew him. He lived among us as though only occasionally and momentarily visible. The kids called him Andy Gump, and feared him. Some sought to prove their bravery by tormenting him. They were the mediaeval bear baiters, and he the lumbering bewildered bear, half blind, only rarely turning to snarl. Everything is to be found in a town like mine. Belsen, writ small but with the same ink.

All of us cast stones in one shape or another. In grade school, among the vulnerable and violet girls we were, the feared and despised were those few girls from what was charmingly termed "the wrong side of the tracks." Tough in talk and tougher in muscle, they were said to be whores already. And may have been, that being about the only profession readily available to them.

The dead lived in that place, too. Not only the grandparents who had, in local parlance, "passed on" and who gloomed, bearded or bonneted, from the sepia photographs in old albums, but also the uncles, forever eighteen or nineteen, whose names were carved on the granite family stones in the cemetery, but whose bones lay in France. My own young mother lay in that graveyard, beside other dead of our kin, and when I was ten, my father, too, only forty, left the living town for the dead dwelling on the hill.

When I was eighteen, I couldn't wait to get out of that town, away from the Prairies. I did not know then that I would carry the land and town all my life within my skull, that they would form the mainspring and source of the writing I was to do, wherever and however far away I might live.

This was my territory in the time of my youth, and in a sense my life since then has been an attempt to look at it, to come to terms with it. Stultifying to the mind it certainly could be, and sometimes was, but not to the imagination. It was many things, but it was never dull.

The same, I now see, could be said for Canada in general. Why on earth did generations of Canadians pretend to believe this country dull? We knew perfectly well it wasn't. Yet for so long we did not proclaim what we knew. If our upsurge of so-called nationalism seems odd or irrelevant to outsiders, and even to some of our own people (*what's all the fuss about?*), they might try to understand that for many years we valued ourselves insufficiently, living as we did under the huge shadows of those two dominating figures, Uncle Sam and Britannia. We have only just begun to value ourselves, our land, our abilities. We have only just begun to recognize our legends and to give shape to our myths.

There are, God knows, enough aspects to deplore about this country. When I see the killing of our lakes and rivers with industrial wastes, I feel rage and despair. When I see our industries and natural resources increasingly taken over by

America, I feel an overwhelming discouragement, especially as I cannot simply say "damn Yankees." It should never be forgotten that it is we ourselves who have sold such a large amount of our birthright for a mess of plastic Progress. When I saw the War Measures Act being invoked in 1970, I lost whatever vestigial remains of the naive wish-belief that repression could not happen here, or would not. And yet, of course, I had known all along in the deepest and often hidden caves of the heart that anything can happen anywhere, even in the microcosm of a prairie town. But in raging against our injustices, our stupidities, I do so *as family*, as I did, and still do in writing, about those aspects of my town which I hated and which are always in some ways aspects of myself.

The land still draws me more than other lands. I have lived in Africa and in England, but splendid as both can be, they do not have the power to move me in the same way as, for example, that part of southern Ontario where I spent four months last summer in a cedar cabin beside a river. "Scratch a Canadian, and you find a phony pioneer," I used to say to myself in warning. But all the same it is true, I think, that we are not yet totally alienated from physical earth, and let us only pray we do not become so. I once thought that my lifelong fear and mistrust of cities made me a kind of old-fashioned freak; now I see it differently.

The cabin has a long window across its front western wall, and sitting at the oak table there in the mornings, I used to look out at the river and at the tall trees beyond, green-gold in the early light. The river was bronze; the sun caught it strangely, reflecting upon its surface the near-shore sand ripples underneath. Suddenly, the crescenting of a fish, gone before the eye could clearly give image to it. The old man next door said these leaping fish were carp. Himself, he preferred muskie, for he was a real fisherman and the muskie gave him a fight. The wind most often blew from the south, and the river flowed toward the south, so when the water was wind-riffled, and the current was strong, the river seemed to be flowing both ways. I liked this, and interpreted it as an omen, a natural symbol.

A few years ago, when I was back in Winnipeg, I gave a talk at my old college. It was open to the public, and afterward a very old man came up to me and asked me if my maiden name had been Wemyss. I said yes, thinking he might have known my father or my grandfather. But no. "When I was a young lad," he said, "I once worked for your great-grandfather, Robert Wemyss, when he had the sheep ranch at Raeburn." I think that was a moment when I realized all over again something of great importance to me. My long-ago families came from Scotland and Ireland, but in a sense, that no longer mattered so much. My true roots were here.[2]

I am not very patriotic in the usual meaning of that word. I cannot say "My country, right or wrong" in any political, social, or literary context. But one thing is inalterable, for better or worse, for life.

This is where my world began. A world which includes the ancestors – both my own and other peoples' ancestors who became mine. A world which formed me, and continues to do so, even while I fought it in some of its aspects, and continue to do so. A world which gave me my own lifework to do, because it was here that I learned the sight of my own particular eyes.

Love and Madness in the Steel Forest

*"Love and Madness in the Steel Forest," contained in the Clara Thomas Archives
and Special Collections, York University, 1980–001/023 (156), was first published
in the* Vancouver Sun *on 18 October 1969, with the following blurb printed at
the end of the article: "*Mrs Laurence, now Writer in residence at the University
of Toronto, won the 1966 Governor General's fiction award for *A Jest of God,
a novel about an unhappy spinster in a prairie town which was made into the
highly successful movie,* Rachel, Rachel. *Her latest book,* The Fire-Dwellers,
reflects some of her experiences when she lived in Kerrisdale. She will write for
the* Sun *from time to time during her Toronto stay."*

*Here Laurence conveys her detestation of cities, especially Toronto, dubbed
"the Vile Metropolis," or "*vm*" for short, where skyscrapers create a "steel forest."
Portraying the urban scene in italics reflects her method for conveying dystopic
science-fiction scenes in* The Fire-Dwellers, *also published in 1969. Climaxing
the essay in the Kafkaesque prison of a television studio, as experts discuss the
possibility of love in the madness of this urban landscape, suggests Laurence's
distrust of technology and dislike of public speaking.*[1]

Being by nature a country person, cities tend to bug me under any circumstances. Now, for the first time in my life, I am living totally on my own in a city
strange to me. The city is Toronto – if it were New York, I would no doubt have
flipped my lid after one week. As it is, things are bizarre enough. I do not drive
a car, and, with my oddly faulty sense of direction, finding my way around by
public transport is slightly traumatic in itself. Then again, I am going in to an
office (my own office – ye gods) for the first time in nearly twenty years.

Walking alone in a city, when one is unaccustomed, has an element of madness and unreality. I have not yet relearned what every city dweller has to do in self-protection – that is, to block out of sight and hearing some of the zoom and flash and screech and rush and buzz and boing and shove and clatter. Still, all this I needed to know. And at least it means I'm viewing things with different eyes and ears than they will be in a month or so, when I'll look back and wonder how everything could have seemed so weird.

Adjustment, or whatever it is – learning the simplest rules of survival perhaps – begins to happen, it seems to me, in pendulum sweeps. One moment the impersonality of the city oppresses me as though I were breathing in some mind-numbing gas. The next moment the ability of people to maintain life as themselves seems nothing short of miraculous. We are a hell of a tough breed, after all – scathed, beat-up, but tough. The wonder is not that so many crack up, but that so many don't.

Morning subway, and there are no songs here, not even sad ones. Hundreds of eyes, focused on train floors, not on each other. Are floors safer to look at? Eglinton Davisville St Clair Summerhill (nostalgically named?) Rosedale and change at Bloor.[2] *Tumult of hurtling anonymous bodies along the early platforms in the subterranean caves of ice masquerading as concrete or false marble, caves of chill, filled with hot lung-used air. All of us ascending escalators like one corporate octopus body, as on a conveyor belt taking us to a destination which may well turn out to be a meat factory run by human-devouring extra-terrestrial cacti.*

Yes, but then I am on a plane going to Ottawa. Sitting next to me is a girl, not more than twenty-two, slender, nearly thin, green eyes darting, suspicious or curious, I can't tell, and a tentative opening smile. She begins to talk. She is a snake dancer.[3]

A *what* dancer?

"A snake dancer," she says, pleased at my astonishment. "I've got this boa constrictor, see, and I do dance numbers with it. No, don't worry – it's not on the plane at this moment. I've played nightclubs all the way from Montreal to Vancouver. Oh – you used to live in Vancouver? I played The Cave there. They said they'd never had a snake dancer before. Isn't that a gas? They loved my show – even old middle-aged guys and their wives, yet, came to see it. I didn't always have the snake. I got it in Mexico. Believe me, I been all over. Before I got the snake, I used to do straight expressive dancing, know what I mean? But I got no use for these strippers who think all they gotta have is big tits and they don't know from nothing how to move. Actually, I'm really an artist. I mean, like, I paint. I work the night clubs so as to get enough money to quit for awhile and do my painting."

What sort of thing does she paint, I inquire.

"Well, I've been doing these feather people lately," she begins hesitantly. Then she frowns a little. "No – I can't say. If I could, I wouldn't be painting what it is with me."

This figures. She really is an artist, then. Godspeed, whoever she is. She never tells me her name.

Traffic is not neutral. Metallic predators prowl and lunge along these streets. I see them as having minds of their own, ignoring their drivers who naively imagine themselves to be in command. These are the big cats of the steel and concrete jungle, voices purring, roaring, sometimes screaming for the blood they live on. (Calm, calm. Let us not become paranoid.)

I am on an express bus, winging happily through the Ontario countryside on my way back to Toronto. The leaves of the maples are turning red, and all I want to do is look, unable to take in enough of that incredible colour. Unfortunately, I begin coughing. The man in the seat behind leans forward and offers a cough drop. He will not take no for an answer, so 1 accept the cough drop and open a book. This is exceedingly mean of me, as it is so clear that he wants to talk. Over the top of the book, I peer out the window at the maple trees. The man sighs, and finally latches onto the guy in the opposite seat.

"C'mon over here and talk, eh? We can talk about anything you like, anything. Whatever you say. We can argue, if you wanna. I'll argue about anything."

He is on his way to Chicago to see his sister, who is dying. She is thirty-seven years old and is dying of cancer. It is likely that she will not be alive by the time he gets there. His plane leaves Toronto at midnight. He does not know a soul in Toronto, not having been there for seventeen years. Of course, he has two brothers in Toronto, but they left home a long time ago and never paid a nickel for their mother's keep. Hell, he'd rather walk the streets from five to midnight than phone one of them. His sister is different. But now he might not get there in time. He is trying to work out what kind of fairness there could be in this life.

The man who is acting as captive audience finally asserts his own tale. He works as an elevator operator and has done so for some forty years. He is black, unmarried, aging. He lives in a small apartment, where nobody bothers him. He has a TV and he keeps a fridge full of beer. At night, he goes home and locks his door, and there he is with his TV and his beer.

"No problems," he says, with seeming belief. "No problems."

The bus arrives in Toronto. The elevator operator, in a gravel voice, almost as though what he were saying were a surprise to himself, invites the other man to go and have a beer with him. I watch them walking together across the street to the nearest bar.

Everywhere, the apartment buildings are spearing the sky, the new tallest dead terribly quick-growing trees, trunks and branches of steel, leaves of concrete. The now forest. If you lived away up there, you could see for miles. For instance, you could see other apartment buildings.

The taxi driver is huge, a man with arms like cedar logs and a belly like some obese Buddha. Last night, he tells me, was a great, great night for him. Why, I ask.[4]

"I beat the world's karate champ," he says, with suitably casual pride. "Come from LA, this guy, and he's the best. I beat him last night. That was quite a moment, I can tell you. I only drive cab part time, see? I teach karate, evenings. I was in the US Marines for three years, in Vietnam, and I killed a hundred Viet Cong with my hands and feet."

Not ninety-four, exactly one hundred. Fate can be quite tidy at times, it appears. How did he feel about doing that, I ask.

"Well, I guess it isn't anything to be exactly proud of," he says, considering the question carefully, "but then again, you gotta think – it was either them or me. Now I teach karate only to women."

To women? He teaches karate only to women?

"I figure it like this," he explains. "A woman needs to be able to defend herself more than a man does, most times. Besides, I'm a masseur, and when my girls get into knots, see, I can straighten them out."

Oh. And whether the whole tale is fact or fantasy, everyone to their own means of survival, I guess.

The TV studio is darker than darkness, out beyond those white sight-destroying spotlights which clutch the four people around the oval table and hold them in Kafkaesque prison. Claustrophobia is everywhere, like a felt presence, something you could touch. Technicians in armies soft-foot around, muttering incomprehensible directions in another language. We are as follows: two psychologists (male), one anthropologist (female) and one novelist who gets angry if anyone calls her a lady novelist, which the announcer of course does in the opening gambit. The lights burn like small suns of hell, unquenchable and forever high noon. We sweat. The water in the drinking glasses grows tepid. We are talking about love and tenderness in urban and depersonalized situations. Is it possible? Who can say? But we must believe or perish.

On the sidewalk, a boy and girl, long hair streaming into the winds of autumn, jeans and old jackets a mock to plastic worlds, to worlds of broadloom, walk with their arms around one another. They see another young couple approaching, people known, others of their tribe. All four embrace on the street, putting their arms around each other, a momentary circle of safeness, of touching.

The newspaper photo shows a sixteen-year-old girl sitting on the steps of the place from which she has just been evicted. She comes from Edmonton, but that was – she can't remember when. She hasn't taken any speed or anything today, she is reported as saying. She did yesterday, but not today, not yet anyway. Maybe she won't tomorrow. No, she doesn't know where to go tonight. Maybe something will happen.

But then again, a small, unexpected gift. Two almost-elderly women wearing those strange flower-petal hats which seem to be made out of starched chiffon, in shades of determined pink and orange, are talking on the subway. One fragment only comes across, but it is sufficient.

"They sure picked the wrong party when they picked Myrtle. Why, Myrtle was so incensed that they hadn't paid their rent that she went out to the garage, and the lady had this piece of marble there, you know, that she was gonna use for a coffee table top. And Myrtle got a sledge-hammer and busted that marble all to smithereens and threw the pieces all over the lawn."

Being one for omens, I immediately get the distinct impression that things are looking up, at least in some few areas. This feeling is reinforced when I get to the office. A letter is waiting for me from a writer friend, saying, "Come and see us. I need the sanity of your insanity."

Survival, as I keep trying to say in my various ways, is all.

Upon a Midnight Clear

Laurence published this essay recalling Christmas traditions in her family homes, including the "agreeable anarchy" of Elm Cottage, in Weekend Magazine *on 21 December 1974, under the title "The Greatest Gift of All." She included it in* Heart of a Stranger *with this introduction: "This article was published in December 1974, just before our first Christmas in my Lakefield house, which is now establishing some of its own traditions, while as always carrying over some of those from the past."*

I would bet a brace of baubles plus a partridge in a pear tree that when Charles Dickens wrote *A Christmas Carol* no one wanted to identify with Scrooge, before he became converted to Christmas. How very different now. One is likely at this time of year to run into all kinds of people who view themselves as the Good Guys and who actually try to make you feel guilty if you celebrate Christmas. "It's become totally commercial," they virtuously say. "We don't have anything to do with it."

All I can reply, borrowing a word from Scrooge, is *Humbug.* Sure, okay, the stores may less-than-subtly put out their Christmas displays immediately after Halloween; the carols may be used to advertise fur coats or washing machines; the amount of phoniness surrounding Christmas in our culture may be astronomical. But Christmas itself remains untouched by all this crassness. It's still a matter of personal choice, and surely it's what happens in your own home that counts. In our house, Christmas has always been a very important time.

My background and heritage are strongly Christian, although I reserve the right to interpret things in my own way. In my interpretation, what Christmas celebrates is grace, a gift given from God to man, not because deserved, just because given. The birth of every wanted and loved child in this world is the same, a gift. The birth of every child should be this way. We're still frighteningly far from that, but maybe this festival can remind us. Christmas also reaches back to pre-Christian times – an ancient festival celebrating the winter solstice. The *Concise Oxford Dictionary* defines solstice very beautifully – "Either time (summer, winter) at which the sun is farthest from the equator and appears to pause before returning." For countless centuries, in the northern lands, this time of year was a festival of faith, the faith that spring would return to the land. It links us with our ancestors a very long way back.

Christmas when I was a child was always a marvellous time. We used to go to the carol service on Christmas Eve, and those hymns still remain my favourites. "Hark the Herald Angels Sing," "Once in Royal David's City," and the one I loved best, "It Came upon a Midnight Clear." It couldn't have been even near midnight when we walked home after those services, but it always seemed to me that I knew exactly what "midnight clear" meant. I had no sense then that there could be any kind of winter other than ours. It was a prairie town, and by Christmas the snow would always be thick and heavy, yet light and clean as well, something to be battled against and respected when it fell in blinding blizzards, but also something which created an upsurge of the heart at times such as those, walking back home on Christmas Eve with the carols still echoing in your head. The evening would be still, almost silent, and the air would be so dry and sharp you could practically touch the coldness. The snow would be dark-shadowed and then suddenly it would look like sprinkled rainbows around the sparse streetlights. Sometimes there were northern lights. My memory, probably faulty, assigns the northern lights to all those Christmas eves, but they must have appeared at least on some, a blazing eerie splendour across the sky, swift-moving, gigantic, like a message. It was easy then to believe in the Word made manifest. Not so easy now. And yet I can't forget, ever, that the child, who was myself then, experienced awe and recognized it.

We always had the ceremony of two Christmas trees. One was in the late afternoon of Christmas Day, and was at the home of my grandparents, my mother's people, at the big brick house. There would be a whole congregation of aunts and uncles and cousins there on that day, and we would *have the tree* (that is how we said it) before dinner. One of my aunts was head of the nursing division in Saskatchewan's public health department, and was a distinguished professional woman. I didn't know that about her then. What I knew was that each Christmas she came back home with an astounding assortment of rare and wonderful things from what I felt must be the centre of the great wide world, namely Regina. She used to bring us those packages of Swiss cheese, each tiny piece wrapped in silver paper, and decorations for the table (a Santa with reindeer and sleigh, pine-cone men painted iridescent white with red felt caps), and chocolate Santas in red and gold paper, and chocolate coins contained in heavy gold foil so that they looked like my idea of Spanish doubloons and pieces of eight, as in *Treasure Island*.

The dinner was enormous and exciting. We had *olives* to begin with. We rarely had olives at any other time, as they were expensive. My grandfather, of course, carved what was always known as The Bird, making the job into an impressive performance. He was never an eminently lovable man, but even he, with his stern ice-blue eyes, managed some degree of pleasantness at Christmas. The children at dinner were served last, which seems odd today. One of my memories is of myself at about six, sighing mightily as the plates were being passed to the adults and murmuring pathetically, "Couldn't I even have a crust?" My sense of drama was highly developed at a young age.

When the dishes were done – a mammoth task, washing all my grandmother's Limoges – we would make preparations to go home. I always had my own private foray into the kitchen then. I would go to the icebox (yes, icebox, with a block of ice delivered daily) and would tear off hunks of turkey, snatch a dozen or so olives, and wrap it all in wax paper. This was so I could have a small feast during the night, in case of sudden hunger, which invariably and improbably occurred each Christmas night.

The day of Christmas, however, began at home. The one I recall the best was the last Christmas we had with my father, for he died the next year. We were then living in my father's family home, a redbrick oddity with a rose window, a big dining room, a dozen nearly hidden cupboards and hidey-holes, and my father's study with the fireplace, above which hung a sinister bronze scimitar brought from India by an ancestor. I was nine that year, and my brother was two. The traditions in our family were strong. The children rose when they wakened (usually about 6 am or earlier) and had their Christmas stockings. In those days, our stockings contained a Japanese orange at the toe, some red-and-white peppermint canes, a bunch of unshelled peanuts, and one or two small presents – a kaleidoscope or a puzzle consisting of two or three interlocked pieces of metal which you had to try to prise apart, and never could.

As my memory tells it to me, my very young brother and myself had our Christmas stockings in our parents' bedroom, and Christmas had officially begun. We were then sent back to bed until the decent hour of 7:30 or 8:00 a.m., at which time I could get dressed in my sweater and my plaid skirt with the straps over the shoulder, while my mother dressed my brother in his sweater and infant overalls. We then went down for breakfast. In our house, you always had breakfast before you had The Tree. This wasn't such a bad thing. Christmas breakfast was sausage rolls, which we never had for breakfast any other time. These had been made weeks before, and frozen in the unheated summer kitchen. We had frozen food years before it became commercially viable. I guess our only amazement about it when it came on the market was that they could do it in summer as well. After breakfast, we all went into the study, where we had to listen to the Empire Broadcast on the radio, a report from all those pink-colored areas on the world map, culminating in the King's speech. The voices seemed to go on forever. I don't recall how my brother was kept pacified – with candy, probably – but I recall myself fidgeting. This was the ritual – The Empire Broadcast *before* The Tree, a practice which now seems to me to have been slightly bizarre, and yet probably was not so. Our parents wanted to hear it, and in those days it wasn't going to be repeated in capsule form on the late night news. I guess it also taught us that you could wait for what you wanted – but that's a concept about which I've always felt pretty ambiguous.

At last, at last, we could go into The Living Room for The Tree. The Living Room, I should say, was the only formal room in that house. We did not live in it; it was totally misnamed. It was For Best. It was the room in which my mother gave the afternoon teas which were then required of people like the wives of lawyers in towns like ours. The Living Room had a lot of stiff upholstered furniture, always just so. It was, as well, chilly. But it was the place for The Tree, and it seemed somehow the right place, something special.

And there it was, The Tree. *Oh.*

I could see now why we'd been so carefully kept out of the room until this moment. There, beside The Tree, were our presents. For my brother, a rocking horse, two horses cut out of wood and painted white with green flecks, joined by a seat between them. Our dad had made it, for he was a very good amateur carpenter. And for me – wow! A desk. A small desk, found in an attic, as I later learned, and painted by our dad, a bright blue with flower patterns, a desk which opened up and had your own private cubbyholes in it. My own desk. My first. That remains the nicest present that anyone ever gave me, the present from my parents when I was nine.

It was only many years later that I realized that the rocking horse and the desk had been our presents then because no one could afford to buy anything much in that depression and drought year of 1935. And it wasn't until long afterwards, either, that I realized how lucky and relatively unscathed we'd been, and how many people in this country that year must have had virtually no Christmas at all.

One other aspect of my childhood Christmases was Lee Ling. He was the man who ran our town's Chinese restaurant, and he lived without his family for all the time he was there. In those days, Chinese wives were scarcely allowed into this country at all. My father did Lee's legal work, and every Christmas Lee gave us a turkey, a large box of chocolates, and a box of lichee nuts. You might possibly say that Lee did it because he hoped to get on the right side of the lawyer. My father wasn't like that, and neither was Lee. The point of this story, however, is that Lee Ling continued at Christmas to give our family a turkey, a box of chocolates, and a box of lichee nuts after my father died, for years, until Lee himself died. To me, that says something valuable about both Lee Ling and my father.

Much later on, when my own children were young and growing up, our Christmases became patterns which reflected my own Christmases many years ago, but with our own additions. We had ten Christmases in our house in England, Elm Cottage, before my children became adults and I moved back home to Canada to stay. Christmas in that house was always something very good and warm, and there were usually a lot of young Canadian visitors there with us at that time.

As in my childhood, the Christmas stockings were opened early in the morning. The difference was, with us, that my kids always made a Christmas stocking for me as well, their own idea. The stockings had candies, including the same kind of chocolate coins, but they also had a variety of joke presents, sometimes kids' books when my kids were no longer children, because we've always liked good children's books and we frequently give them to one another.

Some of the traditions continued. In our house, you always have breakfast before you have The Tree. But in our time, The Tree was in my study, not a "special" place, and we frequently went in wearing housecoats and dressing gowns and bearing large mugs of coffee. The presents were distributed one at a time so everyone could look at each. We made it last about two hours. I don't think gifts need to be meaningless. I love opening presents from people who care about me, and I love giving presents to people I care about, hoping I've chosen something they will really like, something that fits their own personality, something that will be a symbol of my feeling for them.

Our dinner at Elm Cottage was always fairly hectic. I was in charge of what we called The Bird, as it had been called in my own childhood. I twittered and worried over that turkey, wondering if I had put it in the oven soon enough, or if I was going to overcook it to the point of total disaster. It always turned out fine, an amazing fact when one considers that our stove was so small as to be almost ridiculous and that even cramming a 15-pound turkey into it at all was a major task. The turkey, I modestly admit, was accompanied by some of the best sage-and-onion stuffing in the entire world. Our friend Alice always made her super cranberry sauce, which included walnuts and orange, and was the best I've ever tasted. Our friend Sandy always used to do the plum pudding, which she cleverly heated on a small electric burner set up in the hall, as there wasn't room on the stove. My daughter had been the one to organize the cake, a month before, and everyone had given it a stir for luck. It was a very co-operative meal. Yes, the women did prepare all the food. But the men carved The Bird, served the dinner, and did the dishes. It always seemed to me that our efforts meshed pretty well. Our friend Peter once said that Elm Cottage was a scene of "agreeable anarchy." I think it was, and that phrase certainly describes our Christmas dinners, at which we never had less than a dozen people, and sometimes more.

After dinner, we would move to The Music Room, which was our version of The Living Room, except that we really lived in it. It had a good stereo and a feeling that people could come in and sit around the fireplace and play their guitars and sing their own songs. This used to happen a lot, and always at Christmas. We made new traditions. One of my own favourites was a ritual which said that at some point in the evening, our friend Ian would play and sing two songs for me. Corny and out-of-date they may be, but I like them. They were "She Walks These Hills in a Long Black Veil" and "St James Infirmary Blues."

Those Christmases at Elm Cottage had a feeling of real community. For me, this is what this festival is all about – the sense of God's grace, and the sense of our own family and extended family, the sense of human community.

Don't Whisper Sudden; I Scare Easy

"Don't Whisper Sudden; I Scare Easy" is contained in the Clara Thomas Archives and Special Collections, York University Archives, Accession 1980– 001/023 (156), and was first published in the Vancouver Sun *on 20 December 1969. While transitioning from Elm Cottage in Buckinghamshire to North American cities in 1969 renders Laurence accident-prone, a trip to New York City to meet with her American publisher, Alfred Knopf, makes the comparatively clean Toronto seem almost palatable to Laurence, although visiting the lunar landscape of York University, with English professor Clara Thomas, custodian and donor of the manuscripts that form the basis of many essays in this collection, proves absurdly nightmarish.*

Whilst vacationing in the cosy city of Victoria last summer at high noon, cold sober, I walked into a lamppost.

That, apart from being a great opening line for a short story I'll never write, happens to be true fact. One would not believe it possible, but it happened. I was running for a bus and not looking where I was going. I stood there with my life's blood fountaining from a scalp wound onto the sidewalk outside Woolworth's, wondering in a detached desultory fashion what to do next, musing upon the impersonality of cities, and thinking that if *Victoria*, for heaven's sake, could do this to me, how was I going to react to Toronto, after six years of living in a small English village? Perhaps thanks to the subdued size of Victoria, presently a police car drew up and carted me off to the emergency ward of St Joseph's, where a maddeningly calm young doctor did some fancy embroidery on my right eyebrow with black thread and put a band-aid on the scalp wound, which turned out to be the size of five minutes and not, as I had naturally imagined, a gaping gash through which my gray matter could be observed quivering.

In early autumn, I arrived in Toronto, which was to be my dwelling place for the next eight months. With admirable aplomb, I stuck out the traffic, the noise, the ever-presence of cement under the feet, the sense of too much going on all at once, coupled with the conviction that thousands of people were walk-ing these streets totally shut inside the boneyard of their own skulls. I endured the high-rise apartments springing overnight like strange metallic fungi con-taining a plethora of human ants who had no notion of each other's names, the doom-crying (and rightly so) newspapers, the polluted air, the feeling of living in a world made of plastic but not unbreakable – in fact, so brittle it might shatter any moment. I stuck it out all right. For about three weeks. Then I sprained my ankle.

I did not sprain my ankle only once. Oh no. That would not have been enough. I overturned it half a dozen times before I finally went to a doctor, by which time I could hardly walk – the subconscious purpose of the whole nonaccident, no doubt, but it is one thing to recognize these matters and another to do anything about them. The doctor applied an elastic bandage which gave my hitherto presentable-looking ankle the appearance of a baby elephant's leg.

"What shall I do?" I groaned, hoping he would say *Absolute Rest For Two Months.*

"Keep walking," he said, grinning.

Well, probably that is as good a slogan as any in this life. If I must take it upon myself to react thus violently and absurdly in the flesh to the isolations and ter-rors of urban life, all I could hope was that something might ultimately come of it and that I might learn a few things I needed to know.

One thing which was interesting, albeit alarming, to know about was how it really feels not to be able to rely upon the strength of your own legs. This had never happened to me before. How many times had I watched someone whose walk was frail, old, or damaged, snailing themselves onto buses, without knowing that for them each step was a small, precise battlefield?

My friends looked at me oddly when I told them what had happened, or rather *why*, which is often more interesting than what. Some of them could even be heard to murmur that perhaps I had simply sprained my ankle. But they had lived in Trona for a long time. *They* didn't suffer from this sort of accident. Or did they?

"Did I ever tell you," a social worker friend said one evening, "how I ran into a cupboard door last winter and the same evening slipped and fell down the stairs? We'd been terribly busy at the office, and I was absolutely exhausted … "

"Say no more," I intoned in my best Cassandra[1] voice. "I get the picture perfectly."

This picture, as far as my eyes are concerned, continues to be frequently surrealistic, and one is saved only by laughter and the sometime presence of friends. What about those who have gone beyond laughter and friends? It does not bear thinking about, but how can you stop thinking about it?

A friend tells me about an encounter in a bookshop with an old woman.

She comes up to me with a notebook in her hands and a ballpoint pen, all ready. She's – oh, maybe not that old but she gives the impression of being shrivelled, and she's dressed in a man's overcoat like an unintentional maxi, and her hair is grey and frizzy. She asks me if I'll write a letter for her, and it occurs to me then, from her accent, that maybe she can't write in English. So I agree, and she goes into this long tirade, all about how she keeps writing letters to the minister of justice, because she's determined to protect her rights and get back at those who are against her. You know why? Because they have been following her all the way from Chicago to here, and every room she lives in, they put bugs in it. Not electronic bugs, you understand. Real bugs – cockroaches, maybe. She finds the bugs, and that's how she knows they are doing it. What can you do? I wrote the letter for her. What else could I do?

Nothing else.

I am supposed to be seeing young writers and discussing their work with them, and I do. But one day the man who shambles into my office is neither young nor, I think, a writer. His clothes are tidy, but very worn, and his half smile seems poised on some precipice of fear. He isn't employed at the moment, he blurts out, but he intends to be soon. He wants to write a novel – in fact, he has been thinking about it since 1955, but he does not know how to write dialogue. Can I please tell him how to write dialogue? No, I reply, I can't tell him – it's really just a question of listening to how people talk and learning the knack that way. He looks apologetically out of his eyes' depth and then rapidly glances away.

"Well, you see," he says, "I don't often get to talk to people."

After a short while, I chivvy him as tactfully as possible out of the office, and I do not encourage him to return. Am I wrong? No. And then again, Yes.

But laughter, like the grace of God, comes when least expected or deserved. I go out to York University on Keele, which seems a million miles away from Trona proper, to take part in a seminar on Commonwealth literature. I had thought of York, mistakenly, as relatively small. Not so. It is vast, all the colleges connected by baffling and barren corridors, every door the same as every other door, acres of glass and tile, spreading plains of bare walls, great prairies of room after room after room. None of them the right room. On legs of gelatin, I keep walking. Draped here and there are young men and women like beautiful but limp lilies.

"Can you tell me," I inquire, "where I can find the English Department?"

"There's no English Department in this college," is the reply.

"There must be," I say, desperately. "I know someone who works in it."

"Not here, ma'am."

"Listen," I say with some exasperation, "Dr Clara Thomas,[2] whose class I have come to visit, works here. I may add that three of this country's best-known poets – Irving Layton, Miriam Waddington, and Eli Mandel – also work here. And you're telling me *it doesn't exist?*"

"Gee, I'm sorry," the young creature answers with regret. "I wouldn't know."

Kafka and Camus, bend kindly down from your non-heaven. William Burroughs, grotesquerie is at least mini-possible without injections or infusions of any sort.

Three-quarters of an hour later, the patron saint of directionless mariners comes to my rescue and I stumble accidentally upon the correct office. After the seminar is over, Clara Thomas and I try to wend our way to the senior common room of McLaughlin College,[3] where we have arranged to meet a few people for a drink. Easier said than done. Half an hour and innumerable corridors later, we have to admit we are lost. Clara attributes our mutual lack of instinctive direction to the fact that neither of us drives a car. But her Ontario pioneering instincts are aroused. She is a latterday Susanna Moodie,[4] roughing it in a new variety of bush, and she is *not* about to be defeated.

"We will retrace our steps," she says firmly.

Only one difficulty. We have made the major error of neglecting to blaze our trail with bits of paper or notches on the anonymous doors. The next thing we know, we are in a truly giant kitchen, full of exotic stainless steel fixtures and the bubbling grease-spitting noises of cooking food. In one bathtub-sized cauldron the soup is simmering.

"Why go any further?" I suggest. "Let's just jump in and drown ourselves right now."

The kitchen staff gazes with mild eyes upon our inexplicable mirth.

But if Trona often gives me the sense of living in a distorted and sometimes hilarious dream, what will New York be like?

A nightmare. In Manhattan, where my American publishers have their offices, from very high up the view is oddly beautiful – silver and black shafts of buildings, the glass of their windows diamonding in the sun, the waterfront from this distance not displaying its sores. But at street level it is another thing. The city streets are filthy, rubbish-laden, jammed with scurrying humans who hurry eyesdown not daring to look at one another.

Where is the next blow coming from? Who is going to stab me in the back? What enormities will my sheathed eyes be pried open to behold next minute? I don't want to look. I won't look.

This is the way the atmosphere comes across – to me, anyway. The war of all against all.

"Do you mind if I stop off at this bank, to make a deposit?" a cab driver says. "I don't like carrying no more money around than I have to."

This is one of the cab drivers who *speak*. Most don't. I recall, a little fondly, the many fascinating life stories I've heard from cab drivers in Trona. The friends with whom I'm staying live in the Village. They're lucky, they say, because the street on which they live also houses many little old Italian and Sicilian ladies, whom they take to be mothers of the Mafia, so there's not much trouble. The street is, so to speak, under the protective wings of the dark angels.

But other things apart from human hostility create trouble. If the garbage is collected on time, it is cause for celebration. Groceries won't deliver. Doctors won't make house calls. If you are stuck in the house with a young child, and you have flu or a wrenched back, your life becomes so complicated that the nerves stretch to their utmost, and you wonder how much further they can be stretched, even while recognizing that this is nothing compared to what it would be like if your life were that of the black ghettoes.

The city itself seems to be falling apart. For the bizarre beauty of every sky-searing tower, there are in other areas long stretches of streets dilapidated, paint nonexistent or shredded, where the stones of houses seem to be crumbling from some unidentifiable bone disease. One is aware of the day-unseen presence of the rat tribes.

Yet there is still the city where a large proportion of the nation's business is carried on. It is still the centre of the arts, of publishing. It houses many of the most talented, enlightened, and concerned people in America.

My visit, as it happens, is shortly before the mayoral elections. The slogan of one of Lindsay's opponents is FOR A CLEANER CITY, FOR A SAFER CITY, FOR A GREATER CITY. New York *is* a great city.[5] So was Babylon. But who in God's name could pretend to be capable of making it clean or safe?

In the evenings, sitting around after dinner, talking warmly and affectionately of books and mutual friends, the outside world seems perhaps not so threatening after all. Then we turn on the TV and get a shrill series of yelps and puzzling charts. It seems that floods and a hurricane are predicted. Of course. What else? There is only one possible comment. The prose style of the Book of Revelation[6] was better.

We worry for a while, and my friends batten down their back door, as torrential rains have a way of slithering into their kitchen, which is at basement level. The hurricane, fortunately, does not arrive. Better damnation next time, perhaps. I spend some hours the next day trying to get a more balanced perspective on New York (knowing my own tendency to overreact) by reading a collection of Jimmy Breslin's columns. In one of them he says that when the great power blackout came a few years ago, half the people in New York thought it was only their own house because they hadn't paid the light bill. Such is the contact among neighbours?

"The crucial fact about this city," one of my friends says, "is that it has become a place no longer meant for human habitation."

Here, if you have edgy nerves like mine, you are a commonplace. When I go out alone, my sprained ankle becomes instantly almost unable to support me. I walk as though on ice-coated eggs. But my publisher's editor walks jauntily, telling me that if I lived here six months I'd get used to it. And that, I am absolutely certain, is true. I have the feeling that these are a species of new pioneers, all of them, having to learn to live under circumstances which the human central nervous system was never designed to meet.

The plane finally takes off from Kennedy Airport,[7] after nearly an hour's delay while we wait our departure turn.

"Is this usual?" I ask the woman in the next seat.

"Yeh, and getting worse," she responds petulantly.

"I suppose you could say thank God we haven't been hijacked, but as far as I'm concerned, I wouldn't mind even that. At least it wouldn't be boring."

Dear old Toronto at last! *What is that you're saying?* I said Dear Old Trona.

"My, my," I remark ebulliently to the driver, "this is certainly a clean city – you know that?"

He gazes at me in astonishment in the car mirror. And, of course, it *is* an optical illusion, the sudden sense of order and safety here, but all the same, not all comparisons are totally odious. The feeling of having come home won't last – and doesn't. Because, whatever my own particular neuroses on the subject, it is undeniable that life in cities as we know them is becoming less viable every day. The rape of the planet, the poisoning of lakes and air, the impossibilities of massed traffic, the terrifying mutations which over-crowded humans, like grasshoppers, can undergo – these are not demons of any deranged imagination. They are actual, external, and with us.

A week after returning from New York, I buy a piece of land on the Otonabee River, not far from Peterborough.[8] It isn't large, but it has a cedar shack on it, and some trees, and the river passing by. It is not the answer to anything. In fact, in some ways it is downright delusory. I know all this very well. Nonetheless, I'm fortunate – more than usual – to be able to have this personal talisman. I can hold it in the mind, like an area of quiet, even when I am not able to be there.

And gradually I find I am walking again without having to think about walking.

The River Flows Both Ways

"The River Flows Both Ways," first published in the Vancouver Sun *on 11 December 1971, relates to* The Diviners *(1974), which Laurence wrote at her cabin overlooking the Otonabee River near Peterborough, Ontario. In a similar way, Morag Gunn writes her manuscript while looking out onto a river in the first section of the novel, "The River of Now and Then" (9–27), which begins, "The river flowed both ways" (11).*

Returning, one rarely finds the same place. The landscape, outer and inner, has usually changed while one has been away. I had lived in this cedar cabin on the banks of a southern Ontario river a year ago, only for a month. Now I was back for four months, with some apprehension. I had loved it so much before that I was afraid of being disappointed. Also, I had come here to work, and I kept having the nightmare fear that I would spend the entire summer looking at a blank page, unable to set down a word.

The cabin was just the same – better, in a sense, because it had been used by friends in my absence and it had a lived-in feeling which it hadn't had before. In front of the wide front window which overlooked the river was the oak library table which served both as desk and dining table. And here again was my small black woodstove which said *Huron* on the oven door, and my tall old-fashioned chair, the one I'd painted goldenrod the summer before. On the bookshelves which I'd put up in every available corner of the cabin were the books I'd brought here, mostly Canadian fiction, poetry, and history, and some few books from my childhood – my old and much-read copies of *Kim, Kidnapped, Wuthering Heights, Pride and Prejudice*. I knew instantly that I'd returned home. Loneliness, as Richard Hughes has said, is being alone and not talking. I lighted a fire in the stove and realized I could live here alone without feeling lonely. The next day, without any inner hassles, I began work.

Every time I lifted my eyes from the page I was writing, I saw the river. It changed all day long. In the early morning, when I was first wakened by the dawn chorus of yelling birds, I used to totter up and have a look at the river before going back to bed again in the hope that my joyful feathered friends would either get sore throats or become exhausted by their own exuberance. At that ungodly hour, the river had a beautifully spooky appearance, the fragile white mist cloaking it, swirling over it. Later, the world grew light. It actually did *grow* light in both senses of the word, as though the sun were a plant putting forth its tendrils into the sky. Then the river would become alive, the water almost the colour of polished bronze, but lovelier than any metal could be, because unset, moving, fluctuating, taking its own course. Mid-days, the river would often lie still, and then you could see in its mirror the trees beyond, the great maples and oaks, the silvergreen willows. Sometimes you could even see the double flight of swallows – the birds flying in air and on the waterscreen. Evenings, and the river altered once more. The receding sun gave to it a zillion candle flames, and the water ripples carried for an hour or so this armada of moving lights. A river is unceasingly fascinating, almost hypnotic, like the falling of snow or a log burning in a fireplace, but much more so.

Then one day I noticed a peculiar thing. The river flowed both ways. Or appeared to, which was the same thing. The wind came mostly from the south, and the river flowed toward the south, so that when the breeze was high and the watercurrent strong, you could see the river moving both ways. To me this seemed like a message which I might one day be able to interpret.

The previous owner of my shack had had a vegetable garden, nicely fenced against groundhogs and other invaders. After I moved in, the garden went to seed. I am no gardener. I realized almost at once that I would have to make severely threatening gestures in the direction of my Presbyterian conscience. I was not about to grow vegetables, but I had the feeling that there was something pretty reprehensible about this failure. Then the birds helped me out, and indeed relieved me of all guilt. The ex-garden grew a marvellous assortment of grasses, thistles, weeds, and wildflowers, stunning to behold. I have always felt that weeds were unfairly discriminated against and have admired dandelions as much as sunflowers. But it was not until I saw the way in which the birds, especially the goldfinches, adopted my wildflower garden as their free café, feasting on its huge variety of grassfruits and seeds, that I felt magnificently vindicated. My neighbour on one side was a Yugoslav who regarded it as a sin against the earth to have land and not grow anything on it. Whenever I went over to Steve's, to admire the garden in which he laboured mightily every weekend, he would give me both good advice and heaps of giant tomatoes, sweet green peppers, corn, and lettuce. The advice was that if I could only manage to get myself up at 5 a.m., like he did, I, too, could have a marvellous vegetable garden. I used to nod in agreement – *Yes, yes, undoubtedly true.* I never told him that, as long as he insisted, out of the kindness of his heart, in loading me up with all the goodies from *his* garden, I was much less likely to start my own.

My neighbour on the other side was eighty years old, and had come originally, in his own parlance, from *Ioway*. He had homesteaded north of Regina as a young man, and had fought in the First World War. He'd married an English girl at that time, and their marriage had been one of love and trust until she died, some five years ago. He had been a toolmaker in a car factory, and a very skilled work it was. He had also been a garageman, a driver, and many other things. He had weathered the Depression, he and his wife, and had never gone on relief. He was proud about that. He said it was mainly due to her. My Phil, she was really something. She could go down to the market in Toronto and get the leftover vegetables cheap and make a meal on practically nothing. When he'd once said he couldn't take any more and was going to apply for relief, she'd said, No, love, we're not. And they didn't. When she died, his life was cut out from under him. He sold up the house in Toronto and moved out to the river. He had broken his back, once, years ago, but he could still cut up the driftwood with his chainsaw and handle his boat.

He was a fisherman. Whenever he caught a few pickerel, he would come over to my place and give me one, all cleaned and filleted, the best fish I've ever eaten. But he preferred the muskie, because they were tough, like him. They gave him a fight. Listening to him talk about fishing, about the river, about his own life and the early days on the Prairies, I felt I was learning from him many things of great value.

He was careful never to interrupt me during what he knew were my writing hours. But late afternoons, he'd come over sometimes.

"C'mon," he said one day. "I'm going to teach you to run an outboard."

"Me?" I gasped. "I can't. I'm no good with machinery of any kind."

"You never know what you can do," he parried, "until you try."

This concept appealed to me, so out we went. That first trip must have been an awful experience for him. Rigidly, I grasped the lever of the outboard, my jaw set and tense. At the other end of the boat, he grinned encouragement while he spun out his fishing line. At no time during that voyage did he hook a fish, thank goodness. But at one point, owing to circumstances I find difficult to explain, in trying to steer the boat I found I was turning it around in midstream, slow sweeping circles. Help! What's happening? The old man had to leap to his feet in order to prevent his line from becoming impossibly snaggled in the rudder of the motor.

"I told you," I said to him when we finally and mercifully got back home. "I'm no good with motors."

"For the first time," he said gallantly, "you did pretty well."

He didn't press it, though. He began to realize that I really was a first-rate nit-wit with machinery. After three or four attempts, he gave up. Thereafter, I went in his boat only as an appreciative passenger. Once, at the end of a tropically hot August day, we skimmed along the river, catching whatever breeze there was. And there, on every outjutting log and treebranch in the unstirring water, sat all the tribes of the snapping turtles. From youngsters measuring only a few inches across the shell to oldsters measuring some two feet, they sat sunning themselves, a species almost as old as the world, regarding us with unblinking saurian eyes. And once, on one of our river trips, we saw a great blue heron, rearing its gigantic wings and flying with such certainty that you know it didn't have any notion yet what man has done to decimate our mutual home.

One afternoon we landed at a small settlement where they sold gas for boats and ice cream for boaters. The old man and I clambered ashore. We ate ice cream and chatted to the proprietor. During the course of conversation, the old man mentioned that I was a writer.

Fatal revelation.

"What *you* should write about," the proprietor said to me, "is the lady who has this house not more than about three-four miles from here. Daughter of a re-mittance man, she was, but he must've made good because that house there is really a sight – great big old place, chuck full of real antiques, it is. She never mar-ried – real old lady now. Knew lots of famous people, she did. One of them guys who composed one of them great everlovin' hymns – I think it was *What a Friend We Have in Jesus* or like that – well, he's buried there, see, just outside her kitchen doorstep. I kid you not. You should go and see her."

I didn't go and see her. I preferred to imagine her, somewhat macabre in high-button boots, tending the kitchen-doorstep graves of mysterious English clerics.

In the evenings, when I didn't go out in my neighbour's boat, I used to walk. The grainfields undulated on either side of the road, and beside the old split-rail fences the purple and white wild phlox flourished perfumedly. A groundhog would stare curiously at me before scuttling fatly away, and the killdeers would start up out of the grass with their wordlike cry, really saying *killdeer*. The road was a dirt track, and there were very few cars. I sometimes had the momentary feeling that this was a time out of time, and that it might as easily have been a hundred years ago as now.

One day a large parcel arrived. It was a sign which my publisher had had made for my shack, in the interest of my work, he said. At one time he used to be content with saying *Back to your typewriter, slob!* each time I finished a book. But this was going one better. The sign read: "No Visitors Allowed: By Order of the Government of Ontario. By Authority of J.G. McClelland, Servant & Publisher." It included a large coat-of-arms of the provincial government. When Jack McClelland[1] came to see me, I told him the sign had made a great hit with all my visitors. In fact, the visitors were mainly weekend ones. Naturally a lot of them were writers, some my contemporaries and some much younger.

One of the writers who came out during the summer was a poet whose work I had read in *Storm Warning*, an anthology of young Canadian poets. I had been impressed by Dale Zieroth's poems,[2] and when I looked him up in the biographical notes, it turned out he had been born in the same prairie town as I had, twenty years after myself. Talking with him somehow had an extra dimension, like meeting one of your family whom you haven't previously known. To my surprise, he told me that my novels had introduced him to the contemporary writing of his own people. Yet in a way I wasn't surprised. Years ago *As For Me and My House* by Sinclair Ross had done precisely the same for me. With Dale and with all the other young writers that summer, I had the strong feeling of a continuum in life, and the assurance and reassurance that my generation's inheritors are finding their own voices. This feeling went beyond writing, too. It had something to do with the old man next door, and listening to his tales of homesteading in Saskatchewan so long ago.

Perhaps what I was learning was a little about the meaning of the river that flows both ways.

Salute of the Swallows

"Salute of the Swallows," in the Clara Thomas Archives, York University,
1980–001/023 (156), No. 1980–001/023 (156), and first published in the Vancouver
Sun *on 22 May 1971, manifests Laurence's interest in the ancestral past of*
Canada's Indigenous peoples and British settlers and in nature and ecology. It
relates to The Diviners, *where Morag Gunn observes swallows in "The River*
of Now and Then" (9–27) and espies a great blue heron. The following blurb,
presumably written by the Sun *editor, is appended to the article: "Traditionally*
the 24th of May is the weekend to open summer camps in Canada. This year,
Canadian author Margaret Laurence is a long way from her beloved river. She
is living in a cottage in Buckinghamshire, England, writing her new novel.
But she remembers summer in Canada. And the way it was."

The first day of the Muskie season arrives, and the swallows go unaccountably
mad in the morning. I do not really believe there is any connection between
those two facts, but I make a mental note of it nonetheless, as a mysterious possibility, for I am living in this cabin beside an Ontario river for one precious
month only, so I am trying to learn the country, at least a little, while I can.

Never having gone fishing in my life, I wouldn't even have known it was the
first day of the Muskie season if the old man next door hadn't told me. All the
other fish in the river he regards with scorn; he is interested only in catching a
Muskie because they give a fight.

The swallows, truly, are acting demented. Light rose-coloured breastfeathers
flashing, the birds whirl and spin, somersault, pirouette, dip so close to the
water's surface that it seems they must plunge in and be drowned – but no, they
zoom up again, dartingly, in an endless series of crazy manoeuvres. They look

as though they are saluting the old man, who is now detaching his boat from the little dock and setting off on his quest.

Tiring momentarily of the river, the birds try their wings at alarming me as I sit drinking coffee and staring out the large front window of the cabin. *Zing! Whirr! Kapowee!* Cartoon action-captions seem to be written in the air above those reckless wings as they head straight for the glass. They will obviously never reverse in time, and we will have splattered swallow all over the windowpane. But again, no. They turn so swiftly that they seem to be suddenly flying backwards. Maybe they have radar, like bats. My knowledge of nature is not great.

I am what might be termed an enthusiastic amateur, and I tend to interpret all life in human terms, which I recognize as an inaccurate viewpoint, but the only one of which I am capable. In my fashion, then, I have surprisingly become a bird-watcher.

I am not equipped with binoculars or with books that explain the markings, voices, and habits of every member of the species. I simply sit and watch birds, sometimes for hours. Quite often I don't know their names, but I am pleased with myself when I do. Here comes the goldfinch, a tiny streak of yellow and black who perches on top of the tall swaying wild asters at the side of the cabin and fixes his unblinking eye on me. I wonder if goldfinches are long-sighted. If I make even the slightest movement, such as flicking the ash off my cigarette, the goldfinch will be off in a blur of gold. Of course, the minnows in the river scatter frantically, too, at the faintest sign of human activity from the dock, and one wouldn't have thought *they* would be aware at all of what was going on outside their own watery element.

A pair of orioles is building a nest across the river, in one of the huge maple trees. They skim back and forth from one side of the river to the other, toting building materials. The orange feathers are so beacon-like that I can follow them for quite a while as they weave their way through the bending willows on the opposite bank and fly on up to the high green branches of their home. Sometimes they alight for a moment on the branches of one of the dying elms, and then their feathers contrast ironically with the grey wood of the disease-doomed trees.

I have preferences. Birds, I discover, are like other people's children – one does not love or admire them en masse; some are likable and others are not. I cannot feel sympathy toward starlings. In fact, I detest them and consider that they do not deserve the appealing name they bear. Apparently they were first brought to this continent, a hundred years or so ago, as cagebird pets. The day that the first male starling and female starling fled the coop was certainly an evil one. They have shown a positively appalling talent for reproduction, and I am told that they prey on other less aggressive species. I've seen them actually in knockdown, drag-out fights with the robins, who stand up to them with spunk, but unfortunately lack the starlings' murderous determination. There is something sinister to me about these birds with their dark, iridescent feathers and forward-thrusting snake-like heads. They look reptilian, as though their direct ancient ancestors were the pterodactyls. They have also an enormous but stupid curiosity, which leads them to poke into chimneys and come squawking down stovepipes. I am petrified that this may happen when I am alone in the cabin, because if it did, I am pretty certain I would faint. In the early mornings, when I waken to hear the starlings tramping about on my roof, I shoot out of bed and kindle the stove. The theory behind this tactic is that surely to goodness not even a starling would be brainless enough to crawl into a chimney from which smoke is issuing. On the other hand, if one did, there would be a scorched starling, which would be even nastier than the ordinary kind. There appears no way out of this dilemma. It is simply one of those perils of rural life.

My anxiety, for the moment, is quelled by the amazing performance of one of the songbirds. These may, indeed, be the *same* songbird with an impressive repertoire; I do not know. I think of it or them as the song sparrows, but it is quite possible that some of them may belong to families unknown to me – the Con-tralto Oboe-Throated Triller, perhaps. But about the quality of their music there is no possible doubt. Each note is distinct and beautiful, clear as rain. These birds are professionals.

What songs the sparrows sing must of course remain shrouded in their own secrecy, for what those arias mean to them can only be a matter for human spec-ulation. One might be astonished if one could understand the words. But lacking bird language, I sometimes find myself putting selected human words to the tunes. One splendid rebellious Highland-type bird sings *Who Wouldn't Fight for Charlie!* ME.[1]

I am not the only person hereabouts who plays this game. I was listening one day to a songbird with a magnificent (and to me wordless) nine-note song, when my neighbour, Mrs Morag Mellwraith,[2] dropped in.

"Hear that?" she cried. "That's the bird that says *Pres-pres-pres-pres-Presby-terian!*"

Wondering if I would never be free of my background, I mustered only the most meagre smile.[3] Now, of course, I cannot hear the wretched bird without hearing the stern voice of my ancestral past.

The ancestral past is strong here in other ways, however, the ways in which the ancestors are held in common, are in a sense everyone's ancestors, whatever one's personal background. I walk down to the water-bleached wooden dock in front of the cabin and indulge in my other pastime – river watching. Sometimes sitting here on weekdays when there are no motorboats around and when the luxury yachts and the rainbow-painted home-made houseboats of the Sunday trippers are nowhere to be seen, I believe that the river bears a different craft, a flotilla of phantom boats.

Now that the wind has died and the swallows have settled down, when I look at the unruffled and deep-flowing Otonabee, I can almost see the long canoes of the Hurons[4] slipping through these waters in the days when this part of the country was theirs alone.

This was Susanna Moodie's country, too, and that spirited if irascible lady wrote *Roughing It in the Bush* about events that happened a few miles from here, when she and her rather ineffectual husband settled here in the 1830s. A few years earlier, though, Susanna's more admirable sister, Catherine Parr Traill,[5] passed this way as she and her husband made their precarious way by boat to Peterborough. Only a mile or so upriver, their boat went aground and they stumbled ashore and walked through the night forest to the town. It is not difficult to see that boat on the river now, its slow and unwieldy progress, and the young woman perched on a trunk on the deck, having recently recovered from a stupefying and near-fatal fever, trying to trust in the Almighty and her husband, trying to remember that, after all, her brother, Samuel Strickland,[6] was already settled in the area, so it could not be *that* bad, but undoubtedly unable to stave off a great many qualms as well. She did not know then that she would become not only an efficient and caring mother to a large family, but also a distinguished botanist who would record and even give names to many of the wild plants hereabouts, a woman who would in her spare time (*spare time!*) write *A Canadian Settler's Guide*, that classic of good sense and practicality that would inform new settlers how to make bread, cakes, preserves, soap, medicines, and a thousand other items, using local materials and utensils, and which would, as well, give them a few sharp bits of advice, such as the inadvisability of brooding about the homelands they had left behind. No doubt, over the years, her capabilities must have been rather a trial to her less efficient neighbours. Still, she lived here until she was a very old lady, and died, as they say, full of years and honour.

The flotillas of the past drift by, and I look into the water to see what is going on there. The water beetles skim along the surface, making zigzag patters of silvery lines. The minnows waft and flicker through the underwater forests of undulating green algae.

When I first came here, I thought how lovely those bright-dark forests were, their tendrils trailing. Now, observing what appears to be their daily encroachment, I see them differently. That rich heavy slime-green seems poisonous, robbing the river of life for its fish-dwellers. This river, people say, is still relatively unpolluted. Well, "relatively" is a very relative word.

I reach down with a stick and pull three plastic milk jugs and an assorted collection of beer and Coke tins from the water, and think of the weekend speedboats, pouring out their effluvia. I am also thinking of how incredibly beautiful this fragment of the planet still is, the river and the great stands of hardwood trees, the split-rail fences of our grandsires, the farmlands, the early morning sky alive with birds. And I am wondering how long.

The old man is returning. I wave to him and ask him if he's caught a Muskie. No, he admits, as he pulls his boat alongside his dock. He's noticed there aren't many Muskie this year, and wonders if maybe they're kind of dying out. It isn't just him, he says. Others along this stretch of the river are wondering the same.

I recall the swallows earlier today, and some words come into my head. A line that used to be spoken, those centuries ago, by the men set against lions in the Coliseum in ancient Rome. *We who are about to die salute you.*[7]

Of course, I know it isn't really that way. The swallows don't intend it that way. It's just fantasy. I do know. Don't I?

The Shack

Laurence published this essay in Weekend Magazine *on 11 May 1974, with the title "Loneliness Is Something That Doesn't Exist Here," the final phrase of the essay,*[1] *with this introduction:*

When this article was published in 1974, I had spent the three previous summers at my cottage (known as The Shack), working on my novel The Diviners. *A river such as the one here figures largely in the novel, although my cottage is totally different from the protagonist's house, and the novel is not autobiographical. The work circumstances were almost ideal – no interruptions for five days a week and, on weekends, friends coming to visit. They were allowed in despite the joke poster my Canadian publisher sent me, to encourage unremitting toil, and which is still tacked to a wall there. Under a stylized provincial coat-of-arms, it says, "No Visitors Allowed: By Order of the Government of Ontario; By Authority of J.G. McClelland, Servant & Publisher."*[2]

The most loved place, for me, in this country has in fact been many places. It has changed throughout the years, as I and my circumstances have changed. I haven't really lost any of the best places from the past, though. I may no longer inhabit them, but they inhabit me, portions of memory, presences in the mind. One such place was my family's summer cottage at Clear Lake in Riding Mountain National Park, Manitoba. It was known to us simply as The Lake. Before the government piers and the sturdy log staircases down to the shore were put in, we used to slither with an exhilarating sense of peril down the steep homemade branch and dirt shelf-steps, through the stands of thin tall spruce and birch trees slender and graceful as girls, passing moss-hairy fallen logs and the white promise of wild strawberry blossoms, until we reached the sand and the hard bright pebbles of the beach at the edge of the cold spring-fed lake where at night the loons still cried eerily, before too much humanshriek made them move away north.

My best place at the moment is very different, although I guess it has some of the attributes of that long-ago place. It is a small cedar cabin on the Otonabee river in southern Ontario. I've lived three summers there, writing, bird-watching, river-watching. I sometimes feel sorry for the people in speedboats who spend their weekends zinging up and down the river at about a million miles an hour. For all they're able to see, the riverbanks might just as well be green concrete and the river itself flowing with molten plastic.

Before sunup, I'm wakened by birdvoices and, I may say, birdfeet clattering and thumping on the cabin roof. Cursing only slightly, I get up temporarily, for the pre-dawn ritual of lighting a small fire in the old black woodstove (mornings are chilly here, even in summer) and looking out at the early river. The waters have a lovely spooky quality at this hour, entirely mist-covered, a secret meeting of river and sky.

By the time I get up to stay, the mist has vanished and the river is a clear alebrown, shining with sun. I drink my coffee and sit looking out to the opposite shore, where the giant maples are splendidly green now and will be trees of flame in the fall of the year. Oak and ash stand among the maples, and the grey skeletons of the dead elms, gauntly beautiful even in death. At the very edge of the river, the willows are everywhere, water-related trees, magic trees, pale green in early summer, silvergreen in late summer, greengold in autumn.

I begin work, and every time I lift my eyes from the page and glance outside, it is to see some marvel or other. The joyous dance-like flight of the swallows. The orange-black flash of the orioles who nest across the river. The amazing takeoff of a red-winged blackbird, revealing like a swiftly unfolded fan the hidden scarlet in those dark wings. The flittering of the goldfinches, who always travel in domestic pairs, he gorgeous in black-patterned yellow feathers, she (alas) drabber in greenish grey-yellow.

A pair of great blue herons have their huge unwieldy nest about half a mile upriver, and although they are very shy, occasionally through the open door I hear a sudden approaching rush of air (yes, you can hear it) and look up quickly to see the magnificent unhurried sweep of those powerful wings. The only other birds which can move me so much are the Canada geese in their autumn migration flight, their far-off wilderness voices the harbinger of winter.

Many boats ply these waterways, and all of them are given mental gradings of merit or lack of it, by me. Standing low in the estimation of all of us along this stretch of the river are some of the big yachts, whose ego-tripping skippers don't have the courtesy to slow down in cottage areas and whose violent wakes scour out our shorelines. Ranking highest in my good books are the silent unpolluting canoes and rowboats, and next to them, the small outboard motorboats putt-putting along and carrying patient fishermen, and the homemade houseboats, unspeedy and somehow cosy-looking, decorated lovingly with painted birds or flowers or gaudy abstract splodges.

In the quiet of afternoon, if no boats are around, I look out and see the half-moon leap of a fish, carp or muskie, so instantaneous that one has the impression of having seen not a fish but an arc of light.

The day moves on, and about four o'clock Linda and Susan from the nearby farm arrive. I call them the Girls of the Pony Express. Accompanied by dogs and laughter, they ride their horses into my yard, kindly bringing my mail from the rural route postbox up the road. For several summers it was Old Jack who used to drive his battered Volkswagen up to fetch the mail. He was one of the best neighbours and most remarkable men I've ever known. As a boy of eighteen, he had homesteaded a hundred miles north of Regina. Later, he'd been a skilled toolmaker with Ford. He'd travelled to South America and done many amazing things. He was a man whose life had taught him a lot of wisdom. After his much-loved wife died, he moved out here to the river, spending as short a winter as possible in Peterborough, and getting back into his cottage the first of anyone in the spring, when the river was still in flood and he could only get in and out, hazardously, by boat. I used to go out in his boat with him, late afternoons, and we would dawdle along the river, looking at the forest stretches and the open rolling farmlands and vast old barns, and at the smaller things closeby, the heavy luxuriance of ferns at the water's rim, the dozens of snapping turtles with unblinking eyes, all sizes and generations of the turtle tribe, sunning themselves on the fallen logs in the river. One summer, Old Jack's eighty-fourth, he spent some time planting maple saplings on his property. A year later, when I saw him dying, it seemed to me he'd meant those trees as a kind of legacy, a declaration of faith. Those of us along the river, here, won't forget him, nor what he stood for.

After work, I go out walking and weed-inspecting. Weeds and wildflowers impress me as much as any cultivated plant. I've heard that in a year when the milkweed is plentiful, the monarch butterflies will also be plentiful. This year the light pinkish milkweed flowers stand thick and tall, and sure enough, here are the dozens of monarch butterflies, fluttering like dusky orange-gold angels all over the place. I can't identify as many plants as I'd like, but I'm learning. Chickweed, the ragged-leafed lambs' quarters, the purple-and-white wild phlox with its expensive-smelling free perfume, the pink and mauve wild asters, the two-toned yellow of the tiny butter-and-eggs flowers, the burnt orange of devil's paintbrush, the staunch nobility of the huge purple thistles, and, almost best of all, that long stalk covered with clusters of miniature creamy blossoms which I finally tracked down in my wildflower book – this incomparable plant bears the armorial name of the Great Mullein of the Figwort Family. It may not be the absolute prettiest of our wildflowers, but it certainly has the most stunning pedigree.

It is night now, and there are no lights except those of our few cottages. At sunset, an hour or so ago, I watched the sun's last flickers touching the rippling river, making it look as though some underwater world had lighted all its candles down there. Now it is dark. Dinner over, I turn out the electric lights in the cabin so I can see the stars. The black sky-dome (or perhaps skydom, like kingdom) is alive and alight.

Tomorrow the weekend will begin, and friends will arrive. We'll talk all day and probably half the night, and that will be good. But for now, I'm content to be alone, because loneliness is something that doesn't exist here.

A Fantasy Fulfilled

"A Fantasy Fulfilled" is an unpublished, undated essay in the Clara Thomas Archives, York University, 1980–001/023 (155), with the initials "M.L." typed at the end. It celebrates Laurence's sense of self-empowerment in being able to fulfill a childhood fantasy of buying whatever she needed – in this case, to furnish the cabin that she purchased on the Otonabee River in Peterborough County, Ontario, after moving back to Canada from Elm Cottage in Buckinghamshire, England, where she lived from 1967 to 1972.[1]

I have been a lifelong reader of the 2-inch-thick coloured catalogues issued by the big department stores. Any Manitoban of my generation who grew up, as I did, in a small town, will instantly know why.

When I was a kid, it was during the Depression and drought, when there was very little money around. Even when I was a teenager, things did not really improve much until nearly the end of the war, when I was almost grownup and away from home. During most of my childhood, then, we did a certain amount of ordering from the catalogues, but what we mainly did was catalogue *poring*. Whenever a new one arrived, each member of the family would compete for the first look at it. Through those years, I must have spent hundreds of hours, scrutinizing every page and picking out everything I would order if only I had the wherewithal.

I had rather mixed tastes, and the variety of objects which I would have ordered was vast. When quite young, I coveted one of those huge dolls, about the size of a two-year-old child but got up to resemble some glamorous rosebud-mouthed movie midget. She was dressed in formal attire, gown of pink, blue, or green lace – please specify colour by number – and she boasted a coiffure of indescribable blonde curliness. I had straight dark brown hair, which I considered it ungenerous of the Almighty to have given me.[2]

I longed for one of the toy typewriters, on whose tin keys I visualized myself composing odes which would at least privately compensate for the fact that I was a dead loss at baseball (and when I was in grade four or five, to strike out every time was regarded as a kind of social disgrace, even for girls). I would also, if I had had the means, have ordered numerous flashlights, of which the catalogue carried a marvellous selection. These would have supplemented my own supply, for reading at night when I was meant to be asleep. And, as I was in those days a mean hand with a fretsaw, I hankered after one of those red metal boxes full of assorted Tools For Little Carpenters.

Never books, although I was an insatiable reader. From an early age I recognized that the catalogues were rotten in the book department. Mostly what you could get were books like the Bible, *Treasure Island*, and *Black Beauty*, which – worthy and ever fascinating as they were – already resided on our bookshelves, or else horrors like *World Classics In Brief* or The Honey Bunch Series[3] (Honey Bunch being a small girl of staggering smugness).

Later on, my tastes became more predictably feminine, and I examined in minute detail each set of the ruffled bedroom curtains then in vogue, and candlewick bedspreads to match in colour. My bed was covered with one of my grandmother's patchwork quilts, which she had made especially for me, but good heavens, it was only an old homemade thing. Now, naturally, I'd give anything for that long-gone and truly beautiful quilt.

The clothes, of course, were a major interest – those bright dirndl skirts, those winter party dresses in moss-green or sky-blue wool, those pleated plaid skirts for skating, those sloppy-joe sweaters (real cashmere), those beige belted polo coats, those saddle shoes, those flower-printed summer dresses with circular skirts, calculated to make you absolutely irresistible to boys (at least, that's how it appeared in the catalogue pictures).

There was even, if my memory serves me, a strange appliance guaranteed to increase one's bust measurement. Anyone with a 32-inch bust in those days had her moments of profound gloom, for this was the Betty Grable era, when the cult of the cantaloupe breasts was at its height. How I longed to try that developing device, but it was probably about $5.95 or some impossible price.

Of late years, I have sometimes had the opposite kind of pleasure to my early catalogue one. I now like to wander through department stores and observe the enormous quantity of stuff which I *don't* want and indeed wouldn't give house-room to. Nevertheless, when I recently bought a small cedar cabin on the Otonabee River, near Peterborough, I equipped it almost totally from the catalogue. I purposely didn't set myself any top sum. I simply went through and listed everything the cottage needed in the way of linen, dishes, curtains, lamps, cutlery, pots and pans, cushions, bedspreads, blankets, the whole bit.

I *could.* The sum, in fact, came to much less than I thought it might. It was not, in anyone's terms nowadays, such a very great deal of money. I sent off the order, and the boxes began to arrive. It was like Christmas presents multiplied by ten. I don't suppose anyone has ever had more pleasures from such a relatively modest outlay as I did opening those boxes.

My explanation to friends and acquaintances was quite logical and true – this was the easiest and most practical way of outfitting a cottage, when you had to start from scratch.

But any Manitoban of my generation who grew up, as I did, in a small town, will instantly know what it *really* was. It was the fulfillment of a childhood fantasy.

To go through the catalogue and order ANYTHING YOU WANTED.

The More Interesting Country

"The More Interesting Country" is an unpublished, undated essay from the Clara Thomas Archives at York University, No. 1989–039/010 (227), with the name "Margaret Laurence" typed at the end of the typescript. It reflects Laurence's love of the railroad and support of VIA Rail, as she recounts memorable trips on the "iron horse" – from crossing Canada with her husband and infant daughter in 1957 to her last trip along "Nostalgia Road" through her "heartland" of southern Manitoba in August 1983 to visit her half-brother Bob, Robert Wemyss, who was dying of cancer near Calgary, Alberta.

The iron horse is still magical to me. *The iron horse* – the name the prairie Indians gave to it when the first of the great steam locomotives thundered and snorted across the plains in 1885, bringing the green young troops from Upper Canada to quell the Métis'[1] and native peoples' final desperate uprising, their last attempt to prevent the loss of their lands. The steel road would end their traditional way of life forever, although they did not know it then. The railway would also make possible an entity called Canada and would be an integral part of our country's history. Whether the railway will continue to be important in terms of people remains to be seen. The freight trains will keep on, certainly, but the fate of the passenger service is less certain. VIA Rail, that sometimes uneasy coalition of the CPR and CNR,[2] does not seem to be giving the problems the attention they need and deserve.

The signs are ominous. In the past few years, I have read many articles stating that rail travel was safer and more efficient half a century ago, the tracks now being badly maintained and the locomotives outdated and dangerous. A recent report of the Canadian Transport Commission said that there has been a loss of a million passengers between 1982 and 1983, and in the same period costs of maintenance rose by nearly $40 million. These are disturbing figures. Numerous branch lines have been closed in the past decade. My own experience tells me that the service on the passenger trains has deteriorated and that many of the staff seem, not surprisingly, demoralized. I know little of the economics of the situation, but even I can understand that the freights pay better. The freights, of course, take precedence over passenger trains, and on many occasions I have sat in surly boredom while the seemingly endless boxcars flashed by and our train sat like a becalmed sailboat, waiting, waiting. A few years ago, in such a hiatus, I tried to count the number of freight cars, not an easy task as they whipped by my window. The freight had three engines, and I chalked up 111 freight cars, grain and lumber and cattle being moved from the Prairies to the cities of the east. Our passenger train had twelve coaches and one engine. The railway doesn't have to take much care of grain and lumber, and even the cattle must get minimal attention compared to people. [Passengers have to be fed, even if on boring fare, and their basic needs attended to, even if not with alacrity. I become angry when I consider that the steel road, so much a part of our nation, our history, our mythology, our consciousness, is being let go in this way. A great many Canadians want to travel by rail, and indeed, continue to do so despite the decline. And so do people from outside Canada – Japanese, Americans, British. I stubbornly believe the passenger service could pay, or at least break even.]

(The steel road is so much a part of our nation, our history, our mythology, our consciousness. The huge waves of immigration in the late 1800s and early 1900s could not have taken place without the passenger trains that carried settlers from Britain and all over Europe out to western Canada. Those early immigration coaches must have been little better than cattle cars, with families huddled on the wooden benches, travelling to new lives in a strange land whose language many of them were unable to understand, equipped only with their few belongings, their hopes, and their determination. They became the prairie people – my people, wherever their country of origin. It is thanks to their suffering and sweat that western farmland became the nation's breadbasket. The passenger service is simply too important to be let go. A great many Canadians and visitors to Canada *want* to travel by rail and continue to do so. I believe an improvement in service would mean an increase in numbers of passengers.)

Am I being totally unrealistic? Is the railway just Nostalgia Road for me, a part of my childhood that I'm reluctant to relinquish? Possibly, but I don't think so. Rail travel is by far the best and most relaxed way of seeing this country, especially on long trips. Naturally, planes are very much speedier, but if I have the time I will always choose to look at Canada rather than images of Canada on the film. I don't drive a car, but, even if I did, I would prefer the train any day – no jammed highways, no wear and tear on the nerves, no anxiety over where to stop and eat and sleep. Freedom to look out at the passing scene, or simply to read or talk to other passengers. Despite all signs of doom and gloom, the iron horse remains, in some deep and heartfelt ways, magical to me. I hope it will be there for future generations.

My connection with the railway goes back, as it does for so many people of my generation, to my early childhood. Every prairie kid in those days, nearly half a century ago, heard the trains passing through on silent winter nights, as we lay snug in bed under our eiderdowns. The long-drawn wail of the whistle of the steam trains said, "Go away, go away, go away to the world, get out of this town and never come back." Of course, many of us did go away, just as soon as we were grown and able to, not realizing that those towns formed us and would live in us as long as we lived. The train-voice first told us that out there lay undiscovered countries, worlds undreamed of, worlds we dreamed of constantly. My own life's journey has been one that brought me back home, at least in heart, but I had to go away to learn that.

Mine was a railway town in southern Manitoba. A lucky town. It was only much later on that I realized some of the prairie towns had begun in high hopes that the railway would go through and withered when it didn't. Both the CPR and the CNR went through my town. The fathers of many of my school friends were railway men, a respected camaraderie in those days. Two of my friends, a brother and a sister, belonged to a railway family. Their grandfather ran the station in my town, and their father was the station master in a village so close that we could bicycle back and forth on Saturdays. I knew well those solid impressive stations, all built to the same design, with the station master and his family living above the business part. The mysterious tick-tack-tock of the telegrapher sending thrilling (no doubt) messages to heaven knows where is a part of remembered rhythms of childhood. A lot of those small-town stations, including the CPR station in my home town, are gone now, ripped down, the branch line closed, the land made available for profitable developments.

My first long rail trip, when I was about ten, was with an aunt. She had been visiting us at home, and I travelled with her out to her workplace, Regina, to stay with her for a while. I then thought of Regina as the centre of the universe, because my aunt, head of the Nursing Division in Canada's first Public Health Service, had an office in the provincial parliament buildings.[3] I had written my first novel, in no less than three 5-cent scribblers. It was called *Pillars Of The Nation*[4] and was about pioneers, a subject with which I was somewhat less familiar, not then knowing that my own people had been among them. My aunt had promised, and did fulfill that promise, that her secretary would type it all out for me. I was excited beyond measure. The rail journey added to that exultation. I had an upper berth all to myself. There was a little light that you could switch on and off, which I did repeatedly. To gain access to this curtained chamber, you climbed a ladder. Wow! I was safe as churches, of course, but I nonetheless slept in my underwear, with my housecoat on top, in case a sudden derailment or any other dire crisis might make a hasty exit necessary. To tell you the truth, I follow this custom even now. That mighty train rocketing across the Prairies in the darkness seems to me to be moving unconscionably fast, and its swaying motion, so far from lulling me to sleep, often induces in me a wakeful yet pleasurable sense of danger and adventure.

In 1948, my husband and I, married then a year, decided to see the world. He had just graduated in engineering, and I in arts, in Winnipeg.[5] He wanted to see England in peacetime; he had been stationed at an air force base there during the war, before going out to Burma. I had never been outside Canada. We had just enough money to take us by rail to Montreal, and thence by ship to England. Optimistic and young (he was thirty-two and I was twenty-two) we set off. Let me tell you right now that fiction writers who wax ecstatic about making love in a lower berth don't know what they're talking about. The space is that of a single bed, and privacy behind those long canvas curtains is by no means guaranteed. A strange face pops into view … "Oops! Sorry! Wrong berth!"

In those days, there was a Smoking Car. Women were not, or such is my memory, supposed to go there, but I did. Jack and I used to sashay back and have a cigarette with the porters, who at that time were always blacks, then known as negroes, mostly large soft-spoken men who must have been either amused or angry at these two young white liberals who earnestly told them we were in sympathy with the aspirations of their people. Naturally, we didn't know enough to notice how boringly naive we were. They were kind and didn't put us down. We had no money to speak of, so lived on sandwiches and coffee that the vendors brought around, all the way from Winnipeg to Montreal. It sounds awful. I remember it as one of the happiest trips of my life.

When we came back to Canada, in 1954, after having lived in England and in East and West Africa,[6] our daughter was eighteen months old.[7] We travelled by rail from Montreal to Vancouver. It was not a leisurely tourist journey, to say the least, but if you went second-class, as it was then un-charmingly called, there was the boon of a kitchenette at the back of each coach. We could live for what seemed interminable days on sandwiches, but our child could not. In the kitch-enette, on the hot plate, we could heat up tins of baby veg and meat. We took turns looking at the scenery, the other one looking after our curious and sprightly daughter. I remember her, gorgeous kid that she was, and I remember the tins of baby spinach. The Rockies are less clear in my memory. I do, however, have vivid and dizzy recollections of looking out the window and seeing, coaches and coaches ahead, the train's engine as we achieved yet another hairpin bend around those mountains. I will always be awed by the fact that this railway could have been built at all. I believe that some of the most heroic men in our history were those crews of immigrants – Chinese, Japanese, Ukrainian, and so many others who, against all odds, put the long steel through. Living in camps, without their families, and their absent women heroic as well, not able to com-municate in the strange language, English, no doubt underpaid and suffering hardships and dangers, especially in those impossible mountain passes – they made our country *one*, from sea to sea. I respect and honour them more than I do any of our country's leaders, even Sir John A. Macdonald, so-called father of our country.[8]

My children and I lived in England from 1962 to 1973 and took several won-derful trips north to Scotland on such famous trains as The Flying Scotsman and The Highlander. If you had a sleeping compartment, you were wakened early by a steward bearing tea and biscuits, just in time to raise the blind and see the moors and burns of the highlands at first light.

I returned home to Canada in 1973, and a few years later went out to Calgary for a conference on Canadian literature. I decided to travel by rail. I thought I'd paid my dues of uncomfortable travel – a very puritanical concept, I guess. This time I decided to do it in style. Not even the one-person "roomette" for me, in which the toilet is not accessible once the bed is made up. I didn't mind dashing along the corridor during the day, fully clad, but in the middle of the night, at my age, forget it. So I got a "bedroom," a double accommodation, but I had it all to myself. Spacious lower bunk, two chairs in the daytime, washbasin and toilet. It was next to the dining car, so I would only have to wrestle with the two dauntingly heavy railway doors to get meals. I booked, as always, through my local travel agent, well in advance. All was organized, or so I thought. When the woman at the agency phoned to say the tickets were ready, I got a friend to go and collect them, having given him my cheque for the agency. He arrived back at my house, white-faced and shaken.

"A terrible thing has happened," he said. "I got the tickets okay and put them on the car seat. I stopped off to get gas, and the tickets must've blown out when I opened the car door. They're gone."

He was so upset that all I could do was try to reassure him. I phoned my travel agent instantly. She was nearly as stunned as I was. Had the tickets blown out into the snow or had they been stolen? When she regained her breath, she rose to the crisis magnificently. Phone calls to Toronto. Cancellations. New tickets issued. I had to pay again, of course, but later got my money back for the original tickets. I boarded that train at midnight in Toronto in apprehension, half expecting to see some demented ape who had my original tickets. But no. Cancellations had been effective. All was well.

That was some trip. February in the Prairies. Many people think that the Prairies are boring even in the summer, and in the winter, unthinkable. I am prairie, so I think otherwise. My train was the first in nearly two weeks to get through, as there had been an almighty blizzard, and the snow blocked the tracks. Admittedly, I knew enough to feel glad I wasn't out there in the cold, but I saw my heartland with new eyes. The drifts on the tracks had been cleared, but the walls of snow in some places, on each side of the train, were much higher than the window and I had the sense of zooming through a weirdly enchanted white tunnel. At other places the drifts had been wind-carved into magnificent sculptures, the bizarre beauty of which I had forgotten in my years away. The drifts, the snow-sculptures, the lights of the brave towns out there, are very swell from the warmth of the train. Not so swell if you are out there. I wasn't out there at that time, but had been, once.

In 1978, I took the train to Winnipeg. That was the year the CPR and CNR merged the passenger service into VIA. I went out by CPR and back by VIA. Same train, different management. I thought the service had improved greatly – hurrah, no more boiled whitefish on the menu. But the improvement in service and food was, I fear, short-lived. On another trip west, more recently, there were only two choices on the menu for each meal. I didn't object to that, but there was a set price, and you were expected to have every course – soup, salad, main course, dessert. If you didn't want soup, and I never do on the railway, because soup slops, then you had to wait until the next course was served. No blame to the staff – they were overworked and understaffed, and a young Québécois waiter said to me, "Madam, I'm afraid the service will be slow. This train is packed and we have four sittings instead of three for every meal. Our electric dishwasher has gone *phut* and they won't give us another." I am not astounded that the employees of VIA feel discouraged. It's a wonder to me that they do so much and so well.

The 1978 trip was mostly wonderful. The train goes around the north shore of Lake Superior, and I cannot describe adequately the stands of evergreen, the rushing rivers, the rocks speaking this land's antiquity. On the way back, however, there was a delay just south of Thunder Bay. I went into the dining car for lunch and discovered that a freight train containing cattle had been derailed. I was sitting on the side that overlooked it. I didn't want to see. I may be a coward, but I am not a ghoul. A woman on the opposite side of the dining car came over and leaned across me, peering out the window, brushing my shoulder closer than I liked.

"Hey, Harold! Look here! Gee, look at this! All those calves with their necks broken! Get a load of that blood, eh?"

"Florence," her anguished and embarrassed husband said, "Come on and sit down, eh?"

I had been going to order a hamburger for lunch. I changed my mind and didn't eat. We got into Union Station in Toronto two hours late.

I take the railway to have a time to myself, without telephone or mail, a time of thinking and meditation and looking at the scenery out the window. If I can afford to travel with some privacy, that will be my choice from now on. I know writers who love trains because "you meet such interesting people." I meet interesting people every week of my life, in my village and elsewhere. I'm not crazy about chatting on trains.

A pleasant surprise happened a few months ago on a rail trip from Toronto to Windsor. I booked in advance, as I always do, through my travel agent, but I did not realize until I was lined up at the gate in Union Station in Toronto that there was a club car on that run. I asked one of the attendants if I could still get a seat. "Sure," he said. "Just leave your suitcase here and run up and get your ticket upgraded." It cost me only seven dollars extra each way. Frankly, if for seven bucks extra I can have a seat to myself and a hot meal if I want it, I am going to do that. The service was better than on Transcontinental, and I can see that wouldn't be feasible for a family with six kids, but for one person or two, it's perfect. It was October, my favourite time of year in Canada, with the sumac still gloriously crimson, the maples resplendent in their array of colours, yellow, scarlet, pale red. Sipping a gin and tonic and looking out at those dazzling trees is my idea of heaven.

Last year, 1983, I went by rail from Toronto to Calgary. There was only one route this time, not a choice of two. I make a point, when travelling by rail, to keep my watch accurate in the time zones we are moving through, and to consult the timetable and see the names of all the little towns we pass through without stopping. I wakened up in the middle of the night, not knowing where we were. My first thought was "Someone has put poison gas into the air conditioner." The air was vile. I felt sick, and, choking, I hopped out of bed, consulted my watch and timetable. Of course. Dryden, Ontario,⁹ where the paper mill has not only polluted the river but also the air. I never realized how severe it was. But kids are born there and grow up breathing that bad air. On the trip back, I checked the schedule and turned off the air conditioner before we got to Dryden, only turning it on again when we were well past. I could do that. People who live there can't.

When I left Calgary to come home, my brother and sister-in-law took me to the station. I asked them not to wait; I'd rather be by myself at stations. Little did I know that in the heat of August, the train would be two hours late getting into Calgary. It was late late in the night when the train finally chugged in. Not much time for passengers to get on. The bedroom accommodation was neatly placed, as always, in the furthermost coach. I huffed and puffed for miles, or so it seemed, with my two heavy suitcases. When I found approximately the right area of the train, and did not dare wait any longer to get on, there was no one there. The portable steps that are a normal part of railway travel, enabling the passenger to perform athletic wonders, were absent. I was supposed to clamber onto Everest, with two suitcases, unaided. I felt desperate, lest the train would callously pull out of Calgary without me. Just then, two young Alberta women came along.

"Hey, ma'am, can we help you?" they blessedly asked. There is still some camaraderie in rail travel.

"I would be eternally grateful," I said.

They heaved my suitcases on and gave me a hand. I grabbed my suitcases and, gasping with the deep hot air and my panic, wrestled with the railway doors and finally found the right car. A lolling attendant stood there and looked at me with idle curiosity. A prairie man, whose ancestors had come here around the same time as mine? Who could know?

"Yer not breathin' so good, there, lady," he said.

I fixed him with a beady eye. And yes, I know it wasn't fair of me. Passengers yell at the crew; they don't know how to approach or yell at the top brass.

"It's a bloody wonder I'm breathing at all," I snarled.

And yet that rail trip was probably the best among the many good rail trips of my life. On the way out west we went through southern Manitoba in the lovely light of the morning. August, and the crops not quite ripe, the fields green-gold. I sat in my rail-room, looking out the window, near to crying, and I wrote some words, scribbled them down just as I felt them.

"The train is always moving west. For us, always west. For my people, west is the direction our lives take. West is in us. I haven't seen my heartland for years and years at this time of year, the fields of fall nearly ready for harvest, the wind-fingers ruffling wheat oats barley as though these were the goddess's hair. I'm not fooled, even from the safety of a train, because a train of consequence binds me like long-ago binder twine, twining lives and land together. I know the same tender wind can turn destroyer, and what relief when the crops are in, even for those young farmers who don't know *Relief's* other meaning their parents knew, the thirties' years when proud people had to take shame for the paltry dollars the government dole doled out, and the guilt they felt for the ruined lands when the rain did not come and the banks foreclosed. I know all this; I grew up with it; it is in my blood. The Depression and how many themselves in their own depression? I'll not ever know. Although I was a child then, I recall those years, and yet I sing this land, mine, and mourn for that past and love this openness of sky, these waiting fields, these bluffs scrub oak poplar birch maple, these often-stunted but damn tough trees like farmers, like women and men, survivors against all probability."[10]

The train was detained in Winnipeg for two hours. I could not even get a soft drink because the staff were taking stock, so I was told. The railway had thoughtfully laid on an hour's bus excursion for tourists, of whom in my own homeland I did not count myself one, so naturally I didn't go. The train finally took off. I went into the dining car for lunch. I sat at a table with two amiable American ladies.

"Are you a native-born Canadian?" one of them asked me.

I allowed as how I was.

"Then maybe you can tell me and my friend," she said, "when we will get to the more interesting country."

In my mind and heart were all the years, the land that my people and so many others settled long ago, the land that the native people believed belonged to God and was on loan to humankind, the land that inhabits my soul as long as I shall live. But these women were kindly and friendly, and I hope I was gentle.

"Well, you see," I said, "I was born and grew up hereabouts, and to me, this *is* the more interesting country."

Of course, I knew what they meant. They meant the Rockies. They meant sensational scenery, and their question was a legitimate one. For tourists from other countries, our railway means fantastic scenery, and that is as it should be. I think that VIA, with better service, could attract enormous numbers of tourists from away, and I just can't believe it wouldn't pay. For Canadians, the steel road can mean something more, I wish the top brass in VIA could understand. The question may not be "Can Canada afford to keep on the passenger service?", but rather, "Can we, as a people with a history, a past, and a future, afford to let it go?" I wish I could talk to our government about this, and to whoever is in charge at VIA. But I am not an economist, nor a business person. Why would they listen to me?

I know some things that perhaps they do not know so well. We have to maintain not only our business; we have to give thought to our land and soul; otherwise we are nothing. For Canadians, the steel road can mean something more than stunning scenery, as it has for me over many years. A way of getting from one town or city to another, yes. But also the best way of seeing, truly seeing, and perhaps beginning to understand the vastness of this awesome and beloved land.

Down East

"Down East" was first published in the Vancouver Sun *on 20 March 1971 and later collected in* Heart of a Stranger *in 1976 with the following introduction:*

I lived in Toronto for the academic year of 1969–70, as writer-in-residence at the University of Toronto, and acquired a cottage on the Otonabee river, near Peterborough, during that period. When I wrote about Lakefield in this article, I didn't imagine that within a few years one of its old brick houses would be mine and that I would be settled in a small town not un- like the one in which I grew up. In preparing this collection, I was tempted to expand this article and to include some of the things I have since learned and come to feel about this area, but I decided not to do so, and to leave my first impressions intact.[1]

My geographical grasp of Canada was not learned at school. It came straight from the semantic roots of what I now perceive to have been my folk culture, and it was many years before I suspected that in textbook terms it might not be totally accurate. It was, however, very accurate psychologically. A quick glance at the geographical terminology of my youth will reveal my prairie origins.

The West, of course, meant us, that is, the three prairie provinces, especially Manitoba and Saskatchewan. Alberta just barely qualified – it was a little too close to those mountains for our entire trust. We sometimes suspected that Al- bertans had more in common with *The Coast* than they did with us. *The Coast* meant only one thing – British Columbia. As far as we were concerned, there was only one coast. The eastern coast, presumably, was so distant as to be bey- ond our ken. *The Coast* was a kind of Lotus Land which we half scorned and half envied. All prairie people, as was well known, wanted to retire there. Think

of it – a land with no winter, semi-tropical beaches, breezes which were invariably balmy; a land where the apricots and apples virtually dropped into your
mouth. Jerusalem the Golden, with milk and honey blest[2] – that was how we
thought of it. At the same time, we considered in our puritanical hearts that
our climate was healthier, as we sneezed our way through the desperate winter
and thawed our white-frozen ears and knees gently, not too close to the stove,
as we had been taught.

Apart from *The West* and *The Coast*, our country contained only one other
habitable area (*The North*, in our innocent view, being habitable only by the indigenous Eskimo and the occasional mad trapper), and that was *Down East*. This
really meant Ontario. Quebec and the Maritimes existed in geography books but
not in our imaginations, a sad lack in the teaching of Canadian literature, I now
think, being partly responsible. Everyone born on the Prairies has a sense of distance, but there were limitations even to our horizon-accustomed eyes. *Down
East* was within our scope, and upon it we foisted our drought-and-depression
fantasies. The people *Down East* did not know what it meant to be hard up – like
most depressed areas, we had the illusion of solitary suffering. I did not personally suffer very much, if at all, from the depression of the thirties, but I
certainly imbibed the dominant myths of my culture. *Down East* was mainly
composed of banks and mortgage companies, and the principal occupation of
most Ontario people was grinding the faces of the poor. In their spare time, they
attended cocktail parties and made light scornful banter of their impoverished
relatives out west. My only relative *Down East* was an aunt married to a man who
had once, glamorously, been a bush pilot, but of course that was different. This
same aunt told me not long ago that she lived in Ontario for years before the
prairie chip finally fell from her shoulders.

As the years passed, I grew to understand that my early impressions of
Ontario were somewhat distorted, to put it mildly. But something of the old
antagonism toward Upper Canada remained until the past year when I lived
there and discovered something of Ontario for the first time.

Yes, there were many things I didn't like, chief among them the virtually cannibalistic advance of what we are pleased to term, with stunning inaccuracy,
Progress. Toronto, it is true, has more banks than even I dreamed possible in my
youthful condemnation, and one has to drive seemingly endless miles even to
begin to get away from the loathsome high-rise apartments going up everywhere. Yes, you listen to the radio in the morning and hear the city's air-pollution

index and wonder if you should venture as far as Yonge and Bloor without a gas-mask. Yes, water pollution wades deeper and deeper into the Great Lakes. But there are other areas still left, and one prays for their survival.

The land around Bancroft in the fall. I had never seen the hardwood maples in autumn before. The prairie maples turn yellow, marvellously clear and clean-coloured. But these scarlet flames of trees, a shouting of pure colour like some proclamation of glory, have to be seen to be believed. Words won't make a net to catch that picture; nor, I think, will paint. But suddenly I could see why the Group of Seven was so obsessed with trying to get it down, this incredible splen-dour, and why, for so long, many Canadian writers couldn't see the people for the trees. With trees like these, no wonder humans felt overwhelmed. The maples stretched along ridge after ridge, with yellow poplar and speared pine for the eye's variety, as though God had planned it this way. A friend and I walked over the clumps of coarse grass, over the slabs of exposed bronze-brown rock, and there in the small valley was a beaver lake, the camouflaged lodges barely dis-cernible, and only the wind and the birds to be heard, the cold air gold with sun and azure with sky.

"This is my heartland," my friend said, simply and without embarrassment. She did not visualize herself as a wordsmith, yet when she talked about the coun-try around Bancroft, she enabled me to see beyond the trees to the roots which exist always within the minds of humans. Her people farmed this land for gen-erations. Cousins and uncles still lived here, in the farmhouses half hidden away from the gravel or dirt roads. I began to realize that most of the prairie towns and farms I remembered were in fact relatively new compared with this part of the land.

Later, months later, thinking of the blazing cold conflagration of the maples in fall, and the sense of history, of ancestors buried here, I thought of one of Mar-garet Atwood's poems about Susanna Moodie, when that prickly, over-proud pioneer lady's son was drowned. The last line of one poem will always haunt the mind – "I planted him in this country like a flag."[3]

Kitchener and/or Waterloo. I never did discover which part of the town was which, or what to call each. Two towns have merged, but both seem to maintain their separate identities. This is Mennonite country, and in the markets on week-ends you can buy homemade sausage and cheese. I visited a friend who has lived there most of her life, and who writes about the Mennonite people, their cus-toms, their cooking, and, more than anything, their life-view, which is to us amazingly untouched by this century, amazingly simple and related to one another. Naturally, outsiders tend to regard their way of life as archaic, but sometimes one wonders if their view won't endure longer than ours.

Morning came early in the country just outside Kitchener, and I got up despite my hatred of early rising, drawn by the sun on the snow. I tramped along the paths beside Sunfish Lake, thinking that people in Canada really ought to be told that not everywhere does the winter come like this, with this brightness of both air and snow. Through the woods, tangled in among the bushes, a small river tried to take its course, and flowed despite the ice, making bizarre carvings on the frozen parts of itself. Back at the house, looking out the window, I saw a whole contingent of red cardinals, coming for the birdseed my friend put out. Arrogant crimson feathers, sleek against the snow. I never imagined that I would be much of a birdwatcher. But there are moments when one is struck with a sudden intense awareness of the beauty of creatures, and wishes their continuance could be guaranteed. I would like my grandchildren, when they exist, to be able to see cardinals like these.

Peterborough. To me, this small city on the Otonabee River meant Robertson Davies' country – some of his books, *The Diary of Samuel Marchbanks* and others, and himself those years ago as the fiery editor of the *Peterborough Examiner.* The area remains so related, but now I see it as the historical home of Susanna Moodie as well, that snobbish composer of dreadful patriotic poems and writer of *Roughing It in the Bush,* that genteel and self-dramatizing English lady who never really came to terms with what was a very raw land when she settled here in the 1830s. More especially the area now evokes Catharine Parr Traill, who made this land her own, who named many of the wildflowers, and who lived hereabouts until she died at a very old age – a woman both gentle and strong.

Many of the Peterborough streets are maple-edged, and the old houses are square, solid, dignified, redbrick, some with wooden lacework around their elegant verandas. The houses sit in the shade of their trees, cogitating on the past, which in some cases is more than a century. Not long for Europe, but long enough in our terms. These streets do seem to be from another era. One almost expects little kids in knickerbockers or frilly gingham gowns to spring out of the next hedge with homemade stands and one-cent lemonade signs.

In nearby Lakefield, you can buy pine blanket chests made by someone's great-grandfather, and if you're lucky you can hear an old-timer reminiscing about the last of the great paddlewheel steamers that used to ply these waters. In Lakefield, too, they make excellent cheese. You can buy it, in three degrees of sharpness, from the place where it is produced, and the giant cheese wheels smell and taste like your childhood. There is also a place where they still make their own ice cream, in a dozen flavours.

Taking a taxi in Peterborough is a very different matter from taking a taxi in Toronto. In the city, the cab drivers are fluently and instantly conversational, a motley collection of men from nearly all corners of the earth. In Peterborough, when they get to know you a little, then they talk. Most seem to be local men. When they talk over the intercom, it is to people who are their known neighbours. They do not, as in Toronto, say, "Come in, Number 87654321." They say, "Hey, Ron, where the heck are you?" Sometimes a despatcher loses his temper and addresses a particular driver as "sir." "Well, sir, if you can't find that address on Charlotte Street, you've got to have been born yesterday." I listened to these exchanges for quite some time before it dawned on me that "sir" in these parts could sometimes mean an ironic reproach. A legacy, perhaps, from the hordes of bloody-minded Irish who settled this area? The well-driller who divined with a willow wand (yes, it really works) the well for my cottage near Peterborough also had an inflection of those Irish. When asked about the well's potential, he replied, "Lard, woman, you got enough water there to supply halfa Trona." And I was reminded of James Joyce – "Hail Mary, full of grease, the Lard is with thee ... "

Probably I will be accused of sentimentality and nostalgia, writing affectionately about these towns Down East and this countryside, but I don't think this accusation would be entirely true. No era that is gone can ever return, nor would one want it to. I will, however, admit that in looking at towns where some quietness and sense of history remain I am looking at them at least partly as a tourist. I'm aware that under the easily perceivable surface there lurk the same old demons of malice and man's persistent misunderstanding of man. I was born in a small town – I *know* all that. But I would venture to suggest my own theory about such places.

Are they really anachronisms? Or may they possibly turn out to be to our culture what the possession of manuscripts in monasteries was to mediaeval Europe during the dark ages? Maybe some of them will survive, and maybe we will need them. Whatever their limitations, it is really only in communities such as these that the individual is known, assessed, valued, seen, and can breathe without battling for air. They may not be our past so much as our future, if we have one.

Journey from Lakefield

"Journey from Lakefield," headed "Letter from Margaret Laurence," with her name typed at the end, from the Clara Thomas Archives, York University Archives, 1980–001/004 (81), is a dramatic vignette that, whether fiction or fact, demonstrates Laurence's honesty, courtesy, and humility, combined with her dislike of prejudice. It is also a fine example of her skill with dialogue.

The bus trip from Peterborough to Toronto is two hours. It's a trip I take frequently, more frequently than I would like, because the demands of my profession require me to be in the VM (Vile Metropolis) for meetings, book-signings, worthy causes, and the like. The bonus is that I get to see my friends and my daughter and son, who live there. Being a non-driver, I'm an old hand at bus travel. I'm organized. I go from my village to Peterborough, only a few miles away, by local taxi. l get there early, and I'm first or second in the bus lineup. I sit near the back, seats for smokers, window seat, just opposite the lavatory, *in case*. I have never yet had to use the facility on the bus, but proximity gives me peace of mind. I haul out my paperback, usually a who-dun-it, aggressively light a cigarette, hunch toward the window, and hope no one will sit beside me. Bus travel is a time for light reading and meditation, for looking at the land, not for gabby exchanges. I'm lucky sometimes, and sometimes I'm not.

This time was the worst ever.

It was the 11 a.m. bus, which is usually not crowded. This time it was, because it was shortly before Christmas 1980. The lady came stumbling down the aisle and sat beside me. Her husband took the unoccupied seat opposite, next to a young man who already had *his* paperback out and *his* cigarette aggressively lit. If only that young man and I had come to some tacit agreement, beforehand, to share a seat. But then, all us experienced bus travellers go for the window seats.

Off we groan, the bus rumbling and snorting.

The lady is possibly in her late sixties, wearing a checked trouser suit, sunglasses, and a whole lot of lipstick. She is also sloshed. She has numerous shopping bags and purses and other gear, which she stows around her feet and mine.

LADY: Damn bus damn bus damn bus, I jus' don' know how I can *demean* myself to go by this damn bus. Listen here, if you'd of bought a new car, instead of being so damn tightfisted ... hell, I *knew* the car was gonna pack it in, but would you buy a new one? Oh no. Not you. Too much money, you said. Too much goddamn money. So we have to travel by BUS. For godsakes. How I can *demean* myself ...

HUSBAND: Sh, Bertha. It's okay. It's only two hours. Sh, please, eh?

LADY: (fumbling in one of innumerable bags): Oh shit oh shit oh shit. I've lost my cigarette holder. John – JAWN – it was a bran new one! I musta dropped it when I got on this damn bus. Jawn! You just go and ask the driver!

HUSBAND: Sh, Bertha. It's okay. You'll find it.

LADY: I will *not* find it because it is *not* here. I dropped it. Sure, I know. I bet the goddamn driver picked it up and he'll keep it, too. I know those guys. Buses! If you'd of bought a new car ...

HUSBAND: (low, but not so low that he could not be heard) If you could leave the house just once without having six drinks first ...

LADY: Don't you talk to me like that! Don't you dare! Don't you bloody dare!

HUSBAND: Okay dear okay dear okay dear. I'll go and ask the driver.

LADY: (struggling up) Oh no you won't. You damn well won't. I will go myself.

HUSBAND: (terrified) No, dear, it's okay. I'm going. Right now. (Husband climbs out of seat and shuffles to front of bus. Returns.)

HUSBAND: Here it is, Bertha. The driver did pick it up. He was going to ask people when they got off.

LADY: Well, now. Well, isn't that the nicest thing. Well, he sure is a nice person, that driver. Haven't I always said that these bus drivers were really nice guys?

(She lights a cigarette, eats a salmon sandwich from her baggage, announces that she thinks she'll just have a little snooze. I, a smoker, am suddenly aware of the dangers of allowing smoking on public transport. I am eating cough drops. Sure as anything, this bus is going to be set afire by this lady.)

LADY: (mumbling to herself, cig in holder in her hand) Goddamn bus. What a way to travel. How I can *demean* myself by travelling by bus, I jus' don' know. I just DO NOT KNOW.

(Miles and miles of this. I read, hardly seeing a word. The fiction writer in me says that this is a life of awesome complexity. Another part of me just wishes she would shut up.)

LADY: (suddenly leaning toward me) *You* seem awfully interested in that book. How come yer reading? You don' wanna talk? You a student or something? Are you learning English?

ME: (taken aback and by surprise) Well ... uh ... no.

LADY: (scrutinizing me closely; I have high cheekbones and slightly slanted eyes inherited from my long-ago Pictish and Celtic ancestors.) I know what *you* are! You are one of those damn people from Vietnam or Taiwan! Tha's what you are. Boat people! One of *them*. Why did we let you all in? Wha language you speak, parn my curiosity? Chinese? Vie – man – eez? Yer trying to learn English, eh?

ME: No. Actually, I speak English pretty well.

LADY: Then why the hell you're *reading*? Don' deny it. Yer one of the foreigners we let in. You don' fool me any. Where you from, then? Jus' all I ask is one simple question – where you from? You too ashamed to say, or what?

ME: (*Thinking* – what if I *were* from elsewhere? How would I feel about this Lady?) I'm from here. Canada.

LADY: Ha ha. I bet. You cernly aren't from Canada. Where you say you came from, jus' answer me that.

ME: Manitoba.[1]

LADY: Manitoba! Jeez! Well, now I know what *you* are. I shoulda' known. Yer a halfbreed, one of those goddamn halfbreeds. Admit it! You are!

HUSBAND: (quietly, desperately) Bertha, the lady wants to read her book.

LADY: Book! She's a halfbreed and she won't admit it![2]

(How can you talk to somebody who can't be talked to? She could have been sober as a judge and I still couldn't have talked to her. But in the confined space of a bus, and a captive, what to do? I don't think I handled this especially well, but would there have been a good way to handle it? I doubt it. A pitched yelling match on a bus is not my style.)

ME: Madam, if I were a Métis, I would certainly not deny it. I would be proud.

LADY: (snorting; lighting another cig) *Madam*, she says. Madam! My gooness, you trying to be fancy, eh? Halfbreeds.

HUSBAND: Bertha – for pete's sake – she wants to read her book!

LADY: Okay then, whatcha think of Louis Riel, then? A devil. A devil. The worst. Part Indian, I ask you. Whatcha think of *him*, then? I was born and raised on the prairies, myself. Saskatchewan.

ME: He was a great man. (But to my shame, I did not say this loudly. I absolutely *hate* public scenes that have no point.)

LADY: (face close to mine) Lemme tell you something, jus' lemme tell you! Nothing but trouble. Tha's what I tell you. We lived in Montreal for *years*. Had a nice house, good dis'rict, the whole bit. Did those goddam Frenchies ever *appreciate* us? No bloody way. We moved to Ontario. But I tell you, people here don' realize how bad it was in the West. My father worked for a bank ... yessir ... in the old days in Saskatchewan. Gee, I used to go out with him when I was just a kid, and I'd hold the dog inside the car while he talked to the farmers. None of those farms was ever foreclosed on. *None*, I tell you. You better believe it. Of course, people said different, but we know.

ME: (Mumble, mumble.)

LADY: Now you jus' tell me what you think about the goddamn French Canadians! Those damn buggers ...

HUSBAND: (whispering) Bertha ... Bertha ...

LADY: Oh you, shut up! Jus' shut up!

(She turns to me once more.)

LADY: What you *do*, eh? I mean, what do you *do*? You a student or something? What do you (this said with dignity) *intend to do with your life*? Nothing? Nothing?

(Nightmare proportions seem to be taking over. I want earnestly to tell her something quite untrue, but I find I can't. One isn't permitted to tell lies in vital areas.)

ME: (unhappily) I'm a writer.

LADY: Well, my heavens, think of that. And jus' what *do* you write? Is your whatchacallit in the *papers*, pray tell?

ME: (Thinking – she obviously does not believe me, so maybe we are home free) I write books.

LADY: Reely? Books, eh? Well, now, isn' that jus' so *interesting*. What kind of books?

ME: (Thinking – oh hell, is she beginning to believe me, alas?) Novels.

LADY: (Rummaging in one of her innumerable bags) Jus' a minute, here. Where's my pen and a bit of paper? Where? Hm. Wha's this? No. Oh, here we are. Now you jus' write down the names of your books, and your name, so I can jus' go and read them.

(Trapped. At this point, I don't know what to do. So I write my name and the name of one of my books. There is not much chance that she will have heard of me.)

LADY: (peering through her tinted specs) Who? Margaret Laurence? Yer Margaret Laurence? Well, I jus' cannot believe it. I HAVE SEEN YOU ON THE TV! Well, isn't that something, now!

ME: (Mumble)

LADY: Well, it cernly has been *such a pleasure* to meet you and have this *nice frenly talk* here on the bus.

ME: (Cough)

LADY: Well, I sure will tell my frens. Well, I know where you live – in Lakefield![3] Maybe I'll jus' drive up and drop in on you some day. I'd reely enjoy that. That would be very nice. You gotta' meet my husband. John!

(She reaches across the aisle. He is not there.)

LADY: JAWN! Where the hell are you?

ME: I think he's in the lavatory.

LADY: (pounding on lavatory door) Jawn! Are you there? Come out! I want you to meet a *famous* person! She is setting right here, right beside me. I have seen her on the TV!

SEPULCHRAL VOICE FROM BUS TOILET: Bertha, quit it. I'll be out in a minute.

(The bus is drawing into the Toronto station at Bay & Dundas. It halts. I step across the Lady and her baggage, and grab my coat from the rack above. The procession in the aisle, as always, takes awhile to get moving, but when it does, it moves briskly. John, poor refugee, is still in the can.)

LADY: Wait! You gotta meet my husband! He's so literary!

ME: (now telling lies with comfortable abandon) Maybe outside. Gotta get a taxi.

I'm middle-aged, but by heaven I can still sprint when the motivation is strong enough. I sprinted. There was a cab there. Freedom.

I didn't look back.

****

Margaret Laurence

PART THREE

Essays on Canada and Canadian Literature:
"The Case for Canadian Literature"

Canadian Novels:
Change in the Past Decade

"Canadian Novels: Change in the Past Decade," an unpublished essay, dated 1 July 1967, Oxford, from the Clara Thomas Archives and Special Collections, Margaret Laurence Fonds, York University, Accession 1980–001/023 (155), is an original hand-edited draft prepared for the Canadian Centennial. Laurence reviews nineteen recent Canadian novels, explaining how, during the sixties, nationalism takes a back seat to literary merit in Canadian fiction.

Perhaps I should begin by saying that I have no intention of talking about Canadian literature. I'm not really sure, within the framework of the last half-century, what literature *is*, and it is not my business to decide. That is up to the critics and the future. I would like, however, to talk a little about Canadian writing, especially the writing of the last decade, and to outline some of the changes that have taken place in that time. By "Canadian writing," I do not mean all of Canadian writing. I am forced, I regret to say, to confine myself to the area of the novel in English, because that is my own territory and the only one I know anything about. But when I say "the novel in English," I must include, as well, the works of a few Canadian novelists which have become accessible to English readers through translations, because some of these have had a profound effect upon English Canadian writing.

As a people, we do not have a vast background of interesting writing. And that is probably the understatement of the century as far as books are concerned. Perhaps we are spiritually intimidated by England and America. Our national inferiority complex, from which we now appear to be recovering at last, is well known. Or perhaps our writers were simply too isolated, physically isolated, unable to communicate sufficiently with one another and too cut off from the more demanding standards of the outside world. In any event, for a very long time Canadian writing was filled with novels of incomparable dullness, and our literary judgments tended to equate good writing with the presence in a novel of the puritan virtues of plain living and high thinking. If a novelist gave edifying advice to the young, he was obviously a good novelist.

In the 1930s and 40s, Canadian writing at last began to break out of the parochialism and puritanism which had inhibited it for so long. Such novelists as Morley Callaghan, Hugh MacLennan, and Gabrielle Roy made a momentous discovery – many Canadians actually lived in cities. Until then, Canadians had laboured under the strange kind of national fantasy which suggested that urban life was nonexistent. We appeared to believe that we were all country dwellers. The popular and indeed the *self*-image of a Canadian – if I may put it in rather general terms – was that of a man who, when he was not wrestling with the recalcitrant soil or the demon Rum, was busy wrestling with the grizzly bear or stomping out into the Great North Woods in order to tame them with his double-bitted axe. The plain truth of the matter was that most of us had lived in cities or towns for some considerable time, and wouldn't have lasted five minutes in the Great North Woods. The "land" novel – by which I mean the novel whose theme is strictly man in relation to the land rather than man in relation to other men or to God – probably survived longer in Canada than in any other country in the world, and when Morley Callaghan came along to deal it a well-deserved death blow, he was greeted with shrill cries of disapproval in his own country, a disapproval which has taken more than thirty years to subside. Callaghan is one of our best novelists, and until quite recently he has had absurdly insufficient recognition within Canada. At a time when Callaghan was writing his short stories and some of his best novels, such as *More Joy in Heaven*, *They Shall Inherit the Earth*, and *Such Is My Beloved*, and was widely read in both England and America, we were saving our enthusiasm for people like Nellie McClung, sweet songstress of Manitoba, because she was against booze and was sentimental about scenery and little children. Callaghan was concerned with the real matters of his time – with those who walked crowded streets and were yet terribly alone, with doubt-ridden priests and despairing prostitutes, with con men and jailbirds, with the down and out, and with the comfortably situated men who might conceivably and smugly believe that they were their brother's keeper, but could never visualize being their brother's brother. Written from the standpoint of a Roman Catholic, Callaghan's novels also concern the prime matters of Good and

Evil, of man in relation to God. This, I believe, was another reason why for so long his writing was viewed in Canada with something akin to embarrassment. We are – or were – an extraordinarily repressed people. God, like sex, was *there* but largely unmentionable except in the most vapid and empty terms.

Hugh MacLennan's novels – *Each Man's Son, The Precipice, Two Solitudes, Barometer Rising,* and *The Watch That Ends the Night* – were, from the beginning, more widely accepted in Canada than those of Callaghan. MacLennan is an excellent social analyst, writing out of the background of the thirties and forties – the Depression and the war – and one of his main themes has been an exploration of the Canadian identity. The French in relation to the English, the Canadian Scots in relation to their own bleak Gaelic background, the Anglo-Canadian in relation to his American counterpart – MacLennan has dealt with these themes in a probing style which, if it is sometimes too earthbound, is invariably intelligent. And in an age in which many writers are all guts or heart, and no head, let us not undervalue intelligence.

With Gabrielle Roy's *The Tin Flute*, the elements of social realism and the urban life were fused with a true inner grasp of character, an ability to create individual life on the printed page. This story of French-Canadian working-class life in Montreal was published only twenty years ago, and yet in terms of Canadian writing it broke incredibly new ground, for the dilemmas of a society are never in this novel presented as philosophical arguments or sociological explanations, but always through the plight of characters who are realized in depth, and because of this, the images of poverty are unforgettable. One could forget quite easily an abstract statement of deprivation, but what will haunt the mind always is the picture of the exhausted Rose-Anna, washing and ironing her children's clothes every night because they have only one set of garments each, and her pride demands that they wear clean clothes to school.

Sinclair Ross was another writer who appeared in the forties and who was writing out of the background of the drought and depression of the thirties. His novel *As For Me and My House* is set in a small prairie town, and concerns a withdrawn and desperately isolated minister. When I first read it – at about the age of seventeen – it seemed to me the only true thing that I had ever read about my own kind of people, my own kind of place, for it didn't pull any punches about how things really were in the stultifying atmosphere of small and ingrown towns, and yet it was illuminated with a kind of painful compassion. This is something which I imagine English writers or even present-day American writers might find hard to comprehend – this lack of anything that went before. Most literate people's image of their own home – in the broadest sense – is at least partly conditioned by the interpretations and insights of past generations of writers. Shakespeare influences all literate men's view of England, whether they are aware of it or not. But for me, growing up in a small prairie town, there was no background of this kind. I had read other books set in prairie towns, but until I read Sinclair Ross I had never read anything which did not strike me as unutterably phony. If this proves anything, it proves that, although our country cannot be said any longer to be very new, our writing certainly still is.

In this brief sketch of writers of the thirties and forties, I should also like to mention Ethel Wilson. Coming from an English background and writing out of her experience and love of British Columbia, Ethel Wilson's gentle, witty, and wise novels are unique in Canadian writing. In novels such as *Hetty Dorval*, *The Swamp Angel*, and *The Equations of Love*, she does not make any social protest, unlike the other writers I have been speaking about – at least, she never does so in any direct sense. But her novels are filled with real humans involved in real situations. Her economy of style was quite new in Canada, and she was probably the first Canadian novelist to write serious novels that were at the same time not lacking in humour. One small scene I always remember with delight. In *The Innocent Traveller*, which is about Topaz Edgeworth, who lived a full hundred years, Topaz in middle age never quite manages to master the art of riding a bicycle, so she pushes her bike around the streets of Vancouver so as not to waste it.

All of these writers of the thirties and forties and early fifties represented an attempt to break through the confines of provincialism and an attempt to strike closer to the way things actually were. They wrote, generally speaking, out of the background of the Depression and the war, and like writers elsewhere during that period, they tended to write in terms of social realism, with a straightforward narration which was usually analytical and somber. With one or two exceptions, such as the novels of Ethel Wilson, they were careful not to mix the tones in their writing – seriousness and humour did not go together, and so today some of their novels seem overly earnest if we do not read them within the context of their own time.

The writer who really introduced a new idiom into Canadian writing was Roger Lemelin, a French Canadian, with his at-the-time baffling novel *The Town Below*. This was ostensibly a story of life in Quebec City, and when it was first published, in 1948, I think it must have been widely misunderstood. In fact, I honestly wonder now if Roger Lemelin himself fully realizes how new his style was in Canada, for he went on to do a popular TV series about the Plouffe family, which ran for years and was cosy and predictable. But with that first wild and weird novel, he presented life not through its externals but through the grotesque inner interpretations of the people who live it. It was a complete breakaway from the certainties of an external narration, but in Canada it came too soon and was not then seen for what it was.

Within the last ten years, Canadian novels have changed enormously. For one thing, nationalism as a theme has almost entirely disappeared. I take this as a healthy sign. I cannot imagine an English writer starting out to write a novel which would be decisively English, or an American writer trying to write a novel which would be distinctively American – they simply wouldn't be (and wouldn't *need* to be) troubled by this aspect of identity. Thanks partly to our predecessors who settled some of these questions for us, Canadian writers in the past ten years have become mercifully unconcerned with writing "Canadian" novels and mainly concerned simply with writing *good* novels. The meaning of being a Canadian has diminished in writing and is being replaced by the meaning of being a human. This is not to say that Canadian writers do not still have a very strong sense of place. Of course, they do, as writers do everywhere. Characters must be set firmly in some soil, in some climate of values. Even works of fantasy are rooted in a territory which has been to some extent inherited. But Canadian writers these days, it seems to me, are dealing with themes which reach beyond their own boundaries.

The general tone of novels has changed completely. Where the emphasis was once upon social themes, it is now upon individual character, and the characters too have altered. They are not viewed in the same ways any more. The non-hero, in Canadian novels as in novels elsewhere, has taken over simply because it is closer to the way in which many people now see themselves and others. A biting humour and a certain amount of self-mockery have taken the place of the old earnestness. We ourselves as human beings have become more suspect than we once thought we were. Since the last war the lines of demarcation have become blurred. The Sons of Light and the Daughters of Darkness aren't any longer absolutely certain who is who. Everybody proclaims himself a dove these days; everybody secretly wonders if he isn't maybe a hawk, except for the *real* hawks, who *know* they're doves. The dilemmas of persons, like the dilemmas of nations, are now too complicated, not to say sinister, to be spoken of with any earnest assurance.

The Canadian novelist who best represents this fusion of the serious and the ludicrous is Mordecai Richler. In what I believe to be his best novel so far, *The Apprenticeship of Duddy Kravitz*, the main character, Duddy, is the compleat non-hero. Coming from the working class Jewish community of Montreal, Duddy is determined to survive and to be *somebody*. Toward this end, he takes part in many bizarre endeavours, including a hilarious enterprise concerned with the making of Bar Mitzvah films. He is utterly irreverent about the values of the past, with one exception – he cherishes, still, his grandfather's belief that "a man without land is nobody," and he is determined to place himself once and for all upon this planet owning a piece of land. One cannot help feeling sympathy for him. If one of his eyes is always on the main chance, the other is on the stars. He does not demand to be loved. He merely demands not to be ignored. In a world in which the individual is valued less and less, Duddy proclaims – loudly, rudely, and undeniably – his own unique presence.

In Jack Ludwig's novel *Confusions*, the setting is the academic world, but here again we have the self-mocking voice of a non-heroic hero, Joseph Gillis, PhD, battling to survive in what he sees as the lunatic world of the universities, haunted by his visions of the Hassidic rabbi who reproaches him with faithlessness, attempting to keep going somehow his marriage with Nancy, who is a Radcliffe girl and an ex-Unitarian. He has, as you might expect, problems. The tone of the book is perfectly expressed in the final summing-up – "Desire nothing in this world but time to do your work, love, kisses, serious talk, laughter, great works of art, and a white Jaguar so you can get to these things more quickly."

Another recent Canadian novel which creates vividly a central character in the non-hero mould is Robert Kroetsch's *The Words of My Roaring*. Oddly enough, this novel is set in the 1930s, but its idiom is completely contemporary. It could not, in fact, have been written in the thirties or even the forties. But it deals fascinatingly with the Prairies of that period, the drought, the time when political and religious prophets flourished because people in despair will try anything. Kroetsch's main character is Johnnie Backstrom, a small-town undertaker, a large and in his own eyes clumsy man, almost by accident and certainly without belief, running for parliament on the fantastic promise that the leader of his party can actually cause the sky to open and the rain to fall.

As well as this increased emphasis upon individual character and the change of tone with the emergence of the non-hero, Canadian novels in the past decade have presented the environment of cities and towns in very different ways from the novels of the thirties and forties. The descriptions are not any longer done from the external point of view of a narrator who is not personally present in the story. Whether the novel is written in the first or the third person, streets and houses and passers-by and acquaintances now tend to be seen through the eyes of one of the novel's inhabitants – that is, in a frankly biased, rather than a supposedly neutral, manner. The reader sees, therefore, everything with the distortions of the character himself, and this has the dual effect of conveying something about the character and at the same time giving an extra dimension to the streets. I think, for example, of the ways in which Winnipeg is described in Adele Wiseman's novel *The Sacrifice*, sometimes through the eyes of Abraham, the patriarch, sometimes through the eyes of his son, Isaac, or of his grandson, Moses. The city, one realizes, has changed throughout these years, but it has not changed as much as the various views of it. Although description of place is not central to this novel, everything adds to the total effect, for even in brief sketches of rooms or shops we get not only a sense of place but also a knowledge of the tremendously different eyes of three generations.

Mordecai Richler's descriptions of Montreal also have this highly personal flavour, and for a completely different view of Montreal we can turn to Brian Moore's *The Luck of Ginger Coffey*, where the city is seen – ludicrously and yet movingly – through the eyes of an Irish immigrant who finds it difficult to believe that his charm won't really carry him to the promised land of boundless wealth and limitless opportunity which he at first imagines the city to be. He discovers, of course, that Montreal has not been simply waiting with open arms for his presence, but ultimately he gains a kind of genuine dignity when he painfully abandons his self-image as top journalist and goes to work for a diaper service, whose badge saying *Tiny Ones* is humiliatingly embroidered on his uniform.

This highly individual view of places is again found in the short stories and in the third and recent novel of Austin Clarke, a West Indian writer now living in Canada. Clarke, like the other novelists I have mentioned, is not primarily concerned with describing places, but, in his novel *The Meeting Point*, Toronto is presented devastatingly though a pair of eyes very different from those of old Torontonians.

Another interesting aspect of Canadian novels in the past ten years is the growing number of novels written in the first person. The same thing, of course, has been happening with novels in England, America, and Australia, and I do not believe that these parallels are due to any sense of following fashion, on anybody's part, but rather to a necessary abandonment of the god's eye view, together with the novelist's desire to incorporate the narrator as a personality within the novel – to speak, in other words, not with any pretense of objectivity, but committedly, in somebody's voice. Jack Ludwig's novel *Confusions*, Robert Kroetsch's *The Words of My Roaring*, Leonard Cohen's recent and controversial novel *Beautiful Losers*, George Bowering's *Mirror on the Floor*, and Steve Vizinczey's celebrated best-seller *In Praise of Older Women* – all these are first-person novels. So are my own last two novels, *The Stone Angel* and *A Jest of God*. I believe this current tendency springs from an attempt on the part of the novelist to discover how things really *are*, on the inside, for the character in question, and an attempt to communicate somehow this inner geography.

Social themes in recent Canadian novels are rarely dealt with in a direct or expository manner. David Lewis Stein's first novel, *Scratch One Dreamer*, published this year, while it contrasts very perceptively the left-wing movements of the 30s with the protest movements of today, does so always through individual characters caught in their own snarled webs, which are never entirely due to the outside world and are also never over-simplified. Jane Rule's novel *The Desert of the Heart* was reviewed with more understanding in England than it was in Canada, where it was said to be a novel about lesbianism. In fact, it is about love and is a subtle delineating of the relationship between two women. It increases our comprehension simply because its characters live and matter. Perhaps the greatest departure from the hitherto-conventional ways of presenting social themes is to be found in the work of the young French Canadian writer Marie-Claire Blais, who is certainly one of our most talented novelists. In her recent novel *A Season in the Life of Emmanuel*, she abandons the almost-Gothic fantasies of her previous novels and portrays the desperate limitations and brutishness of life within a Quebec farm family. The poverty of body and soul which she shows is never observed from the outside, but rather through the dreams and disturbed musing of such characters as Jean-Le Maigre, who is aware that he will soon die of tuberculosis. The distortions are deliberate, extraordinarily skillful, and – one might say – *spiritually* accurate. We are not shown the scene *in itself*. We are shown it as it is *felt* to be and therefore as it really *is*. We are enabled in this way to grasp it in all its damaging effect.

This novel leads me to make one final observation about recent Canadian novels, for, in all her writing, Marie-Claire Blais rejects the older forms of social realism in favour of reality of a different kind – the inner reality of dream and fantasy, and her earlier novels – *Mad Shadows* and *Tête Blanche* – have a grotesque but compelling power about them. In their own ways, many other Canadian novelists have come to feel that the traditional straightforward narrative is inadequate for their particular purposes and have tried to convey – with varying degrees of success – the fluctuating and ambiguous nature of reality. Sheila Watson, in *The Double Hook*, attempts to communicate the mystery and duplicity of human life and motivations through a poetic imagery which makes extensive use of the old Indian gods. Mordecai Richler, in *The Incomparable Atuk*, swings into far-out fantasy with the tale of an Eskimo sculptor who becomes so wise in the ways of the white man's world that he keeps his entire family imprisoned in a Toronto basement, churning out quantities of extremely bad Eskimo carvings. Douglas Le Pan, in his novel *The Deserter*, tries to pierce through to a deeper reality in his use of intricate symbolism and inner commentary to accompany the story of a young soldier who – paradoxically – deserts after the war is over. George Bowering, a Vancouver poet whose first novel, *Mirror on the Floor*, was published this year, uses sharp visual images in juxtaposition with the transcription of a fictional tape recorder in what seems to me a most successful attempt to unravel the reasons behind a girl's killing of her mother. Leonard Cohen, in his second novel, *Beautiful Losers*, gives a terrifying picture of an old man whose mind is on the brink of collapse, by presenting the external world only in flashes, so that the line between fantasy and so-called reality shifts and hovers in a manner which is highly effective.

These are a few of the changes that have been taking place in Canadian novels. Some of our present problems of survival and growth we share with novelists writing anywhere; some of them are peculiarly our own. Our writers are still too isolated and too few. Too many novels still are written which could not conceivably be of any interest outside Canada. Despite all this, however, the general picture appears to me to be a heartening one.

With reference to the writing of the past decade, I have mentioned nineteen novels, out of the hundreds published during that period. Of these nineteen, fourteen have been published in England as well as in Canada. I don't know how many of them have also been published in America, but I would guess that the number is more than fourteen. I think this is a fairly representative group of novels, so the average publication rate outside Canada is not too bad. Does this matter? Isn't one writing primarily for one's own people? Personally, I think the answer is that one is writing primarily for oneself, but when each relatively small fictional world is complete and open to the public, as it were, then the more visitors the better, partly because of the admission fee. The external aims of novelists anywhere are few but important – to be read as widely as possible, and somehow to earn enough money to pay the rent and write the next book. In these ways, therefore, it is important for Canadian writers to be published not only in Canada but also in England and America.

In any event, never have there been so many novelists of some quality writing in Canada as there are today. The present generation of novelists and a newer generation who are already announcing themselves through short stories and whose novels will no doubt soon be appearing – these writers are no longer self-consciously Canadian. Their themes are both specific and universal, and their responsibility is to themselves, to the sight of their own eyes, to their own vision, whatever it may be.

Canada Still Too Canada-Focused

*"Canada Still Too Canada-Focused," from the Clara Thomas Archives, York
University, No. 1980–001/022 [154]), was first published in the* Montreal Star
*in December 1966. In 1966, Laurence returned from England to visit Canada,
probably on a book-promotion tour for* A Jest of God, *which won the Governor
General's Gold Medal for fiction, and reviewed novelists in Canada's major
centres. As a writer who lived in Africa for seven years and published five books
inspired by that experience, she finds Canada "too Canada-focused" because
insufficiently aware of Commonwealth, or postcolonial, literature in English.*

Montreal – Toronto – Winnipeg – Edmonton – Vancouver. I visited all of them
this summer. One thing that interested me most was to find out what was going
on in writing. How was everybody? How was the work? I received almost too
many impressions. But here are a few of them.

Montreal

Adele Wiseman is working full steam ahead on a second novel. It will have a very
different theme from her distinguished first novel, *The Sacrifice*, but it promises
to be just as good. Sinclair Ross is also working on a new novel. An extremely
modest man, he seems almost unaware that *As For Me and My House*, his first
novel, is now a Canadian classic. I was very glad to be able to tell him at last what
this novel had meant to me, for it was the first prairie novel I ever read in which
the writer really spoke the kind of truth I recognized about life in a small town.
No volume of Ross's short stories has ever been brought out, and I believe this
is long overdue.

Leonard Cohen has recently chucked over a proposed TV series, thank goodness. He seems to be one of those writers who shouldn't work at anything except
writing (and the contemplation of whether or not he's in a state of grace, if he
really feels he must). Irving Layton is still bashing out poems of energetic fury.
I think he is at his best when he doesn't write about his friends and/or enemies
– from the way he writes about them, it's sometimes hard to tell which is which.
M. Charles Cohen is working on a surrealistic TV play which sounds fascinating.
I am sorry not to meet or hear anything about any French-Canadian writers.
One would think there would be some mingling of the two language groups,
among writers, but there doesn't appear to be much.

Toronto

Lots of new young novelists are appearing, among them Scott Symons, whose
novel *Place d'Armes* will almost certainly create the same kind of critical furor
as Cohen's *Beautiful Losers* did. This is Symons' first novel but he has already
got another written. I didn't meet Al Purdy, as he was somewhere up north,
but I read some of his Eskimo poems in *Tamarack Review*, *Parallel*, and *Prism*,
and I think they are terrific. Pierre Burton with his unusual phenomenal energy has just brought out a book of TV interviews, plus editing *The Canadian
Centennial Library*, a series of books which are both beautifully produced and
intensely interesting.

Morley Callaghan is at last getting proper acknowledgment in his own country, thank goodness, after years of recognition in England and America, but less
at home. I have always maintained that Canadians took a long time to get used
to the fact that he deals with prime matters – good and evil as themes tend to
embarrass us, or did once. Charles Israel's novel *The Hostages* has just come out.
He is a tremendously hard-working writer who is one of the few not to yield to
the common current compulsion toward mockery of all against all. Austin
Clarke, having published *Amongst Thistles and Thorns* last year, has now completed another novel.

Earle Birney is now in Toronto and seeming as much as ever a survivor. It's
difficult for poets to be survivors – worse, even, than for prose writers, but he

manages it. His *Collected Poems* came out not long ago, and this year the CBC has published *The Creative Writer*, his essays on how writers work, an exploration of what goes on innerly. Phyllis Gottlieb, as intense in discussion as she is in her poetry, talked about science fiction, which is her other field. She must be one of the very few Canadian writers to tackle SF.

Farley Mowat, bearded and kilted, was about to take off for Siberia or all points North, Northwest, and wild. Having recently scored with *Westviking*, he has now brought out a children's book with the spectacular title of *The Curse of the Viking Grave*. Dave Godfrey is now teaching at Trinity and working on a novel. His stories have been the best ones published in *Tamarack Review* in the past few years. If I had to put my money on a Canadian writer who is most likely to produce some first-rate work in the next decade, I'd bet on Dave.

Winnipeg

From Dr Paul Hiebert I discovered that there is going to be a successor or successors to the immortal *Sarah Binks*. His new book is coming out next year and deals with Saskatchewan's Group of Seven. If Ontario could have a Group of Seven, why not Saskatchewan? But their seven are of course poets and poetesses. Dr Hiebert says for a while he considered calling it the Group of Seven-and-a-Half. He is a marvellously witty and somehow eternally youthful man.

Edmonton

Henry Kriesel, despite his heavy workload as head of the English Department at the University of Alberta, managed to bring out his second novel, *The Betrayal*, last year. He is a fine writer, someone of real wisdom, and I wish he had more time for his own writing. Sheila Watson's novel *The Double Hook* has recently come out in the *New Canadian Library* series, where it certainly belongs, being one of the few Canadian novels to attempt new perceptions of reality. Eli Mandel's latest collection of poems will be published soon by a new publishing venture on the part of a with-it Edmonton bookman.[1]

Vancouver

I cannot express how much it meant to me to see Ethel Wilson again. She is the only person I've ever known whom I'd call a great lady, as well as being a first-rate writer. In her novels she can say in a phrase what most of us take pages to catch. Jane Rule is completing another novel – her first, *Desert of the Heart*, was one of the best to come out of Canada in a long time, and in England it had the good reviews it deserved, although some Canadians still imagined that the theme was lesbianism rather than love. In fact, she is not an "ism" kind of writer.

Robert Harlow, having recently brought out a second novel, *A Gift of Echoes*, is now teaching creative writing at UBC and editing *Prism International*, which has grown since my own first stories were published in it some years ago. Dr Roy Daniells has just arrived back from a year in Rome, and spoke about it with the same gentle comprehension which illuminates all his poems. *Canadian Literature* continues to thrive under the excellent editorship of George Woodcock.

Books This Year

How have they been? Not a bad year, I'd say. The most controversial but possibly also the most worthwhile novel has been Leonard Cohen's *Beautiful Losers*. Thousands would disagree with me, no doubt, but I didn't think it was obscene. It gave a terrifying picture of an old man whose mind is on the brink of collapse. The external world is seen only in flashes and then horrifyingly. The line between fantasy and so-called reality fluctuates and is uncertain, and in this way Cohen is expressing what so many novelists nowadays everywhere are having to try to grapple with. Nobody can be sure, any more, what actually happened, and reality cannot be perceived in the same ways. Another way of handling this dilemma is found in Marie-Claire Blais' novel *A Season in the Life of Emmanuel*. She is surely one of our most talented writers.

This year, also, Gabrielle Roy's *The Road Past Altamont* was published. This book of stories is written with a restraint and tenderness that remind me of *Where Nests the Water-Hen*, and, like the earlier book, this one is also set in Manitoba.

Robert Kroetsch's *The Words of My Roaring* is another good novel, and is a large step forward from his first, *But We Are Exiles*. This new one, while set in the

Prairies during the Depression, speaks in a completely contemporary idiom and creates a truly active character, Johnnie Backstrom, a small-town undertaker and would-be politician. George Ryga's *Ballad of a Stonepicker* is also an improvement on his first novel, and, strangely enough, was better reviewed in England than in Canada.

The big deal of the year has been Stephen Vizinczey's *In Praise of Older Women*. Personally I thought it was a very pleasant young-man's novel, and that's about all. It has not only been a runaway bestseller, however, but also has vastly admiring reviews on both sides of the Atlantic.

What Else

I talked with Malcolm Ross, who is general editor of the New Canadian Library series. He would like to round out the series so that a general impression of Canadian literature could be achieved in it. Some very good titles have come out in this series over the past few years. Publisher Jack McClelland, with his customary enthusiasm, talked about his experiment this fall – putting out his whole list of novels simultaneously in hardcover and paperback. It's hoped that this will mean a wider reading public. Book-jacket designs seem somewhat better than they were. This is especially noticeable with publishers like Macmillan, whose jackets used to be ultra-traditional and who are now trying, like the parent firm in England, to make use of contemporary design.

Tamarack Review is still Canada's leading literary quarterly, and one of the best anywhere. Robert Weaver, of the Canadian Broadcasting Corporation, who has parented *Tamarack* through nearly ten years, has in my opinion done more to help Canadian writers than any other person. *Saturday Night* is continuing the short story contest begun last year, the Belmont Award.

Canada has more bookshops than it had a few years ago. This is especially true in the west, where good bookshops used to be rare. In England, the distinction is made between "bookseller" and "bookman" – the latter really cares about books. Western bookshops tend to be run by "bookmen" – Mel Hurtig in Edmonton, Bill Duthie in Vancouver, and also "bookwomen" – Mary Scorerin in Winnipeg.

In my view, Canada is still too Canada-focused.[2] Lots of people who care about books don't know that good novels in English are coming out of such places as Africa and India. The great distances within Canada are still an isolating factor for Canadian writers, too. I don't mean that any writer wants to talk incessantly with other writers. But it is heartening to see friends in the same line of work from time to time, and this is still difficult for too many Canadian writers. The talk still tends to be local. When you go to Toronto, you talk about the writing that's going on there. When you get to Vancouver, you change groove. Inevitable? Perhaps. The same tendency, after all, is not unknown in London, although it is lessened there by the influx of writers from all over the world.

But things are moving in Canada. The work is getting done – and that's all that really matters.

Voices from Future Places

"Voices from Future Places," in the Clara Thomas Archives and Special Collections, Margaret Laurence Fonds, Accession 1980–001/023 (156), York University, was first published in the Vancouver Sun *in April 1972. Laurence returned from England to Canada to spend the 1969–70 academic year as writer-in-residence at Massey College, University of Toronto, when Robertson Davies was master, an experience she recounts in* Dance on the Earth: A Memoir *(193–5), where she refers to herself as the "Ann Landers of Massey College" (195).*[1]

What, exactly, does a writer-in-residence do?

This question, while admittedly not of a truly vital or mind-boggling nature, has been put to me literally hundreds of times since my stint as writer-in-residence (which I will henceforth call W-in-R for brevity) at the University of Toronto.

The question is usually voiced in a slightly suspicious tone and accompanied by a half-embarrassed smile, as though the questioner finds it absolutely inconceivable that the lucky recipient of such an obvious sinecure might actually *do* anything at all. Or, if any activity does take place, it must surely be of a fairly dubious nature, such as swigging gallons of dry martinis behind locked office doors, or at best scribbling a few dilettante-type haiku on sheets of pale pink paper.

I will not attempt to dispel these interesting concepts, which no doubt afford much vicarious pleasure to those who hold them. (*Lucky old Joe Schmaltz – all those rotten novels, and now nothing to do for a whole year but seduce seductive undergraduates.*) I can't even say what any other W-in-R does or has done, exactly. I can only vouch for what happened to me during that somewhat bizarre year.

When I accepted the job, some months before actually commencing it, I wrote to Mordecai Richler, who was just then beginning his term as W-in-R at Sir George Williams in Montreal.

"What, exactly," I asked him piteously, "does a W-in-R *do*!?"

Mordecai replied sympathetically, in his pithy and to-the-point manner, saying that unfortunately he didn't know any more about it than I did. I next tried Jack Ludwig, whose successor I was to be at the University of Toronto. His reply, although not full of cheery reassurance, was at least abundant in its cautionary admonitions. *On no account*, he advised, be conned into acting as confessor-figure, headshrinker, parent-substitute, money-lender, marriage-broker, etcetera. I began to wonder what I was getting myself into.

Upon arrival at the university, I found there was a Committee relevant to my post. Universities, as such, love committees. It is only the unfortunate individual members of the committees who usually deplore them. This disparity is known as one of life's mysteries. My particular committee was designed to give help, advice, and moral support to the W-in-R. Great. Lovely. Some practical guidelines at last.

"What, exactly," I asked them hopefully, "is a W-in-R supposed to *do*!"

This was about the time when the word *structured* was truly coming into its own as a contemporary obscenity, and in many cases rightly so, when one considers the rigidity of universities in previous times. My committee were all very kind, very encouraging, but they weren't about to tell me what I was supposed to be doing. They smiled gently.

"Well, what would you *like* to do?" they responded.

Nervous as I was, my pioneering instincts began to rise. This business of being given a free hand was heady stuff. Interesting possibilities presented themselves. I fought down the baser of these, such as (a) *Nothing* or (b) *Write a pornographic novel, one chapter each, with a group of students and sell it for four billion dollars.* I said I would like to talk to young writers, should there be any who wanted to talk to me. I also asked where I could get some really flashy posters printed.

The posters turned out a brilliant purple. This was a clever ploy on my part, or so I hoped. I reckoned I would have to have the whole arrangement with students *structured* (you should excuse the expression) to some extent, by asking them to make an appointment to come and see me. Otherwise, if it were total Open House, it might mean nobody one day and six hundred the next, and I had only bought four coffee mugs for my office.

The poster's violent violet was calculated to overcome this unpleasant necessity by disarming disapproval through visual aids. The simple but touching message was that M.L. would like to talk to young writers, so please phone your

friendly neighbourhood W-in-R for appointment. It was posted on every bulletin board in every college in the university. I felt like a beginning General Prac-
titioner, or perhaps Tree Surgeon, who has just hung up the crucial shingle for
the first time.

Having inherited from both my Scots and my Irish ancestors an imagination
which readily visualizes disaster looming around the next corner, I was naturally
convinced that I would spend the whole academic year totally alone in my hand-
some office, brooding savagely over my four coffee mugs and my electric kettle,
while every young writer in the area spurned my brash offer of converse.

I had just finished a book of short stories and a children's book.[2] I didn't want
to do any of my own writing. What in heaven's name would I do? Keep white
mice? Cultivate geraniums? Take up embroidery? I decided I would spend the
year reading Proust and Frantz Fanon.

My office was in Massey College, hitherto a male stronghold – or so popular
opinion had it, but when I arrived and first met Robertson Davies, master of
Massey, he beamed at me from behind his splendid beard and said unequivocally, "Do not believe the idiotic tales you may have heard about Massey. You
are WELCOME." That made me feel better, and it proved to be consistently true.

I was, incidentally, the first woman ever to have had an office in Massey College, and I must say this pleased me. It did, however, give rise to a few misunderstandings related to the word *residence*. Many, looking at the sign on my
door, expressed the opinion that it must be kind of strange to live here. Writers-
in-residence, I now hasten to say, do not actually reside in the college which has
kindly given them office room.

I am certain that the young graduate students (all male) who did reside there
would have been absolutely delighted if I had taken up actual residence, had I
only been nineteen or twenty years of age. But the sight of my middle-aged self
stalking the night halls on the way to the bathroom, like a slightly apologetic
Lady Macbeth in a quilted housecoat, would probably have been too much.

The purple posters proved the truth of that odious saying *It Pays to Advertise*.
Suddenly, there seemed to be no time left in the week, and I, unaccustomed to
this hectic pace, would end up on Friday evenings feeling as though I had been
in training for some kind of Talk Olympics. It was exhausting and fascinating.

Throughout the year, I talked with multitudes of students, most of whom
would send in manuscripts of prose or poetry a few days in advance so I could
read and think about the writing before we met. The kids came to my office one

at a time, because it seemed to me this would work better than any kind of group, and we simply had coffee and talked, mostly about their writing, but often about everything under the sun. I never drank so much coffee in my entire life.

They weren't, of course, all born writers – in fact, hardly any were, or so it seemed to me. But this isn't a matter which anyone can feel sure about. I know which ones I considered the most promising, but I could be wrong even about those few. Not wrong, I think, about their talents. But at this point no one could possibly tell how great or how little their ultimate commitment to writing might turn out to be.

On the other hand, some of the apparently less promising may develop and find their own voices. I don't know. What I do know is that they were infinitely interesting to talk with, all of them, and that I finished the year feeling I had probably learned more from them than they had from me.

They were a very varied lot of people, and they had very varied reasons for writing. Therapy. Loneliness. Exhibitionism. Money. The desperate need to communicate. Even a genuine interest in writing itself. I thought I could generalize about them, but I find I can't. I can only remember them as individuals, not as types.

Every generation of writers has to draw material from its own world. This world is always very different from the one which went before. Within every generation the themes and concerns and obsessions may overlap, but they are basically individual and personal ones, which is why nobody can write for everybody, and also why nobody can generalize about writers.

There was the girl who was writing a novel which dealt with American draft-resisters. And the girl who wanted only to write children's stories and to illustrate them herself, and who said, apologetically (and unnecessarily) about the appealing fantasy creatures of her verbal and visual imagination, "I guess it's escapism, but I really care about these little animals."

Or the boy who wanted to pry from me the magic secret – like, how do you write a novel and be guaranteed that a publisher will accept it and pay you lots of lovely money for it? He may have felt let down when I snarled that there *was* no secret, and he'd be lucky if he got the thing published at all, never mind the money, always supposing he was capable of getting it finished in the first place.

Or the girl who had spent time in a mental hospital and felt she must write about it, about how it feels to be incarcerated with no rights and no power of appeal, for this was how she saw her experience, and then to be released once more into a world which made you wonder who were the insane – people like yourself in mental hospitals, or the military powermen, testing their lethal toys and apparently unaware that the planet is destructible.

Or the young man who had come from the Old Left[3] background, had gone through the drug scene and emerged the other side, and who was now New Left,[4] in his own life taking part in radical, student-protest movements, but in his prose trying to explore and verbalize the drug experience, in a style which he recognized as Burroughs-derived, as yet, but with the faith and determination that he would discover his own voice.

Or the lanky boy from Fairbanks, Alaska, who hated Toronto and was miserable there, and yet wondered if he'd be able to write, back home – was it a sufficiently stimulating milieu? I sometimes think of him, and hope he's back in Fairbanks, where everything happens, just as everything, essentially, happens everywhere.

Most of the kids I saw only once, but there were a few with whom I talked a great deal throughout the year, and I admit to prejudice. These were the ones whose writing most interested me, the ones whose writing I criticized the most harshly, partly because it was worth criticizing and partly because I knew perfectly well that nothing I could say could possibly either help or damage them.

Frank was the son of Italian parents who wanted him to become a lawyer. His great difficulty was that he now knew he didn't have the faintest intention of becoming a lawyer, but he knew this was going to pain his family, and he cared about them. He put off telling them, but he recognized that it would have to be done sometime. His novel, which kept growing at an astonishing rate, was really spooky stuff, the inner geography which sometimes scared him, but with which he had to continue.

"It's about three-quarters done, in the first draft," he said, toward the end of the academic year.

"That's great," I said.

"For me, in one way it's a disaster," he said; "I'm five essays behind."

I had visions of myself being abruptly dismissed, or blackballed, or whatever they do to you, for encouraging students to write novels rather than essays.

Only the other day I opened a Canadian literary publication, and there was a story by a new writer. It was spooky stuff, the inner geography. It was an excerpt from Frank's novel.

Dan, perhaps the most natural-born writer I met all year, had once been a novice in a Jesuit seminary, and had decided the priesthood was not his vocation after all. Boston American, he had been studying in Toronto when he began to write stories. Some of them concerned the seminary experience, and some the experience of being a draft-resister, and how it felt to leave the land of your ancestors, hating its present lunacies but also compelled to love your own roots there. In a recent letter, he tells me a novel is nearly finished. I think it will be a good one.

Paul wrote mainly poetry, and his poems came across to me more strongly than anyone else's that year. He had a very unusual (for his age, about nineteen) sense of connection with his past, and some of his poetry was concerned with an attempt to overcome the stifling effect of that past, while at the same time realizing the reality of his parents and grandparents. Once he came into my office looking both bewildered and furious.

"Just got two acceptances," he said, naming two Canadian literary magazines.

"So why the long face?"

"Well, because it's one poem, actually. Damn, I submitted to both publications at the same time. I never thought even one would accept."

A dreadful warning, as I tried to point out to him when I had stopped laughing.

He and his girl visited us recently in England, and Paul sang some of his songs, which he's doing now. I wish more people could hear those songs. Maybe one day they will.

At this point I would like to give the lie to the scurrilous story, reported in some newspapers, that I was known as the Ann Landers of Massey College. The truth is less spectacular, although quite pleasant in its way. Once a young man from a residence of engineering and medical students arrived in my office and asked me to go over one evening for a talk session. Did they *really* want to talk about writing, I asked him in some puzzlement.

"Oh no," he said, astonished that I should think so. "The guys want to talk about WOMEN."

In fact, we talked about everything from Women's Lib to water pollution, but the story got around. My fault, of course. I made the major error of saying to several people that maybe my initials should be A.L. not M.L.

What, exactly, does a writer-in-residence do?

Well, sometimes they can be a knockdownable parent-figure, a financial consultant, an amateur friend, any number of strange categories. Mostly they just listen, and very occasionally they really do hear voices from future places.

The Case for Canadian Literature

"The Case for Canadian Literature," housed in the Clara Thomas Archives and Special Collections, Margaret Laurence Fonds, Accession 1980–001/023 (156), was a convocation address presented to Simon Fraser University on 28 May 1977 and published in the Simon Fraser University Week. *On several occasions of her being awarded honorary degrees at Canadian universities, Laurence presented convocation addresses wherein she advocated for Canadian literature.*

I'd like to make, to the graduating students today, a statement of faith. This may sound like heavy stuff, but I'll keep it brief.

Some of you will probably become teachers, or members of school boards and library boards in due course of time, and no doubt a number of you will ultimately become parents.

What books will you wish to put into the hands of your young, when the time comes? This is not a statement for censorship, I need hardly say. I am simply expressing the hope that a reasonable proportion of those books which you will read, buy, recommend, teach, or give to your own children will be Canadian books.

Why? Why bother about trying to get more Canadian books into our libraries, bookshops, on high school and university courses, and indeed on primary school courses as well? Why not just include one or two Canadian books in general literature courses? Isn't literature international? Why not let Canadian literature find its place, if at all, among the literatures of the world? There's nothing special about Canadian literature, is there?

Yes. There is something special about it.

The very fact that such a statement needs to be made at all – and it *does* – shows how far we still have to go. The thing that is special about Canadian literature is that it is ours. It speaks to us of our own people, of ourselves, of our connection with the physical reality of our land.

I am, of course, not suggesting in the slightest that we should throw out Shakespeare or any of the great writers of the past from whatever culture. Nor am I suggesting that we should fail to read the best writers in contemporary literature anywhere in the world. Of course we should cast the nets of reading as widely as possible, and gather in a whole multitude of marvellous creations.

I am, however, saying that we do not any longer need to read or teach Canadian writing simply because it *is* Canadian. Nor do we have to do what our colonialist background taught us – which was to ignore our own writers simply because they are Canadian. Many, many people, of course, realize these things now. It's taken us awhile, but we have learned.

The calibre and scope of our literature now is such that it can be read and taught simply because it is interesting, worth reading, and worth teaching. But for us it has an added dimension as well. It is our own: it speaks to us, through its many and varied voices, of things which are close to our hearts; it links us with our ancestors and with one another. This view is equally true of anglophone and francophone writing in this country.

Dr Homer Hogan, of the University of Guelph, Ontario, conducted a survey a couple of years ago, and published his unfortunate findings in an article entitled "Who Cooked the Canadian Goose?"

Dr Hogan took an extended trip throughout Europe, searching for a country that taught less of its own literature than Canada did. Britain, France, Germany, the Scandinavian countries – a dead loss. The teaching of their own literature was taken totally for granted. Dr Hogan finally found himself in his last chance – Luxembourg. Luxembourg is the smallest nation in Europe. He was ushered into the office of an official of the ministry of education. "What can I do for you, Dr Hogan?" the official asked.

"You can save the honour of Canada," Dr Hogan replied.

But it was not to be. It turned out that Luxembourg – which we do not exactly tend to think of as a repository of the greatest literature of mankind – taught one full year of Luxembourg literature, at a secondary school level, and this was a required course. The official apologized to Dr Hogan that only one full year's course was available.

In Canada, I don't know of *any* high schools where Canadian literature is a required course, and although I do not have any figures to support my view, I have visited a great many schools and I would guess that there are very few of our high schools that offer full courses in Canlit as yet.

Of what other people could it be said that they failed in such manner to pass on to their children their own cultural heritage? Why do we take it for granted that other countries – countries such as England, France, America, and yes, even Luxembourg – should perfectly properly be teaching their own literature, and yet teachers here who are interested in Canlit still have to struggle to get it on their courses? That there should even be any question about it is astonishing. This reluctance is, of course, a leftover from colonialist attitudes of the past, and these are attitudes which have no place or relevance in our present and future.

That was the bad news. Now comes the good news.

Happily, things are changing, and changing rapidly. When I attended high school and university, a long time ago, virtually *nothing* Canadian was being taught, although such writers as Sinclair Ross, Hugh MacLennan, Morley Callaghan, and Gabrielle Roy were publishing some of their best works, books which in a later and different climate of thought would be recognized for the splendid novels they are.

Nowadays Canadian writers *do* have an audience among their own people, an informed and growing readership. I have talked with literally hundreds of high school teachers who are trying to get school board agreement to teach more Canadian writing on their courses, and students who are keenly interested in knowing more about the poetry and prose of their own culture. The situation has changed dramatically from even ten years ago.

There has been, as well, an incredible upsurge in Canadian writing, and there is a whole generation of Canadian writers, younger than my generation, who are coming up with splendid works in the areas of fiction, nonfiction, and poetry.

The Writers' Union of Canada, of which I am a founding member, has been in existence now for nearly five years, and we are working very hard to make conditions better for writers in this country, through such projects as a standard contract, public lending rights for library use of our books, and many others. And through this association of writers, there has come about a feeling of true community, of tribe, of family, among the writers of our country.

Is my stance a narrowly nationalistic one? I do not think so. I believe that nationalism and internationalism are not mutually exclusive. I consider myself to be an internationalist. I also define my own brand of nationalism as one which has no desire to control or own or manipulate other lands, other peoples, but which *does* have a great need to possess our own land, to know our own heritage, to value ourselves in relation to a world community.

As one of the European educators said to Dr Hogan, "You must love your own people before you can truly love humanity."

I think it is important to pass on, from generation to generation, a feeling of our own people, of our place of belonging. It is important at this point in our country's history for us to communicate with one another, across this land, from Vancouver Island to Newfoundland, and to feel the true reality of one another. It is important to know that we all come from many different sources, originally, but that in this diversity lies our true strength as a people.

There are many ways in which this passing-on process may be done, and is being done. I have been speaking to you today of one of these ways of communication, one way which I believe to be essential, not only because I myself am a writer, but because writing itself, at the heart of it, is an assertion of faith in the possibilities of human communication.

Canadian Writers: From Neglect to Special Treatment

"Canadian Writers: From Neglect to Special Treatment" was first published in the Toronto Star *in 1970 with the following Editor's Note: "During the past decade Canadian writers have at last had the opportunity of getting into print without 'proving themselves' in England or the US. Margaret Laurence, one of Canada's most respected novelists and writer-in-residence at Massey College, the University of Toronto, explores some of the consequences of this change." While Laurence was a fervent advocate for Canadian literature, she believes literature should be valued for its merit, not for purely patriotic reasons. Although a Canadian nationalist, she suspects that the pendulum has swung too far and cautions reviewers against parochialism.[1]*

Once upon a time, and not so very long ago at that, the old adage "There is no surer path to obscurity than to be a Canadian writer" was unhappily true. Morley Callaghan was writing novels which were widely recognized in England and America, while in Canada people were still naively embarrassed by the fact that he dealt with such prime matters as good and evil, innocence and its loss. Sinclair Ross, having published *As For Me and My House* at the worst possible time, namely during the war, worked in a Montreal bank for years, totally and tragically unaware of the fact that he had written a Canadian classic. Ethel Wilson's novels were read by a devoted minority, but it was years before the delicate brilliance of her writing was properly acknowledged. Young writers wrote in an atmosphere of stealth and gloom, knowing they didn't stand a dog's chance of being published in Canada unless an American or English publisher would take their novel first. Mordecai Richler, despairing of his own country, took off for London, England.

Those days seem pretty distant now. A mere decade, and the whole picture has changed.

I think a portion of the credit must go to McClelland & Stewart, who have always billed themselves unashamedly as "the Canadian publishers." Jack McClelland has introduced more innovations into the Canadian publishing world than any other person. He has been willing to take chances on the work of young writers; he hasn't been afraid to publish controversial books; he has brought the design of books and dust-jackets into this century.

Also, a good many of the painfully traditional publishers in this country are at last beginning to move into new areas. The ancient and honorable House of Macmillan is now bringing out novels with dust jackets that no longer look as though they might be refugees from the Victorian era. Such ultra-establishment houses as Ryerson and Clarke-Irwin are beginning to handle books that a few years ago they wouldn't have touched with a ten-foot pole.

Part of this stir and ferment can be attributed to the upspringing of a number of new young publishing houses. I don't mean the little presses that put out limited editions of poems and which certainly serve a useful function, even though they may rise and fall with the seasons. I mean the new publishing ventures which appear to stand a good chance of surviving and which are making the old-line publishers look to their laurels, the new publishers whose scope is broad and who have entered the field with a considerable grasp of the business requirements, as well as a feeling for what needs doing in Canadian publishing.

The House of Anansi, in Toronto, comes to mind first, with its steadily growing list of poetry, novels, and social commentary, and its knack of imaginative format. Others include New Press of Toronto; Mel Hurtig of Edmonton; *Prism International*, the University of British Columbia literary quarterly; Peter Martin Associates of Toronto; Tundra Press of Montreal; Oberon Press of Ottawa; and Lovat Dickson, a distinguished Canadian who spent many years as a well-known publisher with Macmillan in England and who now has begun his own publishing firm in Toronto. And there are others.

What has all this meant in terms of output? Can we look for a sudden in-all-directions flowering of Canadian writing? Not yet, I think. However, things are moving along with fairly encouraging vigour.

So here we are, at the beginning of another decade, and the writing and publishing picture looks extremely promising. Fiction of some value is being written (poetry, too, of course) and it is being published both by the older publishers and the new publishing houses which are springing up all over. To be a writer in Canada today is certainly a far cry from the discouraging and isolated business it once was.

This is great, and I am all for it. However, there are one or two perils implicit in this burgeoning atmosphere. I think it needs to be pointed out that, whereas Canadian writers were once desperately neglected in their own land, they are now in danger of being overpraised. The blossoming of new publishing houses and the gradual emancipation (hopefully) of the older ones coincides with an upswing of Canadian nationalism the like of which we have not seen before.

Canadians no longer feel they have to put down their nationality at every turn.

People twenty years younger than I am (and I am forty-three) will not even remember when this was the national sport, but I do not forget the old and once-true joke which said that if you ask an Englishman what is the best country in the world, he'll say England; if you ask an American, he'll say America; if you ask a Canadian, he'll say, "any goddamn country except Canada." We are a long way from that stance now, thank goodness. But pendulums have a way of veering too far.

I was depressed the other day to read a review of a first novel by a Canadian writer in which the reviewer actually apologized for panning the novel. I could scarcely have been more depressed if he had praised it only because it was a Canadian novel. What is all this nonsense about Canadian writing? Writers, publishers, and critics, in my view, need to hold strongly onto only one thing – the crucial thing about any novel is whether or not it is a good novel. By this I do not mean that there are absolute standards; of course, there aren't. But a novel should be capable of communicating something – character, dilemmas, themes – to some readers of reasonable intelligence and literacy, both inside and outside the writer's particular culture.

If writers are going to compare their capabilities with anyone else's, there is only one standard of comparison – and that is with the best that is being written in the same language anywhere in the world. If publishers are selecting novels for publication, there is only one yardstick – not "Well, it's fairly decent compared to what else has come along by Canadian writers this month," but does it or does it not stand up on its own, with no props, as a novel. If a reviewer is talking about a novel by a writer who happens to be a Canadian, it is an insult both to writer and readers to give that novel any kind of handicap or special treatment.

The minute we forget that the world is a large place, praise God, then we speak or sing to fewer than those who might be able to hear us and respond to us, to fewer than those who might even need to hear us and to answer.

We can afford to relax about such theoretical and meaningless matters as a national culture. There is no such thing as an instant culture, and we are certainly not going to accumulate a powerful body of Canadian literature overnight or even over a century. So what? It will come – it is already in the forging – if we let it be. It will take shape around us, if only we can stop being so twitchy about the national aspects of the thing and just concentrate both lovingly and critically on the only thing that matters, the work itself.

When You Were Five and I Was Fourteen

"When You Were Five and I Was Fourteen," in the Clara Thomas Archives, York University, No. 1989–039/010 (208), and published in the Fiftieth Anniversary Issue of Quill & Quire *(April 1985), celebrates Laurence's love for this journal. Peggy's Aunt Marg, Margaret Simpson – who returned to Neepawa from Calgary to become her stepmother, her beloved "Mum," after her birth mother, Verna Wemyss, died shortly after Peggy's fourth birthday – allowed Peggy to help select Canadian books from* Quill & Quire *for the Neepawa library.*

It was my good luck to be born into a family of readers. It was my fate to be born in 1926, when the drought and the Depression were about to strike, and to grow up during that time and during the Second World War in a small town in Manitoba. Our house was full of books. I read Kipling, Dickens, and Mark Twain at a young age. I also read, less illuminatingly, *The Boy's Own Annual* and *The Girl's Own Annual*, books that my parents and my aunts and uncles had read when they were young, collections mainly of adventure stories (the boys got to do all the most exciting things) that told us the British Empire was the best thing in the world. Amazingly, I survived those books relatively unscathed and grew up to be vigorously anti-colonialist.

My father was a lawyer, and during the Depression he got paid in eggs and chickens and produce. There was not much money, but there was always a book for me and my brother at Christmas and birthdays. During my early years there was no library in our town. The first library was started when I was fourteen, in 1940. My Dad had died some years before, and my Mum was bringing up my brother and myself by herself. She had been a high-school teacher of English and was determined that her kids would have the chance to read good books. She and a few others in our town, including the splendid teacher of English, Miss

Mildred Musgrove,[1] and Mr Rey, the principal, started the first library. It was first housed in a room over the post office and moved quite a lot in the years to come – to the basement of the drugstore, and so on.

My mother had decided on her policy for her children's reading. We could read anything that came our way, but discussion about books was encouraged. Well do I recall myself reading *Laddie* by Gene Stratton-Porter and my mother saying, "Well, some people think it is sentimental, but I felt the same as you do now about *Tess of the D'Urbervilles*. Let's look at that." (I adopted this same policy of discussion with my own children when they were young.) In those days, recently published books such as *The Grapes of Wrath* by John Steinbeck and *Gone With the Wind* by Margaret Mitchell were thought by some parents to be unsuitable reading for the young prairie violets I and my girlfriends were then (How innocent those books seem now!). My mother disagreed. I read them, and we talked about them.

From 1940, until 1944, when I was eighteen and went away to college,[2] my mother and I used to ponder on a Canadian publication to which our newly hatched library had a subscription. Called *Quill & Quire*, it told us about the Canadian books that were being published. Canadian books then? You bet. My mother was a staunch supporter of having Canadian books in our library; she was, as I realized only much later, an early evangelist for Canadian writing. She did not, of course, realize that her daughter would one day write out of our land and townspeople and that tradition, but perhaps she suspected it, for she gave me a serious critique of everything I wrote.

Quill & Quire then, as I recall, had a smaller format and was a much slimmer magazine. Mum and I read it avidly, and at fourteen, fifteen, and sixteen I actually had some input about which books the town library would buy with its very limited resources. I recall those evenings now with such affection, Mum and I reading *Quill & Quire*, and my practical Mum trying to figure out how we could get the maximum number of books for the minimum amount of money. It was only years later that I knew how privileged I had been. I recall one book especially – Sinclair Ross's *As For Me and My House*. It was published first in 1941, when I was fifteen, and we read the write-up in *Q&Q* and got it for the library. I learned from that book that one could write about where one *was*, even a small prairie town. I never forgot that.

Quill & Quire probably gave me a lifelong addiction to book reviews and perhaps a lifelong addiction to buying books when I could.

When I left Canada, I didn't read *Q&Q* for some time, although I read it whenever I was back. When I came home to stay, in 1973, one of the first subscriptions I took out was to this magazine.

I may possibly be one of the earlier readers of *Q&Q*, and that gives me pleasure. I don't suppose too many people began to read it when they were fourteen years old and *Q&Q* was five.

Books That Mattered to Me

*"Books That Mattered to Me," labelled "Talk for Friends of the Bata Library,
Trent University, 1981," was published in the Friends' Bulletin, No. 4, 1981, and
reprinted in* Margaret Laurence: An Appreciation, *edited by Christl Verduyn.
Laurence recalls her favourite books by Canadian, African, and women writers.*

I confess that the subject of this talk – books that mattered to me – is a little
daunting, to say the least. For those of us to whom books have been a major part
of our lives, the books that mattered to us are legion. This is, of course, a blinding
glimpse of the obvious. I do not need to say to *this* gathering that the books I'm
about to mention are a *very* few of the very, very many that have influenced, en-
riched, disturbed, and changed my life.

There is a family tale – perhaps apocryphal – that my mother and aunts were
fond of telling me. Supposedly, on returning home from my first day of school,
at the age of six, I had as my considered opinion that I didn't think much of it
– *one whole day* and I couldn't yet read.[1] I have since tried to make up for that
early slowness.

I was born in 1926 and grew up in the thirties. Like most people at that time,
we had very little money, although we were much luckier than many. I was an
insatiable reader – (when I *finally* learned, a little later than my first day at
school!). There wasn't much money to buy books, although my family tried val-
iantly, and there was never a birthday or a Christmas when I wasn't given at least
one book I'd wanted.[2] There was no public library in my town until I was about
thirteen – my mother was one of the founders of that first small library, and one
of its volunteer librarians. I did, however, have the immense good fortune to be
born into a family of readers, and our house contained a great many books. One
of the joys of my childhood was the complete set of Rudyard Kipling's books,

most of which I read at a fairly tender age. Looking back now, it seems remarkable to me that, although my reading of Kipling instilled in me a vast desire to travel to far places, his staunch British imperialism made very little impression, thank goodness. I think this is because Kipling – as many people now forget – had an enormous sympathy and even empathy with the peoples of India. It was, after all, his birthplace and remained his heart-place all his life. In any event, *Kim* was one of my best loved books when I was a child, as were, also, *The Jungle Books* and – with their English, historical, mythical, and magical aspects – *Puck of Pook's Hill* and *Rewards and Fairies*. These books were among the many that helped to open my imagination to far-off places and long-ago people.

Two other books stand out in my memory of childhood reading. One is Robert Louis Stevenson's *Kidnapped* and the other is Arthur Conan Doyle's *The White Company*. The former, set just after Culloden, the tragic battle in which the Scots Highland clans were finally broken and the fabric of their society torn forever, probably set me thinking about those historical events, but not in any conscious way at that time. Alan Breck, escaping through the heather, was my ideal of bravery and adventure, and young David Balfour's triumph against his wicked uncle seemed to me to be just the sort of thing I myself would have been very good at, had the opportunity ever presented itself. Conan Doyle's book, with its – as I now see – rather dreadful idealization of the English, and its marvellous evocation of Agincourt and the English bowmen, also had a hero, the lad Alain, with whom I identified totally. Does this seem strange to you? It seems strange to me, now; it did not seem so then. That book was in the grade seven library and I must have borrowed it three or four times that year, when I was twelve. That was the same year – this really dates me – that a young American singer first became popular, and the girls were pretending to swoon all over the place. His name was Frank Sinatra. I wasn't much of a swooner. On odds, I preferred Kim, Alan Breck, David Balfour, and Alain. It was around this time that I began to perceive that I did not fit in with many of my contemporaries, although heaven knows I longed to do so.

Were there no women writers who spoke to my childhood? Not many. I don't recall ever wishing that I had been born a boy, which seems curious, considering that the boys in fiction were the ones who got to have all the exciting adventures. I suppose that, because of my mother, who had been a high school teacher of English and who had once gone as a young woman on an exchange teachership for a year to faraway Bermuda, and my aunts, two of whom were nurses, one a very distinguished nurse who had been for some years head of the Canadian Nurses Association – because of these strong independent-minded women, I always had the vague but powerful feeling that I, too, could participate in exciting events. There were, however, two women writers who were especially important to me, away back then. One was Nellie McClung, and the other was L.M. Montgomery. Both, also, were Canadian writers, people who wrote out of territories not unlike my own, and this was not so usual at that time. Nellie McClung's personal history of strong feminism, the battles she had fought before I was born, to have women proclaimed "persons," her fight for women's right to vote – these were not observed or known to me until I was much older. Only in my young adulthood did I realize how far-reaching was the victory of such women as Nellie McClung and Emily Murphy, to have women recognized as persons. They won in 1929. For the first three years of my life I was not a person, although I was, naturally, unaware of this fact at the time. But *Sowing Seeds in Danny*, sentimental and even positively treacly though it certainly was, in fact was a real influence in my life. The indomitable Pearl, holding the family together against vast difficulties, must have been to me what people now call a role model. Pearlie was young, but she was brave and strong. She had humour and wit, and she put up with no nonsense from snobs. As far as L.M. Montgomery was concerned, my favourite of her books was her first, *Anne of Green Gables*. It remains, to my mind, a children's classic. My own daughter loved it when she was a child. The other of Montgomery's books that stirred me was *Emily of New Moon*. Both Anne and Emily were rebels – intelligent, talented girls who were not about to be put down. Emily had the added appeal of wanting to become a writer – no, of actually *being* a writer, as I myself was, even as a child, although I never dreamed I would someday be published. Of course, as was inevitable when those books were written, both Anne and Emily ended up – in sequels to those novels – by marrying the boy next door and becoming, if memory serves, somewhat more subdued. It is only fair to add, however, that the male characters, Gilbert and Teddie, did respect and acknowledge their wives' intelligence and talents. These two fictional girls gave me, I think, the sense that a woman could be – and it was *all right* for her to be – an intelligent, independent-minded person who was determined to pursue her own vocation, as well as being a wife and mother.

Now we move on to a few of the books that I recall as moments of Recognition and Revelation. I am leaving out, here, purposely, all the truly great and magnificent works of the past to which we all owe so much of our intellectual, emotional, and spiritual development – the Bible, Shakespeare, Milton, John Donne, Melville, Hawthorne, and on and on and on. We can, I think, take those revelations for granted – they must have happened in some way or another to all of us. I know they did to me, especially when I went to college in Winnipeg, at the age of eighteen, and discovered, quite literally, a whole new world. United College[3] – now the University of Winnipeg – was at that time one of the small liberal arts colleges, not unlike Trent now, although much smaller. Those of us who were privileged to go there in the mid-forties will, I think, forever be grateful for the kind of caring, questioning, thoughtful educations we received there. Canadian writing, at that time, was not taught in any courses. But there were teachers – Arthur Phelps, among them, one of the great teachers in our land – who encouraged us to read Canadian writers.[4] He was a personal friend of Frederick Philip Grove, and also of Morley Callaghan, who once visited – to our delight – a meeting of the English Club, a once-a-month event that took place at the Phelps' home, at which those of us who were devoted to English literature took turns in presenting our earnest, youthful, but quite marvellously enthusiastic, papers. Well, we *did* read Canadian books. We couldn't afford to buy them, and they weren't even greatly in evidence at the public library, but we read Gabrielle Roy, Hugh MacLennan, Morley Callaghan, and others, in the book department of the Hudson's Bay Company, just across the road from the college, a chapter at a time, hoping the sales clerks wouldn't notice us standing there, turning the pages. A rather touching footnote to this story is that, when I first met Dale Zieroth, the talented poet who was born in the same town as I was, just twenty years after myself, and who grew up on a farm near Glenella, Manitoba, he told me that when *he* was at United College, he couldn't afford to buy books, either, so he read my novel, *A Jest of God*, in the bookstore at the Bay, a chapter at a time, hoping the sales clerks wouldn't notice.

Recognition, Revelation. The first time this happened to me with great force was when I read Sinclair Ross's novel, *As For Me and My House*. It was published in 1941, and sank without a trace, for that was during the Second World War, and people didn't want to be reminded of the so-called Dirty Thirties. It surfaced some years later as a Canadian classic and at last came into its own. I must have read it, however, in about 1942, because we got it for the Neepawa Library, my mother and a few others being very keen on acquiring Canadian books. I would have been sixteen years old. I saw, reading it, that a writer could write out of a background similar to my own. You didn't need to live in London or

New York. It was all here. Some five or six years later, W.O. Mitchell's novel *Who Has Seen the Wind?* confirmed and strengthened this revelation. My fictional town of Manawaka is different in very many ways from the prairie towns of Ross and Mitchell. Nonetheless, it was these writers who showed me what I would ultimately have to do, namely to write out of my own place, my own time, my own people.

One of my contemporaries, Adele Wiseman, who is also a dear friend and has been so for more than thirty years, wrote a novel that I consider to be one of the finest written in the English language in the past twenty-five years or so. This was her first novel, *The Sacrifice*, published in 1956. It is an amazing piece of work. The vision of Abraham, his terrible anguish and his triumphs, the generations who followed him in this new land – all these spoke to me so deeply that it is impossible for me to honour them sufficiently in a few words. I have in my possession, incidentally, a letter that Adele found among her mother's things when Chaika Wiseman, the doll-maker, that beloved and wise woman, died just over a year ago. It is a letter I wrote from England, in 1950, to Adele's parents in Winnipeg. My husband and I were preparing to go to Somaliland, in East Africa, where Jack was to be in charge of a scheme to build *ballehs*, large earth dug-outs, to catch the once-yearly rainfall across the Haud desert.[5] Adele had not long before arrived in England, where she was working at the Stepney Jewish Girls Hostel in London. She and I were carrying on the same discussions about writing that we had begun a few years before in North Winnipeg. In the letter, I described, somewhat touchingly, Jack's and my preparations to go to an unknown land, my hope that we had bought the right pots and pans, and that my one newly purchased – and very inexpensive – formal dress would prove suitable. I didn't know whether we were in for a giddy round of dances at Government House, or whether it would all be slogging through the desert. Actually, it turned out to be both, and of the two, I soon discovered that I preferred the desert. Anyway, I went on to say: "I was over at Adele's this afternoon. We read each other our manuscripts and told each other that we were going to write the two great novels of the century." Oh, young hopes! I was, of course, speaking in jest, and yet it is true that we both had, at that point, an undeniable sense of vocation. What manuscript of mine I showed to her that day, I can't recall – whatever it was, it came to nothing. But the manuscript of hers that I saw was part of the first draft of *The Sacrifice*. Adele and I had a joke in those days. We used to say to one another, "Just wait, kiddo, until we both win the Governor

General's Award!" Of course we never dreamed that in the years to come, we both *would*.[6]

I'm skipping many years and many books that made profound impressions on me. In 1960, my first novel, *This Side Jordan*, set in West Africa, had just been published. I was working on a number of West African short stories, and also contemplating getting out my old diaries from Somaliland days, and trying to write an account of our experiences there. I was trying to *understand* our African experience, and it was at this point that quite by accident I came across the exact book I needed at the exact time I needed it. This was *Prospero and Caliban: The Psychology of Colonization*, by the French psychologist O. Mannoni. In it, Mannoni describes his own anguished time in Madagascar, and his feeling that at last – terribly, frighteningly – he understood something of the Malagasy people's feelings, often inchoate, toward the French colonialists – the African people's rage, sense of spiritual violation, sense of powerlessness in the face of economic exploitation and social and psychological oppression, in the days before the independence movements were to become organized and politically effective, when the people's anguish expressed itself in unorganized and chaotic uprisings doomed to failure, at that point. To me, this book meant a real, literal revelation. It opened up to me an understanding of some of my own feelings and experiences in East and West Africa, and in the end, perhaps, taught me as much about my own land and the terrible injustices and outrages committed by imperialism against *our* native peoples, as it did about the peoples of Africa. I made use, I hope, of these insights in my West African stories, especially in a story called "The Voices of Adamo,"[7] and in my book on Somaliland, *The Prophet's Camel Bell*. Much later, some of these insights were to return, informed this time with more knowledge of my own land and peoples, in my novel *The Diviners*.[8]

Among the books relating to my own land, one that has meant the most to me is W.L. Morton's *Manitoba: A History*. I knew sadly little of the history of my own part of the country until relatively few years ago. When I was a child we were not taught a great deal of Canadian history, and what we were taught seemed to be mostly Acts of Parliament. It was standard practice to skim over the North-West rebellions in very short order, and to present Louis Riel, Gabriel Dumont, Big Bear, Poundmaker,[9] and others as the bad guys who wanted to impede good old John A. Macdonald's grand design for Progress and the CPR.[10] Yet I was born and grew up in a town called Neepawa, the Cree meaning of which is something like "Land of Plentiful Game." It was through these bluffs and valleys and open prairies that the bi-yearly buffalo hunts of the Métis and Cree swept along in by-gone years. It was not far from here that the events of 1870 took place, when Riel sought to guarantee some rights for his people, and was finally driven into his fifteen-year exile, from which he returned in 1885, to Saskatchewan, to the heroic attempts made by the Indian and Métis peoples to save their land and their way of life, and to ultimate defeat and tragedy. Of these things I knew nothing. My own grandfather had been the first lawyer in our town, and had incorporated the town, the name being interpreted as Land of Plenty, and its symbol being a cornucopia.[11] A cornucopia! A European symbol having nothing to do with the history of the place. When I first read Morton's *Manitoba: A History*, it was with a tremendous sense of excitement, combined with an angry sense of having been deprived, when young, of my own heritage. I have since done a great deal of reading of prairie history, but it was Morton who first gave me the sense of my place's long and dramatic past.

One book I want to mention here, because of the depth of its perceptions and the scope of its vision, is F.R. Scott's *Essays on the Constitution*.[12] Scott, our most distinguished constitutional lawyer and one of our finest poets, wrote these essays over some fifty years. They were collected in a single volume in 1977 and won the Governor General's Award for nonfiction of that year. In these essays Scott discusses issues such as civil liberties, censorship, the rights of minorities, the need for due process of law as against the emotional hysteria of the vigilantes of any historical period. To me, Scott's book can be described in one word: *noble*. Here is one brief quote from an essay written in 1932, entitled "Freedom of Speech": "'The time, it is to be hoped, has gone by,' wrote John Stuart Mill,[13] 'when any defense would be necessary for the principle of freedom of speech.' His hope was vain. The time for defending freedom never goes by. Freedom is a habit that must be kept alive by use."

These are words, I think, that we would do well to ponder deeply in our own times.

I want now to speak a little about a few more novels that have impressed, delighted, and enlightened me, possibly to give you some further indication of my own tastes in reading and also of some of the standards to which I aspire as a novelist, those impossible standards that in our own self-assessment we never meet, those qualities in the writing of others that we instantly recognize.

The British novelist Joyce Cary has meant a very great deal to me. This is true of all his novels, but perhaps especially *The Horse's Mouth*. The artist Gulley Jimson and the immortal Sara Monday will inhabit my mind as long as I live. Here are characters who step right off the printed page and into the reader's mental and spiritual landscape.

Another novel that endures permanently within my mind is *Arrow of God*, by the Nigerian writer Chinua Achebe. This is the story of Ezeulu, priest of his god Ulu, in postcolonial times in Nigeria, shortly after the British took over. At times, Achebe writes with rage and deep irony. Yet he does not write in any didactic way. He is speaking of humankind's dreadful misunderstandings of one another, of man's inhumanity to man, and he is speaking of individuals living within their own cultures and their own isolated skulls and trying – often vainly – to communicate with one another. His character portrayals are nothing short of miraculous. If I may quote my own words, from a book of essays on contemporary Nigerian literature, *Long Drums and Cannons*, this is my conclusion about Ezeulu: "Ezeulu, man and priest, god's man, like Oedipus and like Lear, has the power to reveal not only moving and terrifying aspects of himself, but moving and terrifying aspects of ourselves as well."

The word "great," as applied to writers, is a greatly abused word. There are very few writers, in any historical period, who can be called "great," and usually it is only the passage of time that confirms a writer in that status. However, I will go out on a limb and say that one writer now writing in the English language, whom I consider to be *great*, is Patrick White of Australia. When he was awarded the Nobel Prize, I rejoiced. All his novels have in some way changed my life, by the force of their characters, their sheer quality of alive-ness, their troubling and basically spiritual view of life. I would mention especially *The Tree of Man*, *Voss*, *Riders in the Chariot*, *The Solid Mandala*, *The Vivisector*, and *The Eye of the Storm*. How White can keep on writing novel after novel of such power, with such a huge assemblage of compelling characters, is something one can only marvel at and give thanks for.

Of the large number of contemporary American works of fiction that have touched my life, I want to mention two – and my choice may seem strange, for these two writers are so different, so apparently far apart in subject matter, so totally unalike in style, that one might wonder how I could feel so strongly about both of them.

Kurt Vonnegut's novel *Slaughterhouse Five* I consider to be brilliant. His savage wit, his zaniness which is a cover for a perception so unremittingly honest that it is almost unbearable, his use of Science Fiction techniques to point up the lunacy of our times, his genuine rage against wars and human destruction – all these qualities in his writing I find quite stunning. Vonnegut has proclaimed himself a total pessimist – *Things are going to get worse*, he says, *and they are never going to get better*. And yet, there is a way in which he seems to be saying – it's up to us. To me, the act of writing is itself an act of faith. Vonnegut is totally concerned with human life, and he goes on speaking.

Tillie Olsen is an American writer with whom I feel a deep sense of empathy, tribal kinship, sisterhood. Her book *Tell Me a Riddle* consists of a novella and three short stories. She has written relatively little because of her personal circumstances. She married young, had four children, and for many years had to work at a job outside of her home. Her book *Silences* explores the circumstances that have prevented some writers, both female and male, from fulfilling their life's work. The novella *Tell Me a Riddle* seems to me to be as close to perfection as any contemporary prose I have read. In just fifty printed pages – fifty! – Olsen communicates the story of a long marriage, an entire family, ancestral roots reaching back into a long ago past in other counties, the ways in which humans suffer and hurt one another and yet support and love one another. In my view, it is a small masterpiece.

I want to conclude by mentioning a few more Canadian novels that have moved and impressed me the most.

All of Gabrielle Roy's writing I admire and love.[14] When I read *The Tin Flute* for the first time, I began to understand what a woman writer can do, in portraying women characters. I grew up reading books that had mostly been written by men. The women writers who spoke to my childhood were by no means able to tell all or most of their own truth. When I met the character of Rose-Anna, the mother, in *The Tin Flute*, I was overwhelmed. I believe her to be one of the truly great characters in our literature.

The prairie writer Rudy Wiebe has written some tremendously good fiction. Of all his books, my favourite is *The Temptations of Big Bear*, which tells the story of the North-West Rebellion of 1885, often from the viewpoint of Big Bear, the heroic leader of the Crees, who, tragically, lived to see his people defeated and dispossessed. When the Métis writer Maria Campbell, author of an autobiographical book

Halfbreed, read *The Temptations of Big Bear*, she told Wiebe that she believed the spirit of Big Bear had guided him in the writing. She may well be right.

I could hardly conclude without speaking of Robertson Davies. Of all his writing, his novel *Fifth Business* has meant the most to me. Dunstan Ramsay, who is so much more than the aging, rather fussy schoolteacher that his students and colleagues perceive him to be, is a brilliantly portrayed character. This is, of course, in the broadest sense, a religious novel. I am not qualified to speak of the Jungian framework out of which Davies writes, but to me his are the great themes of good and evil, of humankind's need for grace.

One of the finest novels to have appeared in Canada in recent years, and indeed, one of our finest ever, is Timothy Findley's *The Wars*. This novel is written out of Ontario and the First World War, but Findley is in fact talking about *all* wars, those within the individual human being, those concealed but sometimes deadly ones that can occur within a family, and, finally, those insane slaughterings that constitute wars between nations.

A very recent novel that also speaks powerfully to these issues is Hugh MacLennan's *Voices in Time*. This remarkable novel deals with the insanity of wars, the betrayal of one person by another, the miraculous power of the human spirit to survive.

What, if anything, do all these novelists – Canadian, English, American, West African, Australian – have in common? I think what they have in common is the ability to portray human individuals in all their complexity and ambiguity, in vitally alive terms, compassionately and caringly. They all have a strong sense of justice and of the possibility of human communication, even when these qualities, as so often happens, must be defined by their absence. In fact, the books, whether fiction, nonfiction, or poetry, that have mattered the most to me throughout my adult life have been those that have a sense of our past and a belief that life itself is immeasurably valuable, to be worked for, hoped for, understood, and proclaimed in whatever ways we are given to do.

(a)

Introductions to New Canadian Library Editions

Afterword to Sinclair Ross, *The Lamp at Noon and Other Stories*

Laurence composed the afterword to Sinclair Ross's The Lamp at Noon and Other Stories *for the New Canadian Library Series edition. Her typescript is housed in the Clara Thomas Archives and Special Collections, Margaret Laurence Fonds, York University, Accession 1980–001/023 (156). Ross's stories and novels, which Laurence greatly admired, influenced her own fiction, especially* The Stone Angel.

Although Sinclair Ross's stories and two novels have appeared over a period of some twenty-five years, most of his writing has been done out of the background of the prairie drought and Depression of the thirties, and, as a chronicler of that era, he stands in a class by himself. When I first read his extraordinary and moving novel *As For Me and My House*, at about the age of eighteen, it had an enormous impact on me, for it seemed the only completely genuine one I had ever read about my own people, my own place, my own time. It pulled no punches about life in the stultifying atmosphere of small and ingrown towns, and yet it was illuminated with compassion.

In Ross's short stories, the same society is portrayed, the same themes explored, with the difference that these stories all have completely rural settings. The farms stand far apart, only distantly related to whatever town is the focal point for buying and selling. The human community is, for most of the time, reduced to its smallest unit, one family. The isolation is virtually complete. It is within this extreme condition of human separateness and in the extremes of summer drought and winter blizzard that Ross's characters grapple with their lives and their fate, a fate partly imposed upon them by an uncaring and fickle natural order and partly compelled by their own spiritual inheritance, the pride, and the determination that enable them to refuse defeat, but which also cut them off from nearly all real contact with others.

Appearing almost as chief protagonist is the land itself. In spite of its deceptive moments of calm promise, it is an essentially violent and unpredictable land, quixotic, seeming to bestow grace and favour, then suddenly attacking with arrows of snow, shrieking armies of wind, bludgeons of hail, or the quiet lethal assault of the sun. Indeed, the land sometimes assumes a character as harsh as that of the vengeful God who sorely tried Job, and the farmers who stay on, year after year, seeing their crops spoiled and themselves becoming old in youth, yet still maintaining their obsessive faith in the land, are reminiscent of Job himself – *Though He slay me, yet will I trust in Him*.[1]

Characteristically, and in keeping with his themes, Ross describes the land in strong, broad strokes, and I do not believe that anyone has ever given a better impressionistic view of the Prairies. I think, for example, of his description of drought in "Not by Rain Alone": "The days were still, brassy, pitiless. Swift little whirlwinds scoured across the fields; in their wake there closed a hushed, oppressive immobility. On wheat and fallow land and ripened rye alike lay a dusty-yellow monochrome of haze." Or the hard, sharp description of winter as seen by Ann in "The Painted Door":

The sun was risen above the frost mists now, so keen and hard a glitter on the snow that instead of warmth its rays seemed shedding cold. One of the two-year-old colts that had cantered away when John turned the horses out for water stood covered with rime at the stable door again, head down and body hunched, each breath a little plume of steam against the frosty air. She shivered, but did not turn. In the clear, bitter light the long white miles of prairie landscape seemed a region alien to life. Even the distant farmsteads she could see served only to intensify a sense of isolation. Scattered across the face of so vast and bleak a wilderness it was difficult to conceive them as a testimony of human hardihood and endurance. Rather they seemed futile, lost, to cower before the implacability of snow-swept earth and clear pale sun-chilled sky.

Ross's style is always beautifully matched to his material – spare, lean, honest, with no gimmicks, and yet in its very simplicity setting up continuing echoes in the mind.

The women in these stories have their own personal dilemmas, but they also have many qualities in common. They are farmers' wives, most of them still fairly young, trying to resign themselves to lives of unrelieved drabness. They are without exception terrifyingly lonely, shut into themselves, shut out of their husbands' inner lives. Ann, in "The Painted Door," is trapped both by John's blunt devotion and by his total lack of perception of her real needs. Ellen, in "The Lamp at Noon," feels caged and cannot communicate her feelings to Paul. Their separate pain remains separate, until she, in a final madness of concern about their baby, tries to escape and walks into the windstorm in which the child, ironically and tragically, is smothered both by dust and by his mother's hysterical efforts to protect him.

These women are immensely loyal, and as driven by work-compulsion as their men, but they still long, hopelessly, for communication and tenderness with their husbands – who desperately need the same thing but can never permit or accept it lest it reflect unmanfully upon themselves. Martha, in "A Field of Wheat," thinks that "love was gone; there was only wheat." In lieu of expressed love toward their men, these prairie women take refuge in attempting to instill small, rigid, meaningless, and usually tasteless portions of "culture" into their children's lives. In "A Field of Wheat," Martha's ambitions are described. They are heartbreakingly limited. She would like to see her husband for once unclenched with worry, and to have him shave twice a week, as he used to do when they were first married, and she would like her children to be able to have music lessons. The mother in "Cornet at Night" forces her son to spend dreary hours in the stuffy plush parlour, playing hymns on the piano so that he will not grow up rough. (In this same story, interestingly enough, there is some adumbration of Ross's first novel, for on the parlour wall is a pansy-bordered motto which reads *As For Me and My House We Will Serve the Lord.*)[2]

The men who are portrayed here are painfully inarticulate. They are not able to make themselves known, not even to their women – perhaps especially not to their women. They are basically men with great uncertainties, great inner doubts. But because they believe that a man must be strong, both physically and spiritually, it is quite beyond them to acknowledge any vulnerability to any other human. They must maintain faith in the land's ability to yield, and in their own ability to coax or force it, for in this encounter their essential manhood lies in the balance. They cannot desert the land in its drought because in some way they would die as male beings if they did. Yet their helplessness in the face of drought and blizzard gives them a recurring sense of impotence against which they can only rage inwardly.

Paul, in "The Lamp at Noon," refuses to leave his land, although it is dying all around him. Consciously, the one thing he could not bear would be to become dependent upon his town store-owning in-laws. But at a deeper level, one feels that what he really could not stand would be to prove inadequate to the land. He cannot express his torment verbally. He cannot appeal to his wife for help or re-assurance, and in the end his self-imposed isolation and his shutting-out of Ellen are decisive factors in her final crack up. In "September Snow," Will meets the challenge of wind and snow, only to fail utterly in the area of human contact, for he refuses to admit into his consciousness the realization of his wife's desper-ation. Her horrifying death in childbirth seems bizarrely similar to retribution. These prairie men fail consistently in close relationships. They never perceive what is being asked of them, nor do they see what they themselves might have gained by allowing someone to get close to them. When they suffer, it is doggedly alone. John, in "A Field of Wheat," consoles his wife after the crop has been de-stroyed by hail and assumes a mask of unbreakable strength. It is only by chance that she goes later to the barn and finds him there, sobbing. She goes away with-out letting him see her, knowing this is the kindest thing she can do for him. The real issues will never be mentioned between them, for she is too afraid of being brushed away, and he is too afraid of appearing weak in her eyes.

With the character of Vickers, in "One's a Heifer," there is a sense of real evil, and yet even this sinister man's madness is pictured as a direct result of unbear-able isolation. This is where it can sometimes end, this total non-contact – in a man who, when another human being attempted to touch him even slightly by coming in and cooking his meals, responded by killing her.

The children in Ross's stories are only half aware of the deprivation of their lives, but they long for the colour and excitement that are missing. Tommy, in "Cornet at Night," listens to the unsuitable hired hand playing his cornet, a voice quite literally out of another world. "A harvest, however lean, is certain every year; but a cornet at night is golden only once." He does not know at all what the rest of the world holds, but the notes of the cornet suggest marvels to him, and he will never forget.

Fantasy is these children's solace and place of retreat. For many of the imag-inative youngsters in these stories, horses symbolize freedom, escape, far-off glamour. In "The Outlaw," the mare Isabel is infinitely more feminine and more sophisticated than the prissy girl child Millie, and to the thirteen-year-old boy, the horse represents adventure and the conquering of worlds. "She was one

horse, and she was all horses. Thundering battle chargers, fleet Arabians, un-
tamed mustangs – sitting beside her on her manger I knew and rode them all. I
charged with her at Balaklava, Waterloo, scoured the deserts of Africa and the
steppes of the Ukraine. Conquest and carnage, trumpets and glory – she understood, and carried me triumphantly."

The horse represents something quite different to the men whom the boys
grow up to be. Paul, in "The Lamp at Noon," turns to his horses, strokes their
necks, for the comfort that he cannot seek from his wife. When John, in "A Field
of Wheat," goes to the stable after his wheat has been ruined, he rests his face
against the flanks of one of his horses and sobs his anguish there.

Throughout Ross's stories, the outer situation always mirrors the inner. The
emptiness of the landscape, the bleakness of the land, reflects the inability of
these people to touch another with assurance and gentleness. In "The Painted
Door," Ann finally makes love with Steven, the young bachelor, out of her need
to be noticed once more as a woman and to be allowed to express tenderness.
When her husband discovers what has happened, and in his shock and pain
allows himself to freeze to death, his act, as well as being an appallingly unan-
swerable reproach to her, is in a sense only a final and terrible externalization,
for the process of emotionally freezing to death was begun long before. Ross
never takes sides, and this is one admirable quality of his writing. Blame is not
assigned. Men and women suffer equally. The tragedy is not that they suffer, but
that they suffer alone.

The patterns are those of isolation and loneliness, and gradually, through
these, the underlying spiritual goals of an entire society can be perceived. The
man must prove absolutely strong, in his own eyes. The woman must silently
endure all. If either cannot, then they have failed to themselves. With these
impossible and cruel standards, and in circumstances of drought and depression, it is no wonder that individuals sometimes crack under the strain.

The real wonder is that so many of these men and women continue somehow
– stumbling, perhaps, but still going on. Hope never quite vanishes. In counter-
point to desolation runs the theme of renewal. Tomorrow it may rain. The next
spring will ultimately come. Despite the sombre tone and the dark themes of
Sinclair Ross's short stories, man emerges as a creature that can survive – and
survive with some remaining dignity – against both outer and inner odds that
are almost impossible.

Introduction to Jack Ludwig,
Above Ground

Laurence's introduction to Jack Ludwig's Above Ground *was first published in the 1973 New Canadian Library edition. The typescript is housed in the Clara Thomas Archives and Special Collections, Margaret Laurence Fonds, York University, Accession 1980–001/023 (156). Ludwig's characterization may recall Laurence's in* The Stone Angel, *while his narrator's "double consciousness" may recall her* Bird in the House. *She admires Ludwig's characterization of women and portrayal of sexuality, although her own portrayal of sexuality was attacked in a Canadian literary version of the double standard.*

Joshua, the protagonist of *Above Ground*, learns very young and very thoroughly a basic fact of life – all living creatures are mortal. Death, not as something which happens only to the very old, but as something which can happen anytime to anyone, enters his consciousness truly and permanently when, at the age of five, he has his tonsils out and begins hemorrhaging. Joshua's grandmother died when the boy was three, but death did not yet to him have a name, and possibly in his first hospital experience at five, it still does not have a name, but it is there and is felt, the darkness which he senses when he knows he is bleeding uncontrollably. Jack Ludwig does not dwell on the (literally) gory details in this first scene. He does not have to. Our first glimpse of Josh is of a child in hospital, more frightened than he even realizes himself at the time.

Some years later, the boy fractures his hip. Treatment is bungled by the first doctor; the bone does not mend. Then begin the long sessions in the enclosed world of the hospital, "a city within a city." Here, Josh experiences great physical pain and the fear of death or mutilation (at one point, being taken into the operating theatre, he is convinced they are about to amputate his leg; no one has thought to tell him they are going to put it in a cast). He also experiences the others' pain and witnesses the death of Mae, one of the nearby patients, after an operation. The saving elements in the situation are the kindness and even affection of nurses, all of whom Josh falls in love with, and the visits of his family, especially his Uncle Bim, with his enormous gusto and appetite for life. Uncle Bim has "two categories, *living* and *dying*," and to his nephew he imparts some of his stubborn will to survive, to live joyously, to rise, to fly.

It is typical of the older Joshua, the narrator of this novel, to recount the grim hospital scenes with an incisive and ironic humour – not the saccharine humour of sentimentality, not in any sense a downplaying of the reality of pain and death, but the humour of survival. In fact, this survival humour is one of the marks of Jack Ludwig's writing, not only one of his greatest technical strengths, but also an unstated theme in itself. Man, it is said, is the only creature who knows he must die. Man is also the only creature (or at least as far as we know) who laughs. For Ludwig, the two facts are not unrelated. It may be as well to point out here that Ludwig's ironic humour in this novel is not "sick humour" in the contemporary meaning of those words. It is not cruel or malicious humour. It does not seek to destroy – my sense of it is that it seeks to build, to mend, even to heal.

The type of Ludwig's humour in *Above Ground* meshes perfectly with the general theme of the novel – a person who lives with the knowledge of the reality of death is a person who may be capable of living most fully. Josh's hip never does heal properly. For him, life is a gift. He takes nothing for granted. Uncle Bim sums up his double consciousness when he proposes a toast at Josh and Maggie's engagement party, a toast to all, and "to the angel of death," who "looks just like the angel of life."

Josh's awareness of the fact that he is, fairly miraculously, alive and on his feet, makes him constantly aware of the life around him, both its ugliness and its splendour, and here Ludwig communicates, through Josh, a keen and detailed sense of place and time. Whether in the descriptions of North Winnipeg streets in the thirties depression years, or the war years, or the good sand beaches of California, or the concrete deserts and repulsively artificial apartments and few human oases of New York, Ludwig can paint the picture of a specific place in incredibly few words, so that the reader can see and feel and hear the scene.

Josh does not have an answer to death – who could? But he does have a cry of defiance, and even, in one sense, a kind of magic charm against it. The ancient charm. For Josh, as for every human since our legendary father Adam and mother Eve, probably, the act of love is a defiance of death. It is a talisman, a rune, an act not only of the flesh but an act of faith as well. Josh differs from most humans only in the fact that he knows and verbalizes this aspect of our lives, our deaths. Josh falls in love frequently, but he is no cynical collector of the sexual equivalent of scalps. Which brings us to an interesting aspect of this novel. I think I am fairly alert to most kinds of putdown of women, in fiction as in life, and in *Above Ground* I get no sense of women being regarded as objects. On the contrary, each of the women with whom Josh makes love has totally recognizable individuality; one doesn't get them confused; they speak in their own voices, and what is more, they speak intelligently. When Josh says he loves them, he means it. He does love them, and keeps on loving them even when the affair is over, and, with one exception, Mavra, they don't rely on him to make or save their lives. Zora, the flamboyant girl in Winnipeg, with whom Josh makes love on the evening of his engagement to Maggie, and whom, many years later, he meets again and is saddened by the inevitable fact that she has grown older; Maggie, the constant in his life, whom he marries and who bears his daughter; Alvira, who loses vast amounts of weight in order to experience sex, even if not love, and with whom Josh makes love at least partly out of pity, although he denies this is so; Nina, the Russian woman whom he meets in California, and who remains to him some kind of ideal, a dream-person whose tough-minded reality he sees but does not want to recognize; Gyla, who, as a Jewish child in Europe during the war, was left with nuns and told by her mother to kiss the cross, for survival; and finally the incredible Mavra, disturbed to a degree, Mavra of many roles and many faces – I find all these women understandable and believable.

Perhaps one of the most interesting is Maggie, Josh's wife, about whom less is said than most of the others. Maggie knows all about each of Josh's affairs, and is angry, but never so angry that she considers leaving him, partly because she loves him but also partly because she is shrewd and intelligent and understands a lot of things about Josh – at one point, during Josh's affair with Mavra, Maggie says, "You still believe a great love could heal a hip." We are shown the transformation of Mavra from the rather kooky but pathetic babysitter who latches onto Josh and Maggie and their infant daughter, Bailla, into the desperate and compulsively promiscuous woman who begs Josh to save her, and who is so far gone in being spiritually maimed that she cannot for one instant see outside herself even to recognize Josh's pain when his father dies. But long before Josh finally comes to see Mavra's spiritual disease as one which infects and destroys others as well, Maggie has seen it. Maggie is, as far as the portrayal of her goes, totally believable, and yet I feel somehow that there are whole areas of Maggie's responses to life which aren't dealt with. I have the sense that Josh, as a narrator, is both protecting her and shying away, for his own protection, from some of the aspects of Maggie which might be too upsetting for him to face. Wasn't she ever interested in another man? I can't believe it. Ludwig tries occasionally to get inside the consciousness of Maggie (as he does, once, with Mavra, in the bar scene) but I don't think these attempts are entirely successful, partly because they aren't probed far enough and partly because in a first-person novel this method of taking on another persona seems, at least momentarily, to threaten both the narrative flow and the authenticity of the single voice. With this reservation, however, about the character of Maggie not being looked at deeply enough, I still have to say that the women in his novel are never stereotypes and never caricatures. Josh values these women both as sexual partners and as people. I really like the sex in this novel – there is always a warmth and tenderness about it. Ludwig's portrayal of women is as far from the Bunnygirls of *Playboy* as a field of ripe wheat is from a plastic daffodil.

But if love is Josh's talisman against death, Death is still a constant presence. Life, for Josh, does not mean merely drawing breath. There are two people who live on but do not survive, Evvie and Tamara, both of whom become insane and live out their lives in institutions, the one terrorized by sinister voices despite a lobotomy, the other an inert vegetable. A great many of the characters in *Above Ground* are touched by the angel of death, either death-in-life or actual death. These portraits are done with such a sense of caring, such ironic humour, and in such brief and telling brushstroke that it becomes plain that this kind of character portrayal is Ludwig's finest talent. Wilkoh Joe, who hangs himself because he cannot understand English and imagines the doctor is telling him he has T B; Bibul the fruit peddler, with his old horse and wagon; the chemistry professor, Grover, in the horrific hypnotism scene, who "woke us all," but not quite in the way Grover imagines himself to have done; Uncle Baer and Aunt Teena, in California, who in their hatred of one another carry on the pretense of a perfect marriage, except when the masks slip; Hettie Karousel, who "bought apartment blocks the way some bought coins," and who is run over accidentally by Levitt, her abject husband; Fran, damaged irreparably by her puritanical family; Carson, who can't accept that he's survived the war and who only gains peace when he becomes crippled by polio; and perhaps more than anyone, Mavra, whose urge to destroy spiritually herself and others is so strong that nothing can abate it. All these people suffer, are maimed, and yet the general feeling of the novel is not despair. Once, making love with Nina in the sea, Josh cries, "What a way to go it would be." Nina says, "In the midst of this much life, why death?" Josh can only reply, "A passing thought." For him the thought passes across his consciousness often, maybe always. And because it does, life is not diminished – in fact, the exact reverse.

The final portion of the novel, which includes the death of Josh's father and subsequently the death of his mother, is counterpointed with letters from Mavra, which are idiotic and repellant, and yet because of their very vulgarity and ignorance the most moving part of the book, and one which draws together all the threads. Josh's father dies, quite unexpectedly, of a heart attack, when it was Josh's mother who had had a stroke and was in hospital. Josh realizes at that moment something which he has been on the brink of knowing for a long time. "Irreversible death. Knowledge that flays. I could not be to my father as if he were Lazarus."

No one can save anyone else. We can only try to make them aware of our caring. And yet, when Josh's mother dies, Josh is not there. He has gone back to New York to see Mavra, and doesn't return to his childhood home in time. Josh's Aunt Beatty tells him that his mother has said, "Tell him how hard I waited." Beatty says that "she had a crazy thought in her head – she believed you could keep her alive." Josh says, "Beatty, I couldn't."

Not will, nor love, nor faith, nor any mortal thing can stop Time. Death will not fail to happen. This may seem obvious, but it is not. Some people never know it until death surprises them. Maybe they are the lucky ones, and maybe not. But for Josh, the goal is to stay above ground for as long as possible, hopefully with whatever love it may be his to give and to receive. On the night of his mother's death, Josh thinks of Uncle Bim, who died some years before – "old eaglefaced man, waving his arms to discount the finite." With the constant knowledge of death, perhaps the only way to live is as though we were going to live forever.

Something about legends interests me in *Above Ground*. Ludwig, from time to time, brings in reference to classical myths – Orpheus, Aeneas and Queen Dido, Theseus and Ariadne. I have the feeling that these references may be somewhat extraneous. The true ancestral references are made in the novel, it seems to me, without any comment and without naming sources, and these work very well – these ancestral references, of course, are Old Testament ones, and this is not only because Ludwig is writing out of a Jewish background, but also because for most of us in Canada, I suspect, the Old Testament legends have more relevance than the classical ones. At one point, Josh says, "Miracles I carry in my bones. Not when voice spoke out of whirlwind; or seas parted; or man was swallowed then spewed by a whale." But the voice that spoke to Job, saying, *Where wast thou when I laid the foundations of the earth?* is a voice that one feels this contemporary Joshua would recognize, if not in a purely religious sense, then at least in his realization of the fleeting quality of human life. When the Red Sea parted, and Moses led his people into the wilderness, on the way to the Promised Land – Josh, like nearly everyone in this land, could recognize that parable, ironic though some of its aspects are. As for Jonah, who was swallowed by the whale – Josh, to use the words of Carl Sandburg, "was swallowed one time deep in the dark/ And came out alive after all" ("Losers").[1] Josh, when explaining to Mavra why he has not kept in daily touch with her whilst in the prairie city at the time of his father's death, says, "There was a time to think about you and a time that swept you and everything else out of mind." The echo there is from Ecclesiastes, *To everything there is a season, and a time to every purpose under the heaven. A time to be born, and a time to die.* Josh's words catch that echo and use it like his natural inherited speech. The biblical Joshua, remember, was he who crossed Jordan and entered the new and ancient land. Josh, in *Above Ground*, speaks in his own idiom, for his own time, and miracles he does carry, literally, in his bones. But he also speaks out of his ancestry, and that ancestry is the Old Testament.

Ludwig is doing something else with legends. Some of the characters he portrays – Josh's father and mother, Uncle Bim, Dobrushyn, Uncle Baer, Joseph Czernowski, and many others – these people are part of our own legends, our history, our ancestors, and Ludwig, like a number of Canadian writers at this point, is giving them a form and a voice.

The main theme of *Above Ground*, however, remains that of how to live in the face of an ever-present awareness of death. It might have been an exceedingly sombre novel, but sombre it most certainly is not, and the reason that it is not is only partly due to the swiftness of the currents of humour within it. The other aspect is summed up in the novel's last line – "I fly eastward, where sun rises tomorrow, as I hope to see."

Introduction to Percy Janes,
House of Hate

Laurence's introduction to House of Hate *by Percy Janes was first published in Toronto by McClelland and Stewart in 1976, in the New Canadian Library series, no. 124.*

House of Hate is an apt title for this novel, for it is placed within the confines of the Stone family, and by remaining within these claustrophobic limits the book gains its true strength. In the harsh and bitter character of Saul Stone, and in the varied characters of Saul's wife and children, Percy Janes gives us a complex and totally convincing picture of a family perpetually at war with itself.

We get almost no sense of the outer community, although the Newfoundland background, setting, and history are all integral to the novel's effectiveness. True, the paper mill, which is as dark and satanic as any of Blake's,[1] looms constantly in the background, meaning both livelihood and slavery to many of the towns-people, and we are aware of the town itself as a presence, with its stratified class system, its religious animosities, its petty-mindedness. But the townsfolk are mainly introduced in general group terms (one or another of the Stone sons is often said to be going out with a bunch of the "b'ys"),[2] with the exception of those individuals who marry into the Stone family and become part of its domestic war. Most of the events of the novel take place within the ugly and sprawling house, just as the Stone family itself is held spiritually and mentally there, in unwilling bondage to one another.

Juju, the narrator, is the only Stone to leave Milltown for any length of time, except for Racer, who is forced to be away for six years during World War II. Juju is also the only one to obtain a university education. But we are told little about his wanderings in the years between part one and part two, when he returns home for a year at the age of forty. We *are* told that he "came to realize that in these exotic places I had been seeking to prove to myself my passionate childhood conviction that all the world was not like Milltown." And yet the frightening thought occurs that perhaps "this whole world was essentially a Milltown in which I should find no home nor any place of refuge this side of the grave." In his travels, Juju may have carried only one suitcase, but he has plainly carried his entire family with him in his mind. Juju does not hold back on details of his own life – it is simply that anything not directly relevant to the theme of the warring family is not included. In fact, Juju does explain precisely those details of his adult life which relate to his having been "chilled in childhood," namely his inability to form a lasting personal relationship with a woman, and his dread of fathering children.

The angry and warped relationships of several generations of the Stone family is Janes's theme, and he never loses sight of it, never for an instant allows himself to digress. Initially, it may seem to the reader that this singlemindedness narrows the novel's scope, but I don't think this is so. The Stone family *is* narrow, its members living largely unto themselves, unable (except for Juju) to leave one another but also unable to leave one another alone, in the colloquial sense – forever quarrelling, criticizing, planning elaborate revenges for some slight, real or imagined. The shape of the novel thus has the effect of powerfully conveying the stultifying and tortured atmosphere throughout the years within the Stone house.

The focus and originator of the tensions within the family is, of course, Saul Stone himself, one of the most terrifying and yet tragic father figures in all Canadian literature, and we have had some very strong ones, as any quick glance through the Canadian fiction of this century will show. Saul, with his famine Irish Protestant background, knows only work. He is a compulsive worker and cannot permit himself even those few hours of leisure which his job at the mill might allow. His own obsession with work is something he forces on his wife and children as well. He is, furthermore, illiterate, and believes his family looks down on him because of it, although it is many, many years before Juju gains this crucial insight into his father's character. It is typical of Saul that he should throw his vast energies and frustrations into attempting to build a concrete wall around his house. Not only is he locked tightly into himself, but he also would like to shut the world out entirely. This is a man so enraged and embittered by his early life that he can express only one emotion – anger. Whether it is in bickering with Gertrude, his wife, or in beating the others in the interminable family card games, or in physically beating his sons, Saul Stone trusts only aggression. This is not to say that the only emotion he ever feels is anger. Far from it. His early courtship of Gertrude has had some tenderness, insofar as Saul's clenched nature would allow. And when his son Racer takes off for World War II, the Old Man (as he is known to them all) would clearly like to make amends for the brutal beating he gave the boy not very long before. But he cannot make any gesture which would involve the lowering of his terrible pride or the giving of anything of himself. Instead, he hands the boy a twenty-dollar bill. He is not a verbal man; he is not capable of self-analysis. But in his inchoate way he seems almost to be thinking at this moment that money has value, whereas he, Saul, does not. He is a religious man, forcing the entire family out to church twice every Sunday (with Sunday School as well for the children). But his religion seems more related to those Old Testament prophets who believed in a God of Wrath than it does to any gentler aspects of Christianity. Indeed, within his own house, Saul takes on the aspects of a god of wrath himself. He presents it, of course, as righteous wrath. In fact, it has grown out of despair, and there are moments when Saul seems like a soul in his own inner hell.

His wife, Gertrude, represents the one factor in the Stone children's lives which has any warmth at all. She has a rough humour, a survival humour, which helps all of them to get through the worst of the Old Man's tantrums. She also has great strength of character, a strength which will not allow her to submit without battle to Saul's evil temper. But the price she pays in her life is a higher one than any of her children realize for many years. After Racer has received his murderous beating from Saul, he asks his mother if she has ever loved the Old Man. For the first time, Gertrude breaks down and cries in front of her children. She is once again Gertrude Yeovil, the girl who so hopefully married Saul so many years before. In this, one of the most moving scenes in the novel, the family suddenly sees what their mother's life has been, and the knowledge is almost too much for them to bear. Gertrude is not, however, presented as the ever-loving mother, in contrast with the never-loving father. She, too, is capable of being un-just and harsh with her children, and she taunts her one daughter unmercifully throughout Hilda's adolescence. Saul leaves his indelible mark on his wife's char-acter – in standing up to him, she becomes more like him.

Despite their rocky spiritual background, however, there seems promise in all the Stone children during their childhood – the stalwart Ank, the dashing Racer, the theatrically inclined Crawfie, the studious Juju, the determined Hilda (or Flinksy, as she is nicknamed). Even Fudge, the son born years after all the others, seems in childhood to have some imagination. But none of them escape the damage done through being "chilled in childhood." When we meet them again, years later, they all in their various ways bear the scars of those early wounds, and the scars have deepened and darkened. Even Hilda, whose life has been happier and more rewarding than those of her brothers, still shows the effects of her miserable childhood.

The tone of *House of Hate* is not completely grim. Some humour is achieved through the frequently ironic tone of the narrator, and there are moments when even Saul cannot dampen the naturally high spirits of his youngsters. Yet all too often what passes for humour in the Stone family is in fact thinly veiled verbal violence in the form of mockery or embarrassment. Growing up in such an atmosphere does not encourage kindness even toward the other members of the family who have also suffered at Saul's hands. In the book's final chapters, Juju hears Ank's children refer to Ank as the Old Man, and in the same old scornful and yet fear-ridden way, Ank, through despising his father, has become him.

House of Hate is, its author has declared, semiautobiographical. Because this type of fiction is so frequently misunderstood and read mistakenly as a literal transcription of actual events, I think it should be made quite clear that this is not a separate area of fiction. As Janes himself has said (the quote appears on the dust jacket of the original edition), "I have added, subtracted, altered, arranged, and invented." A novel based on a writer's experience is no less a work of true fiction than a novel which has nothing to do with the writer's own life. The art of fiction lies in the ability to bring to life on the printed page a whole range of characters and events, and to explore meaningful and universal themes. In this sense it has nothing to do with simply recording the events of anyone's life. And, of course, if six members of a family set out and were equipped to forge a work of art out of their childhood's materials, we would get six quite different novels.

The form of this novel resembles a very closely interwoven and interdependent series of short stories. In both of its two sections, each character is given a chapter in which he or she figures largely, although the narrative voice is always that of Juju. But while we are learning some of the essentials of Racer's life, for example, we are also learning about all the other members of the family as well, in their relationships with Racer, and especially we gradually receive a full picture of Saul and Gertrude.

Janes uses the Newfoundland dialect carefully and to good effect. Dialect is difficult to set down, for several reasons. First, the writer must not have the characters speaking in ways which will be unintelligible to a reader who is unfamiliar with the particular dialect. Second, an excessive use of dialect can make caricatures of the people in the book. Janes has avoided these pitfalls.

The language of the narration itself is measured and sombre, in some places ironic, in some places even slightly dated (as in the use of the word "concubine" to describe the woman Crawfie lives with after his wife's mental breakdown), but always suited to the material of the book. I find the family nicknames interesting – Ank, Racer, Juju, Flinksy, Crawfie, Fudge. It is as though some small degree of colour were added to their lives by the conjuring up of names like these.

In the end, one comes to see in depth the dilemmas and the pain of every member of this family, and to see in Saul a man tormenting not only others but himself as well, a man shut into himself totally, a man desperately needing affection but incapable of ever reaching out for it. The novel, finally, has an archetypal quality about it. It deals with some of mankind's greatest fears and greatest anguish. Its pessimism is unflinching, not self-pitying. There is a quality of stone about it (one supposes the family name was not chosen for nothing), a quality both jagged and enduring. On the dust jacket of the original edition, the publishers predicted that *House of Hate* "in time will be regarded as a classic of its kind." That was a bold claim, but in this case, I believe, a justified one.

Introduction to Adele Wiseman, *Crackpot*

Laurence's introduction to Crackpot *by Adele Wiseman was first published in the McClelland and Stewart 1978 edition, and republished as an afterword to* Crackpot *in McClelland and Stewart's New Canadian Library Edition.*

Hoda, the protagonist of *Crackpot* – earthy, bawdy, wisecracking Hoda – is a prostitute. But Adele Wiseman's novel is no more a story simply about a whore than her first novel, *The Sacrifice*, in which the patriarchal Abraham finds himself killing a woman in an agonized parody of a sacrificial act, is a story about a murderer. *Crackpot*, like the earlier novel, takes us deeply into a whole complex world of personal and social relationships in which the tragic misunderstandings and distances between people are both pointed up and to a degree alleviated in a way that art can sometimes accomplish, by allowing us truly to see and feel the pain and the interconnectedness of humankind, with our burden and necessity of ancestors and gods.

In a sense the novel's title expresses in one word the novel's themes, for, like all totally fitting and appropriate titles, it contains meanings and allusions which reverberate through the book. Crackpot is, at one level, Hoda herself, the idiomatic word referring to the neighbourhood's opinion of her, a view both humorous and cruel. By extension, it is also Hoda's father, Danile, whose wise innocence can be mistaken by the clumsy-hearted for simplemindedness. At another level, the title speaks of some of the underlying concepts and the life-view of the novel itself. The epigraph is this:

He stored the Divine Light in a Vessel, but the Vessel, unable to contain the Holy Radiance, burst, and its shards, permeated with sparks of the Divine, scattered through the Universe.

Ari: Kabbalistic legend of creation.

In an article in *Waves* (vol. 3, no. 1), Kenneth Sherman pointed out that Ari was "Ashkenazi Reb Isaac, also known as Isaac Luria (1534–1572), a Jewish mystic born in Jerusalem who developed an extremely significant strain of Kabbalistic theosophy." Sherman went on to say, "In Luria's Kabbalistic work is his creation myth which is divided into three major experiences: *Tsimtsum* – the self-limitation or exile of God; *Shevirah* – the breaking of the vessels; *Tikkun* – harmonious correction and mending of the flaw." Without overemphasizing the ways in which the novel reflects in structure and content this creation myth, it is fascinating to see how *Crackpot* draws upon and is nourished by ancestral creation myths and finally becomes in a contemporary sense its own legend of creation, growth, and reconciliation – the long journey through pain, a journey relieved by joy and accompanied by a survival humour, into a final sense of wholeness and completion. The novel seems to me to be a profoundly religious work, in the very broadest sense, ultimately a celebration of life and of the mystery which is at the heart of life.

Hoda learns the story of her beginnings when she is a child, just before the First World War, in the North Winnipeg hovel where she lives with her parents. Her gentle, unworldly father, Danile, gives her a birthright of pride and love which, told differently, could have been a horror story. In the Old Country, Russia, he and Hoda's mother, Rahel, were more or less forcibly married – in a graveyard, to ward off a plague. The villagers, following ancient superstition, sought among the Jewish community to find the most witless or crippled male and female whose union would magically appease the fates. Hoda's parents were not witless, but Rahel was hunch-backed and Danile was blind. In Danile's skilled and tender telling, the story becomes to the child Hoda a legend, a marvel, with her parents in heroic roles. It is only as the legend weaves its way through Hoda's life that she realizes the true pain and courage of her parents. By this time she has known her own anguish, and is able to understand what an incredible gift her father has given her: out of demeanment, pride; out of the depths, hope. He had, both consciously and intuitively, handed on to her a heritage of strength and belonging.[1]

The portrayal of Danile is done with such sureness of touch, such understanding, that this blind and frail man emerges as enormously wise and strong. In some ways he is a fool of God (and despite Saint Paul's well-known use of this term, it is far from being an exclusively Christian concept: it extends to many faiths and cultures), a person who is not understood in the slightest by most of the society in which he lives, for he is hearing the pulsing of a different drum, a man whose wisdom and spiritual power come from love, from contemplation, from faith, and yet whose naïveté is also real and can be unwittingly damaging. One of Danile's literary antecedents seems to me to be Myshkin, in Dostoevsky's *The Idiot*; one of his contemporaries is Okolo, in *The Voice*, by the Nigerian novelist Gabriel Okara.[2]

Rahel, Hoda's mother, doing domestic work in the houses of middle-class Jewish families, is also portrayed with great depth and complexity. Worrying constantly about her adored child, wanting to do not only well for Hoda but superbly well, Rahel constantly feeds Hoda scraps of food, partly, of course, to keep her quiet while Rahel is cleaning houses, and partly to express the love which, unlike Danile, she cannot express verbally. Rahel's death is one of the most moving parts of the novel. She knows she is leaving her child unprepared for life; she knows it in a way in which Danile does not. Her grief is not only grief for her own early death, but the unbearable anguish of having to leave too soon.

By the time Hoda gets to school, she is already grossly overweight. The other children make fun of her for her size, her poverty, her strange parents. The teachers are no better, not so much out of malice as out of sheer ignorance or – in the case of Miss Boltholmsup, a pathetic and unwittingly cruel WASP – because they are embarrassed and terrified by their often unruly charges.

Hoda is bewildered by the treatment she gets at school. She longs for affection and, romantically, for love, the real thing. What she finds is fumbling sex with the neighbourhood boys. Her sense of shame at her own appearance, her loud-mouthed bravado as a young teenager, her tenderness toward the boys, such as big dumb Morgan, who initiates her into sex – these are shown with an intricate ambiguity. Hoda is trusting and naive; Hoda is also learning that not everyone is to be trusted, and yet, because of Danile's early teaching, she does not easily give up that faith in human creatures. In fact, she never gives it up, even though she ultimately comes to see the fact of evil in the world. Life and society hurt her a great deal. She reacts with puzzlement, anger, pain, humour, and ultimately, with determination to survive and to retain a faith in life itself.

After her mother's death, Hoda leaves school to look after her father. She takes on her role as prostitute almost without realizing it. When the boys come over, a whole group of them, she takes them into her makeshift bedroom one after another. Danile in his blindness believes (or needs to believe) that his clever daughter is helping them with schoolwork. Hoda believes (and needs to believe) that it is only the taking of money that saves her actions from blame – after all, she and her father need the few coins so badly, and, also, sex for pleasure *alone* is something she thinks is not permissible outside marriage. Her ideas of conception are unusual. Brought up in isolation, with no real friends, and by a mother who died too soon and who always told her severely never to discuss such things with anyone, Hoda has had to figure it all out by herself. When a woman is married, the man is finally able to shoot in enough match-ing parts to make a complete baby. As long as she goes with different men, she will not conceive. Here we have almost a parody, and a very touching one, of the crackpot/creation theme – the parts ultimately and hopefully come to-gether to make the whole.

When Hoda becomes pregnant, her notions about biology, and her own amply larded body, conceal her condition from herself. The birth is dark with terror for her.[3] When she realizes what is happening, her main thought is to con-ceal the situation from her father. The scenes in which Hoda, unobserved, leaves the newborn child at the Jewish Orphanage, along with a garbled note which gives rise to wild speculations in the community concerning the child's royal ori-gins (British, at that, for the Prince of Wales has visited Winnipeg an appropriate length of time before) are skilfully handled. The first could have slipped into melodrama and the second into slapstick. Adele Wiseman treads a very fine line here, as she does so often in this novel, and she does not take a false step. The tone is exactly right. We *feel* Hoda's panic, her urgency to get the child out of the house before Danile finds out, and later, her terrible sense of loss, and her at-tempts to submerge the memory. The community's response to what they mistakenly take to be the note's central message, namely that a lovely Jewish girl has slept with the Prince and produced this foundling, is both maddening and hilariously funny – the cynicism, the disapproval, the hope for "an enormous breakthrough in civil rights," the endless gossip and guesswork. This interweav-ing of the humorous and the bizarre with the frightening and the tragic is one of Adele Wiseman's greatest talents, for, of course, life presents all of us with similar simultaneous juxtapositions; but to catch and hold these tones, together, in writing, is something that only an accomplished artist can do.

The clue to the uproar at the orphanage, and a re-statement of some of the novel's themes, are found in the note: "In her note, Hoda had pieced together, out of the confused shards of her dream and desire and the longings of her shattered childhood, the following: TAKE GOOD CARE. A PRINCE IN DISGUISE CAN MAKE A PIECE OF PRINCE, TO SAVE THE JEWS. HE'S PAID FOR."

The themes of crackpot/creation can be seen here again – the vessel which, broken, still contains the sparks of the Divine and the potentiality of wholeness. In this disjointed note we can see many fragments: Hoda's shattering experiences of life; her dreams of love, and the prince in disguise; the "pieces" which would come together to make a child, a new life; perhaps the tales of a Prince of Peace, from her Christian teachers, combined with the sense of her own ancestry, gained from Danile, and hope in the coming of the Messiah, some final reconciliation of life's discordant aspects. Ironically, all Hoda herself means by "HE'S PAID FOR" is a reference to Danile's rich uncle, Nate, who has endowed the Jewish Orphanage, but whose help to Danile and Hoda has been grudging and minimal, despite his emotional demands on them. Hoda feels that her child's keep in the orphanage has been, so to speak, prepaid. The community, of course, does not see this simple fact, as they never connect the child with her. The reader, too, can see other possibilities of meaning. He has indeed been paid for, by Hoda, through her years of labour and her solitary birth-labour.

The boy is named, appropriately enough, David Ben Zion. His nickname is Pipick because his navel protrudes, as Hoda herself tied the cord around, imperfectly. Hoda tries to refrain from wondering and thinking about the boy, and sometimes she succeeds. Sometimes, however, she experiences feelings alien to her, the desire to scream aloud and to run and keep on running, the breaking up and the cracking of the basic human earthen pot, the skull, the brain, the psyche. But she never breaks up totally, not ever.

At this point it should be said that this novel, among very many other things, is at one level a political novel, in the broadest sense. It portrays a whole community, North Winnipeg, with its influx of immigrants at various points in its history, spanning the years from World War I to the end of World War II.[4] We are shown, through Hoda's eyes, the Winnipeg General Strike of 1919, the political groups and union organizers, the factories and sweatshops of that era, the poverty and despair of the depression of the 30s. None of these historical events, however, is presented in any didactic way. They are seen through individual experiences. We feel it all as though it were happening right now, and to us.

The narrative is in the third person, but the voice is usually that of Hoda, and her idiom and changing modes of thought are caught exactly. The use of language throughout the book is extraordinarily interesting. Hoda's concepts when speaking with her father (in Yiddish, as we are meant to realize) and when speaking with her contemporaries (in English) are very different. We may speak what we are thinking, but the particular tongue in which we are speaking also determines and forms our thoughts. The lovely ambiguities, too, of the English language occur again and again. Danile, after the death of Rahel, is "wrapped in his darkness, rapping on his darkness, rapt and listening in his darkness for an explanation."

This is a sombre novel in very many ways, and yet it is full of a surging and irrepressible humour. Hoda's humour is to her a protection, an armour, but it is really felt and genuine, even though it sometimes has its darkly ironic side. There are marvellously funny scenes, such as those in which Hoda turns up, brash and uninvited, at weddings, dancing with gusto despite her girth and nabbing a customer or two in the process.

Seldom does one find in a novel a character who is so alive and who is portrayed with such change and development as Hoda. As her understanding expands, she sees in retrospect what her early life was really like. She doesn't pity herself in the present, but she is able to feel pity for that child she once was, the child without a childhood. And over the years, the thoughts of her son haunt her. Under Hoda's jokey surface there is an area of darkness, the accumulation of years of bewildered pain and uncomprehended rejection.

Her final encounter with her son, who comes to her as a young man to a neighbourhood whore, is one of the most shattering scenes in contemporary fiction. If Hoda refuses the boy, he will either feel that he is unacceptable as a man, or he will have to be told who he is. Her choices are real, but they are narrow. What can she do to hurt him the least? This is Hoda's greatest act of love and greatest moment of suffering. Until now, she has had something of Danile's terrifying innocence, but not any more. She assumes here the dimensions of a truly tragic character, drawing into herself all the ancestral myths, all the strength and anguish of the centuries. She is even "denied that loss of responsibility in suffering, which is the gift of madness." Yet to the outside world, as she realizes, she will always be crackpot Hoda.[5]

She still, however, has her life to complete. Lazar presents himself, the Lazarus who has risen, literally, from the grave itself, who has climbed over the dead of his family and his village in war-torn Europe, and has survived.[6] His hurt and his need finally match with Hoda's, and the world may begin again.

In a wish-fulfilling or prophetic dream at the end of the novel, Hoda sees her-self and her son and her people rising again, out of the holocaust which encompasses and is yet more than the Jewish holocaust – man's inhumanity to man finally overcome. The nightmare element, however, and the bitterness are present here, too. Hoda, about to marry Lazar, cries out in sleep "CONDOMS PRURIENCE INCESTRY," an agonized comment on her own life as well as an ironically twisted version of Winnipeg's motto – *Commerce Prudence Industry*.[7]

But at last, in the dream, there is wholeness: "Hoda curtseyed deep, arose. With a magnanimous gesture she drew the magic circle around them, showing them all she knew. Soon, she promised extravagantly, in the ardour of her vision, they would all be stirring the muddy waters in the brimming pot together."

The shards, to continue to speak in the novel's metaphor, are many in this culmination, and they finally come together and fuse in a complete vision. The allusions occur on many levels. The Indian name *Winnipeg* means "muddy waters." In Hoda's experience, the community in which she grew up, with its mixture of immigrant peoples of different backgrounds and different degrees of wealth and poverty, was indeed a milieu of muddy waters. But she dares to hope, to look forward to the time when "they would all be stirring the muddy waters in the brimming pot together." In a wider sense, Hoda's dream embraces a whole area of world myth, in which the "magic circle" may be seen as the unending cycle of life and death, and the "brimming pot" as the fullness of creation in all its forms. Hoda herself finally becomes an archetypal figure, the earth mother, the Wise Woman of the tribes.[8] Her son David, forever lost to her and yet never lost, says of her in the dream, "She occupies her past; she inhabits her life."

She does indeed. And as one of the greatest characters in our literature, she helps us more fully to occupy our own past and to inhabit our lives.

(b)
Unpublished Speeches and Tributes

W.L. Morton – A Tribute

"W.L. Morton – A Tribute" is an unpublished address by Margaret Laurence housed in the York University Archives and Special Collections, Margaret Laurence Fonds, No. 1986–006/001 (47) and delivered at Trent University, where Laurence succeeded Morton as chancellor in 1981. Morton (1908–1980), first master of Champlain College at Trent University from 1961 and chancellor of Trent from 1977 until his death in 1980, influenced Laurence's last Manawaka novel, The Diviners *(1974), through his 1957 history of Manitoba.*

As the new chancellor of Trent University and also as a friend, I would like to pay tribute to my predecessor, Dr W.L. Morton, whose recent death has saddened so many of us.

It was through the Mortons that my association with Trent began, eleven years ago. Bill was then master of Champlain College. That fine and strong lady, Peg Morton, whom I later grew to value so much as a friend, invited me to address the University Women's Club in Peterborough. I stayed with the Mortons and discovered that Trent was a small and excellent liberal arts university of the type I most admired. This was indeed a factor in my ultimately settling in this area. I will always remember the warm welcome that Bill and Peg Morton gave me on that first visit. I was naturally somewhat in awe of Dr Morton, one of our most distinguished historians. I soon discovered, however, that he was a true gentleman, a gentle man, proud in the best possible way and yet possessing a quality of humility that is the mark of the genuinely great.

As fellow Manitobans, we had grown up in towns only a few miles apart. This prairie background gave us much in common, but there was something else as well. Throughout the years, I was privileged to discuss with Bill Morton the relationship between history and fiction. We agreed that the two disciplines were closely related. The fiction writer seeks to create a world that has been experienced both as an external "real" world and as an internal one. The historian selects the facts and landscapes of the real world and brings to them his own perceptions and interpretations. Both try to arrive at some kind of truth which can never be complete but which will possess its own integrity.

For the Autumn 1978 issue of *The Journal of Canadian Studies*, Dr Clara Thomas wrote an article dealing with myth and Manitoba in my novel *The Diviners*.[1] In it she discusses my considerable debt to W.L. Morton. She quotes Morton writing about the writing of history: "The difficulty was to reconcile a landscape actually seen and realistically experienced with an internal landscape formed by reading. How could these be brought into a single authentic vision in which neither would deny, but rather clarify the other?"

That statement could serve as my basic perception of my own work, too. The article goes on to quote my own feelings of a common aim: "I did in fact read *Manitoba: A History* the summer that I began writing *The Diviners*. Morton's history gave me not only a great many facts that I needed ... but also a sense of the sweep of history, the overview which I think I share. What I share, most of all, with Morton is the sense of my *place*, the Prairies, and of my *people* (meaning all prairie peoples), within the context of their many and varied histories and the desire to make all these things come alive in the reader's mind.

I owe a deep debt of gratitude to W.L. Morton. I am honoured to follow him as chancellor of Trent University. He was a great human being, a great historian, a great and beloved Canadian.

Tribute to Malcolm Ross

Laurence's unpublished "Tribute to Malcolm Ross," in the Clara Thomas Archives, York University, No. 1980–006/023 (156), presented on his retirement as Thomas McCullogh Professor of English at Dalhousie University in 1982, celebrates this renowned teacher, critic, and founder of the New Canadian Library.

In 1946, as a fourth-year university student in Winnipeg, I took a course in seventeenth-century thought from Dr Malcolm Ross.[1] It was a small class in Honours English, scarcely more than a dozen of us, if memory serves, and we met informally, sitting around a large table, heatedly discussing such things as the poetry of John Donne and the influence on his work of the cosmology of Copernicus and Galileo. We talked about these matters as though they had happened only the day before yesterday. Our sense of the *immediacy* of great literature we owed in no small measure to Malcolm Ross. He encouraged – indeed, insisted upon – our thinking for ourselves. He made accessible to us many aspects of the literature we were examining, but he also helped us to trust our own responses to it. Now, so many years later, I still recall with great clarity the excitement and enthusiasm of those classes.

I would have been astounded then to know that thirty-five years later I, like so many of Malcolm Ross's students, would have kept up an association with him, and that he would become, over the years, my friend and colleague. Those of us who became writers, such as myself and Adele Wiseman, would have much cause to be grateful to him for his unfailing encouragement.

The first story of mine to be published in a professional journal came out in *Queen's Quarterly*, in 1956, when Malcolm Ross was editor. I had submitted a story to this publication about a year before, and Ross had sent it back, saying that he believed I would one day write a story that he could proudly publish in

Queen's Quarterly, but this one wasn't it. Try harder, he said. I did, and ultimately he accepted my first West African story, "The Drummer of All the World."[2]

I recall meeting Malcolm Ross in Toronto in 1961, when my first novel, *This Side Jordan*, had won the Beta Sigma Phi First Novel Award.[3] I was living in Vancouver at that time, but because the award carried with it some *money* – ye gods! – I decided to go to Toronto to pick up the loot. I had lunch with *Dr* Ross, as he still was to me then. He looked at me with that quirky humour, that ironic lift of the eyebrows, and told me in his brusque voice that perhaps I should learn to call him by his first name, as I was grown up now! I remember telling him then how surprised I was to realize that he wasn't nearly as old as I had thought he was when I was at university. Of course, when one is a student one's professors do tend to seem nearly as old as God. He confessed to me that when he first went to teach at the University of Manitoba he had grown a moustache to make himself look older!

I do not need to say much about Malcolm's role in the New Canadian Library series, because it must be known to everyone who cares about the teaching of our literature. Malcolm Ross and Jack McClelland brought the NCL into being. Its purpose was to put back into print the best novels of our past and to print in paperback some contemporary novels. Without the NCL series, the teaching of Canadian novels in our high schools and universities would never have become possible. Now there are a number of publishers who print Canadian novels in paperback and try to keep them in print, for the academic market, but the NCL was the first and remains the most extensive of its kind.

As a teacher, as an editor, as a literary critic, as a person who has always encouraged young writers and academics, Malcolm Ross has earned our very deepest gratitude. On the occasion of his retirement, I want to extend my own personal thanks to him for all his help to me.

Clara Thomas ... Biographer, Teacher, Critic ... and Pioneer

In "Clara Thomas ... Biographer, Teacher, Critic ... and Pioneer," an unpublished address from the Clara Thomas Archives, York University, No. 1986–006/ 001 (15), Laurence celebrates Thomas on her retirement as professor of English at York University in June 1984.

In 1968, when I was living in England, I received a letter from a professor at York University in Toronto. She was writing a short book on my work for the New Canadian Library series, Canadian Writers, and she wanted to check on a few biographical details. I was astounded, although naturally pleased, that anyone would be writing a book on my work. Thus, my correspondence with Clara Thomas began with a business letter, but it soon became apparent that we had a great deal in common and that, indeed, we spoke the same language, with all that the phrase implies. We were both professional women, who had also married and brought up two children, with all the difficulties and joys that managing two virtually full-time jobs entailed. We were both passionately interested in and concerned with Canadian literature, I as a novelist and Clara as a biographer, teacher, and literary critic. We had both come from small Canadian towns, mine in Manitoba and hers in Ontario, and we shared a great deal of the Scots/Irish heritage of those towns. We both had a strong sense of ancestry and of family. From that first exchange of letters there developed a deep and lasting friendship that became and is one of the most valued I have ever known.

Subsequently, Clara Thomas went on to expand her commentary on my work in her book *The Manawaka World of Margaret Laurence*, and she has written many critical articles on my books, articles published in journals in Canada, America, France, and elsewhere. She has never hesitated, in regard to my work or any other of the many Canadian writers whose works she has examined, to point out the limitations and flaws, but neither has she ever written negatively for its own sake or been "clever" at a writer's expense. Her belief is that a critic and teacher should write about those books that capture her/his own imagination and speak to the mind and heart. Such teaching and critical analysis can open a book to students and general readers, can point out themes, use of language, symbolic structures, and what is being spoken underneath the words. I myself believe that a teacher and critic is basically a highly skilled reader who passes on some of those skills with care and enthusiasm. Clara Thomas's analyses of my own writing and the writing of many other Canadian writers seems to me to be among the most perceptive, searching, and communicative of all the commentaries done on our literature. Her book *Our Nature, Our Voices* has been an extremely valuable guide to the teaching of Canadian literature. She has presented critical papers at numerous conferences, both in Canada and abroad, and has done a very great deal to get Canadian writing known within our boundaries and beyond them.

As a biographer, Clara Thomas's work has added honourably to our knowledge of our own literary heritage and some of the people who helped to form it. The biographies of Egerton Ryerson and of Anna Jameson, and now, the biography of William Arthur Deacon, which she wrote with her colleague John Lennox,[1] have contributed to the art and indeed the acceptance of biography in this country. I have often thought that biography, like the writing of history, is closely allied to the art of fiction. At first glance this statement may sound ludicrous, but it is not. I have discussed this matter often with Clara Thomas, just as in bygone years I discussed it with our great historian, the late W.L. Morton. In all these disciplines, the writer must select aspects of the characters and events, whether the people and events are real or imagined, and must try to be as true as possible, through the inevitably subjective sight of our own eyes, to the subjects. The demands and the sometimes frightening responsibility involved in these apparently quite different kinds of writing are in fact very similar. As a biographer, Clara Thomas has sought to be true to her subject, bringing to the work not only a scrupulous scholarship but also an understanding of the human individual whose life she was portraying.

Clara Thomas's very considerable body of work, the biographies and the critical books and articles she has written on various aspects of Canadian literature, has always been closely connected with her other and perhaps most cherished professional role, that of teacher. I believe she is one of our truly great teachers.

For her, teaching is not only a profession; it is a vocation. I have heard her, many times, talk about her students. She cares about them so deeply that any kind of help she is able to give them is given with total generosity. At the same time, she constantly challenges them and demands from them high standards of scholarship. If I were asked to describe her work in only three words, those words would be – generosity, integrity, and professionalism. I have attended and taken part in a number of her classes, throughout the years, both Canadian literature and Third World literature classes. Another whole area of her interest and concern has been the promoting of the teaching of West Indian and African contemporary literature, and she is one among the relatively few Canadian university teachers who are extremely knowledgable in that field. I have been impressed most of all with the warmth with which her students regard her, and with the way in which they are encouraged to think independently, to express their own responses to a book, to defend their own viewpoints, and to participate in a general exchange of ideas. This, to me, is what a liberal education is all about.

I have spoken of Clara Thomas as a critic, a biographer, and a teacher. I should add another category. Pioneer. Sometimes I think people tend to forget now that it was not many years ago that Canadian novels, short stories, and poetry were nowhere to be found in courses in Canadian universities. British, yes. American, yes. Canadian, no. Can you imagine a British or American university that offered no courses in the literature of that country? It is said that we started late, that we are still a young country, that we must look to "international" standards, which does not mean international at all, but rather British or American. We have all heard this argument many times, and we still hear it. It usually comes from people who have never read a Canadian book in their lives. It is only through the devoted efforts of a handful of Canadian academics that we now have Canadian literature courses in our universities. When Dr Malcolm Ross and J.G. McClelland decided that a paperback series of Canadian fiction and poetry books was a necessity, with some out-of-print books being reprinted and some new books gradually added, the New Canadian Library was begun in 1957, and for the first time the teaching of Canlit was made a practical possibility. I might be tempted to say – the rest was history. But it wasn't. Even now, there is opposition to the teaching of our own writers' work in our own land. The colonial attitude is not yet totally a thing of the past. Teachers still need to go on proclaiming that our young people have a right to their own heritage. It has been a difficult, sometimes discouraging, and always ongoing struggle for those who believe that the teaching of Canadian literature is vital and necessary. Clara Thomas has been for many years in the forefront of that struggle. Great strides have been made, but there will be no resting on laurels. I have to say here that there is another way in which Clara Thomas was a pioneer, and that one is the area of women's rights in the academic field. When we look at the number of women professors in our universities, the picture is depressing, even now. She has never ceased from trying to gain a more just situation for women academics and to help younger women colleagues. She knows what that subtle discrimination is like, for she has been there herself. I recall, once, talking with her about the whole question of the teaching of Canlit and the fact that women academics were so frequently not given a fair deal in terms of tenure, promotion, and salaries. I will never forget what Clara Thomas said then. Calmly, firmly, committedly, and with true feeling.

"Metaphorically speaking, we just go on from barricade to barricade. We don't ever give up."

Often, in my own life, both in my writing and in my support of the causes in which I passionately believe, I have repeated that line to myself. *We just go on, from barricade to barricade. We don't ever give up.*

That is a message of strength, of faith, of hope, and of love. It is a conviction that Clara Thomas has not only spoken but has lived.

Lois Wilson[1]

"Lois Wilson: Trent University, Peterborough, Ontario" is an unpublished address from the York University Archives and Special Collections, Margaret Laurence Fonds, No. 1986–006/001 (13). On 1 June 1984 Laurence, chancellor of Trent University from 1981 to 1983, presented Dr Wilson for an honorary degree, celebrating Dr Wilson's many achievements. Laurence and Wilson, friends and classmates at United College, shared a Christian faith expressed in terms of the social gospel, condemned nuclear weapons, supported the equality of women in the church, and actively participated in Project Ploughshares and Energy Probe.

Mr Chancellor, it is my privilege to present to you today a person who is both a pilgrim of faith and a pioneer. Lois Wilson is originally a prairie person, born in Winnipeg, the daughter of a United Church minister. She took her Bachelor of Arts degree at United College, now the University of Winnipeg, in 1947. (I, too, was in that same graduating class. Lois and I share many affectionate memories of our college years, and of our contemporaries and our professors.) She then went on to take theology. In a lecture given in 1958, her father, Dr E.G.D. Freeman, then dean of theology at United College, quoted from a letter written to him by Lois after her first year of theology, when she was serving that summer as a student minister in a rural Manitoba community. In it, she said, "We met in a school house. There was no organ or piano. I saw big husky farmers and their wives, trying to sit in small seats designed for small children. There was neither beauty nor comfort. You know, Dad, I got a new notion of the Church and of what is basic in it, that Sunday. Here was the Church in its bare essentials, a group of toil-worn men and women sitting facing the minister and expecting from me some Word of God that would speak to their needs." That sense of the Church, that sense of connection with a congregation at a grassroots – or grainroots – level has remained with Lois throughout her life. Even when she has filled some of the Church's highest posts, she has never failed to identify with the so-called "ordinary" people of this world, who most profoundly are her sisters and brothers. In 1950 she married the Rev. Roy Wilson, a fellow graduate of the United College theological school. She has said that she was "a typical minister's wife for fifteen years," although it is difficult to imagine Lois being a *typical* anything. The Wilsons' two daughters and two sons were born, and for many years Lois worked as a volunteer pastoral assistant. On the Wilsons' fifteenth wedding anniversary a great step was taken, one must say, by both Lois and Roy when she was ordained at last as a United Church minister and proceeded to work in team ministry with her husband. It is appropriate here to recognize the *team* quality of Lois and Roy in their marriage and in their ministries.

It is quite impossible to sum up Lois Wilson's work in a few sentences. *Active* and *faithful* are the key words. As a young woman, she was a moving force in the Student Christian Movement. She has been a TV producer, shaping many faith-related and ecumenical programs. She has been a minister in a number of pastoral charges. She initiated *Tourism with Insight*, an alternate international tourism in the context of Christian faith. She has worked with the Elizabeth Fry Society on behalf of prisoners and their families,[2] and with community projects such as Children's Aid/Oxfam Daycare centres. She is a board member of Energy Probe.[3] She has recruited, trained, and directed volunteers for many Church projects – including sixteen wilderness canoe trips. She has travelled widely in India, Central and South America, Africa, and the Far East, where her areas of commitment have been communication with Christians of widely different cultural backgrounds; social justice; and the dialogue with people of other faiths. In 1976, she was the first woman to be elected president of the Canadian Council of Churches. In 1978 and 1982, she was the spokesperson for Project Ploughshares, an inter-faith peace and disarmament group,[4] at the first and second sessions of the United Nations on disarmament.[5] She was the first woman moderator of the United Church of Canada,[6] from 1980 to 1982, an enormously demanding post that took her not only to many parts of our country but also to many parts of the world. She is now a president of the World Council of Churches and is presently working as a co-director of the Ecumenical Forum of Canada.[7] A simple listing of these incredible and indeed trail-blazing achievements does not do justice to the nature and spirit of the woman. Her deepest concerns have been the place of the Church and of faith in a world that is desperately hurting and threatened. Social justice; the terrible plight of people in countries suffering from thirst, starvation, and the oppression of brutal regimes; human rights so often trampled on, even in our own land; the spectre of nuclear war that hangs over us all and which she believes must be passionately opposed if we love our earth, our children, and honour God's creation – all these are issues to which she has addressed herself. She has long been concerned with the place of women in the church and in our society, a place that for centuries has not been one of equality. She has worked tirelessly for an ongoing dialogue with people of all faiths. In her book of poem/prayers *Like a Mighty River*, published in 1981, she has spoken of her feelings about this dialogue: "It's so easy/ and so arrogant/ to think that God/ speaks only English/ and works only through Christians./ Help me, O God to relate to those/ of other living faiths/ with openness and trust." Lois Wilson has lived her life by the social gospel. Grieving over suffering, determined to help and to help heal, she has yet known always that human warmth and laughter are gifts of grace. In our land and abroad she has participated in the joy of fellowship. Despite the terrors of our world, she has been able, in the words of the hymn, to "sing to the Lord with cheerful voice."

Mr Chancellor, on behalf of the Senate of Trent University, I have the honour to present to you, for the degree of Doctor of Laws, *Honoris Causa*, the Very Reverend Lois Wilson.

For Marian Passmore Engel

"For Marian Passmore Engel," in the Clara Thomas Archives, York University, No. 1986–006.001 (21), was first published in an issue of Ethos *dedicated to the memory of Engel.*

Marian Passmore Engel (1933–1985) is most famous for her controversial fifth novel, Bear *(1976), which portrays a lonely librarian who has an erotic relationship with a bear, and which won the Governor General's Award. She was the first chair of the Writers' Union of Canada (1973–74) and was made an Officer of the Order of Canada in 1982.*

This issue of *Ethos* is dedicated to the memory of Marian Engel. A beloved and devoted member of the Canadian writing community, Marian is missed tremendously. It is still very difficult to realize and to accept the fact that she is no longer among us. I cannot pay adequate tribute to a person I loved as a friend and valued as a colleague. Marian had an incredible amount of courage, wit, and understanding. She combined her gift of writing with her life as a caring mother, a caring person who struggled for all the good causes she believed in. Often it was like a juggling act – as women writers' lives are apt to be – a juggling act performed sometimes with discouragement and sheer weariness, but always with a determination and what I can only call a kind of grace. It is astounding and awesome that she kept on writing until so shortly before her death, and that she went with her children to Paris last Christmas. I spoke with her on the phone after that trip. Her voice was strong, a strength that told of her willpower, not her failing physical condition. She never once spoke of her pain. She spoke of the city she had loved over so many years. She longed for faith, I think, and yet in so many ways she did have it, perhaps more than ever she realized – faith in good causes, faith in all the children and in younger writers, faith in a writing community for which she never ceased to work, faith in her own honest work of writing, perhaps faith in some kind of holy spirit that through her works she proclaimed. Her writing speaks of the wonder and love and saving humour in the midst of the muddle of our lives. She honours the human individual and especially women whose stories and whose hardiness have cried out, often so silently, for expression. Hers was and continues to be a strong and passionate voice. I think of St Paul's words, when he was close to death, and yet, I know that Marian would have had a good laugh over my quoting St Paul, who was not exactly a great supporter of women, but she would have understood, too. Paul said "I have fought a good fight; I have finished my course; I have kept the faith."[1] Marian Engel's course was all too short. But in her writing and in her life, she fought a good fight; she kept the faith. She lives on among us, in her books.

Madeleine Wilkie Dumont

"Madeleine Wilkie Dumont," an undated talk in the Clara Thomas Archives, York University. No. 1986–006/001 (04), was presented by Margaret Laurence on the Canadian Broadcasting Corporation's radio show As It Happens. *Madeleine Dumont (née Wilkie) was born in 1840 in Pembina, Dakota Territory, and died in 1886 in Lewistown, Montana. "Man of Our People," Laurence's essay about Gabriel Dumont, is reprinted in* Heart of a Stranger.

If I could choose a real-life person that I might have liked to be, among the many heroic possibilities, I think it would be a Métis woman called Madeleine Wilkie. She was a fantastic person, who deserves to be known for herself, not just because of her famous husband. She was the wife of Gabriel Dumont, the great buffalo hunter, leader of the Saskatchewan Métis for many years, and Louis Riel's right-hand man in the last tragic uprising in 1885, when the Métis tried in vain to keep their ancestral lands. Dumont has been restored to his rightful place in our history, but we know all too little about his wife. We don't even know what she looked like. If she ever had her photograph taken, it has not survived. She married Dumont in 1858, when both were quite young. To their mutual sorrow, they never had children, but they adopted a child in 1863, and Madeleine protected and loved this daughter, Annie. For years, when Gabriel's duties did not permit him to leave Saskatchewan, Madeleine made the long trek to the Hudson's Bay post at the junction of the Red and Assiniboine rivers to sell the haul of furs and hides. She would be accompanied by a few Métis men, but was the only woman. Those treks must have been excruciatingly difficult. Think of travelling from North Battleford, say, to Winnipeg, by horseback in summer and by snowshoes in winter. As well as speaking French and several Indian dialects, Madeleine also spoke English, which would have been a great advantage when bargaining at the trading posts. Gabriel established a ferry at Gabriel's Crossing, near Batoche,[1] in 1872, and for a time prospered. Madeleine even got a treadle washing machine! In 1884, when Riel returned to Canada with his wife and family, Madeleine took them in and looked after them. In the fatal battle of Batoche, in the spring of 1885, Madeleine tended the wounded in her own home, and when Gabriel had to choose between staying and dying on the scaffold with Riel or going to the USA and keeping on protesting and fighting, Madeleine urged him to live. She took blankets and bannock to him in the woods, risking capture by Middleton's soldiers, and helped him to prepare for exile. She later joined him in Montana. She must have been heartbroken at his humiliation, when he briefly joined Buffalo Bill Cody's Wild West Circus.[2] She died in America in 1886, far from her beloved Saskatchewan. Dumont returned to Canada not long afterwards, with a government pardon, and died at Batoche in 1906. He is buried there, and his memorial stone stands in the little cemetery. There is no memorial for Madeleine Wilkie Dumont. She was one of our bravest foremothers, whose story, like those of so many women, has been largely unrecorded and is now almost lost to history. I don't know if I'd really have liked to be Madeleine, but I certainly would have liked to possess her courage, her determination, and her steadfastness.[3]

YWCA Woman of the Year Award

This unpublished talk from the Clara Thomas Archives, York University, No. 1986–006/001 (51), delivered by Laurence to the Peterborough YWCA *on 14 June 1985, reflects her interest in feminism and the Nisei.[1]*

I am honoured to have been asked to speak tonight at the Peterborough YWCA's Woman of the Year Award dinner. This award, in my view, is part of a tradition that has been carried on for a long time, by the YWCA here and in many places in our land and in other countries, a tradition of support – emotional, spiritual, and at all times practical – given to women in every walk of life, a steadfast recognition of women's rights and needs, of women's immeasurable contribution to all societies, and our ongoing struggle for equality. I will return to that point in a moment.

I thought you might be entertained tonight to hear of my long-ago and very valuable connection with the YWCA. Not many people know about this aspect of my life, but it was extremely important to me. I will have to give you a bit of my background: I married at the age of twenty-one, in Manitoba, in 1947. My husband, a veteran of both the RAF and the RCAF[2] in World War II, took engineering at the University of Manitoba after the war. I had graduated in arts, the year we got married, and worked for nearly a year at the old *Winnipeg Citizen*, a daily co-operative newspaper that, alas, folded after a year – an idea whose time had not yet come. After that, I had the good luck to get a job with the Winnipeg YWCA. Astoundingly, I got the job of registrar. They knew I was a young woman who had ideals. They knew I had attended United College, the United Church College. They knew I wanted to be a writer, as I made no secret of that. They knew I was a young married woman devoted to her husband. I looked okay to the executive director of the Y and to the program director, the two women who interviewed me for the job. What they did NOT know, however, was that I was a total klutz at mathematics. I was honest as the day is long, but I couldn't add up a column of figures to save my life. That was in the days before pocket calculators, alas.

I managed well on a day-to-day basis. I loved talking to the young women who came in for courses, and to the young mothers who came in for the "Mother and Daughter Swim." Today, I do not doubt, the swimming classes are more mixed, but in those days *we* had the "Mother and Daughter Swims," and *they*, the YMCA, a block away, had the "Father and Son Swims."

The large registrations, which took place every six months, if memory serves, were my downfall. All the staff of the Y helped out, and during one mad frantic afternoon and evening we registered people for the swimming, the dancing, the crafts, the Teen Clubs, the study groups in this, that, and the other.

Women – young, middle-aged, and elderly – waited in lineups, cracking jokes to while away the time. Little kids tore around with sprightly glee. Mums tried to register for their chosen programs whilst keeping an eye on their energetic darlings who were having a swell time getting lost in the crowds in the big old auditorium at the Y where we did these registrations. At the end of the evening, all the staff turned over the money and the registration slips to me, the registrar. When the crowds departed, I breathed a sigh of relief. For about one minute. Then I had to make it all balance. Coffee and a sandwich, instead of dinner. I never got out of there until about midnight. Never, however, was I left alone to do this difficult balancing act. Always, some of my colleagues would be there to help me. The books were never balanced perfectly. We were usually about six dollars out, one way or another. We're not talking big bucks, here. If we ended up out of cash, we would all, finally, sigh and put in a few quarters each to make it up. If we ended up ahead, we would give the money to the staff canteen, hoping this was not dishonesty. We preferred to be short on cash rather than have $2.95 more than we were supposed to have. Those were thrilling times, I tell you. A confession I can now make, after some forty years, is that during those toting-up hours I used to sneak out to the women's lavatory and have a cigarette.

My most profound memory of the year I spent as register at the YWCA in Winnipeg, in 1948/49, concerns the Japanese Canadians. Although the war had ended in 1945, it was not until 1947 and 1948 that the Japanese Canadians, so wrongly and with such terrible injustice incarcerated in camps in British Columbia, many of them third-generation Canadians, were at last released and dispersed to many places throughout Canada. This is one part of our country's history that is forever disgraceful. In 1948, a large number of Japanese-Canadians arrived in Winnipeg. My recollection is that the Winnipeg YWCA was one of the very few organizations that welcomed them. The Y started a Teen Club for Japanese-Canadian kids, and tried, gradually, to get those kids to take part in other Teen Clubs there, dancing and music and talk and coffee. Of course, it was difficult. Of course, those kids, Canadian kids, born here, having been shut up for some years in camps and treated like enemy aliens because they were of Japanese ancestry, were hurt and withdrawn. Who wouldn't be? Can you imagine how they must have felt? Cast out, imprisoned, in their own country, the only country they had? At least away back then in 1948 and 1949, the YWCA did try to reach out to those hurting kids, even if sometimes clumsily, and try to help heal their pain.

Although it was nearly forty years ago now, one of the most vivid memories is that of a young Japanese-Canadian man coming into my office frequently to show me with exuberance his latest paintings. I was twenty-one. He must have been not that much younger. I knew virtually nothing about art and painting, but even I could see from his work that it was inspired, mightily talented, marvellous. His name was Takao Tanabe.[3] He is, all these years on, one of our best artists, acclaimed here and throughout the entire world. I think upon all these things now, and I think how privileged I was to see Tak Tanabe's paintings when he was a young artist, and I was a young writer. That year at the YWCA in Winnipeg was a very formative year for me.

I want to return now to this evening's award. Our county of Peterborough has a long tradition of determined and talented and devoted women. The tradition reaches back to Catharine Parr Traill and Susanna Moodie, and it encompasses all the women since those pioneering times, women who have struggled and who have been strong in times of trouble, women who have served this community and by implication the human community everywhere, in the many areas of the arts, of medicine, of law, of history, of social science, of education, and more. I also want to pay tribute tonight to the many women who are not named, unknown in our annals, who through the centuries have reared their children, have suffered adversity, have passed on to their daughters and their sons a sense of responsibility and caring. Those are the true heroines, our mothers, our grandmothers, our great-grandmothers.

I would like to applaud the YWCA for giving this award to a woman who cares, who works in our own community, and who, in this terrifying world, still

believes that our efforts to make a better world *can* make a difference, *are* profoundly worthwhile. I do not know who this year's Woman of the Year will be.
But I know many women in this area who have served their causes faithfully. The
Woman of the Year will speak for all of them – all of us. Sisters, I celebrate tonight
our faith, our strength, and our caring.

PART FOUR

Essays on Nuclear Disarmament: "The Most
Pressing Practical, Moral, and Spiritual
Issue of Our Times"

A Message to the Inheritors

"A Message to the Inheritors," an undated typescript in the York University Archives and Special Collections, Margaret Laurence Fonds, No. 1980–001/004 (87), with "M. Laurence" typed at the end, parallels her convocation address delivered at York University in June 1980, published in Dance on the Earth *in 1989.*

I graduated from university thirty-three years ago, in 1947. I am tempted to say that it was a very different world from the present one. I'm not sure that such a statement would be true. In some ways it was a very different world, but it was by no means the cosy, optimistic, jitterbugging world that some of the purveyors of late 1940s and early 1950s nostalgia would have us believe.

My world had emerged two years earlier from a six-year period of world war. Most of us had lost a member of our family, or friends and schoolmates. These were the young men of my generation who died on the beaches at Dieppe or in France and Italy in the final stages of the European war, or in North Africa or Hong Kong, or in the ruins of their shot-down planes or torpedoed ships. Some of them were the boys from my town and surrounding towns, the kids I'd grown up with, several years older than I was. When Dieppe happened, in 1942, and so many of them were killed or spent the rest of the war in prison camps, I was sixteen years old. That was when I first realized – really realized – what war meant. It meant that many of the people you had known were dead at a very young age and had died horribly.

Those of my generation who were Jewish had, almost without exception, lost entire branches of their families – grandparents, uncle and aunts, cousins – in the Holocaust, in which all but a fraction of the European Jewish communities were exterminated in the gas chambers of death camps such as

Auschwitz and Belsen. Innocence was no longer a possibility. The gates of whatever Eden our childhoods might have contained had clanged shut forever. We did not want to recognize, but we had to recognize, that humankind is indeed capable of an evil so all-encompassing that no words could possibly describe it. No mourning for those millions of murdered innocent people will ever be enough, will ever be over.

There was, of course, one other trauma that all those of my generation underwent. We had grown up taking totally for granted that the generations of humankind and of all creatures are like the leaves on a tree – they fall, but a *new* generation arises, and the earth endures forever. August 6th, 1945, made it impossible ever again to take that reassuring belief for granted. That was the day the first atomic bomb was dropped by the Allies on Hiroshima.[1] Eight days later the Second World War ended. My generation had the dubious distinction of being the first in the whole history of humankind to emerge into young adulthood knowing that our species had the technological power to destroy all life on earth and possibly our earth itself.

In the face of this knowledge, it was difficult not to give way to depression or despair, not to give up entirely to the draining feeling that we were helpless. Some people I knew did indeed give up, and I mourn those casualties of peace as much as I mourn the casualties of war. Most of us have had to struggle intermittently through the years with the awful temptation to give up the struggle, to cease caring. But a great many of us have in fact gone on amidst struggles that are both inner and outer, and have tried to do our work as best we can, to raise our children as caringly as we could, and in our extremely flawed and imperfect ways to express our beliefs in social justice, in human relationships of love and value, and in the possibility and necessity of peoples of different cultures communicating with one another and trying to understand one another. We have proclaimed the insanity of wars, and the necessity of defending civil liberties. To our voices have been joined the voices of many of a younger generation. It cannot be said that in any world sense we have met with spectacular success. In more than thirty years there has not been a time when peace has prevailed everywhere. Still, I cannot believe we have entirely failed, either. Without these voices, it is possible that the world might be in a worse way than it is.

Young people leaving our universities today are graduating into a world that is truly terrifying. It is difficult not to give way to despair. Not long ago, we were told by an official of the Federal Energy Management Agency in Washington that the "good news" is that in a nuclear war, not all the population of America (and presumably Canada) would die. Only half would be killed. The audacity, the blindness, of calling this "good news"! One of the candidates in the American presidential nominations, some time ago, was reported to have said that he could visualize a nuclear war in which America could declare itself the victor – with two-thirds of its population dead. Have these men no feelings or simply no imagination? Thornton Wilder once said that cruelty is in essence a failure of the imagination, in other words a failure to recognize the reality of other people, a failure to feel the pain of others as though it were one's own and to know it could become one's own. If the hawks everywhere have no concern for the lives of so-called "ordinary" people – that is, all of us – does it not ever occur to them to wonder what kind of a world they would emerge back into from their pro-tected bunkers, at the end of such an unthinkable global war? The disaster business is said to be flourishing right now. Requests are pouring in to Ottawa, to the Department of Public Works, for blueprints for bomb shelters. What a cruel farce all of this is. In Ontario, the regional director of Emergency Prepa-redness sends out to frightened people a twenty-year-old pamphlet entitled "Eleven Steps to Survival,"[2] to – in quotes – "assuage their fears." The pamphlet purports to tell citizens how to "rig up a temporary but effective shelter against atomic fallout." I really wonder how anyone can fail to realize that the only safe-guard against nuclear war is not to have a nuclear war.

Recently, in Ontario, the film censorship board made a tremendous fuss about the possibility of offending public morals with such a film as *The Tin Drum*. "Obscenity" seems to be defined as anything that has to do with sex. It seems to me that the real obscenities of our age are the irresponsible and brutal statements on the acceptability of a global war, statements that treat human individuals as numbers, statistics, figures on a graph, worthless and unvalued as living crea-tures. How far is this from the thinking that instituted the Holocaust? Not far, I think. Have people so soon forgotten the horrors of the Vietnam War?

In Argentina, hundreds of thousands of men and women have "disappeared" – that is, they have been tortured and killed, and in the name of "Western Christian civilization." To me, it is an obscenity to use the word "Christian" in connection with such gruesome wholesale murder. The leaders in that greatly afflicted country have presumably never given thought to the commandment of Jesus – "Thou shalt love thy neighbour as thyself." At the other side of the political spectrum, in Russia countless victims who dared protest the system

have also been imprisoned or killed, in the name of socialism and the brotherhood of man.

The last thirty years have seen an increasing demeanment of language itself,
as words and slogans denoting freedom and justice and brotherhood and faith
are being used to practise the precise opposite. This is, of course, not a new
phenomenon. It has always been true that integrity must be judged not only by
what people say, but more importantly by what they do, how they live their lives
in relation to others.

We are not immune, in Canada, to these injustices and acts of inhumanity.
Racism, violence, oppression, violations of civil liberties – all these exist in some
measure or other here, too. Lastly, and individually, the enemy is always to some
extent within. We are all prey to anger; we are all capable of hurting other people
and of violating our own principles of integrity and humanity. We are all capable
of giving way to self-righteousness, to spiritual pride. And yes, we are all too
capable of giving way to despair. I believe that the early Church Fathers were
quite right in designating despair as one of the deadly sins. In our present and
threatening world, it is only too easy to feel hopeless and helpless, to withdraw
into lethargy or a concern only with our own personal lives, forgetting that we
are an integral part of all humanity everywhere. It is my profound belief that
we must not yield to such a withdrawal.

It is my hope for the generation that has come after mine that they will somehow be able to sustain hope within themselves. I think we must take responsibility for our own individual selves. We must take responsibility for the work
that we have chosen to do. We must try to honour whatever gifts of talent and
ability we have been given, and whatever gifts of knowledge we have acquired.
I believe we must also not ever forget our responsibilities as citizens of our
land and citizens of the world. We must continue in every way we can to protest
nonviolently against social injustice, infringements of civil liberties, cruelties,
and the indifference of governments, wherever these occur. We must continue
to proclaim those things we believe in – the possibility of true communication
between human individuals and among people of all cultures; the responsibility
of those of us in lands rich in food and natural resources to help people in lands
suffering from famine and deprivation; the sheer necessity – if life on earth and
our earth itself are to survive – of peoples to live in peaceful coexistence with
one another and with the other creatures that share our planet, and our responsibility to protect and restore the earth itself.

F.R. Scott, our most distinguished constitutional lawyer and one of our very finest writers and poets, once wrote an essay "Freedom of Speech in Canada." This essay was reprinted in his book *Essays on the Constitution*, published in 1977 and winner of the Governor General's Award for nonfiction that year. In it, he said, "'The time, it is to be hoped, has gone by,' wrote John Stuart Mill,[3] 'when any defence would be necessary for the principle of freedom of speech.' His hope was vain. The time for defending freedom never goes by. Freedom is a habit that must be kept alive by use." Those words were written in 1932.

My generation inherited the legacy of a world war, of the Holocaust, of Hiroshima. We also inherited the legacy of all the men and women who have throughout the centuries stood up and struggled for those human values in which they believed. Frank Scott's words are as true and as relevant today as they were when he first wrote them. They will always be true and relevant.

The struggles for justice, the necessity to proclaim – in the words of St Paul – the qualities of faith, hope, and love, and the necessity to proclaim passionately to all governments everywhere the evils of wars and of destruction, the absolute impossibility of a nuclear war – these struggles are never over, and I believe we must never give up. Our struggle is not going to be won quickly. It goes on from one generation to the next.

My generation's inheritors inherit a deeply troubled world. We are certainly not passing on a secure heritage. But I hope we are passing on, even in the midst of a terrifying world, some sense of hope, some sense that these lifelong struggles are worthwhile because life itself is worthwhile and is given to each of us for a short time – to protect, to honour, and to celebrate.

A Matter of Life or Death

"A Matter of Life or Death" is a 1982 convocation address given at Emmanuel College, Victoria College, University of Toronto, 6 May 1982, and first published in Woodcock, A Place to Stand On, *56–60. An undated typescript in the Margaret Laurence Fonds in the York University Archives and Special Collections is headed by the words a "talk given to church groups, service clubs, universities, etc."*

Laurence sympathized with the social gospel as interpreted by Winnipeg's Old Left from her time at United College until the end of her life. The social gospel was a socio-religious movement that drew on evangelical Protestantism and attempted to apply Christian ideals to social ills caused by industrialization – including economic inequality, child labour, alcoholism, crime, and environmental degradation. It gained popularity in Canada, especially on the Prairies, from the late nineteenth century to the 1930s (Allen, "Social Gospel").

Ours is a terrifying world. Injustice, suffering, and fear are everywhere to be found. It is difficult to maintain hope in such a world, and yet I believe there is hope. I want to proclaim and affirm my profound belief in the social gospel. I speak as a Christian, a woman, a writer, a mother, a member of humanity, and a sharer in life itself, a life I believe to be informed by and infused with the Holy Spirit. I do not think it is enough to hope and pray that our own lives and souls will know grace, even though my entire life as a writer has been concerned with my belief that all human individuals matter, that no one is ordinary. Our Lord's new commandment speaks very clearly: "Thou shalt love thy neighbour as thyself."

The social gospel is no easier now than it ever was. My generation was the first in human history to come into young adulthood knowing that the human race now had the dreadful ability to destroy all life on earth and possibly the earth it-self. Only later did we realize the full extent of the destruction of life, a continuing destruction passed on to the then-unborn children of survivors, but we *did* know that after Hiroshima, August 6th, 1945, the world would never be the same again. The annihilation caused by the first atomic bombs was unthinkable, but it had happened. Also, we had taken it for granted that through wars, through disasters, yet would the earth endure forever. It was clear to many of us in 1945 that this was no longer to be taken for granted. We have lived with that thought ever since, and have yet borne our children, lived our lives, done our work. The will to sur-vive and to pass on important caring to future generations is very strong. But today we have to realize that the bombs used at Hiroshima and Nagasaki were small bombs, compared to today's nuclear weapons.

Our lives and the lives of all generations as yet unborn are being threatened, as never before, by the increasing possibility of nuclear war. I believe that the question of disarmament is the most pressing practical, moral, and spiritual issue of our times. If we value our own lives and the lives of our children and all children everywhere, if we honour both the past and the future, then we must do everything in our power to work nonviolently for peace. These beliefs are not only an integral part of my social and moral stance, but of my religious faith as well. Human society now possesses the terrible ability to destroy all life on earth, and our planet itself. Can anyone who has ever marvelled at the mi-racle of creation fail to feel concerned and indeed anguished, every single day, at this thought?

A central disagreement, of course, exists between those who think that more and yet more nuclear arms will ensure that nuclear arms will never be used, and those of us who believe that the proliferation of nuclear weapons brings us closer all the time to the actuality of nuclear war – a war that no side could possibly win; a war that would be so devastating that we cannot begin to imagine that horror. Whatever we are being told about a "limited" or "winnable" nuclear war, the fact remains that such a war could destroy all that we, as humankind, have aspired to, all that we have achieved. It could destroy the future, not only of the world's peoples but of all creatures that share our planet with us.

As both America and Russia develop more and more nuclear arms, so the other inevitably responds in kind. Nuclear arms have long since ceased to be a "deterrent," if indeed they were ever so, and have become by their very existence a monstrous threat. Daily, the chances are increasing for a nuclear war to break out by accident, by a failure of the intricate control and warning systems, or simply by human panic and a mutual mistrust between the superpowers.

Dr Helen Caldicott,[1] that courageous woman who has done so much in the struggle against nuclear arms, has said that both America and Russia now have enough nuclear weapons to "overkill every person on earth sixteen times." Think of that for a moment. Do the world's leaders really suppose that it would all happen on TV, and that the dead would get up again and take on a different role in another popular series so they might be killed again and again? I fear greatly that many world leaders have so little imagination and so little real caring that they cannot visualize at all what a nuclear holocaust would mean. Do they really think that they and their families and executive staffs would survive, in deep-buried bunkers? And if, by any unlikely chance they did, what kind of a world do they think they would emerge back into? It would be a dead and putrefying world. Dr Helen Caldicott says, "If we look behind the headlines and understand the historical perspective, we realize that America is preparing to fight a nuclear war. Now, that should make us all distinctly uncomfortable. In fact, we should be screaming in the streets, if we really care about ourselves, our children, and those people we love, and if we really love this planet." With well-researched figures, Dr Caldicott also says, "In the event of a nuclear war, we predict that within thirty days after an exchange, 90 percent of Americans will be dead. So will Canadians, probably Mexicans, certainly Russians, certainly Europeans, the British, and probably the Chinese."

Roger Molander, a former White House nuclear strategist for the National Security Council, in an article in the *Guardian* in April of 1982, tells of one of the many things that made him decide to give up that job.[2] He is now executive director of Ground Zero, an anti-nuclear-weapons education project.[3] He says, "The final chance event that confirmed my determination to help correct our flaws involved another military officer. It happened at a meeting in the Pentagon when a navy captain offered the view that in America and Europe people were getting too excited over nuclear war. He argued that people were talking as if nuclear war would be the end of the world, when in fact only 500 million people would be killed. Only 500 million. I remember repeating to myself ... Only 500 million people ... "

Exactly. These are figures, statistics. It takes no time at all to say 500 million. But it all looks different, as it did to Roger Molander, if we think of each one of those people as our own children, ourselves, our parents, our friends.

It is precisely this failure of the imagination on the part of militarists and leaders that is so dangerous today, the failure to visualize what a nuclear holocaust would mean, the apparent inability to imagine the scorched and charred bodies of children – *our* children or children of Russian parents or parents anywhere, and to know, by an extension of imagination, that *all* children are our children. The jargon of the militarists is a distortion and a twisting of language, of our human ability to communicate. Language itself becomes the vehicle of concealment and deception. Such words as "overkill" and "megadeath" do not convey in any sense at all what would really happen – the dead, mutilated, and dying people clogging the ruined cities and towns like so much unvalued discarded rubbish, the suffering humans screaming for help with no medical help available, no water, no relief at all for the unbearable pain of millions of humans except finally the dark relief of death for all. Any shelters that the few might reach would in time turn into tombs. Civil defence plans are a sham. In a nuclear war there would be nowhere to hide.

Canada could and must, I believe, have a real impact in bringing about world disarmament. We are not powerless; nor are we without significance in a world sense. Yet our present government appears to be willing to let the Cruise missile be tested over our land, in Alberta. The Cruise missile, an American nuclear weapon, was not designed as a deterrent weapon – it was designed as a "first-strike" weapon.[4] The Litton plant in Ontario[5] is producing, with the aid of millions of *our* tax dollars, guidance systems for the Cruise missile. Canada has sold nuclear reactors to such repressive regimes as Argentina, and is delivering fuel for those reactors, despite the fact that our government is aware that nuclear weapons could soon be within Argentina's capability.[6] These are only a few examples of Canada's complicity in the nuclear arms race.

Do we care so little about our children? Do we honour the Holy Spirit and the creator of life so little that we will not speak out? I believe we *do* care, passionately and profoundly. Indeed, one thing that gives me hope is that so many of our churches and synagogues, so many people of all faiths, are speaking out against the arms race and the descent into total madness.

Recently I read that $550 billion dollars are being spent, worldwide, on armaments, including nuclear arms. That sum is so vast that we really cannot comprehend it. I think of the people in the world who are suffering from thirst, from starvation, from disease, from ceaseless fighting and the brutality of oppressive regimes. I think, too, of the growing number of unemployed people in our own land. I think of the Reagan program in America – more and yet more money spent on nuclear arms; less and less spent on social programs and help to the poor and the disabled.[7]

In our own land, Canada, what can we do?

I believe that our land should be declared a nuclear-weapons-free zone, with absolutely no testing of nuclear arms or production of parts for those arms allowed in our country. I think that Canada could do a great deal to bring about a gradual and verifiable reduction of nuclear arms by both sides, monitored by neutral countries such as the Scandinavian countries, and to bring about a freeze on the production and testing of nuclear weapons. Canada could be a strong influence for a "no-first-strike" agreement among nations, for multilateral disarmament, and for world peace. To me, this goes beyond any political party views; indeed, it goes beyond any national feelings. It means, in the most profound sense, survival. It means the future. We must not give way to despair, or to what Dr Helen Caldicott calls "psychic numbing," the sense that we cannot do anything, that we are helpless. We cannot afford passivity. We must take on responsibility for our lives and our world and we must be prepared to make our government listen and hear us. We must, in every nonviolent way, cause our voices to be heard, listened to, and acted upon.

As human beings, surely, we have the responsibility to pray and work and speak out strongly in whatever ways we can, with our words and work, our time and money contributions, whatever we can give, for human and caring justice and for peace for all people that on earth do dwell.[8]

The Artist Then, Now, and Always

"The Artist Then, Now, and Always," dated 1984 in a typescript in the Clara Thomas Archives, York University, was published in Trace: Prairie Writers on Writing, *edited by Birk Sproxton.*

I have to speak about how I feel as a writer. I don't like calling myself "an artist," but I guess I am, and I would join with my tribal sisters and brothers in many ways. I believe that as a writer – an artist, if you will – I have a responsibility, a moral responsibility, to work against the nuclear arms race, to work for a recognition on the part of governments and military leaders that nuclear weapons must never be used and must systematically be reduced. Throughout human history, artists have affirmed and celebrated life. Whether we work in words, in music, in paint, in film, in bronze or stone or whatever our medium may be, the artist affirms the value of life itself and of our only home, the planet Earth. Art mirrors and ponders the pain and joy of our experience as human beings. In many parts of the world, and over many centuries, artists have risked and even given their own lives to portray the society around them as they perceived it, and to speak out against injustices. Since the most ancient times, artists have passed on to succeeding generations the tales, the histories, the songs, the sagas, the skills of their trade. Can we conceive of a world in which there would be no succeeding generations? A world in which all the powerful works of the human imagination would be destroyed, would never again be seen or listened to or experienced? We must conceive that this is now a possibility, and one not too far in our uncertain future, either. We must not, as artists, or so I feel, stand by and passively allow this to happen. The death of the individual is the end that we will all one day meet, but in the knowledge that our children and their children will live, that *someone's* children will go on, that the great works of humankind will endure in

art, in recorded history, in medicine, in the sciences and philosophies and technologies that our species has developed with devotion and a sense of vocation
throughout the ages. The individual is the leaf on the tree. The leaves fall, but
the tree endures. New leaves are born. This concept has been the mainstay of
our species from time immemorial. Now the tree itself is threatened. All art is a
product of the human imagination. It is, deeply, an honouring of the past, a perception of the present in one way or another, and a looking toward the future.
Whatever the medium of any particular artist, art is reaching out, an attempt to
communicate those things which most concern us seriously in our sojourn here
on earth. Artists, the real ones, the committed ones, have always sought, sometimes in ways prophetic and beyond their own times, to clarify and proclaim and
enhance life, not to obscure and demean and destroy it. Even the so-called literature of despair is not really that at all. Despair is total silence, total withdrawal.
Art, by its very nature of necessary expression, is an act of faith, an acknowledgment of the profound mystery at the core of life.

As a writer, therefore, I feel I have a responsibility. Not to write pamphlets, not
to write didactic fiction. That would be, in many ways, a betrayal of how I feel
about my work. But my responsibility seems to be to write as truthfully as I can
about human individuals and their dilemmas, to honour them as living, suffering, and sometimes joyful people. My responsibility also must extend into my
life as a citizen of my own land and ultimately of the world.

I do not claim to have done this well. There are no personal victories in those
areas. The individual, here, becomes part of a community, and only as a part of
that community can one person ever be effective and true to herself or himself.
There has to be the resolve not to give up, and to join with all others who believe
that life itself is more important than our individual lives, important though
these certainly are.

Dr Helen Caldicott speaks of "psychic numbing,"[1] the temptation to shut out
from our minds and hearts all the terrifying things in our world. To think that
the problems may just possibly go away if we ignore them. To feel that we are
totally helpless, and so ... why bother trying to do anything? What Dr Caldicott
calls "psychic numbing" I would call "despair," and, although I would take issue
with the early Church Fathers[2] on many things, I would agree that despair is
rightly placed as one of the deadly sins. The problems of our world will not go
away if we ignore them. It is not all happening on TV. It is happening on our
earth, and we, humankind, are the custodians of that earth. We cannot afford

passivity. We must take on responsibility for our lives, and our world, and we must be prepared to make our government listen to and hear us. Our aim must be no less than human and caring justice, and peace ... *for all people that on earth do dwell.*

A Statement of Faith

"A Statement of Faith," in the Clara Thomas Archives, York University No. 1986–006/001 (17), originally presented as a convocation address to Emmanuel College, University of Toronto, on 6 May 1982, was first published in A Place to Stand On, *with the epigraph, "Pray and work ... and speak out for peace." Laurence proclaims her Christian faith, expressed in the terms of the social gospel, as the basis for her advocacy for nuclear disarmament.* [1]

This is the first time I have ever had the privilege of addressing graduating students who are candidates to the ministry of the church. I must admit to feelings of nervousness in standing here and making a statement of personal belief. In accepting this invitation, I requested that a solid lectern be provided – something I could lean on. I told a friend about this need, and she said, "Margaret, what you really want is not a lectern but a pulpit." Well, I don't think that is the case at all, but it is true that in speaking to you now, I feel the need of something solid to lean on, physically, but also the need – not just now but every day – of something spiritual to lean on. The sustaining force is faith.

Ours is a terrifying world. Injustice, suffering, and fear are everywhere to be found. It is difficult to maintain hope in such a world, and yet I believe there is hope. I want to proclaim and affirm my profound belief in the social gospel. I speak as a Christian, a woman, a writer, a parent, a member of humanity, and a sharer in life itself, a life I believe to be informed by and infused with the Holy Spirit. I do not think it is enough to hope and pray that our own lives and souls will know grace, even though my entire life as a writer has been concerned with my belief that all human individuals matter, that no one is ordinary. Our Lord's new commandment speaks very clearly. "Thou shalt love thy neighbour as thyself."

The social gospel is no easier now than it was then. My generation was the first in human history to come into young adulthood knowing that the human race now had the dreadful ability to destroy all life on earth and possibly the earth itself. Only later did we realize the full extent of the destruction of life, a continuing destruction passed on to the then-unborn children of survivors, but we did know that after Hiroshima, August 6th, 1945, the world would never be the same again. The annihilation caused by the first atomic bombs was unthinkable, but it had happened. Also, we had taken it for granted that through wars, through disasters, yet would the earth endure forever. It was clear to many of us in 1945 that this was no longer to be taken for granted. We have lived with that thought ever since, and have yet borne our children, lived our lives, done our work. The will to survive and to pass on important caring to future generations is very strong. But today we have to realize that the bombs used at Hiroshima and Nagasaki were small bombs, compared to today's nuclear weapons.

Think of the Holocaust in Europe, when the Nazis murdered a very large part of all the Jewish communities. The horror must never be forgotten. No mourning will ever be enough for those millions of children, women, and men whose unique and irreplaceable lives were torn away by the de-humanized humans who had taken power in Hitler's Germany. Despite the lessons of Hiroshima and of the Holocaust, today's leaders can speak with apparent complacency of "winning a nuclear war" or of "a limited nuclear war," or – in a jargon that demeans language itself – of "overkill." [2] Such concepts must be called by their true name, and that name is Evil.

Dr Helen Caldicott, that courageous woman who has done so much in the struggle against nuclear arms, has said that both America and Russia now have enough nuclear arms to "overkill every person on earth sixteen times." Think of that for a moment. Do the world's leaders really suppose that it would all happen on TV, and that the dead would get up again and take on a different role in another popular series so they might be killed again and again? I fear greatly that many world leaders have so little imagination and so little caring that they cannot visualize at all what a nuclear holocaust would mean. Do they really think that they and their families would survive, in deep-buried bunkers? And if by any unlikely chance they did, what kind of a world do they imagine they would emerge back into? Dr Helen Caldicott says, "If we look behind the headlines and understand the historical perspective, we realize that America is preparing to fight a nuclear war. Now, that should make us all distinctly uncomfortable. In fact, we should be screaming in the streets, if we really care about ourselves, our children, and those people we love, and if we really love this planet." With well-researched figures, Dr Caldicott also says, "In the event of a nuclear war, we predict that within thirty days after an exchange, 90 percent of Americans will be dead. So will Canadians, probably Mexicans, certainly Russians, certainly Europeans, the British, and probably the Chinese."

Roger Molander, a former White House nuclear strategist for the National Security Council, in an article in the *Guardian* in April of this year, tells of one of the many things that made him decide to give up that job. He is now executive director of Ground Zero, a nuclear education project. He says, "The final chance event that confirmed my determination to help correct our flaws involved another military officer. It happened at a meeting in the Pentagon when a navy captain offered the view that in America and Europe people were getting too excited over nuclear war. He argued that people were talking as if nuclear war would be the end of the world, when in fact only 500 million people would be killed. Only 500 million people. I remember repeating it to myself. Only 500 million people ...."

Precisely. These are figures. It takes no time at all to say 500 million. But it all looks different, as it did to Roger Molander, if we think of each one of those people as our children, ourselves, our parents, our friends.

Increasingly, we are being told that the concept of a "first strike capability" is a viable and acceptable one. If America strikes first, the Soviet Union would be wiped out and America would not, or vice versa. I believe this to be a murderously dangerous fantasy, but even if it were not – what kind of mentality could conceive of the death of countless millions of helpless human beings, whatever their government's ideology? It seems clear that, whether America or Russia develops more and more nuclear arms, the other will respond in kind. I do not believe that the possession of more and more nuclear arms will guarantee peace. I think precisely the opposite is true. What must be aimed at is a lowering of hysteria on both sides, a recognition by world governments that a nuclear war could not be won by any nation, any power.

Canada could have a real impact in bringing about world disarmament. We are not powerless and we are not without significance in the world. Yet our government has agreed to allow the Cruise missile to be tested above Alberta. The Litton plant in Ontario produces parts for the Cruise missile. Canada has sold nuclear reactors to Argentina, a country with a repressive regime and little apparent respect for international law. Now we learn that within a few years Argentina may have developed nuclear weapons, and has not pledged itself not to use such weapons. Canada could and should be a strong force for world peace. We should declare our country a nuclear-weapons-free area, with no nuclear arms or parts being produced here or transported through our land. Canada should to the utmost degree encourage a global freeze on the production and testing of nuclear arms. We should do all in our power to encourage and persuade all nations everywhere never to consider the "first strike."

Do we care so little about our children? Do we honour the Holy Spirit and the creator of life so little that we will not speak out? I believe we *do* care, passionately and profoundly. Indeed, one thing that gives me hope is that so many of our churches and synagogues, so many people of all faiths are speaking out against the arms race and descent into total destruction.

Recently I read that 550 billion dollars are being spent, worldwide, on armaments, including nuclear weapons. That sum is so vast we cannot really comprehend it. I think of the people of the world who are suffering from thirst, from starvation, from disease, from ceaseless fighting, and the oppression of brutal regimes.

In Somaliland, many years ago, I saw people, I saw children, who were dying of thirst. I can never forget. Now, in that area, things are much, much worse. The late Dr Barbara Ward,[3] the great economist, in one of her books put forward the thesis that, if the world's economy could be geared less toward arms production and more toward helping people, it would be possible for everyone in the world to have enough fresh water. Dr Helen Caldicott says that for one-third of the cost of a Trident nuclear submarine, malaria could be eliminated from the world. In East and in West Africa I saw children who were desperately ill with malaria. My own two children had malaria, as babies, in Ghana.[4] They were fortunate. They had medical help, and had previously been given anti-malarial medication, and they recovered. But I remember as though it were yesterday – and it was in fact nearly thirty years ago – my own sense of helplessness and anguish. How many parents in malarial areas, now as then, mourn their children, killed by a disease that could have been eradicated years ago? One-third of the cost of a Trident submarine! Here in Canada, native people in such places as Grassy Narrows[5] are slowly and painfully dying of Minamata disease,[6] caused by mercury poisoning in the fish they must eat for lack of other food. These are only a few, a very few, of the tragic issues in this desperately hurting world. These sufferings and deaths could be halted, could be prevented. Yet worldwide spending on instruments designed only for killing goes on and is escalating.

Dr Helen Caldicott speaks of "psychic numbing" – the temptation to shut our from our minds and hearts all the horrifying things in our world. To think that the problems may just possibly go away if we ignore them. They will not go away. It is not all happening on TV. It is happening on our earth, and we are the custodians of that earth.

"Thou shalt love thy neighbour as thyself." I believe the word "neighbour" in our present world cannot have any limited geographical, racial, national, or religious meaning. Here is a poem/prayer from the Rev. Lois Wilson's splendid book, *Like a Mighty River*:

> It's so easy
> and so arrogant
> to think that God
> speaks only English
> and works only through Christians.
> Help me, O God,
> to relate to those
> other living faiths
> with openness and trust.

Only with such openness and trust will we ever even begin to overcome the dilemmas of our world, only by joining our efforts and our voices with those of concerned peoples everywhere. We must not give way to despair. We must have faith. We must hope. We must try to love, to proclaim humanity and the Holy Spirit indwelling in life. I believe that faith must mean not only a holding onto, but also a reaching out. We must make world leaders and governments know and hear and act upon our determination that life on our earth must not be put into jeopardy, that human suffering can and must be relieved. If we have been given any commandment, as I believe we have, then surely it must mean that we pray and work and speak out for peace, and for human and caring justice for all people that on earth do dwell.

"Peace": A Word's Meaning

"'Peace': A Word's Meaning," in the Clara Thomas Archives, York University. No. 1986–006/001 (37), first published in What Peace Means to Me, *External Affairs Canada, 1986, 27, reflects Laurence's respect for language and dislike of its misuse by militarists.*

The United Nations designates a calendar year to issues of global concern as part of its mandate to encourage international cooperation; 1986 was designated the International Year of Peace. Thus, Laurence's essay was probably composed in 1986.

As a writer, I naturally place a high value on the meanings of words, humanity's main means of communication, despite the difficulty of translation. I rejoice in the rich ambiguities of my own language, in which a word, almost without my meaning to, can take on several true and relevant meanings in the same context of writing. Yet all around us we witness language demeaned, words used to mean virtually their opposites.

Advertising often uses words to mislead, to offer meaningless promises. Politicians often use words not to clarify but to conceal what they mean to do. Militarists often use jargon in perhaps the meanest way of all, to obscure the appalling meanings of their statements: in predicting the results of nuclear war they speak of "megadeaths" or "overkill," cold statistical words that actually refer to the possible horrible deaths of millions of children, women, and men, real and helpless humans.

I suggest that "Peace" is a word whose meaning is in danger of being forgotten in our present world, at least by the powers-that-be. I heartily endorse the United Nations' decision to make this year the International Year of Peace. Perhaps, just perhaps, a few more persons in governments, a few more people everywhere, will give thought to this all-encompassing word, "Peace," and even act upon it. Yet it is a word that nearly everyone in the world would claim to believe in. Both superpowers and a whole range of less powerful nations pay lip-service to peace, whilst either waging war or spending billions of whatever currency on nuclear arms or nuclear-weapons-related industries. Peace isn't a great money-making industry. All it might mean, if truly achieved, would be the survival of human life with some measure of social justice and well-being, some means of ensuring the survival of our only home, Earth, and the survival of other creatures who share this planet with us.

"Blessed are the peacemakers, for they shall be called the children of God."[1] These words of Jesus strike a painful and ironic note in today's world. Individuals and groups in the peace movement throughout the world are being called "subversive" in the Eastern European countries and "naive" or "dupes" in Western Europe and North America by governments that purport to believe in peace but are doing little to achieve it in any long-term sense and are meanwhile adding to the arsenals. I am a long-time member of the peace movement, and I am sickened at having it called "naive" and having our motives questioned. It has become suspect in some quarters to believe in the achievable goal of peace and to believe that the violence and fear now endemic in our world need not go on. "Thou shalt love thy neighbour as thyself," said Jesus, preaching love and nonviolence in a world then dominated by Roman military power.[2] In our time, everyone in a much wider world is our neighbour.

Hundreds of billions of dollars are being spent, worldwide, on nuclear weapons. These sums are so vast that we cannot comprehend them. Suffice it to say that, for the cost of one nuclear submarine, the scourge of malaria could be wiped out. Ours is a terrified and terrifying world, suffering and engendering suffering. Violence, brutality, corruption, starvation, thirst, preventable diseases, homelessness, unemployment, pollution of air and water: all are rife, and many are known increasingly in Canada and our cousin-country, America. Reducing these sufferings does not seem to be high on governments' lists of priorities. More and more, nuclear technology takes precedence.

There are two genuinely held and totally opposite points of view.

One is that more and more nuclear weapons will make all of us safer. The other, my own view, is that more nuclear weapons are putting all of us in greater jeopardy every day. Both superpowers now have enough nuclear arms to destroy all life on earth several times over. Both are paranoid, filled with fear and suspicion of the other. Millions of ordinary Americans and Russians, far from politics, must feel as I do, a sense of terror at the intransigence of both regimes. The simple and difficult truth is that whole populations are not "evil Godless communists" or "cruel grasping capitalists." Most ordinary people everywhere just want to live their lives, do their work, have homes and food and a chance at education, bring up beloved children in health, give and receive love and friendship, and be free of the threat of nuclear or any other war. People everywhere *justly* desire the life that true peace could mean.

Canada could have some real effect in lowering the pressures in this potentially lethal arms race. Our commitment to the North Atlantic Treaty Organization does not require our agreement to the testing of American military weapons here, nor does it demand that we sell nuclear materials or manufacture parts for nuclear weapons. Yet Cruise missiles are being tested over Canada; firms here are producing parts with financial aid from our tax dollars. Canada's complicity in the arms race gives our land far lower credibility in a world sense than we could have. I would like Canada to be declared a nuclear-weapons-free land, with no testing of these weapons or manufacture of parts allowed. Canada could play a significant role as mediator, in an attempt to de-escalate the nuclear arms race and to establish a mutual and verifiable reduction of nuclear weapons by both America and Russia. I and many others will keep trying to make our voices heard by our government.

PEACE. A word reverberating with meanings, achievable meanings.

Operation Dismantle

"Operation Dismantle," an unpublished speech in the York University Archives and Special Collections, Margaret Laurence Fonds, No. 1986–006/001 (03), was presented by Laurence on a panel on disarmament in Toronto on 22 October 1982.

I believe that our lives and those of all generations as yet unborn are in deadly peril because of the increasing threat of nuclear war. I believe that the question of disarmament is the most pressing practical, moral, and spiritual issue of our times. I believe that, if we value our own lives and the lives of our children and *all* children, then we must do everything in our power to work nonviolently for the cause of peace. These beliefs are not only an integral part of my ethical and moral stance, but of my religious faith as well.

A central conflict is, of course, the one between two totally opposed points of view. On the one hand, there are those who believe that more and yet more nuclear arms will ensure that nuclear arms will not be used. Peace will be the outcome of a proliferation of the weapons of total destruction. This point of view, I have to admit, both grieves and angers me. I call it the Precipice Theory: the closer we step toward a precipice, the closer we come to the edge, the more we put one foot over and lean out toward the chasm, the less likely we are to fall to our deaths. To me, this makes absolutely no sense at all. In fact, I think it is a deadly fantasy.

The other point of view – that of peace groups everywhere – is that the proliferation of nuclear arms brings us closer every day to the terrifying prospect of nuclear war – a war which no side could win; a war that would be so devastating that even a close reading of a huge amount of factual material and the utmost exercise of our imaginations fail to bring home to us the true extent of that horror – those millions upon millions upon millions of children, women, and men dead and dying, burned, destroyed senselessly, our civilization and our arts and sciences wiped out forever. Increasingly, we are being told that a nuclear war could be "won," or that a nuclear war could be "limited." We are being told that "a first strike capability" is a viable and acceptable concept. No American president has yet shown himself willing to pledge "no first strike" in the use of nuclear arms. The first strike concept is a very simple one – if America were to strike first, Russia would be wiped out and America would not. Or vice versa. I believe this to be a murderously dangerous misconception, and, in any event, what kind of mentality could conceive of the death of countless millions of helpless human beings, whatever their government's ideology? Other factors enter in: the continued and escalating build-up of nuclear arms daily increases the chances of a nuclear holocaust being started by accident, by a failure of the intricate control and warning systems, or simply by human panic. Both America and Russia now possess a nuclear capability that would, in the jargon of the era, "overkill" every creature on earth many times over. We can, however, die but once. Why, then, even from the hawks' point of view, do we need this escalation in the production of nuclear weapons?

Social services are being cut drastically in America and may soon be cut in our own country. Our universities are suffering cut-backs. Unemployment is rife. People throughout the world suffer from preventable diseases, from starvation, from thirst, from homelessness, from hopelessness. Yet 550 *billion* dollars are spent worldwide on armaments, including nuclear arms, and the sum is increasing. To me this is not only insanity; it is brutality.

Yet the peace movement *is* growing, and growing rapidly, throughout the world. Many of our leading scientists and physicians are raising their voices, as are scholars and teachers and artists. The Physicians for Social Responsibility[1] have some 20,000 members in America alone, and these men and women are telling us that civil defence and medical help plans are a sham and a deception: in a nuclear war there would be no help for those horribly mutilated and burned people who had not died immediately, because all of society, including its medical resources, would have broken down. There would be no place to go and no help. Many of our churches and synagogues, too, are speaking out for disarmament and an end to the threat of nuclear war. In Canada, for example, Project Ploughshares is carrying on valuable educational work and peaceful protests. The recent United Nations Second Special Session on Disarmament[2] saw hundreds of thousands of peaceful protesters in New York and in other places proclaiming their conviction that our governments *must* listen to our voices and *must* bring a halt to the arms race. The two recent Nobel Peace Prize winners, Alva Myrdal of Sweden and Alfonso Garcia Robles of Mexico, have long been tireless workers in the cause of disarmament.[3] One could go on and on: Dr Helen Caldicott, Roger Molander, Daniel Ellsberg,[4] and the millions of ordinary women and men throughout the world – people like ourselves, who love our children and our earth – who see that we must make governments hear us, and act. Our goals are nuclear-free areas: a freeze on the production and testing of nuclear arms; a refusal on the part of our government to sell nuclear reactors to unstable regimes; a gradual reduction of nuclear weapons by both sides, monitored by neutral countries. Canada could have enormous effect for good in this situation, and for a start I believe we should pressure our government to refuse the testing of the Cruise missile in Canada and the production of parts for that missile in our country. Many groups, including the Cruise Missile Conversion Project,[5] are devoted to doing everything possible – in a committedly *nonviolent* way – in this cause. Canada could exert considerable influence in lowering the hysteria level between the two major powers, and in bringing about a considered, gradual, and effectively monitored reduction in nuclear arms.

I believe that all groups working for peace by peaceful means must cooperate. This brings me to Operation Dismantle.[6] Why a referendum? The objection to a referendum held on a municipal level has been, of course, that the disarmament issue is not the proper concern of cities and towns, of average citizens, of *us*. I say, if it is not the concern of every one of us, whose concern is it? In a nuclear war, we and our children would die. Our towns and our cities would be destroyed. More and more towns and cities are holding such a referendum, and whatever may come of those projects, they will give individuals a chance to voice their views on an issue that concerns us all. Dr Helen Caldicott, that courageous woman who has done so much in the struggle against nuclear arms, speaks of "psychic numbing" – the temptation to shut out from our minds and hearts all the horrifying implications of the possibility of nuclear war. It is difficult not to feel helpless, not to experience despair, when faced with the enormity of the problem. But I believe that a referendum held at the municipal level can indeed give us a chance to speak out, to register our views, to challenge our government, and, we hope, to communicate with our leaders.

It will not, however, be enough for people simply to vote once and then feel we need not do anything more. There will be an ongoing need for greater education in the whole area of international politics and nuclear armaments and their implications for the future of humankind. There will be – and there will *always* be – a need for a continued commitment to the cause of world peace.

As a writer, I believe that artists have a moral responsibility to work against the nuclear arms race, to work for a recognition on the part of governments and military leaders that nuclear weapons must never be used and must be steadily and systematically refused everywhere. Throughout human history, artists have affirmed and celebrated life. Whether we work in words, in music, in painting, in bronze or stone or whatever our medium, the artist affirms the value of life itself and of our home, Earth. Art mirrors and ponders the pain and joy of our experience as human beings. In many parts of the world, and over many centuries, artists have risked their own lives to portray the societies around them as they perceived them, and to speak out against injustice.

I believe it is imperative that artists join our voices and our efforts to those of all others the world over who feel as we do. In closing, I want to quote one verse from that mighty book, or rather, library, that Dr Northrop Frye has called "The Great Code" and which has so shaped the imagination and the art of the western world. This verse is from Deuteronomy, chapter 30.[7]

"I have set before you life and death, blessing and cursing; therefore choose life, that both thou and thy seed may live."

My Final Hour

"My Final Hour," presented to the Philosophy Society of Trent University in 1983, was first published in Canadian Literature *in 1984.*

I am being given a unique opportunity. I will not have to postpone until my last gasp the imparting of the wisdom of my accumulated years to a breathlessly awaiting world. Just as well, as I have never been much of a believer in "famous last words." I suppose this is why King Lear's words, "Prithee, undo this button,"[1] seem infinitely more moving to me than any high-flown rhetoric purportedly uttered by some well-known person when on the point of departing this vale of tears. Anyway, here I am, faced with the prospect of delivering the message of My Final Hour. I do not promise that it will be My Finest Hour, but I will do my best.

First, I would like to pass on one piece of advice. If, as you grow older, you feel you are also growing stupider, do not worry. This is normal, and usually occurs around the time when your children, now grown, are discovering the opposite – they now see that you aren't nearly as stupid as they had believed when they were young teenagers. Take heart from that. True, your new-found sense of stupidity will no doubt be partly due to the fact that the technology of the age has far outstripped any feeble knowledge of it that you may once have felt you had. It may, however, also be due to the fact that at last you may be learning a little healthy humility – humility in its true and indeed religious sense, which of course has nothing at all to do with self-effacement, but with a recognition of your human limitations. I would not claim that I have learned that kind of humility – that struggle to learn will never cease. But at least I now can accept with some sort of equanimity that many things are beyond my power. I can try to help friends or family or strangers, but I can never "save" another in the profoundest sense. I can do what is within my human power; that is all. Anything else is delusion or spiritual pride, or so I believe. My limitations extend to many fields. I know now that I will never know an enormous amount about music or painting. My knowledge of science is likely to remain minuscule. I will never know as much as I would like to about the planets and their patterned courses. Even in my own area of so-called expertise, I will never read all the novels I would like to read, even though I read great numbers of them yearly. I will also never write a novel with which I am really satisfied. There is so much to do, so much to learn and experience, and one lifetime, however long it may be, is so short. I think of the verse from Psalm 39: "Hear my prayer, O Lord, and give ear unto my cry; hold not thy peace at my tears; for I am a stranger with thee, and a sojourner, as all my fathers were."[2] Mothers, too, I feel compelled to add. Sojourner, yes, but this need not mean "tourist." My lifetime here is a short span, but I am not here as a visitor. Earth is my home. I have tried to read as widely as I can; I have always believed I had to live as well as write, to be a citizen and a person and a mother and a friend, as well as a writer. But basically, I have spent a great part of my adult life in learning a profession – or, as I prefer to call it, a trade – that can never be mastered in its complexity and richness. I am fond of the story about the brain surgeon, who, meeting a novelist at a party, says, "Oh … you're a novelist, eh? When I retire, I plan to take up novel writing." "How interesting," the novelist replies. "When *I* retire, I plan to take up brain surgery."

Well, an acceptance of limitations does not mean that one is not constantly trying to extend the boundaries of knowledge and accomplishment. And it certainly does not mean an acceptance of defeat, in whatever fields our endeavours take place. It is my feeling that as we grow older we should become not *less* radical but *more* so. I do not, of course, mean this in any political-party sense, but in a willingness to struggle for those things in which we passionately believe. Social activism and the struggle for social justice are often thought of as natural activities of the young, but not of the middle-aged or elderly. In fact, I don't think this was ever true, and certainly in our own era we are seeing an enormous upsurge of people of all ages who are deeply and committedly concerned about the state of our hurting and endangered world. There is a line from the old Anglo-Saxon poem "The Battle of Maldon"[3] that I think of frequently. It is this: "Mind must be the firmer, heart the more fierce, courage the greater, as our strength diminishes."

So the basic message of My Final Hour would have to be: do not despair. Act. Speak out. In the words of one of my heroines, Catharine Parr Traill, "In cases of emergency, it is folly to fold one's hands and sit down to bewail in abject terror. It is better to be up and doing."[4]

We are faced now with an emergency that concerns not only our own personal lives but the lives of all people and all creatures on earth. Ours is a terrifying world. Injustice, suffering, and fear are everywhere to be found. It is difficult to maintain hope in such a world, and yet I believe there must be hope. I want to proclaim my belief in the social gospel, as a Christian, a woman, a writer, a mother, and a member of humanity, a sharer in a life that I believe in some way to be informed by the Holy Spirit. I do not think it is enough to hope and pray that our own lives and souls will know grace, even though my entire life as a writer has been concerned with my belief that all individual human beings matter, that no one is ordinary. The new commandment of the man of Nazareth speaks very clearly: "Thou shalt love thy neighbour as thyself."[5]

The social gospel is no easier now than it ever was. My generation was the first in human history to come into young adulthood knowing that the human race now had the dreadful ability to destroy all life on earth and possibly the earth itself. Only later did we realize the full extent of the destruction of life, a continuing destruction passed on to the then-unborn children of survivors, but we *did* know that after Hiroshima, August 6th, 1945, the world would never be the same again. The annihilation caused by the first atomic bombs was unthinkable, but it had happened. Also, we had taken it for granted that, through wars, through disasters, yet would the earth endure forever. It was clear to many of us in 1945 that this was no longer to be taken for granted. We have lived with that thought ever since, and have yet borne our children, lived our lives, done our work. The will to survive and to pass on important caring to future generations is very strong. But today we have to realize that the bombs used at Hiroshima and Nagasaki were *small* bombs, compared to today's nuclear weapons.

I ask you to think of the Holocaust in Europe, when the Nazis murdered a very great part of all the Jewish communities. That horror, surely, must *never* be forgotten. No amount of mourning will *ever* be enough for those millions of children, women, and men whose lives were torn from them by the group of de-humanized humans who had taken power in Hitler's Germany. Are we to remember the Holocaust and the horrors of Hiroshima and Nagasaki and yet remain silent when we hear today about a "winnable" nuclear war or a "limited" nuclear war? I think not.

Our lives and the lives of all generations as yet unborn are being threatened, as never before, by the increasing possibility of a nuclear war. I believe that the question of disarmament is the most pressing practical, moral, and spiritual issue of our times. I'm not talking about abstractions. I'm talking about my life and your life and my kids' lives and the lives of people everywhere. If we value our own lives, and the lives of our children and all children everywhere, if we honour both the past and the future, then we must do everything in our power to work nonviolently for peace. These beliefs are not only an integral part of my social and moral stance, but of my religious faith as well. Human society now possesses the terrible ability to destroy all life on earth, and our planet itself. Can anyone who has ever marvelled at the miracle of creation – who has ever borne or fathered a beloved child, who has even looked closely at a tree or a plant or a river – fail to feel concerned and indeed anguished, every single day, at this thought?

A central disagreement, of course, exists between those who think that more and yet more nuclear arms will ensure that nuclear arms will never be used, and those of us who believe that the proliferation of nuclear weapons brings us closer all the time to the actuality of nuclear war – a war that no side could possibly win, a war that would be so devastating that we cannot begin to imagine that horror. Whatever we are being told about it, the fact remains that such a war could destroy all that we, as humankind, have aspired to, have achieved. It could destroy the future, not only of the world's peoples, but of all creatures that share our planet with us.

As America and Russia develop more and more nuclear arms, so the other will inevitably respond in kind. Nuclear arms have long since ceased to be a "deterrent," if indeed they were ever so, and have become by their very existence a monstrous threat. Daily, the chances are increasing for a nuclear war to break out by accident, by a failure of the intricate and not totally reliable control and warning systems on either side, or simply by human panic and a mutual mistrust between the superpowers.[6]

It is precisely this failure of the imagination on the part of militarists and leaders that is so dangerous today, the failure to visualize what a nuclear holocaust would mean, the apparent inability to imagine the scorched and charred bodies of children – our children or children of Russian parents or parents anywhere – and to know, by an extension of imagination that *all* children are our children. The jargon of the militarists is a distortion and a twisting of language, of our human ability to communicate. Language itself becomes the vehicle of concealment and deception. Such words as "overkill" and "megadeath" do not convey in any sense at all what would really happen – the dead, mutilated, and dying people clogging the ruined cities and towns like so much unvalued discarded rubbish, the suffering humans screaming for help with no medical help available, no water, no relief at all for the unbearable pain of millions of humans except finally the dark relief of death for all. Any shelters that the few might reach would in time turn into tombs. Civil defence plans are a sham. In a nuclear war there would be nowhere to hide, and nowhere except a dead and contaminated world to emerge back into.

I profoundly believe that we must proclaim that *this must not happen.*

Yes, but what about the Russians? If we try to persuade our government to refuse Cruise missile testing, aren't we playing into the hands of the bad guys? Won't the Soviet Union, as soon as they have clear superiority in nuclear arms, blow us all to hell without a second's thought? I do not think so. Isn't it necessary to have more and ever more nuclear weapons in the hands of the Americans so that we can feel *safe?* I do not think so. Let me make it clear that I hold no brief for the present Russian system of government. I hold no brief for any system of government that is repressive and cruel, and this includes those far-right regimes in countries such as El Salvador, to whom the USA is determinedly giving so much military aid. The USA and Russia, the two superpowers, must, I believe, coexist in this world, even if there are some terrible things wrong in *both* systems, and *there are.* Russia suffered horribly in World War II, whereas war has not been fought on American soil since the Civil War. I cannot believe that the Russian leaders are all that anxious to begin nuclear war in which the Soviet Union would be, if not totally annihilated, then certainly decimated beyond any hope of recovery. George Kennan, formerly US ambassador to Russia, who has been awarded both the Pulitzer Prize and the Albert Einstein Peace Prize, and who is a distinguished diplomat, academic, and writer, says in his book *The Nuclear Delusion*:

> Aren't we then ... being unrealistic in the amount of attention we devote to protecting ourselves from the Russians who, God knows, are not ten feet tall, who have all sorts of troubles of their own, who can't run an agricultural system that really works, who can't adequately house their population, who are rapidly losing their prestige and leadership in the world Communist movement, and have to reckon with China on their long fron-

tier in the East? Isn't it grotesque to spend so much of our energy on opposing such a Russia in order to save a West which is honeycombed with
bewilderment and a profound sense of internal decay?

Quite frankly, I can't believe that Russia any longer has hopes of a world revolution. I can believe, though, that the Russian people, the ordinary people who
love their children just as much as I love mine, are frightened, just as I am
frightened, just as a very large proportion of the American people are frightened
and are expressing that fear and outrage. The American people are indeed our
cousins, and a very great many of them, young and old, are saying virtually the
same things as I am saying here.

No American president has as yet declared himself willing to embrace a policy
of "no first strike" in terms of nuclear weapons. President Reagan recently made
the statement that America must reduce Marxism-Leninism "to the ash heap of
history." If he proposed to do this by making his country such a true and fine
example of social justice, of caring for the poor, of equal rights for women, of
peace-making on the international scene, and of a refusal to support corrupt and
violent regimes in, say, Central and South America, so that people the world over
would look to America, as indeed once they did, as the home of the free, then I
would say – *Great*. But I do not think that is what he had in mind. The president
also, not long ago, addressed a group of fundamentalist Christians and told them
that good and evil exist in the world and that the good must utterly destroy the
evil. By evil, he was not referring to organized crime in his own land, or unemployment or poverty in the richest nation in the world. He was talking about
America as wearing the white cowboy hat (to use a metaphor from his Holly-
wood days) and Russia wearing the black one. Good guys and bad guys. George
Kennan says: "I find the view of the Soviet Union that prevails today in large portions of our governmental and journalistic establishments so extreme, so
subjective, so far removed from what any sober scrutiny of external reality would
reveal, that it is not only ineffective but dangerous as a guide to political action."[7]
He concludes this portion of an essay written in 1981 by saying:

And we shall not be able to turn these things around as they should be
turned, in the plane of military and nuclear rivalry, until we learn to correct
these childish distortions ... until we correct our tendency to see in the Soviet Union only a mirror in which we look for the reflection of our own

virtue – until we consent to see there another great people, one of the world's greatest, in all its complexity and variety, embracing the good with the bad, a people whose life, whose views, whose habits, whose fears and aspirations, whose successes and failures, are the products, just as ours are the products, not of any inherent iniquity but of the relentless discipline of history, tradition, and national experience. Above all, we must learn to see the behavior of the leadership of that country as partly the reflection of our own treatment of it. If we insist on demonizing these Soviet leaders ... on viewing them as total and incorrigible enemies, consumed only with their fear or hatred of us and dedicated to nothing other than our destruction – that, in the end, is the way we shall assuredly have them, if for no other reason than that our view of them allows for nothing else, either for them or for us.

In a moving essay written in 1982, entitled "A Christian's View of the Arms Race," Kennan also says, "utterly unacceptable, from the Christian viewpoint as I see it, is the holding of innocent people hostage to the policies of their government, and the readiness, or the threat to punish them as a means of punishing their government."

Our prime minister [Pierre Elliot Trudeau] recently asked the New Democratic Party leader, Ed Broadbent, who was seeking to have the whole issue of the Cruise missile testing debated in the Commons, if he, Broadbent, had written to Soviet leader Andropov to tell *him* to stop testing, too. This snide remark was, of course, beside the point. Our federal government, at the present time talking out of both sides of its collective mouth, says that on the one hand the actual testing of the Cruise hasn't yet been agreed upon and on the other hand Canada must honour its commitment to NATO. According to Pauline Jewett,[8] NDP defence critic, who has done much research on this matter, Canada's commitment to NATO does *not* include the necessity of our allowing *America* – America, not NATO – to test nuclear weapons here. My point is that Canada could have – and must have, in my view – considerable impact as a mediator in nuclear arms talks, as a non-nuclear nation, as a country that might conceivably be helpful in lowering the present climate of hysteria between the two superpowers, and in bringing about world disarmament.

This is why I think we must keep on trying to make our government hear us. Why would I write to Andropov or Reagan? I don't have a vote or a voice in those countries. I have both vote and voice here, though.

I believe that our land should be declared a nuclear-weapons-free zone, with absolutely no testing of nuclear arms or production of parts for those arms allowed in our country. I think that Canada could do a great deal to bring about a gradual and verifiable reduction of nuclear arms by both sides, monitored by neutral countries such as the Scandinavian countries, and to bring about a freeze on the production and testing of nuclear weapons. Canada could be a strong influence for a "no-first-strike" agreement among nations, for multilateral disarmament, and for world peace.

Canada is not powerless; nor are we insignificant in a world sense. Yet our present government appears to be quite willing to allow the Cruise missile to be tested over our land, in Alberta. The Cruise missile, an American nuclear weapon, was not designed as a deterrent weapon; it was designed as a "first-strike weapon." Its presence in the nuclear arsenal will not be verifiable, thus making any kind of nuclear-weapons control virtually impossible. The Litton plant in Ontario is producing, with the aid of millions of *our* tax dollars, guidance systems for the Cruise missile. Canada has sold nuclear reactors to such repressive regimes as Argentina, and is delivering fuel for those reactors, despite the fact that our government is aware that nuclear weapons could soon be within Argentina's capability. These are only a few of the many examples of Canada's complicity in the nuclear arms race.

Do we care so little about our children? Do we honour life so little that we will not speak out? I believe we do care, passionately and profoundly. Indeed, one thing that gives me hope is that so many of our churches and synagogues, so many people of all faiths, of all professions and trades, of all ages, are speaking out against the arms race and the descent into total madness. Physicians for Social Responsibility, active in this country as well as in America and elsewhere, are telling us what human damage would be done, and how impossible any thought of medical aid would be in a nuclear war. Inter-church groups such as Project Ploughshares are making strong representations to our government, as are labour unions, academics, and indeed, and perhaps most importantly, women and men everywhere, in every walk of life. This is true in so very many places in the world today. When I speak of lobbying our own government, that is because we must begin where we are. But we join our voices with those everywhere who believe as we do.

The money spent on arms, including nuclear arms, continues to mount. Recently I read that $550 billion dollars are being spent, worldwide, yearly, on arms.

An even more recent estimate puts it at $600 billion dollars. That sum is so great we cannot really comprehend it. But we *can* comprehend that, for the cost of *one* Trident nuclear submarine, malaria could be wiped out from the world. Think of that for one minute. I think of the people in the world who are suffering from thirst, from starvation, from preventable diseases, from ceaseless fighting, and the brutality of oppressive regimes. I think, too, of the growing number of un-employed people in our own land. I think of the Reagan program in America: more and yet more money spent on nuclear arms; less and less spent on social programs and help to the poor and the disabled.

I have to speak about how I feel as a writer. I don't like calling myself "an artist," but I guess I am, and I would join with my tribal sisters and brothers in many ways. I believe that as a writer – an artist, if you will – I have a responsi-bility, a moral responsibility, to work against the nuclear arms race, to work for recognition on the part of governments and military leaders that nuclear weapons must never be used and must systematically be reduced. Throughout human history, artists have affirmed and celebrated life. Whether we work in words, in music, in painting, in film, in bronze or stone or whatever our me-dium may be, the artist affirms the value of life itself and of our only home, the planet Earth. Art mirrors and ponders the pain and joy of our experience as human beings. In many parts of the world, and over many centuries, artists have risked and even given their own lives to portray the society around them as they perceived it, and to speak out against injustices. Since the most ancient times, artists have passed on to succeeding generations the tales, the histories, the songs, the sagas, the skills of their trade. Can we conceive of a world in which there would be no succeeding generations? A world in which all the powerful works of the human imagination would be destroyed, would never again be seen or listened to or experienced? We must conceive that this is now a possi-bility, and one not too far in our uncertain future, either. We must not, as artists, or so I feel, stand by and passively allow this to happen. The death of the indi-vidual is the end which we will all one day meet, but in the knowledge that our children and their children will live, that *someone's* children will go on, that the great works of humankind will endure in art, in recorded history, in medicine, in the sciences and philosophies and technologies that our species has developed with devotion and a sense of vocation throughout the ages. The individual is the leaf on the tree. The leaves fall, but the tree endures. New leaves are born. This concept has been the mainstay of our species from time immemorial. Now the tree itself is threatened. All art is a product of the human imagination. It is, deeply, an honouring of the past, a perception of the present in one way or another, and a looking toward the future. Whatever the medium of any particular artist, art is a reaching out, an attempt to communicate those things which most concern us seriously in our sojourn here on earth. Artists, the real ones, the committed ones, have always sought, sometimes in ways prophetic and beyond their own times, to clarify and proclaim and enhance life, not to obscure and demean and destroy it. Even the so-called literature of despair is not really that at all. Despair is total silence, total withdrawal. Art, by its very nature of necessary expression, is an act of faith, an acknowledgment of the profound mystery at the core of life.[9]

As a writer, therefore, I feel I have a responsibility. Not to write pamphlets, not to write didactic fiction. That would be, in many ways, a betrayal of how I feel about my work. But my responsibility seems to me to be to write as truthfully as I can about human individuals and their dilemmas, to honour them as living, suffering, and sometimes joyful people. My responsibility also must extend into my life as a citizen of my own land and ultimately of the world.

I do not claim to have done this well. There are no personal victories in those areas. The individual, here, becomes part of a community and only as a part of that community can one person ever be effective and true to herself or himself. There has to be the resolve not to give up, and to join with all others who believe that life itself is more important than our own individual lives, important though these certainly are.

Dr Helen Caldicott speaks of "psychic numbing," the temptation to shut out from our minds and hearts all the terrifying things in our world. To think that the problems may just possibly go away if we ignore them. To feel that we are totally helpless, and so ... why bother trying to do anything? What Dr Caldicott calls "psychic numbing" I would call "despair," and although I would take issue with the early Church Fathers on many things, I would agree that despair is rightly placed as one of the deadly sins. The problems of our world will not go away if we ignore them. It is not all happening on TV. It is happening on our earth, and we, humankind, are the custodians of that earth. We cannot afford passivity. We must take on responsibility for our lives and our world and we must be prepared to make our government listen to and hear us. Our aim must be no less than human and caring justice, and peace ... *for all people that on earth do dwell.*

So, if this were indeed my Final Hour, these would be my words to you. I would not claim to pass on any secret of life, for there is none, or any wisdom except the passionate plea of caring. In your dedication to your own life's work, whatever it may be, live as though you had forever, for no amount of careful and devoted doing is too great in carrying out that work to which you have set your hands. Cultivate in your work and your life the art of patience, and come to terms with your inevitable human limitations, while striving also to extend the boundaries of your understanding, your knowledge, and your compassion. These words are easily said; they are not easily lived. Learn from those who are older than you are; learn from your contemporaries; and never cease to learn from children. Try to feel, in your heart's core, the reality of others. This is the most painful thing in the world, probably, and the most necessary. In times of personal adversity, know that you are not alone. Know that, although in the eternal scheme of things you are small, you are also unique and irreplaceable, as are all your fellow humans everywhere in the world. Know that your commitment is above all to life itself. Your own life and work and friendships and loves will come to an end, because one day you will die, and whatever happens after that, or if anything happens at all, it will not be on this earth. But life and work and friendship and love will go on, in others, your inheritors. The struggle for peace and for social justice will go on – provided that our earth survives and that caring humans still live. It is up to you, now, to do all that you can, and that means a commitment, at this perilous moment in our human history, to ensure that life itself *will* go on.

In closing, I want to quote one verse from that mighty book – more like a vast library – that Dr Northrop Frye calls "The Great Code," and which has so shaped, sometimes so ambiguously, the imagination, the art, and the many facets of faith in our world. This verse is from Deuteronomy, chapter 30:

"I have set before you life and death, blessing and cursing; therefore choose life, that both thou and thy seed may live."

PART FIVE

Socio-political Essays: "Listen, Just Listen"

"Listen, Just Listen"

"Listen, Just Listen," in the Clara Thomas Archives, York University, No. 1980–001/004 (87), was first published in Divided We Stand, *edited by Gary Geddes in 1977.*

On a raw and windy day in March 1977, with the sky a speckless prairie blue and the snow now unseasonably scant on the black Saskatchewan soil, I made a pilgrimage. I had wanted to make it for many years. I walked over the rough ground where the battle of Batoche took place in the spring of 1885, the last battle when the regiments and cannons of the Canadian government forces took three days to overcome the hungry, ill-equipped forces of the Métis people under the leadership of Louis Riel and the heroic Gabriel Dumont. The pleas of the Métis for rights to their ancestral lands had been persistently ignored by Sir John A. Macdonald and his government, and it was only out of desperation that the Métis finally resorted to battle. Middleton's cannon and the well-armed although poorly trained boys from Upper Canada fought the Métis buffalo hunters, who, running out of ammunition, used the last of their powder to fire nails and stones from their rifles.[1] After that defeat, the voices of the Métis fell into silence for years, only to rise again with the present-day descendants of those courageous men and women.

But the old voices are here yet, and anyone who comes here must surely hear them. They are everywhere in the wind. The Métis people who live here now hear those voices and respect them. Only fairly recently was the area officially declared a historic site, but it has always been cared for by the local people. Around the battle area there are fences made in the old way, poplar poles bound with willow strips. No crops are ever planted in that place. It is a sacred ground, in a sense.

The small, white-painted timber church, built in 1884, is still here. Riel and Gabriel must have prayed here, and Gabriel, when he returned home out of exile, must have spent many hours here, remembering.

In the Métis graveyard at Batoche a rough wooden cross stands blunt and huge against the sky. The tombstone of Gabriel Dumont is a slab of red-gray fieldstone, put up a few years ago by the government of the province. The people hereabouts, I am told, preferred the old grave marker, a small plain wooden cross. The big fieldstone, they say, is suitable enough as a gravestone, but it obscures Gabriel's favourite view of his river, the slow-moving, broad South Saskatchewan, where he ran a ferry during some of the years when he served as leader of the South Saskatchewan Métis.

Standing there in the wind, in the prairie spring, in my own land, I said Gabriel's prayer, for myself and as homage to him, and probably for my people and my land as well. Gabriel composed this prayer on his way back from Montana to Saskatchewan with Louis Riel in 1884, and he thereafter said it every day of his life. "Lord, strengthen my courage, my faith, and my honour, that I may profit in my life from the blessing I have received in Thy Holy Name."

I thought of a previous pilgrimage I had made, to the grave of Louis Riel, just outside of St Boniface Cathedral in Manitoba, my home province. Riel's body was brought back to his home, to the province which he, more than anyone else, brought into Confederation, despite the fact that, as an elected member of the House of Commons, he was turned out and refused entry, given over into the years of exile in Montana until he returned in 1884, at his people's request, to Saskatchewan. The stone in St Boniface cemetery is inscribed:

RIEL

16 novembre

1885

No first names, no birth date, no epitaph. This is enough. No more need be said. Those who know of him know how much is said here. The date is the date of his death in Regina, on the scaffold, when he very consciously gave his death to his people and his soul into the keeping of his God.

Why should I feel so strongly about these men, about their people? They were Métis, French-Cree. My people were Celts, Scots, and Irish, who had no reason to love imperialism, either. But there are more and deeper things between myself and Riel, myself and Dumont. We are prairie.

That day at Batoche, I thought of another form of the name Gabriel. Gabrielle. Like myself, a writer, a woman, a person prairie born and raised. Gabrielle Roy, who has now lived for many years in Quebec. I have not met her, but we have corresponded and read each other's writing. I am honoured to call her my friend.[2]

We are, all of us, it seems to me, bound up in one another's history.

I am prairie. I am by ancestry Scots-Irish. I am Canadian.

I first learned my view of the world in my place of birth. I honour my ancestors and I also feel that there is a profound sense in which the ancestors ultimately become all our ancestors. We, in spirit, being linked to the land, are also linked to the ancestral voices which arise out of many sources.

When I think of my own birth area of this land, I think of prairie writers. In this one area alone, our names are Cree, French, Scots, Irish, Métis, English, Jewish, Ukrainian, Hungarian, Mennonite,[3] Icelandic, German, and more. Such diversity is found everywhere in anglophone Canada.

I find myself desperately wanting to explain to the people of Quebec my sense of my own people's reality. "English Canada" is, of course, a misnomer. We are a mixed people who use the English language as a language of communication. For a great many of us, the English language may not be that of our ancestors, but it is our birth language or one of our birth languages, and we love it. It is for us no longer the language of England, nor does it have the connotations of colonialism, for we have changed it and made it our own. I am linked in many ways with the language and literature of Britain, just like every other person who writes in this language. But in a profound sense what I speak and write is Canadian, a form of the language which emanated from England, a form of it which makes use of our own idiom, our own frames of reference, our own perceptions of the life around us.

We, in anglophone Canada, are a nation, just as the Québécois are a nation. I pray that this country will continue to be one, from Vancouver Island to Newfoundland. But if Quebec does ultimately decide to separate, I want to proclaim my belief that the rest of Canada would continue to remain together. Despite all our differences, and despite all the legitimate grievances of the west, say, or the Atlantic Provinces, we have a common cause. We are a very varied family, but we are a family. We will not, I think, permit this land of ours to go by default to our powerful neighbour and cousin to the south of us. Our identity? To me it is as rich and many-faceted as the names of our people. There has never been any doubt about that identity in my mind. Further, I feel no more need of defining it than I do of defining God. I simply know it is there. I can see it and feel it and relate to it in the works of our writers. Wole Soyinka, the Nigerian writer, once said in reference to "négritude," "Does a tiger have to define its tigritude?" If this identity, this sense of belonging, were not there, why else would I feel such a sense of connection with my tribal sisters and brothers, the writers all across this land who are writing in my language? Because we are all writers? True, but I have known writers in England and have felt a common bond of writing with them, and yet not the same deep bond as I do with those of my own people. I would like to feel this bond with the writers of Quebec as well, and I *do* feel it through those of their works which I have read. I would like to see many more translations, going both ways, for surely the reading of our two nations' writing is one of the best means of getting to feel one another's deepest reality.

I find myself wanting to say to the people of Quebec – *Listen. Just listen.* Please. We are the people of anglophone Canada, and our real views aren't being communicated to you by governments, either about your situation or our own. We are teachers and fishermen, farmers and writers, housewives and storekeepers. We care about this land. Our ancestors came from all over the world. Within our diversity lies our strength. It is not a strength which desires to control or devour other lands. It is a growing strength which wishes to free ourselves and our own land from control by other powers. It is a rising strength which wants to reclaim those parts of our land and our resources which have been subject to the neocolonialism of American governments and corporations, and this in no way affects our feeling of cousinhood with the American people themselves. Cannot yourselves and ourselves, our two nations in Canada, join as we never yet have? My barometer, my gauge of the spiritual and emotional weather, is the writing of my contemporaries in both languages, Canadian and Canadien. We are different. Differences are to be honoured, recognized, and understood on both sides. I cannot, quite honestly, visualize a course in the literature of this country in which the writings of either of our two nations could be excluded.

Yet how dare I presume to try to speak to the Québécois, and how dare I ask them to listen to the reality of my people, of all my people in our incredible variety? I dare to do so because I would like to proclaim that we are real, too, and that we are not unacquainted with suffering. I want to speak of the prairie farmers who weathered somehow, or who did not weather, the drought and the Depression of the 1930s, of the bone-poor Newfoundland outporters who lost their men to the sea and their children to the murderous cities, of the West Coast Japanese Canadians who totally without justice or reason (under the iniquitous War Measures Act) [4] in the Second World War were in their thousands wrenched from their homes and put into detention camps and who to this day have never received compensation for their property which was seized from them, and – more than anything – in the beginning of this country as a "country," the taking away of the land from the native peoples by colonialists who believed men could actually *own* the land, whereas the original inhabitants believed that the land belonged to God, the Great Spirit, and was for mankind's shared use.

The oppression – and God knows it has gone on long – of the Québécois is part of an entire system of colonialism and oppression, and I think it must be seen as such.

Despite all these aspects of our common history, I would not presume to try to speak to the Québécois if I were not, first and foremost, wanting to address myself to myself and to my own people.

How shall we speak what is in our hearts? How shall we find ways in which to communicate, really communicate, our deepest feelings to the other nation in this land? Will they listen? Will they believe that a very great many of us do care, do sympathize and agree with their feelings of nationhood? We must go on speaking, reaching out, and hoping.

But we must first listen to them. My hope is that someday we will not have to say "Us" and "Them," [5] but that the people of this country may be able to live in equality and diversity.

Listen. Just Listen.

In anglophone Canada, we have not listened well in the past. That is indisputable. The grievances and the true anger of the people of Quebec, those who have ancestral roots there, have been a long time smouldering. The dried leaves of their discontent have now burst into flames. Why should anyone be surprised? It is time, and more than time, that such a thing happened.

Is there still time? I must believe that there is always time, for everything. And also that there is not much time at all.

If we are to listen truly to what they are saying, we must take into ourselves views which are passionate, though passionately different from our own, views which extend beyond our experience, but which also encompass our history.

And yet I still pray that this country, from Vancouver Island to Newfoundland, may remain one. Not in its present constitutional form, for the grievances of the Québécois, and also those of the Prairies and the Atlantic Provinces and the West Coast, are real and go deep.

We are faced with a turning point sharper than any in our history. If we can communicate well and truly, if we can listen to and hear one another, at the grassroots level, then the present situation could become our greatest opportunity yet, to right old wrongs and to learn about one another. I believe this is possible. I do not place my faith in governments, and yet I think that we must influence governments, or replace them.

Just before I went to Batoche, I was talking with Rudy Wiebe. He is prairie, Mennonite, and one of our finest writers. His novel *The Temptations of Big Bear* is the best work I know which deals with the Indians' uprising of 1885, and his new novel about Riel and Dumont, called *The Scorched-Wood People*, will soon be published. He knows Batoche well.

"When you get there," he said, "listen. Just listen."

The voices in the wind at the Métis cemetery that day spoke of courage and of faith and of injustice. They spoke of our intertwined history, of our ancestors, of our children.

Listen. Just Listen.

Quebec's "Freedom" Is a Vital Concern, but Freedom Itself Is That and More

"Quebec's 'Freedom' Is a Vital Concern, but Freedom Itself Is That and More"
was first published in Maclean's *on 17 April 1978. It conveys Laurence's belief in*
Canadian Confederation and her sympathy with Quebec's nationalist impulses.

In the Canadian unity debate, what is beginning to concern me greatly is the question of civil liberties and civil rights. We now discover that the Security Service of the Royal Canadian Mounted Police[1] has been carrying out, for some years, a host of illegal activities. Prime Minister Trudeau[2] tells us that he doesn't want to know what the RCMP is up to, and he doesn't think we should want to know, either.

Is the RCMP then to be allowed to be a virtually autonomous force, responsible only to its own concepts of what may constitute a national threat, and using whatever methods its top security officers may deem justifiable? Even to contemplate such a setup frightens me a lot. Among our aspirations for our country, is the formation of a police state really one? The revelation that the RCMP acted in 1971 as *agents provocateurs*, with a false communiqué purporting to come from the Front de Libération du Québec,[3] inciting violence, does nothing to reassure me. And what are they up to right this minute in Quebec? Pierre Trudeau may not be curious, but I certainly am.

The notorious War Measures Act, too, has again reared its unlovely head. The act can, by a Cabinet decision, deprive all Canadians of their civil rights. Mr Trudeau says he would not be "shy of using the sword if something illegal is attempted by the province of Quebec." He speaks proudly of his use of the War Measures Act in 1970.[4] Surely most Canadians would now concede that in 1970 no national crisis happened; the FLQ was not a broadly based revolutionary organization. Yet hundreds of innocent citizens were imprisoned and held without either bail or trial. The history of the War Measures Act is not an honourable one.

Admittedly, Mr Trudeau, in reference to the possibility of again invoking the act, was speaking of circumstances in which the Parti Québécois[5] might attempt to seize federal property. But as far as I know, the PQ has never suggested even the remote possibility of such a thing. So why the talk of the War Measures Act? Why the metaphors of war?

With elegant timing, the now defunct *Le Jour*[6] then published a report by a former army officer, now a separatist, on the need for Quebec to have its own army. As it turned out, the report had been written two years earlier and on the ex-officer's own initiative, but no doubt it added more fuel to the fire. So does the process of escalation take place.

I worry about the rights of anglophones in Quebec, about the rights of minority groups, whether they have lived there a long time or not, not only those of English descent, of course, but the Jews, the Italians, and all the others. I also worry greatly about a denial of their right to have their children educated in the English language if they should want to do so.

But can anyone deny that the Québécois have been short-changed in their own area for generations? Or that the language rights of francophone Canadians in other provinces have been virtually ignored? Only one province in anglophone Canada, namely New Brunswick, is officially bilingual. Premier William Davis[7] has made it clear that he isn't going to be in a hurry to make French an official language in Ontario. In my native province of Manitoba, the large French-speaking community lost its language rights – in education, in the provincial legislature, in the courts – after a prolonged and bitter struggle in the late 1800s. The record, in English-speaking Canada, of guaranteeing language rights to the other founding nation in the country has been consistently abysmal.

René Lévesque[8] says that if the Quebec referendum[9] goes against separation, he will not feel bound by it. Trudeau says that, if the Quebec referendum goes in favour of separation, he will not feel bound by it. What have we here? Who are these men who would so blithely go against the expressed will of the total population of Quebec, if such expression went against their own hopes? What is the point in asking the people of Quebec their view if, whichever way this goes, it will be ignored either by the federal or by the provincial government? Both these leaders are declaring a basic disregard for the will of the people.

I do not think it is too late to remedy old wrongs. But if this land is to remain one, it certainly cannot do so under the present form of federalism. Any new constitution will have to recognize the fact that the Québécois are a nation, bound together by ancestral roots, culture, language, religion. It will also have to recognize the legitimate and longtime grievances and needs of other regions – the West Coast, the Prairies, the Atlantic Provinces, and above all, the grievances, needs, and rights of the native peoples, who have suffered more injustice than any other people in this land. But such discussions, if they are to have any chance of success, must be carried out with as much calm and mutual respect as can possibly be brought to bear.

I believe that without Quebec this country would be poorer in spirit and in culture than it is, or than it has the potential of becoming. I do not, however, believe that without Quebec this country would disintegrate and fall prey to the United States. The one unthinkable thought to me would be the use of violence to keep Quebec within Confederation. If an external invader attacked my country I would be prepared to defend it to the last breath, but as a citizen I would never willingly see violence used to keep in Confederation any part of this country that did not want to remain. I would grieve if Quebec were to part from the rest of Canada, but I have to state unequivocally that the entire cause of Canadian Confederation would never be worth the life of my son or of any of our sons on either side.

Whatever the future holds for us, both Canadians and Québécois, we must surely try to understand the reality of one another and to honour one another's differences. We must be aware of our civil liberties; if we are not willing to speak up and defend them, one day they may not be there.

Open Letter to the Mother of Joe Bass

This essay, first published in Al Purdy's The New Romans: Candid Canadian *Opinions of the* USA *in 1968 and republished in* Maclean's *in October 1968, was collected in* Heart of a Stranger *in 1976 with the following introduction: "In 1967 Al Purdy was putting together a collection by Canadian writers on the theme of our views of America. Taking time out from writing his own poetry, sighing and swearing and smoking his innumerable cigars, Purdy was conning or charming a lot of Canadian writers into contributing. What it turned out to be, in the end, was an extremely diverse and interesting collection of essays and poems, published in 1968 under the title of* The New Romans."[1]

Joe Bass was shot unintentionally by police when they shot at Bill Furr, who was stealing beer from a liquor store. Although rumoured to have been killed, Bass survived, while Furr died. The 7 July 1967 incident was featured in Life Magazine *on 28 July 1967.*

I don't know what you look like. We will not meet. I don't know how old you are. About my age, I would guess, which is forty-one. I don't know how many kids you have. I have two. My daughter is fifteen, and my son is twelve. You have a twelve-year-old son also.

My son was born in Ghana, and there was no doctor present. The doctor was overworked, and I was okay and normal, so there was only a midwife in attendance. She was a Ghanaian matriarch, four kids of her own, and no male doctor could have known what she knew.

"It will be a boy," she promised me as the hours passed by. "Only a man could be so stubborn."

When I was in pain she put out her hands to me and let me clench them, and I held to those hands as though they were my hope of life.

"It will be soon over," she said. "Would I lie to you? Look, I know. I have borne."

She did know. I had no anaesthetic, and when she delivered him, she laid him, damp and thin and blood-smeared, across my belly.

"There," she said. "What did I tell you? Your boy, he is here."

She was the only other person present when I looked over God's shoulder at the birth of my son. She had had her children too, and she knew what it was that was happening. She knew that it had to be felt in the flesh to be really known.

In twelve years so far, touch wood, my son has been lucky. Once in Africa he had malaria, and a few other times, in Canada and England, he had such things as throat infections or chicken pox. Each time I have been afraid in that one way, guts-of-ice feeling that I could probably face anything at all except that something really bad should happen to one of my kids.

He has lived life so far among people who were basically friendly toward him. That is not to say that he has never felt pain. He has. More, even, than I know, and I know some of it. But at least until this point in his life, his pain has been something which he could, in some way, deal with by himself.

I have seen your son only once, Mrs Bass. That was in a newspaper photograph. In Detroit, he went out one evening when his playmates asked him to. It was not an evening to be out. Your son was shot by the police. By accident, the paper said. Shot by accident in the neck. The police were aiming at Billy Furr, who was walking out of Mack Liquors, not with a fortune in his hands but with precisely six tins of stolen beer. When Billy Furr saw the police, something told him to run and keep on running, so he did that, and he was shot dead. But the police had fired more than once, and Joe Bass happened to be in the way. The papers did not say whether he was expected to recover or not, nor how much a twelve-year-old could recover from something like that. A Negro twelve-year-old.

Your son looked a skinny kid, a little taller than my twelve-year-old but not as robust. He was lying on the sidewalk, and his eyes were open. He was seeing everything, I guess, including himself. He was bleeding, and one of his hands lay languidly outstretched in a spillage of blood. His face didn't have any expression at all. I looked at the picture for quite a long time. Then I put it away, but it would not be put away. The blank kid-face there kept fluctuating in my mind. Sometimes it was the face of your son, sometimes of mine.

Then I recalled another newspaper photograph. It was of a North Vietnamese woman. Some marvellous new kind of napalm had just come into use. I do not understand the technicalities. This substance, when it alights, flaming, onto skin, cannot be removed. It adheres. The woman was holding a child who looked about eighteen months old, and she was trying to pluck something away from the burn-blackening area of the child's face. I wondered how she felt when her child newly took on life and emerged, and if she had almost imagined she was looking over God's shoulder then.

Mrs Bass, these are the two pictures. I know they are not fair. I know the many-sidedness of that country in which you live. I know the people I love there, who are more heartbroken than I at the descent into lunacy. Also, I am a North American – I cannot exclude myself from the dilemma. I cannot say *them*. It is forced upon me to say *us*. Perhaps you know who the enemy is – and perhaps it is I.

Once, a long time ago, from the eyes of twenty, I wrote a poem about my father, or maybe about the local cemetery, in which the words said, "Under the stone lies my father, ten years dead, who would never know as his this bastard world he sired." It did not occur to me then that I would one day stand in that same relation to the world – no longer as a child, but as a parent.

I am not even sure who is responsible. Responsibility seems to have become too diffuse, and a whole continent (if not, indeed, a whole world) appears to be spinning in automation. The wheels turn, but no one admits to turning them. People with actual names and places of belonging are killed, and there is increasingly little difference between these acts and the fake deaths of the cowboys who never were. The fantasy is taking over, like the strangler vines of the jungle taking over the trees. It is all happening on TV.

Except that it isn't. You know, because you felt the pain in your own flesh, that evening when the police shot your son. Is it necessary to feel pain in our own flesh before we really know? More and more, I think that it probably is.

I have spent fifteen years of my life writing novels and other things. I have had, if any faith at all, a faith in the word. *In the beginning was the Word, and the Word was with God, and the Word was God*. The kind of belief that many writers have – the belief that if we are to make ourselves known to one another, if we are really to know the reality of another, we must communicate with what is almost the only means we have – human speech. There are other means of communication, I know, but they are limited because they are so personal and individual. We can make love; we can hold and comfort our children. Otherwise, we are stuck with words. We have to try to talk to one another, because this imperfect means is the only one we have.

And yet – I look at the picture of your twelve-year-old son on the sidewalks of Detroit, pillowed in blood. And I wonder – if it were in physical fact *my* son, of the same age, would I be able to go on writing novels, in the belief that this was a worthwhile thing to be doing in this year (as they say) of our Lord? Mrs Bass, I do not think I can answer that question.

I am afraid for all our children.

The Greater Evil: Pornography or Censorship?

"The Greater Evil" was first published in Toronto Life *(September 1984) and reprinted in* Dance on the Earth.

I have a troubled feeling that I may be capable of doublethink, the ability to hold two opposing beliefs simultaneously. In the matter of censorship, doublethink seems, alas, appropriate. As a writer, my response to censorship of any kind is that I am totally opposed to it. But when I consider some of the vile material that is being peddled freely, I want to see some kind of control. I don't think I am being hypocritical. I have a sense of honest bewilderment. I have struggled with this inner problem for years, and now, with the spate of really bad video films and porn magazines flooding the market, my sense of ambivalence grows. I am certain of one thing, though. I cannot be alone in my uncertainty.

I have good reason to mistrust and fear censorship. I have been burned by the would-be book censors. Not burned in effigy, nor suffered my books being burned, not yet anyhow. But burned nonetheless, scorched mentally and emotionally. This has happened in more than one part of Canada, but the worst experience for me was in my own county of Peterborough a few years ago, when a group of people, sincere within their limited scope, no doubt, sought to have my novel *The Diviners* banned from the grade 13 course and the school libraries.[1] The book was attacked as obscene, pornographic, immoral, and blasphemous. It is, I need hardly say, none of these things. Open meetings of the school board were held. Letters, pro and con, appeared in the local newspaper. Some awful things were said about the book and about me personally, mostly by people who had not read the book or met me. In retrospect, some of the comments seem pretty funny, but at the time I was hurt and furious. One person confidently stated, "Margaret Laurence's aim in life is to destroy the home and the family." In an interview, another person claimed that the novel contained a detailed account, calculated to titillate, of the sex life of the housefly. I couldn't recollect any such scene. Then I remembered that when Morag, as a child, is embarrassed by the sad, self-deprecating talk of her stepmother, the gentle, obese Prin, the girl seeks anything at all to focus on, so she need not listen. "She looked at two flies fucking, buzzing as they did it." Beginning and end of sensational scene. The reporter asked if the fundamentalist minister himself had found the scene sexually stimulating. "Oh no," was the reply. "I'm a happily married man." At one open meeting, a man rose to condemn the novel and said that he spoke for a delegation of seven: himself, his wife, their four children – and God. In another county, a bachelor pharmacist accused me of adding to the rate of venereal disease in Canada by writing my books. He claimed that young people should not be given any information about sex until they are physically mature – "at about the age of twenty-one." I hope his knowledge of pharmacy was greater than his knowledge of biology.

Many readers, teachers, and students did speak out for the novel, which was ultimately restored to the grade 13 course. But the entire episode was enough to make me come down heavily against censorship, and especially against self-appointed groups of vigilantes. At the time I made a statement, which said, in part, "Surely it cannot do other than help in the growing toward a responsible maturity, for our young people to read novels in which many aspects of human life are dealt with, by writers whose basic faith is in the unique and irreplaceable value of the human individual."

I hold to that position. Artists of all kinds have been persecuted, imprisoned, tortured, and killed, in many countries and at many times throughout history, for portraying life as they honestly saw it. Artistic suppression and political suppression go hand in hand, and always have. I would not advocate the banning of even such an evil and obscene book as Hitler's *Mein Kampf*. I think we must learn to recognize our enemies, to counter inhuman ranting with human and humane beliefs and practices. With censorship, the really bad stuff would tend to go underground and flourish covertly, while works of genuine artistic merit might get the axe (and yes, I know that "genuine artistic merit" is very difficult to define). I worry that censorship of any kind might lead to the suppression of anyone who speaks out against anything in our society, the suppression of artists, and the eventual clamping down on ideas, human perceptions, questionings. I think of our distinguished constitutional lawyer and poet F.R. Scott. In an essay written in 1933, he said: "'The time, it is to be hoped, has gone by,' wrote John Stuart Mill, 'when any defence would be necessary of the principle of freedom of speech.' His hope was vain. The time for defending freedom never goes by. Freedom is a habit that must be kept alive by use."

And yet – my ambivalence remains. The pornography industry is now enormous and includes so-called "kiddie porn." Most of us do not look at this stuff, nor do we have any notion how widespread it is, nor how degrading and brutal toward women and children, for it is they who are the chief victims in such magazines and films. Let me make one thing clear. I do not object to books or films or anything else that deals with sex, if those scenes are between two adults who are entering into this relationship of their own free will. (You may well say – what about *Lolita*? I hated the book, as a matter of fact, and, no, I wouldn't advocate banning Nabokov. Ambivalence.) I do not object to the portrayal of social injustice, of terrible things done to one human by another or by governments or groups of whatever kind, as long as this is shown for what it is. But when we see films and photographs, *making use of real live women and children*, that portray horrifying violence, whether associated with sex or simply violence on its own, as being acceptable, on-turning, a thrill a minute, then I object.

The distinction must be made between erotic and pornographic. Eroticism is the portrayal of sexual expression between two people who desire each other and who have entered into this relationship with mutual agreement. Pornography, on the other hand, is the portrayal of coercion and violence, usually with sexual connotations, and like rape in real life, it has less to do with sex than with subjugation and cruelty. Pornography is not in any sense life affirming. It is a denial of life. It is a repudiation of any feelings of love and tenderness and mutual passion. It is about hurting people, mainly women, and having that brutality seen as socially acceptable, even desirable.

As a woman, a mother, a writer, I cannot express adequately my feelings of fear, anger, and outrage at this material. I have to say that I consider visual material to be more dangerous than any printed verbal material. Possibly I will be accused of being elitist and of favouring my own medium, the printed word, and possibly such a charge could be true. I just don't know. The reason I feel this way, however, is that these films and photographs make use of living women and children – not only a degradation of them, but also a strong suggestion to the viewer that violence against women and children, real persons, is acceptable. One of the most sinister aspects of these films and photographs is that they frequently communicate the idea that not only is violence against women okay – women actually *enjoy* being the subject of insanely brutal treatment, actually enjoy being chained, beaten, mutilated, and even killed. This aspect of pornography, of course, reinforces and purports to excuse the behaviour of some men who do indeed hate women. I could weep in grief and rage when I think of this attitude. As for the use of children in pornography, this is unspeakable and should be forbidden by law. The effect of this material is a matter of some dispute, and nothing can be proved either way, but many people believe that such scenes have been frighteningly re-enacted in real life in one way or another.

But is censorship, in any of the media involved, the answer? I think of John Milton's *Areopagitica: A Speech for the Liberty of Unlicensed Printing, to the Parliament of England*, in 1644, in which these words appear: "He that can apprehend and consider vice with all her baits and seeming pleasures, and yet abstain, and yet distinguish, and yet prefer that which is truly better, he is the true wayfaring Christian. I cannot praise a fugitive and cloistered virtue, unexercised and unbreathed, that never sallies out and sees her adversary, but slinks out of the race, where that immortal garland is to be run for, not without dust and heat." Obviously, Milton was not thinking of the sort of video films that anyone can now show at home, where any passing boy child can perhaps get the message that cruelty is ok and fun, and any passing girl child may wonder if that is what will be expected of her, to be a victim. All the same, we forget Milton's words at our peril.

The situation is not without its ironies. It has created some very strange comrades-in-arms. We find a number of feminists taking a strong stand *for* censorship and being praised and applauded by people whose own stance is light-years away from feminism – the same people who would like my books, Alice Munro's books, W.O. Mitchell's books, banned from our high schools. We see civil libertarians who are *against* censorship and for free expression arguing that "anything goes," a view that must rejoice the hearts of purveyors of this inhumane material, but certainly distresses mine.

I consider myself to be both a feminist and a strong supporter of civil liberties and free speech, but there is no way I want to be on the same team as the would-be book-banning groups who claim that no contemporary novels should be taught or read in our schools. There is no way, either, that I want to be on the same team as the pornographers.

What position can a person like myself honestly take? The whole subject is enormously complex, but I must finally come down against a censorship board, whether for the visual media or for the printed word. I think that such boards tend to operate by vague and ill-defined standards. What can "acceptable community standards" possibly mean? It depends on which community you're talking about, and within any one community, even the smallest village, there are always going to be wide differences. Censorship boards tend to be insufficiently accountable. I believe that, in cases of obscenity, test cases have to be brought before the courts and tried openly in accordance with our federal obscenity laws. The long-term solution, of course, is to educate our children of both sexes to realize that violence against women and children, against anyone, is not acceptable, and to equalize the status of women in our society.

What about Section 159 of the Criminal Code,[2] "Offences Tending to Corrupt Morals"? My impression of federal law in this area is that its intentions are certainly right, its aims are toward justice, and it is indeed in some ways woefully outdated and in need of clarification. Clarification and amendment have not been and will not be easy. The clause that is most widely known to the general public is Section 159 (8): "For the purpose of this Act, any publication a dominant characteristic of which is the undue exploitation of sex, or of sex and any one or more of the following subjects, namely, crime, horror, cruelty and violence, shall be deemed to be obscene." I think the first use of the words "of sex" could be deleted. How much sex between consenting adults is too much? Are three scenes okay, but ten excessive? Frankly, among the many things I worry about in my life, as a citizen and as a writer, this is not one of them. But how are we to enshrine in our laws the idea that the degradation and coercion of women and children, of anyone, is dreadful, without putting into jeopardy the portrayal of social injustice seen as injustice? How are we to formulate a law that says the use of real women and children in situations of demeanment and violence, shown as desirable fun stuff, is not acceptable, while at the same time not making it possible for people who don't like artists questioning the status quo to bring charges against those who must continue to speak out against the violation of the human person and spirit?

In one case cited in the Criminal Code, the judge declares: "The onus of proof upon the Crown may be discharged by simply producing the publication without expert opinion evidence. Furthermore, where, although the book has certain literary merit particularly for the more sophisticated reader, it was available for the general public to whom the book was neither symbolism nor a psychological study the accused cannot rely on the defense of public good." "Public good" is later defined as "necessary or advantageous to religion or morality, to the administration of justice, the pursuit of science, literature or art, or other objects of general interest." If this precedent means what it appears to say, it alarms me. It appears to put works of "literary merit" into some jeopardy, especially as expert opinion evidence need not be heard. If a book of mine were on trial, I would certainly want expert opinion evidence. I do not always agree with the views of the literary critics, or of teachers, but at least, and reassuringly, many of them know how to read with informed skill.

Realizing the difficulty of accurate definitions, I think that violence itself, shown as desirable, must be dealt with in some way in this law. It is *not* all right for men to beat and torture women. *It is wrong.* I also think that the exploitation of real live children for "kiddie porn" should be dealt with as a separate issue in law and should not be allowed, ever.

The more I think about it, the more the whole question becomes disturbingly complicated. Yet I believe it is a question that citizens, Parliament, and the legal profession must continue to grapple with. It is not enough for citizens to dismiss our obscenity laws as inadequate and outdated, and then turn the whole matter over to censorship boards. Our laws are not engraved on stone. They have been formulated carefully, although sometimes not well, but with a regard to a general justice. The law is not perfect, but it *is* public. It can be changed, but not upon the whim of a few. An informed and alert public is a necessary component of democracy. When laws need revisions, we must seek to have them revised, not toward any narrowing down, but toward a greater justice for all people, children, women, and men, so that our lives may be lived without our being victimized, terrorized, or exploited. Freedom is more fragile than any of us in Canada would like to believe. I think again of F.R. Scott's words: "Freedom is a habit that must be kept alive by use." Freedom, however, means responsibility and concern toward others. It does not mean that unscrupulous persons are permitted to exploit, demean, and coerce others. It is said, correctly, that there is a demand for pornography. But should this demand be used to justify its unchallenged existence and distribution? Some men are said to "need" pornography. To me this is like saying some men "need" to beat up their wives or commit murder. Must women and children be victims in order to assuage the fears and insecurities of those men who want to feel they are totally powerful in a quite unreal way? I don't think so. If some men "need" pornography, then I as a woman will never be a party to it, not even by the tacit agreement of silence. We and they had better try together to control and redirect those needs. I think that citizens can and should protest in any nonviolent way possible against the brutalities and callousness of pornography, including one area I haven't even been able to deal with here, the demeanment of women in many advertisements.

In the long run, it is all-important to raise our children to know the reality of others; to let them know that sex can and should be an expression of love and tenderness and mutual caring, not hatred and domination of the victor/victim kind; to communicate to our daughters and our sons that to be truly human is to try to be loving and responsible, strong not because of power but because of self-respect and respect for others.

In *Areopagitica*, Milton said: "That which purifies us is trial, and trial is by what is contrary." In the final analysis, we and our society will not stand or fall by what we are "permitted" to see or hear or read, but by what we ourselves choose. We must, however, have some societal agreement as to what is acceptable in the widest frame of reference possible, but still within the basic concept that *damaging people is wrong.* Murder is not acceptable, and neither is the abasement, demeanment, and exploitation of human persons, whatever their race, religion, age, or gender. Not all of this can be enshrined in law. Laws can never make people more understanding and compassionate toward one another. That is what individual people try to do, in our imperfect and familial ways. What the law *can* do is attempt to curb, by open process in public courts, the worst excesses of humankind's always-in-some-way-present inhumanity to humankind.

This is as close as I can get to formulating my own beliefs. It is an incomplete and in many ways a contradictory formulation, and I am well aware of that. Perhaps this isn't such a bad thing. I don't think we can or should ever get to a point where we feel we know, probably in a simplistic way, what all the answers are or that we ourselves hold them and no one else does. The struggle will probably always go on, as it always has in one way or another. The new technology has brought its own intricacies. I doubt that the human heart and conscience will ever be relieved of their burdens, and I certainly hope they are not. This particular struggle, *for* human freedom and *against* the awfulness that seeks to masquerade as freedom but is really slavery, will not ever be easy or simple, but it is a struggle that those of us who are concerned must never cease to enter into, even though it will continue to be, in Milton's words, "not without dust and heat."

Statement – PEN

Laurence's unpublished "Statement – PEN," in the Clara Thomas Archives, York University. No. 1986–006/001 (41) and 1989–039/010 (207), was read in her absence by Timothy Findley at the Harbourfront Centre, Toronto, Ontario on 7 May 1985.

Dear Friends – I am sorry I cannot be with you tonight, but I am with you in spirit. What we have to realize is that we *can* make a difference by raising our voices in protest against the imprisonment, torturing, and silencing of our fellow writers in many parts of the world. Members of PEN International[1] have been doing so for many years. We can focus attention on the injustices and horrors committed by repressive regimes against those most vocal and least submissive persons, writers. And we *can* help to get some of those incarcerated writers released.

We must continue to speak out on behalf of our colleagues everywhere, who are being oppressed because they have presented a view of their society and of life itself from the sight of their own unblinking eyes, a view that is against jargon and the distortion of words, a view that is passionately *for* all suffering humanity. Whether the oppression of writers is done by regimes of the extreme Right or the extreme Left, the effect is the same – men and women cruelly abused and their words silenced.

I stand with all writers who care about the human condition, who feel our-selves to be a part of all humanity, who desire justice for all persons. I stand with writers everywhere who believe, as a basic moral precept, that *hurting people is wrong*, who despise racism and militarism and the demeanment and exploita-tion of women, children, and men, anywhere, any time.

In Canada, we are fortunate. As writers, we are not imprisoned, tortured, killed. But let us not deceive ourselves. Anything that could happen anywhere could happen here. Writers here are under attack, too. Remember the old saying: "Sticks and stones can break my bones, but names can never hurt me"? The saying is untrue. The accusations against a serious writer who is called, by a virulent minority, "dirty," "disgusting," "disrespectful of humanity," "blasphemous," "pornographic," and so on, although levelled by people who are, to put it charitably, very unskilled readers, *can hurt*, as I know to my sorrow. When those people say those things about my books, they are saying them about me. And yes, although I have not been physically hurt, I have been emotionally and psychically hurt by all this. The school board in my own county of Peterborough, after four months of hearing such accusations and also hearing many statements of support for my books and J.D. Salinger's *Catcher in the Rye*, has now restored these books to the local high school courses. I received hundreds and hundreds of letters of support, from all over Canada and indeed from America and England. The Textbook Review Committee, set up to examine these books, also received some 800 letters of support for the books, from local people and from readers across the land. I was extraordinarily grateful. The thing about this latest controversy over my books in my own country, for it has happened before eight years ago, is that it was all out in the open. It was covered by the press. The meetings of the Textbook Review Committee and the school board were open meetings. Nothing was done behind closed doors. For this process, I give thanks. We need not think, however, that the problem is laid to rest, here or anywhere. In so-called "safe" Canada, we are not and never will be immune to the attacks of people who would like our books banned and who see nothing wrong in character assassination.

But let us not deceive ourselves. We are not and never will be immune from the attacks of people who would like to have our books banned and ourselves subjected to character assassination. They are not going to go away. The attacks on the serious writer who presents her view of the world in as honest a way as she can will always go on. We must never cease from this struggle, the struggle of Athens against Sparta, the struggle to maintain freedom of speech against those who would clamp down and kill the words of the wordsmiths who try to write about and explore and celebrate life.

I have not suffered in the flesh, as my sisters and brothers in Eastern Europe, in Central and South America, in South Africa, have done. But I have known enough attacks on my work, enough misunderstanding of my writing, enough hate directed toward me by people who proudly proclaim that they haven't read my books – only a few paragraphs here and there – to see and know the plight of writers everywhere. Members of our tribe of scribes and storytellers, of poets, essayists, and novelists, must forever stand together, for in this struggle there are no national boundaries.

A Constant Hope: Women in the Now and Future High Tech Age

In "A Constant Hope: Women in the Now and Future High Tech Age," first pub-lished in Canadian Woman Studies / Les Cahiers de la Femme *in 1985, and reprinted in* Dance on the Earth, *Laurence responds to Marian Kester's article, "The Awful Price of the Computer Age," published in the* Toronto Globe and Mail, *9 August 1984, in which Kester begins by lamenting the time children spend with violent and dehumanizing television and video games and ends by asking who will teach children to be human.*

Any speculation about women in the future must be preceded by a question. Will there be a future, not only for women but for everyone, for the planet itself? Un-less the nuclear arms race can be halted, unless the nations that possess nuclear weapons, and especially the two superpowers, can be persuaded to make genuine efforts to end this lunacy, the prospects do not look promising. Women have taken a large part in the growing peace and disarmament movement, and I be-lieve we must take an even greater part in the future and on behalf of the future. For this article, I am assuming there will be a future for life itself, and this is no longer something we can take for granted. We are living in an age of high tech-nology, an age in which computers and other intricate machines are seen as humankind's salvation. The new religion comes to us complete with its own priesthood and even its own language. Those who have not yet learned this lan-guage, and who do not own or have access to these pieces of sophisticated equipment, are made to feel inadequate and threatened. If we do not have a com-puter, or cannot afford one, will we not become obsolete, irrelevant? This issue affects women deeply now, and will continue to do so, as does the use to which a lot of the high tech stuff is being put and will be put in the future. The new technology can do some marvellous things, but it cannot take the place of human wisdom, compassion, common sense, and conscience, and these values now seem to be at risk in the face of the ubiquitous machines. The technology is still largely male-dominated. I believe that women must take a very level look at the problems of the new technology before they overwhelm us. We must not be intimidated by the sales pitches that imply that everyone must buy a home computer or be left far behind. On the other hand, as many women are realizing, we need to be informed about these tools, because otherwise we will be at an even greater disadvantage in the work force than we are now, and the machines will be used to control us, our bodies and lives, and the minds of our children. In cases where possession of machinery isn't the question, and learning their use isn't possible for most women, as with much hospital equipment, we must familiarize ourselves with procedures, so we can have much more of a voice in the use of these wonderful but by no means miraculous or infallible machines.

Women have already learned, to their sorrow, that a pregnant woman's prolonged exposure to video-display terminals may damage her unborn child. Women of all ages must not look passively on while even a few of our sisters and daughters run the risk of either losing their jobs or bearing damaged babies. Nothing has yet been conclusively proved, but any risk is outrageous if it is preventable. Another and related area of risk is the enormous array of high tech devices now routinely used during childbirth, by doctors who often seem to put more faith in machinery than in the mother's ability and right to deliver her own child, with as much encouragement and human help as medical staff can provide, and as little mechanical intervention as possible. "Labour" means hard work. Too often, now, in childbirth, it means passivity and even total unconsciousness. Male doctors, especially, have long tried, with much success, alas, to make the birth of children *their* achievement, as though the mother were simply a vessel, full of child but soon to be emptied efficiently by the doctor and his machinery, instead of an active participant in what can be one of the most awesome experiences of life. When the Caesarian section is necessary, obviously it saves the lives of children and mothers. No one would deny or fail to be grateful for the magnificent accomplishments of modern medical science. But there are many occasions now when the C-section is not necessary and is performed more for the convenience (and monetary reward) of the doctor than for the safety and well-being, physical and emotional, of mother and child. This practice will continue and even escalate in the future unless women take a very active part in informing themselves and in proclaiming their rights. The thought of routinely monitoring the foetal heart by fancy machinery, in normal deliveries, or putting electrodes into the nearly born infant's skull, fills me with doubts and questions. Not all women want to have their children by natural childbirth, of course, but in cases where the pregnancy has been normal and the delivery promises to be so, mothers must surely have the option of a natural delivery, with the child's father supportedly present if both parents wish it. More women are now opting for a home delivery, with a trained midwife, but the medical profession is still overwhelmingly hostile to this practice, although these births are known to be, on average, as safe as hospital births with all the machinery.

What about bringing up children in the future? That future is now with us, and its effect, in terms of certain aspects of technology, can only increase in a negative way unless women (and more and more men, it is to be hoped and prayed) take a strong stand. In an article in the Toronto *Globe and Mail* (9 August 1984) entitled "The Awful Price of the Computer Age," Marian Kester, a freelance journalist based in Washington, wrote: "If children are separated from their parents by hours of TV, from their playmates by video games and from their teachers by teaching machines, where are they supposed to learn how to be human? Maybe that's just it. There's no percentage in being human anymore." I understand her feelings of dismay, and yet I believe that we must not now or in the future give way to this awful feeling of helplessness. There was a time when TV was regarded (and still is, by some parents) as a handy babysitter. We are beginning to know just how dire can be the effect of children's growing up watching countless hours of TV violence. We have yet fully to see the effects of countless hours of their playing video war and violence games. These games don't make children smarter, and certainly not kinder and wiser. They tend to make kids (and the games are said to be more popular with male children) oriented toward winning at the expense of everything else. They encourage an attitude of "good guys" and "bad guys" in an absolute sense, and often the so-called good guys are performing acts of horrendous brutality. The war games encourage and sanctify cruelty, especially toward women and minority groups. They separate a child from the real world of family and friends, of beauty and tragedy. What appears to be action is really passivity. Hit all those little buttons and save the world from the monsters! Advertising, of course, is making these games super-popular among the young. Meantime, outside, the powers are preparing for war. If it happens, it will not be the first time in our era for the young to stride off to war, whistling a merry tune, in the belief that it is all happening on the screen, and they can't get hurt because they're the good guys. Later, they learn otherwise, when it's too late. The softening-up process of the young, in preparing them to accept readily the idea of war, will not cease until and unless we do something about it. Of course, if nuclear war happens, our children won't be conscripted or recruited. There will be no time or need. For both sides, it will be game over. Forever. Many young people have resisted and will resist being turned into zombies in the glitzy world of the video games and films and are only too aware of the terrible possibility of nuclear destruction. Sometimes I think that many kids are more aware than their parents. Doesn't anyone wonder why the suicide rate among *children* is now so high?[1] Counsellors and commentators speak about broken homes, worries over studies, unhappy loves. But another factor must be that many kids don't feel there will be a future. If they feel despair, we must tell them we understand and are afraid, too, but have to struggle for the survival of the world and all of us.

Vileness and violence threaten women and children in much of the media. As with pornography, so with the really bad video games or whatever, we must now and in the future take legal action and fight these things openly in the courts, not by censorship boards operating without sufficient accountability. Above all, the alienation from other people, fostered by these machines that make billions of bucks for their producers and distributors, must be countered by the human values of love, tolerance, individual worth, compassion, responsibility.

I ponder the situation of women writers in the future. Marian Kester's article also said, "a boom in word processor sales has been occurring among writers. Some say they couldn't function without their Apple II. The belief seems to be that the machine, if it will not actually write the material, is at least conducive to writing. That's like saying a crutch is conducive to walking." The point is well taken. Nevertheless, I don't think it's correct. I know a number of writers, including women writers, who have word processors. I don't think they feel that the machines make *writing* easier but rather that they make copying and inserting revisions a less arduous task. For women writers, with all too often a limited time to spend on their work, this could be a godsend. Over some thirty years, I have typed many books and stories and articles and lectures and book reviews, in manuscript, many times over, on a manual typewriter, doing revisions and ending up by doing two or more fair copies with carbons, in the days when the xerox machine was not widely present, or even if it was, when I couldn't afford xerox copies. A long and laborious job. I don't have a word processor now, although I have an electric typewriter. I don't feel that at this point in my professional life I really need a word processor, but I welcome their use by my younger sisters. All I hope is that in the future women writers will be able to afford such technical aids as they need.

Home computers may, at least in the near future, be another matter for women writers. In an article by Ann Silversides, entitled "Literature Goes Electronic from Coast to Coast," in the *Toronto Globe and Mail* (13 July 1984), we were told that "about thirty-five Canadian writers who own their own home computers will begin sending their work electronically across the country to be criticized, revised, or simply read by other members of the new network." Based at York University, Toronto, and founded by Professor Frank Davey, the venture is called "Swift Current," and it is "described variously as a Canadian literary data base or an electronic literary magazine."[2] There will be some writing available to subscribers, for public viewing and printouts, and subscribers will be mainly libraries and universities. This seems to me to be an interesting experiment, although I would question some of its aims (*revising* other writers' work? Can this really be what is intended?). The comment that specially interested me, however, was this: "there already is one group of writers – women writers – who are almost entirely absent from the project. Davey said he approached a number of women 'who just couldn't see themselves in the project.' He offered the explanation that most women writers are more privately focused on their writing, have less money and hence can't afford home computers, and also are 'conditioned not to participate in the machinery of a culture.'" I was one of the women writers who was approached, and I declined for a variety of reasons, one of which was certainly my lack of familiarity with computers. There were other reasons, however, and perhaps I can make a guess about the reasons other women had.

I don't think women writers are any more "privately focused" on their writing than male writers, and I certainly hope not, out of concern for the quality of writing by either sex. I always thought all writers were privately focused on their writing; this in no way implies an obsession with self. I agree that women writers tend to have less money. Not so many of us teach in universities or have other well-paid jobs outside the home. It is to be hoped that the financial situation of women writers, and women in general, will improve in the future, but it seems likely that a home computer will be relatively low on the list of priorities for some time. A Canadian woman writer of real distinction once told me that when her children were young, she spent most of her first and quite modest Canada Council grant on a washing machine. I understood perfectly. I wonder how many male writers would understand. As for being "conditioned not to participate in the machinery of a culture," I admit that I do find the world of computers mysterious and daunting, but at this stage in my life I'm not highly motivated to learn that world. If I were, I imagine I would be able to do it. I do not think this conditioning, if it really exists, would prove a stumbling block for most women writers. I would guess that a more relevant reason for women writers' almost complete absence is *lack of time*. As in so many other professions, women in my profession have often been expected to choose between career and children, and we have often refused to choose and have opted for both. Women writers, like women in other areas of work, have usually had numerous other jobs – child-rearing with its vast emotional needs gladly given, shopping, cleaning, cooking, laundry, and a host of others, including doing their own business correspondence, without the access to typing and secretarial services that male writers, especially if associated with a university, have frequently enjoyed. Many women writers, if they have been single parents, separated or divorced, have also had to supplement meagre incomes with freelance journalism. Male writers who don't hold teaching positions have done freelance journalism as well, but not in addition to child-rearing and housework – their wives have seen to that. I don't know who originally said that every writer needs a good wife, but my own addition to the saying has always been that if you are a female heterosexual writer it's not so easy to find an understanding and unpaid housekeeper. My own children have been adults for some years, but even now I simply would not have the time to plug in to all or even some of the work being done by the writers in this experiment, and as for commenting on it and pondering other writers' comments on my work, heaven forbid. In addition to doing my writing, I am still my own housekeeper, secretary, and business manager. I would like to see more women taking part in such projects as "Swift Current" because I think the voices of women are needed in every area. All I can hope is that in the future my younger sisters will be able to solve that persistent problem – lack of time. A more equitable distribution of housework and childcare may ultimately be a partial solution, but it won't help single mothers and won't take care of the domestic work or business work for women writers living alone, who can't afford secretarial or domestic help. More and better day-care centres, at affordable prices, are of course a top priority for women with young children, anywhere in the work force. We need not deceive ourselves that this is a top priority for men in our society. Perhaps in the future men may really come to understand that child care is their responsibility, too, and that good child care is important because children are important, as well as the fact that mothers working at other jobs not only need help but have a *right* to it.

Quite apart from the electronic experiment I've been discussing, I want to take another look at the statement that women writers are "'conditioned not to participate in the machinery of a culture.'" I am certainly not taking issue with Professor Davey here. Indeed, when I first read those words, I thought, sadly, *how true*. The statement is thought provoking because it is almost universally believed, not only about women writers but about women in general, all women, and it is believed both by men and by women themselves. In an abstract sense, women have all too often had a self-image of being a klutz as far as machinery is concerned, and men have all too often believed that women just aren't very good at learning any kind of technology. A quick look at history and reality shows otherwise. For a long time, and even now, the operation of such machines as typewriters, washing machines, vacuum cleaners, has been seen as "women's work," as have the jobs of telephone operators and many other jobs involving complex machinery. What people operate the computers in your neighbourhood bank? Not the (male) manager. The tellers, who are almost all women. Women have operated machinery in factories since the industrial revolution. For many years, it was difficult for women to get into medical schools, but it was acceptable for them to become lab technicians, working with highly sophisticated machines. During World Wars I and II, women in their tens of thousands went into heavy industries and also into work involving an understanding of the most intricate technology, and at the end of those wars, were told to get back into the kitchen (which they'd never left, having done, as usual, more than one full-time job). The prairie farmwomen of my generation and older worked alongside their men and were no strangers to the operation of machines. What is the common denominator here? It is, I believe, that women have always operated machinery of all kinds, *when it was to the advantage of society for them to do so*, while at the same time believing in the abstract, a myth (women aren't much good with machinery) that in particular ways *they knew to be untrue.* Second, the jobs women have done, involving machinery, have almost always been *lower paid and of lower prestige than those held by men.*

I hope in the future this situation will change radically, as it is already beginning to do, although not rapidly enough. I hope women will have the confidence and the strength of purpose to learn the operation of whatever kinds of technical equipment they choose and will assert vigorously their right to whatever opportunities the technology may offer. Finally, and most of all, I hope that women will take a decisive part in choosing how and when the machinery of the future is to be used, and for what purposes, in order that machines of increasing intricacy may be used for human benefit and convenience, but never seen as gods, and in order that the human values of caring and compassion and conscience will prevail. I am not in any way excluding men from this difficult struggle, but men, whatever their stances or philosophies, are already involved with the new technology, at higher levels and in greater numbers than women are at the present time. I hope for a greater balance in the future.

Who will teach our children what it means to be human? Humans will. In my novel *The Diviners,* the protagonist, Morag, receives a symbol of her ancestors, a symbol that also points to the future, a Scots plaid pin with the motto: "My Hope Is Constant in Thee."[3]

To women in the future, I have to say: *My Hope Is Constant in Thee.*

Afterword
Rediscovering Margaret Laurence

The writings of Margaret Laurence are so much a part of the Canadian literary tradition that her words and her image continue to hover in the background of a literature that grows increasingly and wonderfully diverse. Some have relegated her work to the mid-twentieth century, but stalwart readers know that Laurence represents a breakthrough in Canadian words that cannot be accurately measured.

Every Canadian reader harbours a memory of the moment when they first encountered the work of Margaret Laurence. My own was in 1973, when I read *The Stone Angel*, a marvellously furious book about one woman's rejection of growing old juxtaposed with her powerful memories of her past. I still have that paperback, an NCL edition, with my marks in the margins, and my name inside the front cover. Laurence's voice was not only distinctive but indelible, and I can still recite sentences from that novel. "Gainsay who dare!"

In these essays, her voice rings out again, as powerfully as when the writings collected here were first published or heard. Nora Foster Stovel's comprehensive and carefully curated compendium of these pieces invaluably ties together Laurence's fiction, life, and activism. As Stovel says, "her essays [are] important because they can illuminate her novels," and she suggests that Laurence "was in the habit of working out issues in essays before dramatizing them in novels." Seeing Laurence's musings and ambivalence playing against one another on the page is both a measure of her method and a suggestion of how complex her process was. The active practice of such a writer reminds readers and writers alike of how much of writing requires introspection and redirection, careful thought and re-evaluation, digression and doubling back.

The essays addressing social and political concerns are less polemical in their approach than clear, balanced, and beautifully uncertain. Laurence was not a

writer who pronounced, or who dispensed unalterable opinions, but a thoughtful and considering observer of her world. Unsurprisingly, she was, as Nora
Foster Stovel's meticulous commentary unfolds, ahead of the pack in terms of
her awareness of postcolonial writing, her resistance to exploitative power structures, and her anti-colonialism. As early as 1982, she made public the fact that
Indigenous people were suffering from disease caused by mercury poisoning
in fish.

She was keenly aware of the power imbalance that women continue to wrestle
with, directly addressing "my growing awareness of the dilemma and powerlessness of women, the tendency of women to accept male definition of ourselves,
to be self-deprecating and uncertain, and to rage inwardly." She is particularly
sensitive to the work of women and how women writers are dismissed as interior, "privately focused" rather than universal in their subject matter. She knows
the cost of "shopping, cleaning, cooking, laundry," and adds, "if you are a female
heterosexual writer it's not so easy to find an understanding and unpaid housekeeper." Her wry appraisal of the differences between men and women concludes
with the trenchant summary, "In addition to doing my writing, I am still my own
housekeeper, secretary, and business manager."

What is richest about these essays is that they capture Laurence's astonishing
life experience. She worked in offices, on a newspaper, in a London employment
agency, and she marked English essays for the University of British Columbia.
She lived in Ghana, Somaliland, the United Kingdom, and she saw Canada, both
widely and well, with an avid eye. She even spent some months at Fort St John,
in northern British Columbia, where her husband was working on the dismant-
ling of the old Peace River Bridge. Ultimately, she acknowledges that her "life's
journey has been one that brought me back home, at least in heart, but I had
to go away to learn that." That recursive motif for writers – the journey home
– rings both honest and true from Laurence's perspective.

Laurence's keen awareness of economic disparity was forged in her depression
childhood; its long shadow is most strikingly exhibited in her wonderful essay
on the joy of furnishing her cabin by ordering everything – "linen, dishes, curtains, lamps, cutlery, pots and pans, cushions, bedspreads, blankets" – from the
catalogue, an experience in direct contradiction to her memory of childhood
when she pored over those wish book pages filled with tantalizing and unattain-
able items.

Powerfully evident too is Laurence's mentorship, as a key founder of the Writers' Union of Canada and someone who supported others with enormous generosity through letters, telephone calls, and "survival humour." Two of the most interesting pieces here are about her stint as writer-in-residence at the University of Toronto. She had never had an office, and she found the experience both exhilarating for its connection with young writers, and daunting for the difficulty of living in Toronto and negotiating "the old brigade" of critical men. Most telling is her final list of what a writer in residence is: "a knockdownable parent-figure, a financial consultant, an amateur friend." She was frustrated by students' astonishing ignorance of Canadian literary publications, but still patiently performed her expected role. Her staunch and unapologetic advocacy of Canadian literature is a thread throughout.

Laurence's observations on writing and genre, and how those elements interact with perception and discernment, reveal incalculable wisdom: "writing itself, at the heart of it, is an assertion of faith in the possibilities of human communication." Her strong sense of justice and her respect for the past reiterate her sense that fiction and history work together, "twin disciplines" that "include biography and autobiography." She believed that the future, the present, and the past contain similar cadences, and that both historian and novelist are challenged to negotiate ambivalent versions of truth.

Striking too are her ready friendships (her meeting and subsequent connection to Clara Thomas is especially vivid), and her generosity to other writers, coupled with gently acerbic humour. "Leonard Cohen has recently chucked over a proposed TV series, thank goodness. He seems to be one of those writers who shouldn't work at anything except writing." She is kind to writers who might now be categorized as unfashionable, Morley Callaghan, Ethel Wilson, and Jack Ludwig, alongside her delight in her close friends, Timothy Findley, Marian Engel, and Adele Wiseman.

Fascinating details outline Laurence's character, her shape-changing shyness, and her awareness that she does not "fit in," even though she longs to. How she chose writing over her marriage and her husband, the true test of a writer. How much she hated Toronto, and her observations on life in cities as dense and difficult. She was a people listener; her ears pick up the comments around her with marvellous acuity. She did not drive, she took public transport regularly, and she loved train journeys. Her evocation of small-town railway stations and their sad

demise, gone now, torn down or repurposed, haunts her travels. And most compelling, her awareness that "The train is always moving west. For us, always west.
For my people, west is the direction our lives take. West is in us." That yearning
west, ineffable as it might be, imbues her writing, as much as her determination
to work with words to understand "the mystery at the core of life."

What is obvious in these essays is that Laurence is no retro thinker, a writer
to relegate to Canada's history, but a woman who was both of her time and
ahead of her time. Her support for unpopular causes, her sensitivity to racism
and prejudice, her strong feminism and pacifism, her advocacy for peace and
against censorship, altogether remark an imagination whose influence goes
beyond momentary context.

The final essay included here, on machinery, compares typewriters (which
she used with avid tenacity) to computers (which she was suspicious of).

That piece reminds me of a story that Marian Engel told me, about visiting a
graduate class at the University of Alberta (probably in 1978) that was studying
Laurence's *The Diviners*. Engel and Laurence were close friends who shared many
of the same challenges – parenthood, financial exigency, and the stress of constant demands, always aware that they were both "famous," and too much was
expected of them.

Marian told me the class distressed her so much that she had thrown a tan-
trum.

"Why?" I inquired.

The members of the graduate class, along with their professor, had apparently
come to the consentient conclusion that *The Diviners* was a flawed novel, too
chronological, and not sufficiently experimental, that it was "not very good."

This dismissal upset Marian beyond vehemence.

"What did you do?" I asked.

"I was furious," she said. "I threw my glasses against the wall. They broke. And
I shouted, 'Do you know how long it took just to type this novel, you sniveling
little runts?'"

I laughed with delight, because of course, Laurence did type and retype her
work, over and over, a ritual that most academics do not partake of.

"The truth is," said Marian, and she was NOT shame-faced, "I had broken my
glasses that morning, and glued them together with crazy glue, so I knew they
were already broken, but the class didn't know that. I shocked them into silence."

It is not easy to type over and over again, words that capture intense feelings, history, emotion, doubt, and grief.

Such was the spirit that Laurence incited. The battle cry she shared with Adele Wiseman, "*Coraggio. Avanti*," says it all.

To this day, Margaret Laurence commands our attention, our passion, makes us rethink what we thought we knew about Canadian writing and its contours. Her generous gathering of Canadian values, her huge-hearted sense of the country, all contributed to her literary legacy and the indubitable fact that all writers here are inheritors of Laurence's journey. This volume contributes enormously to our awareness of the complexity that was Margaret Laurence. Nora Foster Stovel has given, with her beautiful editing of these writings, the gift of reminder and memory, reviving for readers Laurence's "desire to make all these things come alive in the reader's mind."

ARITHA VAN HERK
Calgary, Alberta

Annotations

Introduction

1   In her foreword to *Heart of a Stranger*, Laurence refers to her "articles and essays" as "travels and entertainments" (4) and states in an unpublished preface, "they are all, in one way or another, travel articles" (xii). Because I prepared an edition of *Heart of a Stranger* in 2003, I decided not to include all nineteen essays, especially not the travel essays. Instead, I include six essays, including the foundational essays that frame her collection – "Sources," which she reprinted under the revised title "A Place to Stand On" as the opening essay, and "Where the World Began" as the last – plus four texts that complement the creative and socio-political essays that I collect here: "Upon a Midnight Clear," "The Shack," "Down East," and "Open Letter to the Mother of Joe Bass."

2   In her foreword to *Heart of a Stranger*, Laurence writes, "Many [articles] also deal with themes that I dealt with later in my fiction. Although I did not fully realize it at the time, in a sense I was working out these themes in a nonfiction way before I was ready to deal with them in the broader form of the novel" (4).

3   See Donez Xiques, *Margaret Laurence: The Making of a Writer*.

4   *A Jest of God* was adapted as a film – *Rachel, Rachel* (1969) – directed by Paul Newman and starring Joanne Woodward. It was nominated for four Academy Awards – best movie, best actress, best supporting actress, and best adapted screenplay.

5   See Christian Riegel's *Writing Grief: Margaret Laurence and the Work of Mourning*.

6   See Laurence's *Dance on the Earth: A Memoir*, 8.

7   Laurence praised Trent University, founded in 1961, as the ideal small liberal arts and science university, and the admiration was mutual: Trent University, on its website, declares that Laurence embodied the values and ideals to

which the university itself aspires: "humanitarianism, justice, informed criticism, creativity, and self-examination."

8   Although "Canadian Third Track" is not included in this collection, since it
repeats material in other essays, these particular points are worth recording.

9   This item, along with two dozen other occasional pieces, was deemed too
slight to include in this collection; nevertheless, these sentences are worth
quoting, especially the last sentence, which goes to the heart of Laurence's
humanitarian aims.

10 Laurence refers to the great commandment, or the summary of the law, as
Jesus's new commandment. However, the latter comes from John's gospel.
"A new commandment I give unto you, That ye love one another; as I have
loved you, that ye also love one another" (John 13:34, King James Version).

11 See Lyall Powers, *Alien Heart: The Life and Work of Margaret Laurence*.

12 See Laurence's essay "Road from the Isles" in *Heart of a Stranger*, 113–22.

13 See Stovel, "Mourning Becomes Margaret: Laurence's Farewell to Fiction
in Her Final, Unfinished Novel, 'Dance on the Earth.'" Laurence may have
planned the publication of this projected novel to coincide with the bicenten-
nial of Batoche.

14 "Tribalism as Us Versus Them" was likely intended for inclusion in the original 1976 publication of *Heart of a Stranger*, and thus I included it in the 2003
edition (179–8).

15 While Laurence's letter "Are Holocaust victims expected to die again and
again?" was not included in this collection, these quotations seemed worthy
of inclusion.

16 This article was written in 1978, after the election of the first Parti Québécois
government and the passage of Bill 101, but before the first referendum.

17 Canada, in 1978, was still subject to the British North America Act of 1867.

18 For further discussion of this subject, see Patricia Morley, *The Long Journey
Home*; Donez Xiques, *Margaret Laurence: The Making of a Writer*; and Laura
Davis, *Margaret Laurence Writes Africa and Canada*.

Sources

1   Margaret Laurence's typescript of *Heart of a Stranger* is in box 4, file 1, of the
Laurence Archives at the Mills Memorial Library, at McMaster University,
Hamilton, Ontario. Margaret Atwood published *Survival: A Thematic Guide
to Canadian Literature* in 1972, after Laurence published this essay in 1970.

Laurence excised the final sentences of her introduction to this essay: "It seems we were thinking along similar lines. It is true that survival is a common theme in Canadian fiction, although naturally every serious novel contains a complexity of themes, as Atwood of course recognizes."

2   Laurence was researching Nigerian literature for a BBC radio program. Ultimately, this research produced her only full-length critical study, *Long Drums and Cannons: Nigerian Dramatists and Novelists, 1952–66*, in 1968, edited by Nora Foster Stovel in 2001.

3   Neepawa, Manitoba, Laurence's birthplace, is one hundred miles northwest of Winnipeg. "The cemetery on the hill" is based on Neepawa's Riverside Cemetery, and the "Wachakwa River" is the name Laurence gives to the Whitemud River.

4   "Manawaka" may unite the names "Manitoba," meaning "Great Spirit," and "Neepawa," meaning "Land of Plenty." It may suggest the concept of "Man awaken." For a fuller discussion of Laurence's Manawaka, see Stovel, "'A Town of the Mind': Margaret Laurence's Mythical Microcosm of Manawaka" in *Divining Margaret Laurence: A Study of Her Complete Writings*, 155–71.

5   Laurence did go far away: to England in 1949, Somaliland in 1950, and the Gold Coast in 1952, before returning to Canada, from 1957 to 1962, as she needed distance to write. Her Somali experience is recorded in her travel memoir *The Prophet's Camel Bell* (1963).

6   *A Bird in the House* was first published by McClelland and Stewart in 1970, although all the stories, except the last, "Jericho's Brick Battlements," were previously published in journals and magazines. The quoted sentence is the third-from-last of that story and occurs on page 191 of the New Canadian Library edition. Vanessa MacLeod's maternal grandfather, Timothy Connor, is modelled on Laurence's maternal grandfather, John Simpson, who inspired rebelliousness in his granddaughter.

7   Al Purdy (1918–2000) was a Canadian poet whose close friendship with Laurence is recorded in *Margaret Laurence – Al Purdy: A Friendship in Letters*. Laurence quotes the last lines of Purdy's poem "Roblin's Mills, Circa 1842" as the epigraph for *The Diviners* and later as the title of this essay, originally titled "Sources," which opens *Heart of a Stranger*, 5–9. Purdy's poem first appeared in *Wild Grape Wine*, 46–7, was republished as "Roblin's Mills" in *The Cariboo Horses*, 70–1, and was collected as "Roblin's Mills [II]" in *The Collected Poems of Al Purdy*, 132–3.

Ten Years' Sentences

1   Sherman Baker, editor-in-chief at St Martin's Press, New York, Laurence's first
    American publisher, sent her comments from three readers.

2   Adele Wiseman (1928–1992) was a fellow Manitoban writer and life-long
    friend of Laurence. Both writers addressed similar themes concerning myth-
    ology and morality, which is most evident in Wiseman's 1974 novel *Crackpot*,
    for which Laurence wrote an introduction for the New Canadian Library
    Series. See Laurence's correspondence with Wiseman, edited by John Lennox
    and Ruth Panofsky.

3   *Queen's Quarterly* was founded as the first scholarly journal in Canada at
    Queen's University in 1893.

4   Malcolm Ross (1911–2002), winner of the Lorne Pierce Medal, was a Canadian
    teacher, literary critic, and founding editor of the New Canadian Library. He
    taught Laurence in a course on seventeenth-century poetry at the University
    of Manitoba in 1946. He later published and edited her story "The Drummer
    of All the World" for *Queen's Quarterly*. See Laurence's "Tribute to Malcolm
    Ross" in this collection.

5   *Prism International* (popularly styled PRISM), established in 1959, is a
    quarterly literary publication based in Vancouver, British Columbia.

6   Ethel Wilson (1888–1980), best known for her 1954 novel *Swamp Angel*, which
    helped inspire Laurence's novel *The Stone Angel*, was a source of support for
    female writers in Canada. She mentored Laurence, encouraging her work,
    admiring *The Tomorrow-Tamer*, and describing *The Stone Angel* as "glorious"
    and "great" (quoted in Powers, *Alien Heart*, 218).

7   This quotation is found on page 282 of the NCL edition.

8   Christopher Ifekandu Okigbo (1932–1967) was a Nigerian poet and activist
    who died defending the Republic of Biafra in the Nigerian Civil War.

9   The Igbo, also referred to as Ibo, one of three major ethnic groups inhabiting
    Nigeria, are farming people living in the southeast region of Nigeria. The
    "massacre" Laurence mentions is likely a reference to the first of four anti-
    Igbo pogroms in North Nigeria. Thousands of Igbo people in Nigeria were
    murdered on the directive of the federal military government in the summer
    of 1966.

10 Wole Soyinka (b.1934) is a prolific Nigerian playwright, author, and activist
    who was awarded the Nobel Prize in Literature in 1986. Soyinka is one of the

subjects of Laurence's *Long Drums and Cannons: Nigerian Dramatists and Novelists, 1952–1966.*

11   Biafra, a secessionist state in eastern Nigeria, 1967–70, primarily populated by Igbo nationalists who declared their independence from Nigeria, due to economic, ethnic, and political conflict with other Nigerian peoples, ceased to exist after the Nigerian Civil War (6 July 1967 to 15 January 1970).

12   Chinua Achebe (1930–2013) was a Nigerian writer best known for his first novel, *Things Fall Apart* (1958).

13   The Hausa comprise the largest ethnic group in the northwestern and southern Niger regions. The Hausa culture is partially derived from Islam.

Time and the Narrative Voice

1   Laurence's term "Method writer" is based on the Stanislavski theory of the Method Actor, developed by Russian character actor Constantin Stanislavski (1863–1938).

2   See Jonathan Kertzer, "*That House in Manawaka*": *Margaret Laurence's* A Bird in the House, and Bruce Stovel, "Coherence in *A Bird in the House*."

3   The Métis, persons of mixed European and Indigenous ancestry who formed distinctive cultural and collective ethnic identities throughout Canadian history, were recognized under Section 35 of the *Constitution Act, 1982* as one of three "Aboriginal peoples in Canada."

4   Louis Riel (1844–1885) helped establish Manitoba as part of Confederation. A Métis leader in the Red River and North-West resistance movements, he was executed for high treason against the Canadian government on 16 November 1885.

5   Batoche, established as a Métis settlement in 1872, was the site of a three-day battle during the North-West Rebellion of 1885, which ended in the defeat of the Métis and the collapse of the insurgent Provisional Government of Saskatchewan led by Louis Riel and Gabriel Dumont.

Half War – Half Peace

1   Judith Jones (1924–2017) was an editor at Knopf from 1957 to 2011, known for editing culinary authors, including Julia Child. I interviewed Jones about Laurence in 1998.

2   Laurence's first novel, *This Side Jordan*, was published simultaneously by

Macmillan in England, St Martin's in the United States, and McClelland and Stewart in Canada in 1960. Laurence signed a new contract with Knopf in 1962.

3 Laurence lived in the Gold Coast, soon to become Ghana, from 1952 to 1957, while her husband, Jack Laurence, was employed in constructing the port at Tema.

4 As *A Bird in the House* was published in 1970, this statement suggests that this undated holograph manuscript was composed soon after 1970.

5 This section parallels a passage in "Living Dangerously by Mail" in *Heart of a Stranger* (141–6), especially the final section, pages 144–6.

6 *This Side Jordan* (1960), set in the Gold Coast, alternates between the viewpoints of the African teacher, Nathaniel Amegbe, and the Englishman, Johnnie Kestoe.

7 Knopf published *This Side Jordan*, *The Prophet's Camel Bell*, and *The Tomorrow-Tamer and Other Stories* in 1964 – a venture expressing great confidence in Laurence.

8 "For I am become like a bottle in the smoke; yet do I not forget thy statutes" (King James Bible, Psalm 119:83).

9 "As with a sword in my bones, mine enemies reproach me; while they say daily unto me, Where is thy God?" (King James Bible, Psalm 42:10).

10 Laurence's paternal grandfather believed their family name, "Wemyss," signified "Cave-dweller" in Gaelic.

11 Carl Sandburg's *Losers* provides the epigraph for both Laurence's sister novels, *A Jest of God* (1966) and *The Fire-Dwellers* (1969).

Gadgetry or Growing

1 Graham Greene (1904–1991) was a British novelist whose works explored the paradoxes of Christian morality in the modern world. Laurence may refer here to "The Young Dickens" in *The Lost Childhood and Other Essays* (1952), the essay by Graham Greene that she quotes at the outset of "Sources."

2 "Angry Young Men" refers to certain British novelists and playwrights, including Kingsley Amis, John Osborne, and Harold Pinter, who expressed their disillusion with British society in the 1950s.

3 For a review of the critical reception of *A Jest of God*, see Stovel, *Rachel's Children: Margaret Laurence's* A Jest of God.

4 See Stovel, *Stacey's Choice: Margaret Laurence's* The Fire-Dwellers.

Eye on Books

1 Helen Hutchinson (CTV), Carole Taylor (CTV), and Adrienne Clarkson (CBC) are Canadian journalists and broadcasters who interviewed Laurence numerous times.

2 See "Inside the Idiot Box" in *Heart of a Stranger* (133) for another discussion of this incident. *Verbascum thapsus,* the Common Mullein, or Aron's Rod, is a biennial herb of the North American Figwort Family.

3 Founded in 1973, the Writers' Union of Canada, of which Laurence served as chair, advanced writing as a profession in Canada, both economically and legally (Atwood, "Writers' Union of Canada").

4 Roderick Haig-Brown (1908–1976) was a Canadian writer and conservationist known for his depictions of nature and his dedication to preserving the Fraser River.

A Tale of Typewriters

1 "Peggy Wemyss," as the young Laurence was called, signed letters "Prairie Crocus."

2 Laurence's "Mum" was her adopted mother, Margaret Simpson, her Aunt Marg, who left her position as an English teacher in Calgary to care for young Peggy following the death of her birth mother, Verna Simpson Wemyss, and who later married Peggy's father.

3 Mildred Musgrove was Laurence's English teacher at Viscount Collegiate in Neepawa. She told me in a 1988 interview that Margaret demonstrated literary talent as a student.

4 Morag Gunn, heroine of *The Diviners*, works at Leckie's Ladies' Wear in Manawaka.

5 After the publication of her first book, *A Tree for Poverty* (1954), Laurence asked people to address her by her true name, "Margaret," rather than the familiar "Peggy."

6 Laurence demonstrated a lifelong commitment to the New Democratic Party, self-identifying as a "Christian Socialist," in line with Tommy Douglas, the first NDP leader.

7 Laurence's interpolations – "… see p. 2 for next thrilling episode," "… more …" and "… see p. 4 for explanation" – are included on her typescript.

8 As Laurence notes later, "that extra l will be explained soon."

9 "M.L.'s dear friend Adele, also a prairie flower and a writer," is Adele Wiseman.

10   Laurence's paternal grandfather, John Wemyss, an immigrant from Scotland, was a lawyer who incorporated the town of Neepawa. Her Scottish ancestry made a deep impression on Laurence, as she visited Scotland in adulthood, an experience reflected in *The Diviners* and in her essay "Road from the Isles" (1966) in *Heart of a Stranger*.

11   In *The Diviners* Christie Logan gives Morag Gunn *The Clans and Tartans of Scotland*, first published in 1900 by Robert Bain and republished by Collins of London in 1956.

12   Pictish, the extinct language of the Picts, inhabitants of the north and central regions of Scotland in the Middle Ages, was replaced by Gaelic when Pictland was integrated with the Scottish kingdom in the tenth century.

13   "Chaika" was the name of Adele Wiseman's mother, one of Laurence's "wise-women."

14   Jocelyn and David are Laurence's children, and Sonia was David's then partner. Adele is Adele Wiseman, Dmitry her husband, and Tamara her daughter.

Ivory Tower or Grassroots?

1   Laurence names authors she discusses in *Long Drums and Cannons: Nigerian Dramatists and Novelists 1952–1966* (1968).

2   Matthew Arnold's 1867 poem "Dover Beach" includes the phrase "ignorant armies clash by night."

3   *The Stone Angel* (1964) was the first of Laurence's Manawaka cycle of novels and her first fiction set in Canada.

4   The Highland Clearances involved the forced eviction of Scottish Highlanders from the mid-eighteenth century to the mid-nineteenth century. The eviction of the Highlanders led to the destruction of the traditional clan system and considerable emigration from Scotland over the next century.

5   Lazarus Tonnerre, Christie Logan, Bram Shipley, and Lottie Dreiser are all characters in Laurence's Manawaka Cycle – Bram Shipley and Lottie Dreiser in *The Stone Angel*, and Lazarus Tonnerre and Christie Logan in *The Diviners*.

6   The Dieppe Raid on 19 August 1942, resulting in the death of over nine hundred Canadian soldiers and the imprisonment and wounding of thousands, was a disaster for the Allies and a tragedy for Canada. Dieppe features prominently in Laurence's works: "In one sense Dieppe perpetually has happened only yesterday. It runs as a leitmotif through all my so-called Manawaka

fiction and, in a way, it runs through my whole life, in my hatred of war so profound I can't find words to express my outrage" (*Dance on the Earth*, 84).

Where the World Began

1 Laurence inserted, but then excised, the following sentence: "This theme appears more than once in these articles. I did not realize this repetitiveness or obsessiveness when I wrote them. Now, however, having finally expressed this theme, among others, in *The Diviners*, I don't feel obsessed by it any more. I think it's found its place in me." She replaced this sentence with the sentence that concludes her introduction as published. See *Heart of a Stranger* for an excised introductory paragraph that is excerpted here: "[E]very writer of fiction writes out of the place where, for them, the world began, and most writers of fiction also in some way write out of the land of their ancestors, which in the end is the same world as where the writer's own sight was formed. The journey takes us a long way, and the land of our distant ancestors may be a long way off ... All of us – if the human race survives – are going to be ancestors some day" (*Heart of a Stranger*, 224).

2 Laurence excised the end of this sentence: "and would remain so, whatever happened."

Love and Madness in the Steel Forest

1 *A Jest of God* and *The Fire-Dwellers* (1969), sister novels about Rachel and Stacey Cameron, overlapped in composition.

2 Eglinton, Davisville, St Clair, Summerhill, Rosedale, and Bloor are the names of stops on Toronto's Yonge Street subway line, heading south.

3 This snake dancer may have inspired the figure of Fan, an exotic dancer with a pet python, Tiny, whom Morag Gunn encounters in *The Diviners*.

4 Laurence enjoyed conversing with taxi drivers, as she explains in "I Am a Taxi" in *Heart of a Stranger*, 135–40.

Don't Whisper Sudden

1 Cassandra, also known as Alexandra or Kassandra, was a daughter of King Priam and Queen Hecuba of Troy. Her name is employed as a rhetorical device to indicate someone whose accurate prophecies are not believed by those around them.

2 Dr Clara Thomas (1919–2013), an authority on Canadian women writers, taught in the English Department at York University from 1961 to 1984. Through Thomas, a scholar and friend of Laurence, York University acquired Laurence's papers, which provide many of the essays in this collection. See Laurence's tribute to Thomas in this collection.

3 McLaughlin College, founded in 1968, is the Public Policy College at York University, with Political Science, Global Political Studies, and Work and Labour Studies programs.

4 Susanna Moodie (1803–1885) emigrated from England in 1832 with her husband, John Moodie, to the Coburg area of Upper Canada, near her sister Catherine Parr Traill on the Otonabee River, but later moved to Belleville, where she published fictional and nonfictional works, including her account of Canadian settler life, *Roughing It in the Bush*, in 1852.

5 John Lindsay was mayor of New York City from 1966 to 1973.

6 The Book of Revelation is an apocalyptic section of the New Testament wherein John records his account of a revelation granted to him by Christ through an angel, the most widely recognized references being the "The Four Horsemen of the Apocalypse" (6:1–8), "The Whore of Babylon" (17:1–18), and "The Fall of Babylon" (18:1–24).

7 John F. Kennedy International Airport, originally named Idlewild Airport, is located in Queens, New York City.

8 Part of the Trent-Severn Waterway, the Otonabee River runs 55 kilometres from Katchewanooka Lake near Lakefield, Ontario, along the east side of Peterborough and into Rice Lake, Ontario. Laurence spent summers at her cabin on the river, where she wrote *The Diviners*, from 1971 until her death in 1987. See "The Shack" in this edition.

The River Flows Both Ways

1 Jack McClelland (1922–2004) was president of McClelland & Stewart Ltd, founded by his father, from 1961 to 1982. He promoted Canadian literature, fostering writers Margaret Atwood, Marian Engel, Mordecai Richler, and Laurence, among many others.

2 David Dale Zieroth (b.1946) won the Governor General's Award for his poetry collection *The Fly in Autumn* in 2009.

Salute of the Swallows

1 Charles Edward Stuart (1720–1788), known as the "Pretender" and "Bonnie Prince Charlie," laid claim, as the grandson of Stuart king James II, to the British throne in the Jacobite uprising of 1745. "Wha Wedna Fecht fa' Charlie," or "Who Wouldn't Fight for Charlie," is a Scottish song supporting him (Waltz, *An Introduction to Braid Scots*, 53). Laurence's "Road from the Isles" (*Heart of a Stranger* 113–22) describes her visit to Scotland, which is also reflected in *The Diviners*.

2 The name "Morag Mellwraith" anticipates *The Diviners*, as the protagonist of Laurence's novel is named Morag, her high school English teacher is named Miss Melrose, and her Scottish lover, Dan, is surnamed McRaith.

3 Laurence's family's religious affiliation was Scottish Presbyterian, until Presbyterians merged with Methodists and Congregationalists to become the United Church of Canada in 1925.

4 The Huron-Wendat was a confederacy of five Iroquoian-speaking nations located in what is now south-central Ontario, which the Huron-Wendat occupied until about 1650 when they were defeated and dispersed by the Iroquois-Haudenosaunee nations.

5 Catherine Parr Traill neé Strickland (1802–1899) emigrated from England to Canada in 1832 with her husband Lieutenant Thomas Traill, settling on the Otonabee River. She published her housekeeping manual, *A Canadian Settler's Guide* (also published as *The Female Emigrant's Guide*), in 1854. Traill lived in Lakefield, where Laurence eventually settled, and her house still stands. One of the colleges of Trent University, where Laurence was chancellor from 1981 to 1983, is named for her. Traill is the "Saint Catherine" to whom Morag Gunn prays in *The Diviners* (109).

6 Samuel Strickland (1804–1867) immigrated to Canada in 1825 to work as a surveyor for the Black family in Durham County, Ontario. He settled on a farm near Lakefield, Ontario, where his sisters, Susanna Moodie and Catherine Parr Traill, joined him.

7 Roman gladiators addressed the audience before battle with the Latin phrase *Morituri te salutamus*, translated as "We who are about to die salute you."

The Shack

1 Perhaps the editor of *Weekend Magazine* selected the final phrase of Laurence's essay for its title.

2   See *Heart of a Stranger*, 219, for an introduction to this essay which Laurence
    composed but did not publish, and which contains the following passage: "I
    was coming home rapidly and somehow had to write about how it felt. It felt
    incredibly good – I could hardly believe it. Now that I'm settled here, in a
    two-story yellowbrick house, which seems to have been waiting for me and
    which now has the same kind of open and warming feeling that I think our
    house in England did, I am, of course, more critical. Paradise is nowhere. But
    at least you fight the stupidities and the heartlessness on your own ground,
    and always within, as well." The McMaster Archives also include a version
    of this essay titled "The River Flows Both Ways," the title of another essay
    included in this collection.

A Fantasy Fulfilled

1   For a discussion of Laurence's cabin, see "The Shack" in this edition. For a
    discussion of Elmcot, see "Put Out One or Two More Flags" (*Heart of a
    Stranger*, 107–12).
2   Morag Gunn, protagonist of *The Diviners*, envisions her fictional character,
    Peony, as having rosebud lips, "like the unreachable dolls in Eaton's Cata-
    logue," while Rosa Picardy, her "alter ego," is sturdy like Morag herself
    (*Diviners* 21).
3   The Honey Bunch series, beginning with *Honey Bunch: Just a Little Girl*
    (1923), by Helen Louise Thorndyke and published under the Stratemeyer
    Syndicate – famous for its Nancy Drew and Hardy Boys series – follows
    Honey Bunch on her various girlhood adventures.

The More Interesting Country

1   This involved the rising led by Louis Riel that ended in the Battle of Batoche
    in 1885.
2   The Canadian National Railway (CNR) and Canadian Pacific Railway (CPR)
    passenger services were merged into the independent Crown corporation VIA
    Rail Canada in 1977 and 1978, respectively.
3   Laurence's Aunt Ruby Simpson, her mother's elder sister, was head of the
    Nursing Division in Canada's first Public Health Service in Saskatchewan.
4   *Pillars Of The Nation* is referenced in *A Bird in the House*. See Stovel, "'Death
    and Love': Romance and Reality in Margaret Laurence's *A Bird in the House*,"
    225–44.

5 Margaret's husband, John Fergus Laurence, graduated from the University of
   Manitoba and Margaret from United College, now the University of Winnipeg, in 1947. Jack enlisted in the Royal Air Force and was stationed for four
   years in Burma, where he worked as a truck mechanic, becoming known as
   "Driver" Laurence (*Dance on the Earth*, 102).

6 The Laurences lived in London, England, 1949–50, in the British Protectorate
   of Somaliland, 1950–51, and in Gold Coast, soon to become Ghana, 1951–57,
   where Jack was employed by the Department of Public Works to build
   ballehs, or reservoirs, in the desert of the Haud, as Laurence describes in
   her travel memoir *The Prophet's Camel Bell*.

7 The Laurences' daughter, Jocelyn Laurence, was born in 1952 and died in 2015.

8 Sir John A. Macdonald was the first prime minister of Canada from 1867.
   One of the Fathers of Confederation, Macdonald assisted in the unification
   of Upper and Lower Canada, Nova Scotia, and New Brunswick under the
   1867 British North American Act.

9 The Dryden Paper Mill, established in 1909 on the Wabigoon River in Ontario, and a major supporter of the local economy until the early 2000s, has
   been cited for numerous environmental issues, including depositing mercury
   and other chemical waste into the river between 1962 and 1970.

10 This passage is reflected in Laurence's poem "Via Rail and Via Memory" –
   dated "August 1983" and collected in the appendix of Laurence's memoir
   Dance on the Earth, 275–7 – which ends thus: "for me/ this is the more interesting country" (277).

Down East

1 Laurence excised the following passage from the sentence that ends, "I
   would be settled in a small town not unlike the one in which I grew up":
   "and from which I departed at the age of eighteen, vowing never to live in
   a small town again. One's views change with the years, and endings often
   have a remarkable resemblance to beginnings." See *Heart of a Stranger*
   (213–14) for an introduction that Laurence composed but did not publish
   and that contains the following sentence: "I think now that this article was
   partly to explain to myself how I, a prairie person, could contemplate settling in Ontario, and, as such, it amuses me. But I guess I finally got the
   prairie chip off my shoulder."

2 Laurence is quoting the first line of a hymn by Bernard of Cluny.

3 Laurence quotes the concluding lines of Atwood's poem, "Death of a Young
   Son by Drowning" in "Journal II: 1840–1871," 72–3.

Journey from Lakefield

1 The Cree and Assiniboine lived in the Neepawa area prior to Irish, English,
   and Scottish nineteenth-century settlement.
2 Laurence's high cheek bones and slanted eyes, which she attributes to her
   Pictish and Celtic ancestors, calling herself a "Black Celt," have led people,
   including her Métis friend Alice Williams, to suspect she had Anishnaabe
   heritage.
3 Lakefield, Ontario, the small town on the Otonabee River, where Laurence
   bought a house on Regent Street in the 1970s, is near Peterborough.

Canada Still Too Canada-Focused

1 This may be Mel Hurtig, whom Laurence identifies as Edmonton's major
   "bookman," and who published Eli Mandel's *An Idiot Joy* in 1967.
2 "Canada is still too Canada-focused" is the statement that gives this essay its
   title – a title that, although drawn from the text, may have been applied by the
   Montreal Star editors, rather than by Laurence herself, as newspaper headlines are normally written by editors, not authors, and as Laurence's attitude
   in this essay is primarily positive.

Voices from Future Places

1 A blurb below the article, presumably written by the *Sun* editor, states,
   "Margaret Laurence once told an interviewer: 'I cannot start another novel
   immediately after one is finished. I need a change of pace for at least a year.'
   She got the change of pace while lecturing as writer-in-residence at the
   University of Toronto in 1969–70. Today, she remembers her sabbatical year
   very fondly. Occasional articles by Mrs Laurence will continue to appear
   on page six."
2 *A Bird in the House* (1970) and *Jason's Quest* (1970) are the books referred
   to here.
3 Winnipeg's Old Left, combining the Social Democratic Party and Co-
   operative Commonwealth Federation, involved a socialist approach that
   Laurence approved.

4 In 1972, the "New Left" involved anti-establishment and Canadian nationalist sentiments, especially opposition to American involvement in Vietnam.

Canadian Writers

1 Laurence was writer-in-residence at Massey College, University of Toronto, from 1969 to 1970.

When You Were Five and I Was Fourteen

1 Mildred Musgrove taught Laurence at Viscount High School in Neepawa. She was the model for Miss Melrose, Morag Gunn's high-school English teacher in *The Diviners*.

2 Laurence completed an Honours BA in English at United College in 1947.

Books That Mattered to Me

1 Laurence reflects this experience in *The Diviners*, which she terms a "spiritual autobiography," in Morag's frustration at not learning to read on her first day of school.

2 See "Upon a Midnight Clear" in this volume.

3 In 1938, Manitoba College and Wesley College merged under the enjoining United College, which was affiliated with the University of Manitoba until 1967, when United received a charter and became the University of Winnipeg.

4 Arthur Phelps, a former minister turned radio broadcaster and professor of English at Wesley College and later United College, influenced Laurence's literary interests and introduced her to United College's English Club.

5 Laurence describes this experience in her Somali memoir *The Prophet's Camel Bell*.

6 Adele Wiseman won the Governor General's Award for *The Sacrifice* in 1956, and Laurence won it for *A Jest of God* in 1966 and *The Diviners* in 1974.

7 "The Voices of Adamo" is published in *The Tomorrow-Tamer and Other Stories* (205–24).

8 Laurence's empathy with African peoples' struggle for independence influenced her vision of Canada's Indigenous peoples' fight for justice and women's battle for equality.

9 The North-West Uprising of 1885, culminating in the Battle of Batoche, caused the defeat of the Métis and collapse of the Provisional Government of Saskatchewan led by Louis Riel and Gabriel Dumont.

Mistahimaskwa (c.1825–1886), known as Big Bear, leading chief of the Prairie River People in the 1870s and 1880s, resisted signing Treaty No. Six for six years, eventually signing an adhesion to the treaty on 8 December 1882 (Wiebe, "Mistahimaskwa"). Pitikwahanapiwiyin (c.1842–1886), also known as Poundmaker, was a Plains Cree chief in the late 1870s, who, like Mistahimaskwa, questioned the creation of Treaty No. 6, but signed it two years after its proposal (Dempsey, "Pitikwahanapiwiyin").

10   John A. Macdonald and his Conservative government proposed the construction of the transcontinental Canadian Pacific Railway (CPR) to help create a unified nation. The Pacific Scandal involved Macdonald's using election funds for contracts. Canada contracted Chinese labourers and violated their human rights by exploitative working conditions. The last spike was driven on 7 November 1885 (Lavallé, "Canadian Pacific Railway").

11   Laurence's Scots grandfather, John Wemyss, incorporated Neepawa as a town.

12   Laurence quotes F.R. Scott's essay "Freedom of Speech in Canada," which is reprinted in his *Essays on the Constitution*.

13   John Stuart Mill's 1859 essay "On Liberty" is a treatise on the rights of the collective versus the individual in relation to civil and social liberties; the "harm principle," or acts that constitute harm to the individual, is often discussed in relation to freedom of speech.

14   See *Intimate Strangers: The Letters of Margaret Laurence and Gabrielle Roy*, edited by Paul Socken, for the correspondence of Gabrielle Roy and Margaret Laurence.

Afterword to Sinclair Ross

1   Job 13:15.

2   Joshua 24:15.

Introduction to Jack Ludwig

1   Carl Sandburg (1878–1967) won three Pulitzer prizes – two for poetry and one for his biography of Abraham Lincoln.

Introduction to Percy Janes

1   William Blake (1757–1827) referred to England's "dark Satanic mills" in the preface to *Milton: A Poem* (c.1810).

2   Janes employs a Newfoundland dialect wherein the word "b'ys" is a phonetic version of "boys."

Introduction to Adele Wiseman

1   In *The Diviners*, Christie Logan performs a similar service for the orphaned Morag.

2   Laurence discusses Nigerian novelist Gabriel Okara in *Long Drums and Cannons: Nigerian Dramatists and Novelists, 1952–1966* (171–5).

3   Carol Shields employs a similar situation in her 1993 novel *The Stone Diaries* when Mercy Stonewall Goodwill, unaware that she is pregnant, gives birth to Daisy Goodwill.

4   Laurence depicts North Winnipeg in "North Main Car," included in *Colors of Speech: Margaret Laurence's Early Writings*.

5   This incest theme reflects that in Laurence's dystopic story "A Queen in Thebes."

6   The father of the Tonnerre family in Laurence's Manawaka saga is named Lazarus.

7   *Commerce Prudence Industry* was the original motto of Winnipeg in 1884. In 1972, it changed to "*Unum Cum Virtute Multorum*," meaning "one with the strength of many."

8   Laurence called Adele Wiseman's mother a "Wisewoman," and employed the term in *Dance on the Earth*. She often referred to her fellow Canadian writers as her "tribe."

W.L. Morton – A Tribute

1   Thomas wrote "The Chariot of Ossian: Myth and Manitoba in *The Diviners*."

Tribute to Malcolm Ross

1   See note 26.

2   "The Drummer of All the World," collected in *The Tomorrow-Tamer and Other Stories*, first appeared in the Winter 1956 issue of *Queen's Quarterly*.

3   The Beta Sigma Phi First Novel Award was awarded for a Canadian debut novel from 1956 to 1967. Margaret Laurence, Sheila Watson, and Brian Moore were all winners.

Clara Thomas

1 See Clara Thomas and John Lennox's biography *William Arthur Deacon: A Canadian Literary Life* (Toronto: University of Toronto Press, 1982).

Lois Wilson

1 The Reverend Dr Lois Wilson (b. 1927) was the first female president of the Canadian Council of Churches (1976–79), the first woman moderator of the United Church of Canada (1980–82), co-director of the Ecumenical Forum of Canada, and chancellor of Lakehead University (1991–2000). In 1998, Prime Minister Jean Chrétien appointed her to the senate where she served as an independent until her retirement in 2002.

2 The Canadian Association of Elizabeth Fry Societies is a nonprofit organization assisting women in the criminal justice system.

3 Energy Probe, founded in 1969, researches areas relating to climate and conservation, nuclear power and radiation, and fossil fuels and transportation. Wilson was on the board from 1981 to 1987, and Laurence also joined from 1982 to 1987.

4 Project Ploughshares, founded in 1976, an organization advocating for disarmament and proffering peaceful resolutions as solutions to political conflict, is supported by the Canadian Council of Churches, among other community organizations.

5 The UN General Assembly's first Special Session on disarmament occurred in 1978 and reaffirmed that effective measures for nuclear disarmament are the highest priority.

6 The United Church of Canada was formed in 1925 as a union of the Presbyterian Church in Canada, the Methodist Church, the Congregational Churches of Canada, and the General Council of Local Union Churches.

7 The Ecumenical Forum of Canada, or the Canadian Churches Forum for Global Ministries, focused on missionary training programs to develop faith-based ministry.

For Marian Passmore Engel

1 2 Timothy 4:7.

Madeleine Wilkie Dumont

1 Batoche was established as a Métis settlement in 1872, the year Gabriel

Dumont established a ferry service near the settlement on the Saskatchewan River under the name "Gabriel's Crossing," which became the Dumonts' homestead.

2 William Frederick "Buffalo Bill" Cody (1846–1917), an American buffalo hunter, soldier, and lawman turned showman, organized "Buffalo Bill's Wild West and Congress of Rough Riders of the World" in 1883.

3 Laurence's desire to possess the courage of Madeleine Wilkie Dumont reflects her heroine, Morag Gunn of *The Diviners*, who imagines a foremother who shares her name and strengthens and inspires her.

YWCA Woman of the Year Award

1 Rosemary Ganley, who taught English at Lakefield College School and served on the national board of Amnesty International Canada, was named YWCA Woman of the Year in 1985 and won the Canada 150 Medal in 1992 for outstanding community service.

2 Margaret Laurence's husband, John Fergus Laurence, was a sergeant and mechanic in the Royal Air Force (RAF) before he was transferred to the Royal Canadian Air Force (RCAF) toward the end of World War II. Both the RAF and RCAF had established stations on the western edge of Neepawa and Carberry, Manitoba (Powers, *Alien Heart*, 42).

3 Takao Tanabe (b.1926), a Canadian artist from Prince Rupert, British Columbia, who was interned as a Japanese-Canadian during World War II, studied art at the Winnipeg School of Art, Hans Hofmann Central School of Arts and Crafts, and Tokyo University of Fine Arts. He paints primarily Western Canadian landscapes.

A Message to the Inheritors

1 On 6 August 1945, the American military dropped the atomic bomb Little Boy on Hiroshima, killing between 90,000 and 166,000 people within the first few months. A second bomb, Fat Man, was deployed by the American military on 9 August, killing between 60,000 and 80,000 people in Nagasaki.

2 This pamphlet was produced by a Canada emergency measures organization.

3 F.R. Scott is quoting John Stuart Mill's 1859 essay "On Liberty."

A Matter of Life or Death

1 Dr Helen Mary Caldicott (b.1938), an Australian physician and anti-nuclear

activist who founded the Women's Action for Nuclear Disarmament (WAND),
rose to fame in 1982 with her Academy Award–winning documentary about
the dangers of nuclear warfare, *If You Love This Planet*. She published *A Desperate Passion: An Autobiography* in 1992 and *If You Love This Planet: A Plan
to Save the Earth* in 2009.

2   Brummer, "Week of Protest," 6.

3   Ground Zero, founded in 1982 by Roger Molander to raise public awareness
of the dangers of nuclear warfare, organized a week-long protest against nuclear war in April 1982, with nearly a million participants. Molander later
edited *Who Will Stop the Bomb? A Primer on Nuclear Proliferation* (1985).

4   On 10 February 1983, the United States and Canada established the Canada-
US Test and Evaluation Program, a five-year agreement allowing the US to
request the testing of unarmed air-launched Cruise missiles in Canada. In
July 1983, Canada agreed to test the AGM–86B air-launched Cruise missile
in the Northwest Territories, British Columbia, Alberta, and Saskatchewan.
Cruise missiles are global-positioning, system-guided, pilotless, jet-propelled
aircraft designed to attack military targets (Pike, "Cruise Missiles").

5   Litton Industries was a US defence contractor specializing in production of
military communications equipment. In 1978 it was revealed that the Litton
plant in Rexdale, Ontario, received a $26.4 million grant from the federal
Canadian government to manufacture navigation systems for the Tomahawk
cruise missile.

6   In 1972 Atomic Energy of Canada Limited (AECL) began negotiations to sell
the CANDU (Canada Deuterium Uranium) reactor (a Canadian-designed
nuclear reactor) to Argentina. The Argentinian plant was only made operable
in 1984, production having been stalled by the 1976 coup. The reactor has also
been sold abroad to other countries, including South Korea, Romania, India,
Pakistan, and China.

7   US president Ronald Reagan's economic policies, now referred to as Reaga-
nomics, decreased government regulation and reduced government
spending. Instead, Reagan increased public expenditures for the Department
of Defense in particular, and prioritized the development of strategic nuclear
modernization plans and a national missile defence system that would "provide greater military and political leverage vis-à-vis the Soviets," thus inviting
widespread anti-nuclear protest and criticism (Kimball, "Looking Back").

8   "All People That on Earth Do Dwell" is the first line of the hymn now known
    as "Old Hundredth," composed by Loys Bourgeois (c.1510–1560). It is the par-
    aphrase of Psalm 134 in the Genevan Psalter. Laurence's favourite, it is the
    hymn that Hagar asks Mr Troy to sing in *The Stone Angel* and that catalyzes
    her epiphany (291–2).

The Artist Then, Now, and Always

1   Dr Helen Caldicott borrowed the term "psychic numbing" from Robert
    Lifton, who coined the phrase after studying the psychic trauma experienced
    by those affected by the bombing in Hiroshima and Nagasaki, to explain the
    tendency among North Americans to deny the possibility of nuclear warfare
    (Caldicott, *A Desperate Passion*, 172).
2   The seven deadly sins are lust, gluttony, greed, sloth, wrath, envy, and pride.
    Laurence's inclusion of despair concerns the work of fourth-century Greek
    theologian Evagrius Ponticus, who included despair among his "evil
    thoughts."

A Statement of Faith

1   Laurence declares, "My background and heritage are strongly Christian"
    (*Heart of a Stranger*, 151).
2   In 1957 the *New York Times* wrote, "the military has come up with a new word
    – 'overkill.' This is the term for the surplus in nuclear weapons beyond the
    number believed to be necessary to demolish all key Soviet targets" ("Over-
    kill," def. n.1a., *Oxford English Dictionary*).
3   Barbara Ward (1914–1981) was an economic theorist known for her pioneer-
    ing work supporting sustainable development.
4   Laurence's five years in the Gold Coast, later Ghana, inspired her novel *This
    Side Jordan* and short story collection, *The Tomorrow-Tamer and Other
    Stories*.
5   Grassy Narrows, or Asubpeeschoseewagong, First Nation, is an Ojibway com-
    munity located near Kenora, Ontario.
6   Ontario Minamata disease is a neurological syndrome caused by heightened
    levels of mercury ingestion resulting from consumption of contaminated
    local fish.

"Peace": A Word's Meaning

1 Matthew 5:9.

2 Matthew 22:39.

Operation Dismantle

1 Physicians for Social Responsibility, formed in 1971, gained momentum in 1973 by advocating for prevention of nuclear warfare through focusing on its potential effects on public health and medicine. Dr Helen Caldicott was president of PSR from 1978 to 1984.

2 The United Nations convened three sessions on disarmament in 1978, 1982, and 1988.

3 Alva Myrdal (1902–1986), a Swedish sociologist and political diplomat who won the Nobel Peace Prize in 1982 for her work in nuclear disarmament and peace movements, was Sweden's representative for the United Nations Disarmament Conference in Geneva, becoming minister of disarmament and chairing the 1972 UN committee on disarmament and development. Alfonso Garcia Robles (1911–1991) was a Mexican diplomat and politician. He became Mexico's permanent representative to the UN Committee on Disarmament and was the leading force in the Treaty of Tlatelolco, which set up a nuclear-free zone in Latin America and the Caribbean.

4 Roger Molander was a senior member of the United States National Security Council until his resignation in 1981 following frustration with the American government and the public's ignorance regarding the threat of nuclear war. Daniel Ellsberg is a journalist and activist who published on nuclear disarmament and leaked the Pentagon Papers in 1971, thus providing incriminating details of a top-secret study of US administrative decisions during the Vietnam War.

5 The Cruise Missile Conversion Project (CMCP) was a 1980s grassroots organization aiming to halt production of guidance systems for Cruise missiles through nonviolently protesting the Litton contract and mobilizing Litton workers.

6 Operation Dismantle, a nonprofit organization founded in 1977, dedicated to collectivizing public opinion to urge national governments to halt the nuclear arms race, created municipal Canadian referenda on disarmament and led a coalition to stop testing Cruise missiles over Canada.

7 Deuteronomy 30:19.

My Final Hour

1 William Shakespeare, *King Lear* 5:3:311.

2 Laurence employs the phrase "heart of a stranger" from Psalm 39 as the title for her 1976 collection of travel essays (Psalm 39:12 KJV).

3 The Battle of Maldon is an Old English poem commemorating Anglo-Saxon heroism in a battle against Vikings.

4 Morag Gunn cites this quotation from Traill's *A Canadian Settler's Guide*, also published as *The Female Emigrant's Guide* in 1854 (196), in *The Diviners* (97).

5 The "man of Nazareth" is Jesus Christ. Laurence calls the second part of the summary of the law – "Thou shalt love thy neighbour as thyself" (Matthew 23:39, also in Mark and Luke) – the "new commandment," and considers it the basis of the social gospel. This is slightly inaccurate. The new commandment appears in John's gospel: "A new commandment I give unto you, that ye love one another; just as I have loved you, ye are to love one another" (John 13:34 KJV).

6 I have excised two paragraphs about Helen Caldicott and Roger Molander that replicate, practically verbatim, two paragraphs in "A Statement of Faith."

7 I have excised one short section of Laurence's three-part quotation from Kennan that does not say much of note, while retaining the two longer, more important sections.

8 After quitting the Liberal Party over Prime Minister Trudeau's invocation of the War Measures Act during the October Crisis, Pauline Jewett (1922–1992) joined the New Democratic Party in 1972. A political science scholar, she was the first female president of Simon Fraser University and chancellor of Carleton University.

9 This section parallels Laurence's 1967 essay "The Artist Then, Now, and Always."

"Listen, Just Listen"

1 As commander of the Northwest Field Force, Major-General Fredrick Middleton (1825–1898), charged with suppressing the Métis uprising, led the assault on Batoche and is said to have spent the battle in camp, eating his lunch. "Métis" is a term used in Canada, generically, to describe persons of mixed European and Indigenous ancestry. However, the Métis, who formed distinctive cultural and collective ethnic identities throughout Canadian

history, were recognized under Section 35 of the Constitution Act, 1982 as one
of three "Aboriginal peoples in Canada." (Government of Canada. "Métis."
Library and Archives Canada. http://www.bac-lac.gc.ca/eng/discover/
aboriginal-heritage/metis/pages/introduction.aspx.)

2 Gabrielle Roy, born in St Boniface, Manitoba, in 1909, died in Quebec in 1983.
   The author of numerous novels, stories, and memoirs, including *The Tin
   Flute*, which won the Governor General's Award for fiction in 1947, she
   corresponded with Laurence.

3 Mennonites, a cultural and religious group affiliated with the Germanic
   Protestant Reformers of the sixteenth century, began to emigrate to Upper
   Canada from Germanic-speaking countries in 1776.

4 Under the War Measures Act, West Coast Japanese Canadians were detained
   in camps and their property confiscated by the Canadian government.

5 Laurence addresses this issue in her essay "Tribalism as Us Versus Them"
   collected in *Heart of a Stranger*, 179–88.

Quebec's "Freedom"

1 The Royal Canadian Mounted Police were implicated in several scandals in
   Quebec in the 1970s, including failed bombing attempts and theft of the Parti
   Québécois members list. The Quebec government enacted the Keable Inquiry
   into Illegal Police Activities in 1977, resulting in the conviction of seventeen
   RCMP officers (Bélanger, "Chronology of the October Crisis").

2 Pierre Elliott Trudeau was the Liberal prime minister of Canada, 1968–79
   and 1980–84. He advocated for Canadian federalism, including defeat of the
   Quebec separatist movement in the 1970s and 1980s.

3 In April 1971, RCMP officers stole dynamite, hiding it in Mont Saint-Grégoire
   to link the theft to the Front de Libération du Québéc (FLQ). The FLQ,
   founded in 1963, was a separatist paramilitary group supporting Quebec
   sovereignty that gained a reputation as a terrorist organization for its radical
   tactics, culminating in the kidnapping and murder of Pierre Laporte, minister of labour, in 1970, known as the October Crisis (Laurendeau, "Front
   de libération").

4 The War Measures Act, first employed by Parliament in 1914, "gave broad
   powers to the Canadian government to maintain security and order during

war or insurrection" (Smith, "The War Measures Act"). During the October Crisis, the government resurrected the act.

5 The Parti Québécois (PQ), established in 1968 as a nationalist political party under the leadership of René Lévesque, defeated the Liberals in 1976 and passed the Charter of the French Language, with other acts, in its first term.

6 Founded by René Lévesque, Jacques Parizeau, and Yves Michaud, who served as editor, *Le Jour* was a Quebec-based independent newspaper running daily from 1974 to 1976 and weekly from 1977 to 1978.

7 William "Bill" Davis, premier of Ontario, 1971–85, disapproved of Trudeau's offering Ontario's francophone population official bilingual status (Granatstein, "Bill Davis").

8 René Lévesque, founder of the Mouvement souveraineté-association, later the Parti Québécois, headed the PQ majority government in 1976 and 1981, but lost Quebec's first referendum on sovereignty in 1980.

9 The first Quebec Referendum, called by the PQ, which asked Québécois to vote on the future of succession, was defeated by a 59.56 percent majority on 20 May 1980. A second referendum, called in 1995, was also defeated.

Open Letter to the Mother of Joe Bass

1 See *Heart of a Stranger*, 220–1, for an introduction to this essay that Laurence composed but did not publish, and that contains the following passage:

I am a Canadian nationalist in the sense that I believe profoundly that my place, my people, my land, matter. And I believe that it is our selves, Canadians, who should control our industries and our natural resources. This, if it ever comes to be, will be no guarantee of anything – Canadians are no worse and certainly no better than people elsewhere. But at least the means of controlling the resources of a country should be within the hands of the people of that country, or so I believe. We have, in my land, gone through two colonial experiences, and we are still in the second. We have been colonized by, first Britain, and later and more subtly by America. The latter is in most ways our own fault. America wanted to buy our resources; it was we who sold. I think the time has come now for us to regain our land and our resources and I also think that we, at the very least, are cousins to America. As this article says, we cannot say Them – we have to say Us. I guess that is why I concentrated on writing about the children, my son and Mrs Bass's son, in particular. I am not alone in being afraid for all our children.

Laurence inserted and then excised the following sentence: "Perhaps we – Canadians and Americans – must try to develop the sense of Tribe as *Us in Relation to Them* in which both groups' identity is respected and truly recognized." This passage echoes her 1969 essay "Tribalism as Us Versus Them" which is included in the 2003 edition.

The Greater Evil

1   Both Jim Telford, a board of education trustee in Peterborough, and the Reverend Sam Buick openly opposed placing Laurence's novel *The Diviners* (1974) and Alice Munro's *Lives of Girls and Women* (1971) on the Ontario grade 13 curriculum (Cohen, *Censorship in Canadian Literature*, 117).

2   Section 163 of the Criminal Code of Canada, entitled "Offences Tending to Corrupt Morals," formerly titled under Section 159, pertains to an individual who "makes, prints, publishes, distributes, circulates, or has possession for the purpose of publication, distribution, or circulation any obscene written matter, picture, model."

Statement – PEN

1   PEN International, founded in 1921, is a global association of writers that promotes literature and defends freedom of expression. Originally, PEN stood for "Poets, Essayists, Novelists," but it now stands for "Poets, Playwrights, Editors, Essayists, Novelists." Canada's PEN Centre, which opened in 1926, includes Margaret Atwood and Yann Martel as members.

A Constant Hope

1   The national suicide rate rose during the 1960s and 1970s, peaking at 15.1 deaths per 100,000 in 1983, two years before Laurence's essay was first published ("Study: Suicide Rates," *Statistics Canada*).

2   *Swift Current* (1984–90), edited by Frank Davey and Fred Wah, was Canada's first electronic literary magazine. The goal was to allow "authors to post works-in-progress and to receive feedback in a way that print simply did not permit" (Herbert, "Technology," 1090).

3 The plaid pin motto, "*My Hope Is Constant in Thee*," occurs on page 458 of the NCL edition of *The Diviners*. By concluding with this motto, which provides the title of her essay, Laurence brings her argument full circle, as she does in *The Diviners*.

Works Cited

Allen, Richard. "Social Gospel." *The Canadian Encyclopedia*. Toronto: Historica Canada, 2006.

Arnold, Matthew. "Dover Beach." In *The Poems of Matthew Arnold, 1840–1867*. London, New York: Oxford University Press, 1909. www.bartleby.com/254./

Atwood, Margaret. *The Burgess Shale: The Canadian Writing Landscape of the 1960s*. Edmonton: University of Alberta Press, 2017.

– "Death of a Young Son by Drowning." In *The Journals of Susanna Moodie. Margaret Atwood: Selected Poems 1966–1984*, 72–3. Toronto: Oxford University Press, 1970.

– *A Writer's Life: The Margaret Laurence Lectures*, 215–38. Writers' Trust of Canada. Toronto: McClelland and Stewart, 2011.

– "Writers' Union of Canada." *The Canadian Encyclopedia*. Toronto: Historica Canada, 2006. Last modified 8 February 2006.

Bain, Robert. *The Clans and Tartans of Scotland*. 1900. Reprint, London: Collins, 1956.

Bélanger, Claude. "Chronology of the October Crisis and Its Aftermath – Quebec History." http://faculty.marianopolis.edu/c.belanger/quebechistory/chronos/october.htm.

Brummer, Alex. "Week of Protest against Nuclear Warfare." *Guardian*, 20 April 1982.

Caldicott, Helen. *A Desperate Passion: An Autobiography*. New York: W.W. Norton, 1992.

– *If You Love This Planet: A Plan to Save the Earth*. New York: W.W. Norton, 2009.

Coger, Greta, ed. *New Perspectives on Margaret Laurence: Poetic Narrative, Multiculturalism, and Feminism*. Westport: Greenwood, 1996.

Cohen, Mark. *Censorship in Canadian Literature*. Montreal & Kingston: McGill-Queen's University Press, 2001.

The Concise Oxford Dictionary, 12th ed. Oxford: Oxford University Press, 2011.

Davis, Laura K. "Margaret Laurence's Correspondence with Imperial Oil: An Anti-Imperialist at Work." *Journal of Canadian Studies/Revue d'études candiennes* 44, no. 1 (2010): 60–74. https://muse.jhu.edu/article/391495.

– *Margaret Laurence Writes Africa and Canada*. Waterloo: Wilfrid Laurier University Press, 2017.

Davis, Laura K., and Linda M. Morra, eds. *Margaret Laurence and Jack McClelland, Letters*. Edmonton: University of Albert Press, 2018.

Government of Canada. "Métis." *Library and Archives Canada*. http://www.bac-lac. gc.ca/eng/discover/aboriginal-heritage/metis/pages/introduction.aspx.

– "Study: Suicide Rates, an Overview, 1950 to 2009." *Statistics Canada*, http://www. statcan.gc.ca/daily-quotidien/120725/dq120725a-eng.htm.

Granatstein, J.I. "Bill Davis." In *The Canadian Encyclopedia*. Historica Canada. http://www.thecanadianencyclopedia.ca/en/article/bill-davis.

Greene, Graham. "The Young Dickens." *Collected Essays*, 79–86. London: Penguin Books, 1970.

Herbert, William, ed. "Technology, Communications, and Canadian Literature." *Encyclopedia of Literature in Canada*. Toronto: University of Toronto Press, 2002, 1090.

Janes, Percy. *House of Hate*. New Canadian Library, no. 124. Toronto: McClelland and Stewart, 1976.

Kennan, George F. "A Christian's View of the Arms Race." *Theology Today* (July 1982): 162–70.

– *The Nuclear Delusion: Soviet-American Relations in the Atomic Age*. New York: Pantheon Books, 1982.

Kertzer, Jonathan. *"That House in Manawaka": Margaret Laurence's* A Bird in the House. Toronto: ECW Press, 1992.

Kester, Marian. "The Awful Price of the Computer Age." *Globe and Mail*, 9 August 1984, 7.

Kimball, Daryl K. "Looking Back: The Nuclear Arms Control Legacy of Ronald Reagan." Arms Control Association. 1 July 2004. https://www.armscontrol.org/act/2004_07_08/Reagan.

Laurence, Margaret. Afterword to Sinclair Ross's *The Lamp at Noon and Other Stories*, 157–64. New Canadian Library Series. Toronto: McClelland and Stewart, 1968.

– "Are Holocaust Victims Expected to Die Again and Again … ?" *Toronto Star*, 5 March 1985. Clara Thomas Archives, York University. No. 1986–006/001 (26).

– "The Artist Then, Now, and Always." 1967. Reprint, *Trace: Prairie Writers on Writing*, edited by Birk Sproxton, 61–3. Winnipeg: Turnstone Press, 1986.

– *A Bird in the House*. Toronto: McClelland and Stewart, 1970.

– "Books That Mattered to Me." Talk for Friends of the Bata Library, Trent University, 1981. Reprint, *Margaret Laurence: An Appreciation*, edited by Christl Verduyn, 239–41. Peterborough: Broadview Press, 1988.

– "Canada Still Too Canada-Focused." *Montreal Star*, 3 December 1966, 2.

– "Canadian Third Track." Clara Thomas Archives, York University. No. 1986–006/001 (08).

– "Canadian Writers: From Neglect to Special Treatment." *Toronto Star*, 30 January 1970.

– "The Case for Canadian Literature." Convocation Address, Simon Fraser University. Reprint, *Simon Fraser University Week* 8.5, Spring 1977.

– *The Christmas Birthday Story*. Toronto: McClelland and Stewart, 1980.

– "Clara Thomas … Biographer, Teacher, Critic … and Pioneer." MS. Clara Thomas Archives, York University, No. 1986–006/001 (15).

– *Colors of Speech: Margaret Laurence's Early Writings*, edited by Nora Foster Stovel. Edmonton: Juvenilia Press, 2000.

– "A Constant Hope: Women in the Now and Future High Tech Age." *Canadian Woman Studies / Les Cahiers de la Femme*, 1985, 12–15. Reprint, *Dance on the Earth*, 278–83.

– "Convocation Address, York University, Toronto, June 1980." *Dance on the Earth*, 278–83.

– *Dance on the Earth: A Memoir*, edited by Jocelyn Laurence. Toronto: McClelland and Stewart, 1989.

– *The Diviners*. Toronto: McClelland and Stewart, 1974.

– "Don't Whisper Sudden; I Scare Easy." *Vancouver Sun*, 20 December 1969, 6. Clara Thomas Archives and Special Collections, York University.

– "Down East." *Vancouver Sun*, 20 March 1971. Reprint, Stovel, *Margaret Laurence's Heart of a Stranger*, 123–8.

– "The Drummer of All the World." In *The Tomorrow-Tamer and Other Stories*, 1–19. London: Macmillan, 1963.

– "Eye on Books: The Writer as Performer" Clara Thomas Archives, York University.

– "A Fantasy Fulfilled." Clara Thomas Archives, York University. No. 1980–001/023 (157).
– *The Fire-Dwellers*. Toronto: McClelland and Stewart, 1969.
– "For Marian Passmore Engel." *Ethos*. Clara Thomas Archives, York University. No. 1986–006.001 (21).
– "Gadgetry or Growing: Form and Voice in the Novel." *Journal of Canadian Fiction* no. 27 (1980): 54–62. Reprint, Woodcock, *A Place to Stand On*, 80–9.
– "The Greater Evil: Pornography or Censorship?" *Toronto Life*, September 1984. Reprint, *Dance on the Earth: A Memoir*, 278–83.
– "Half War – Half Peace." MS. York University Archives and Special Collections, Margaret Laurence Fonds 1980–0011023.
– "I Am a Taxi." In Stovel, *Margaret Laurence's Heart of a Stranger*, 135–40.
– Introduction to *Above Ground*, by Jack Ludwig. New Canadian Library. Toronto: McClelland and Steward, 1973.
– Introduction to *Crackpot*, by Adele Wiseman, 3–8. New Canadian Library. Toronto: McClelland and Stewart, 1978. Afterword to *Crackpot*, by Adele Wiseman, 473–82. Toronto: McClelland and Stewart, 1978.
– Introduction to *House of Hate*, by Percy Janes, vii–xi. New Canadian Library. Toronto: McClelland and Stewart, 1976.
– "Ivory Tower or Grassroots? The Novelist as Socio-political Being." In *A Political Art: Essays and Images in Honour of George Woodcock*, edited by William H. New, 15–25. Vancouver: University of British Columbia Press, 1978.
– *Jason's Quest*. Toronto: McClelland and Stewart, 1970.
– "Jericho's Brick Battlements." In *A Bird in the House*, 161–91. Toronto: McClelland and Stewart, 1970.
– *A Jest of God*. Toronto: McClelland and Stewart, 1966.
– "Journey from Lakefield." Clara Thomas Archives, York University Archives, 1980–001/004.
– "Listen, Just Listen." *Divided We Stand*, edited by Gary Geddes, 20–5. Toronto: Peter Martin, 1977.
– "Living Dangerously ... by Mail." *Vancouver Sun*, 23 September 1972. In Stovel, *Margaret Laurence's Heart of a Stranger*, 141–6.
– "Lois Wilson: Trent University, Peterborough, Ontario." 1 June 1984. MS. York University Archives and Special Collections, Margaret Laurence Fonds.
– *Long Drums and Cannons: Nigerian Dramatists and Novelists, 1952–66*. London:

Macmillan, 1968. Edited by Nora Foster Stovel. Edmonton: University of Alberta Press, 2001.

– "The Loons." In *A Bird in the House*, 108–20. Toronto: McClelland and Stewart, 1970.

– "Love and Madness in the Steel Forest." *Vancouver Sun*, 18 October 1969, 6.

– "Madeleine Wilkie Dumont." *As It Happens*. Clara Thomas Archives, York University. No. 1986–006/001 (04).

– "Man of Our People." In Stovel, *Margaret Laurence's Heart of a Stranger*, 161–7.

– *Margaret Laurence's Heart of a Stranger*, edited by Nora Foster Stovel. Edmonton: University of Alberta Press, 2003.

– *Margaret Laurence's Long Drums and Cannons: Nigerian Dramatists and Novelists, 1952–66*, edited by Nora Foster Stovel. Edmonton: University of Alberta Press, 2001.

– "A Matter of Life or Death." MS. York University Archives and Special Collections, Margaret Laurence Fonds.

– "Message to the Inheritors." Convocation address, York University, June 1980. Reprint, *Dance on the Earth*, 278–83.

– "My Final Hour." *Canadian Literature*, 25th Anniversary Issue (Spring 1984): 187–97. Address, Trent University Philosophy Society, 29 March 1983.

– *New Wind in a Dry Land: An Account of a Sojourn among the Nomads of Somaliland*. New York: Knopf Inc., 1964.

– "North Main Car." In *Colors of Speech*, 11–28.

– "On 'The Loons.'" In *The Art of Short Fiction: An International Anthology*, edited by Gary Geddes, 805–6. Toronto: Harper Collins, 1993.

– "Open Letter to the Mother of Joe Bass." In Stovel, *Margaret Laurence's Heart of a Stranger*, 157–60.

– "Operation Dismantle." Toronto, 22 October 1982. MS. York University Archives and Special Collections, Margaret Laurence Fonds.

– "'Peace' – A Word's Meaning." Clara Thomas Archives, York University. No. 1986–006/001 (37). In *What Peace Means to Me*. Canada, External Affairs, 1986, 27.

– "A Place to Stand On." In Stovel, *Margaret Laurence's Heart of a Stranger*, 5–10.

– "The Poem and the Spear." In Stovel, *Margaret Laurence's Heart of a Stranger*, 31–57.

– *The Prophet's Camel Bell*. Toronto: McClelland and Stewart, 1963.

– "Put Out One or Two More Flags." In Stovel, *Margaret Laurence's Heart of a Stranger*, 107–12.

– "Quebec's 'Freedom' Is a Vital Concern, but Freedom Itself Is That and More."
  Maclean's, 17 April 1978, 18.
– "A Queen in Thebes." *Tamarack Review* 32 (Summer 1964): 25–37.
– "Reply to the Toast to Canada." The Canadian Association for Irish Studies.
  Conference at Trent University. 21 March 1981. York University Archives and
  Special Collections, Margaret Laurence Fonds.
– "The River Flows Both Ways." *Vancouver Sun*, 11 December 1971.
– "River of Now and Then." In *The Diviners*, 9–27. Toronto: McClelland and
  Stewart, 1974.
– "Road from the Isles." In Stovel, *Margaret Laurence's Heart of a Stranger*, 113–22.
– "Salute of the Swallows." *Vancouver Sun*, 22 May 1971.
– "The Shack." In Stovel, *Margaret Laurence's Heart of a Stranger*, 147–50.
– *Six Darn Cows*. Toronto: Lorimer, 1979.
– "Sources." *Mosaic*, no. 3 (Spring 1970): 80–4. Reprint, "A Place to Stand On,"
  in Stovel, *Margaret Laurence's Heart of a Stranger*, 5–10.
– "A Statement of Faith." Convocation address, Emmanuel College, Victoria Uni-
  versity, Toronto, 6 May 1982. Reprint, Woodcock, *A Place to Stand On*, 56–60.
– *The Stone Angel*. Toronto: McClelland and Stewart, 1964.
– "A Tale of Typewriters." Clara Thomas Archives, York University. No. 1986–006/
  001 (43).
– "Ten Years' Sentences." *Canadian Literature*, no. 41 (Summer 1969): 10–16.
  Reprint, Woodcock, *A Place to Stand On*, 28–34.
– *This Side Jordan*. New York: St Martin's Press, 1960.
– "Time and the Narrative Voice." In *Narrative Voice: Short Stories and Reflections
  by Canadian Writers*, edited by John Metcalf, 126–30. Toronto: McGraw-Hill
  Ryerson, 1972.
– *The Tomorrow-Tamer and Other Stories*. London: Macmillan, 1963.
– *A Tree for Poverty: Somali Poetry and Prose*. McMaster University Library Press,
  1970.
– "Tribalism as Us Versus Them." In Stovel, *Margaret Laurence's Heart of a
  Stranger*, 179–88.
– "Tribute to Malcolm Ross." MS. York University Archives and Special Collections,
  Margaret Laurence Fonds.
– "Upon a Midnight Clear." In Stovel, *Margaret Laurence's Heart of a Stranger*,
  151–6.
– "Via Rail and Via Memory." In *Dance on the Earth*, 275–7.

– "Voices from Future Places." *Vancouver Sun*, 22 April 1972, 6.

– "When You Were Five and I Was Fourteen." *Quill & Quire*, Fiftieth Anniversary Issue (April 1985). Reprint, *Dance on the Earth*, 278–83.

– "Where the World Began." *Maclean's*, December 1972, 23, 80. Reprint, Stovel, *Margaret Laurence's Heart of a Stranger*, 169–74.

– "W.L. Morton – A Tribute." MS. York University Archives and Special Collections, Margaret Laurence Fonds.

– "YWCA Woman of the Year Award." MS. York University Archives and Special Collections, Margaret Laurence Fonds.

Laurendeau, Marc. "Front de libération du Quebec." *The Canadian Encyclopedia*. Toronto: Historica Canada, 2013. Web. 11 August 2013.

Lennox, John, and Ruth Panofsky, eds. *Selected Letters of Margaret Laurence and Adele Wiseman*. Toronto: University of Toronto Press, 1997.

Ludwig, Jack. *Above Ground*. Toronto: Little, Brown and Co., 1968.

Mill, John Stuart. "On Liberty." In *Essays on the Constitution*, edited by Frank R. Scott. Toronto: University of Toronto Press, 1977.

Milton, John. *Areopagitica; A Speech for the Liberty of Unlicensed Printing, to the Parliament of England*. London: S.N., 1644.

Molander, Roger, and Robbie Nichols, eds. *Who Will Stop the Bomb? A Primer on Nuclear Proliferation*. New York: Facts on File, 1985.

Morton, William Lewis. *Manitoba: A History.* Toronto: University of Toronto Press, 1957.

Pike, "Cruise Missiles." Federation of American Sciences. 2015. http://fas.org/nuke/intro./cm/.

Powers, Lyall. *Alien Heart: The Life and Work of Margaret Laurence*. Winnipeg: University of Manitoba Press, 2003.

Purdy, Al W. "Roblin's Mills (circa 1842)." In *Wild Grape Wine*, 46–7. Toronto: McClelland and Stewart, 1968.

Riegel, Christian. *Writing Grief: Margaret Laurence and the Work of Mourning*. Winnipeg: University of Manitoba Press, 2003.

Ross, Sinclair. *The Lamp at Noon and Other Stories*. Toronto: McClelland and Stewart, 1968.

Sandburg, Carl. "Losers." In *Smoke and Steel: Complete Poems of Carl Sandburg*, 87. New York: Harcourt Brace, 1920.

Scott, Frank R. *Essays on the Constitution*. Toronto: University of Toronto Press, 1977.

– "Freedom of Speech in Canada." In *Essays on the Constitution*, 60.

Shakespeare, William. *The Tragedy of King Lear*. Vol. 46, Part 3. The Harvard
    Classics. New York: P.F. Collier & Son, 1909–14. 2001. www.bartleby.com/46/3/.

Sherman, Kenneth. "*Crackpot*: A Lurianic Myth." *Waves* 3, no. 1 (1974): 5–10.

Shields, Carol. "Canadian Writing." *Startle and Illuminate: Carol Shields on
    Writing*, edited by Anne Giardini and Nicholas Giardini, 133–41. Toronto:
    Random House, 2016.

Silversides, Ann. "Literature Goes Electronic from Coast to Coast." *Globe and Mail*,
    30 June 1984.

Smith, Denis. "The War Measures Act." In *The Canadian Encyclopedia*. Historica
    Canada. http://www.thecanadianencyclopedia.ca/en/article/war-measures-act.

Socken, Paul, ed. *Intimate Strangers: The Letters of Margaret Laurence and Gabrielle
    Roy*. Winnipeg: University of Manitoba Press, 2004.

Stovel, Bruce. "Coherence in *A Bird in the House*." In Coger, *New Perspectives on
    Margaret Laurence*, 81–96.

Stovel, Nora Foster. "'Death and Love': Romance and Reality in Margaret Lau-
    rence's *A Bird in the House*." In *Dominant Impressions: Essays on the Canadian
    Short Story*, edited by Gerald Lynch and Angela Arnold Robbeson, 99–114.
    Ottawa: University of Ottawa Press, 1999.

– *Divining Margaret Laurence: A Study of Her Complete Writings*. Montreal &
    Kingston: McGill-Queen's University Press, 2008.

– "Mourning Becomes Margaret: Laurence's Farewell to Fiction in Her Final,
    Unfinished Novel, 'Dance on the Earth.'" *Journal of Canadian Studies: Myth and
    Ideology: Contributions of Canadian Thinkers*, Special Association of Canadian
    Studies Issue 34, no. 4 (2000): 105–20.

– *Rachel's Children: Margaret Laurence's* A Jest of God, edited by Robert Lecker.
    Toronto: ECW Press, 1992.

– *Stacey's Choice: Margaret Laurence's* The Fire-Dwellers, edited by Robert Lecker.
    Toronto: ECW Press, 1993.

Thomas, Clara. "The Chariot of Ossian: Myth and Manitoba in *The Diviners*."
    Journal of Canadian Studies 13, no. 3 (Autumn 1978): 55–63.

– *The Manawaka World of Margaret Laurence*. Toronto: McClelland and Stewart,
    1975.

Parr Traill, Catharine. *The Canadian Settler's Guide*. 1857. London: E. Stanford,
    1860.

Verduyn, Christl, "(Es)saying It Her Way: Carol Shields as Essayist." In *Carol Shields and the Extra-Ordinary*, edited by Marta Dvorak and Manina Jones, 59–79. Montreal & Kingston: McGill-Queen's University Press, 2007.

Waltz, Robert B. *An Introduction to Braid Scots*. Minnesota: Robert B. Waltz, 2013.

Wilson, Lois. *Like a Mighty River*. Kelowna: Wood Lake Books, Inc., 1981.

Wiseman, Adele. *Crackpot*. Toronto: McClelland and Stewart, 1978.

Woodcock, George, ed. *A Place to Stand On: Essays in Honour of Margaret Laurence*. Edmonton: NeWest Press, 1983.

Xiques, Donez. *Margaret Laurence: The Making of a Writer*. Toronto: Dundurn Press, 2005.

Index

Aboriginal peoples. *See* Indigenous peoples

Above Ground (Ludwig), introduction by Laurence, xxviii, 178–83; on Biblical and classical references, 182–3; on living in the face of death, 178–80, 181–2, 183; on women and sex in, 180–1

accidents and injuries, 80–2

Achebe, Chinua, xxii, xxiv, xl, 11, 54–7, 301n12; *Arrow of God*, 55–6, 168; *A Man of the People*, 56; *No Longer at Ease*, 56; *Things Fall Apart*, 55, 301n12

Africa: colonialism in, 52, 166; lessons and inspiration from, xxii, xli–xlii, 30, 57, 166; Nigerian writers, 4, 10–11, 53; reflections on books about, xxii, 9–11, 14; support for, xxxvii. *See also* Achebe, Chinua; Ghana; Nigeria; Somaliland; Soyinka, Wole

African-Americans, xxxviii

aging, 246–8, 256

air travel, 70–1, 85–6

Aluko, T.M., 53

Amadi, Elechi, 53

Angry Young Men (writing school), 29, 302n2

Argentina, xxxiv–xxxv, 223, 229, 236–7, 253, 316n6

Arnold, Matthew: "Dover Beach," 57, 304n2

artists, and nuclear disarmament, 231–2, 245, 254–5

Assiniboine people, 310n1

Asubpeeschoseewagong (Grassy Narrows) First Nation, 237, 292, 317n5

Atlantic Advocate, 38

Atomic Energy of Canada Limited (AECL), 316n6

Atwood, Margaret, xxvi–xxvii, xxxix, 54; *The Burgess Shale*, xxviii; "Death of a Young Son by Drowning," 116, 310n3; *Survival*, 3, 298n1

autobiographical fiction, 4, 6, 38–9, 187

Baker, Sherman, 300n1

Bancroft (Ontario), 116

Bass, Joe, 268, 269–70, 271

Batoche (Saskatchewan), xxxviii, 259–60, 264, 301n5, 314n1

Batoche, Battle of, 213, 298n13, 301n5, 308n1, 311n9, 319n1

"The Battle of Maldon" (Anglo-Saxon poem), 247, 319n3

belief, fiction as, 51

Belmont Award (*Saturday Night*), 141

Beta Sigma Phi First Novel Award, 202, 313n3

Biafra, 11, 55, 56, 301n11

Bible: allusions in *Above Ground* (Ludwig), 182–3; Deuteronomy 30:19, xxxv, 245, 256; John 13:34, 298n10, 319n5; Matthew 22:37–9, xxxvi, Matthew 5:9, 318n1, Matthew 22:39, 318n2, Matthew 23:39, 319n5; Psalm 39, 247, 319n2; Revelation, 85, 6:1–8, 17:1–18, 18:1–24, 306n6; titles from, 25, 26. *See also* Christianity; Jesus

Big Bear (Mistahimaskwa), 166, 169–70, 311n9

biography, 51, 204

bird-watching, 88, 92–5, 98, 117

Birney, Earle, 138–9; *Collected Poems*, 139; *The Creative Writer*, 139

Blais, Marie-Claire, xxix, 134–5; *Mad Shadows*, 135; *A Season in the Life of Emmanuel*, 134–5, 140; *Tête Blanche*, 135

Blake, William, 184, 312n1

bookshops, 141

Bowering, George: *Mirror on the Floor*, 134, 135

Boy's Own Annual, 158

British Columbia, 114–15. *See also* Vancouver

British North America Act, 298n17, 309n8

Broadbent, Ed, 252

Buckler, Ernest: *The Mountain and the Valley*, 53

Buick, Sam, 40, 322n1

Burton, Pierre, 138
bus travel, 71–2, 119–23

Caldicott, Helen: about, 315n1; on nuclear
weapons and disarmament, 228, 235–6, 237,
244; Physicians for Social Responsibility
and, 318n1; on psychic numbing, xxxiv, 230,
232, 238, 244, 255, 317n1
Callaghan, Morley, xxvii, xxix, 53, 128–9, 138,
152, 154, 164, 293; *More Joy in Heaven*, 128;
Such Is My Beloved, 128; *They Shall Inherit
the Earth*, 128
Campbell, Maria, 169–70
Canada: British North America Act, 298n17,
309n8; censorship and attacks on writers
in, 281; colonialism in, 52, 57–8, 263, 321n1;
devaluation of, 66–7; geographic understanding of, 114–15; nuclear disarmament
and, 229–30, 236–7, 241, 244, 252–3; railway
and, 104, 105. *See also* Prairies; Quebec
Canada Council grants, xli, 288
Canada-US Test and Evaluation Program,
316n4
Canadian Association of Elizabeth Fry
Societies, 208, 314n2
Canadian Centennial Library series, 138
Canadian Council of Churches, 208, 314n4
Canadian Forum, 52
Canadian literature: in 1930s and 1940s, 128–
31; in 1960s, xxvii–xxix, 131–6, 140–1; advocacy for, 152; cities, portrayal of, 128, 133–4;
definition, 127; development of, 53–4, 127–
8, 152, 154–6; in Edmonton, 139; in education system, 151–2, 205–6; essays on,
xxvi–xxx; first-person narrative, 134;
"land" novel, 128; Laurence, relations with
fellow CanLit writers, xxvi, xxx, 91, 262,
293, 313n8; Laurence's favourites, 163, 164–7,
169–70; in Montreal, 137–8; nationalism
and parochialism, xxix, 131, 141–2, 156–7;
New Canadian Library series, xxvii, 53, 139,
141, 202, 205; non-hero, 131–3; publication
overseas, 136; *Quill & Quire* and, 159–60;
reality, portrayal of, 135; social themes, 134–
5; Third World and, xxiv, 52; in Toronto,
138–9; value of, xxvii, 150–1, 153; in Vancouver, 140; in Winnipeg, 139
Canadian Literature (journal), 140
Canadian National Railway (CNR), 106, 109,
308n2. *See also* railway

Canadian Pacific Railway (CPR), 106, 109,
308n2, 312n10. *See also* railway
CANDU (Canada Deuterium Uranium)
reactor, 316n6
Cary, Joyce: *The Horse's Mouth*, 168
Cassandra, 82, 305n1
catalogues, mail-order, 101–3, 292
censorship: arguments against, 273–4; Criminal Code and, 276–7, 322n2; Laurence's
position on, 272, 275–6, 278–9; of Laurence's work, xxi, 40, 272–3, 281, 322n1;
pornography and, 274–5
characters: narrative voice and, 16–17, 19, 32;
non-hero, 131–3
children: childbirth, 268–9, 284–5; child care,
289; fear for, 269–71; in *The Lamp at Noon
and Other Stories* (Ross), 176–7; new technologies and, 285–6; pornography and,
275, 276, 277, 278
Chinese Canadians, 78
Christianity: bare essentials of Church, 207–
8; Lois Wilson's work within, 207–9; nuclear disarmament and religious faith, 237,
238, 253; social gospel, xxxvi, 226, 234–5,
248. *See also* Bible; Jesus
Christmas, 74–9; childhood memories, 75–8;
devaluation of, 74; in Elm Cottage, 78–9;
meaning of, 74–5, 79
cities: in New York, 84–6; portrayal in fiction,
128, 133–4; in Toronto, xxiv–xxv, 69–70, 72–
3, 81–4, 86, 115–16, 119; in Victoria, 80–1
Clark, John Pepper, xxii, 53
Clarke, Austin, 138; *Among Thistles and
Thorns*, 138; *The Meeting Point*, 133–4
Clarke-Irwin (publisher), 155
Clarkson, Adrienne, 41, 42, 303n1
Clear Lake, Riding Mountain National Park
(Manitoba), 39, 97–8
Cody, William Frederick "Buffalo Bill," 213,
315n2
Cohen, Leonard, 138, 293; *Beautiful Losers*,
134, 135, 140
Cohen, M. Charles, 138
Cole, Jean Murray, xxxix
colonialism, 52–3, 57–8, 166, 263, 321n1
computers, 286–8. *See also* technologies, new
"The Controversy," xxi, xxvi, 40, 272–3, 281,
322n1. *See also* censorship
Co-operative Commonwealth Federation,
xxxvi, 310n3. *See also* New Democratic
Party

Crackpot (Wiseman), introduction by Laurence, xxviii, 189–95; on narrative voice, 193–4; on parental figures, 190–1; on protagonist's journey, 191–3, 194–5; on themes, 189–90; on Winnipeg, 193
Cree peoples, 166–7, 310n1
Criminal Code, 276–7, 322n2
Cruise Missile Conversion Project (CMCP), 244, 318n5
Cruise missiles, 229, 236, 241, 244, 252, 253

Daniells, Roy, 140
Davey, Frank, 287, 289, 322n2
Davies, Robertson, 117, 145; *The Diary of Samuel Marchbanks*, 117; *Fifth Business*, 170
Davis, Laura, xxxiii
Davis, William "Bill," 266, 321n7
Depression, 64, 78, 101
despair, 224, 230, 232, 255, 317n2
dialect, 188
Diamond Lake (fictional), xxiii, 19, 39
Dickens, Charles, 158; *A Christmas Carol*, 74
Dickson, Lovat, 155
Dieppe, Battle of, xxxiii, 59, 221, 304n6
dispossession, theme of, 59
Diviners, The (Laurence): autobiographical elements, 39, 311n1; Battle of Dieppe and, xxxiii; censorship controversy, xxi, 40, 272–3, 322n1; *The Clans and Tartans of Scotland* in, 304n11; comparison to *Crackpot* (Wiseman), 313n1; dispossession theme, xxxvii, 59; four-letter words in, 43; Governor General's Award, 311n6; graduate class on, 294; narrative structure, xxiii; river and, xxv; Scots plaid pin with motto, xli, 290; snake dancer and, 305n3; W.L. Morton and, 200. *See also* Morag Gunn (fictional)
Dostoevsky, Fyodor: *The Idiot*, 191
Doyle, Arthur Conan: *The White Company*, 162
Dryden Paper Mill, 111, 309n9
Dumont, Gabriel, xxxvii, 166, 212–13, 259–61, 314n1
Dumont, Madeleine Wilkie, xxxix, 212–13, 315n3
Duthie, Bill, 141

Ecumenical Forum of Canada (Canadian Churches Forum for Global Ministries), 208, 314n7
editing process, 21–4

Edmonton, 139
education: author visits to schools, 42; Canadian literature taught in, 151–2, 205–6
Ekwensi, Cyprian, xxii, 53
Ellsberg, Daniel, 244, 318n4
Elm Cottage (England), xxvi, 78–9
Energy Probe, xxxv, 208, 314n3
Engel, Marian Passmore, xxx, 54, 210–11, 293, 294; *Bear*, 210
England, 78–9, 108
environmentalism, xxxi–xxxiii, 66–7, 86, 115–16. *See also* nuclear disarmament
essays, xx
Ethos (magazine), 210
Evagrius Ponticus, 317n2
Evans, Hubert, 53

feminism. *See* women
fiction: autobiographical fiction, 4, 6, 38–9, 187; biography and, 51, 204; exploring the self through, 3–4, 6, 7; facets of, 51–2, 60; flashbacks, 12; groundedness and universality, 7; history and, 51, 199–200; influences on, 29, 50–1, 54, 305n1; lessons learned, 9, 14; narrative forms and voice, 28–37; narrative voice and time, 15–19; people influences, 5–6, 14; place influences, 5
films, based on books, 34
Findley, Timothy, 280, 293; *The Wars*, 170
Fire-Dwellers, The (Laurence): autobiographical elements, 39; composition, 305n1; defence of, xx; epigraph, 302n11; narrative form and voice, xxii, xxiii, 13–14, 16, 34–7; revisions, 23–4; Stacey character, 13; theme, 6–7, 59; title, 26–7
First Lady of Manawaka (film), xxi
first-person narrative, 16, 30–1, 32, 33, 134
flashbacks, 12
fools of God, 190–1
form. *See* narrative form
freedom, 58–9, 167, 225, 274, 277
Freeman, E.G.D., 207
Front de Libération du Québec (FLQ), 265, 320n3
Frye, Northrop, 245, 256
Furr, Bill, 268, 269

Ganley, Rosemary, 315n1
gardening, 88–9
Ghana (Gold Coast), xxii, xxxvii, xli–xlii, 237, 268–9, 302n3, 317n4

Gibson, Graeme, xxvi, 54
Girl's Own Annual, 158
gladiators, Roman, 307n7
Godfrey, Dave, 54, 139
Gold Coast. *See* Ghana
Gottlieb, Phyllis, 139
Governor General's Award, xx, xxiii, xxvii, xxviii, 165–6, 167, 210, 225, 311n6
Grassy Narrows (Asubpeeschoseewagong) First Nation, 237, 292, 317n5
Greene, Graham, 3, 5, 7, 28, 302n1
Ground Zero (anti-nuclear-weapons education project), 228, 236, 316n3
Group of Seven, xxxii, 116
Grove, Frederick Philip, 164

Hagar Shipley (fictional): development of, xxii, 4–5, 11–12; groundedness and universality of, 7; Laurence's divorce and, xxiii; narrative voice of, 30–2; "Old Hundredth" (hymn) and, xxxv, 317n8; self-empowerment of, xlii, 59
Haig-Brown, Roderick, 44, 303n4
Harlow, Robert, 140
Hasan, Mahammed 'Abdille, xxxvii
Hausa people, 301n13
Hiebert, Paul, 139
Hiroshima, 222, 227, 235, 248, 315n1
history, and fiction, 51, 199–200
Hitler, Adolf: *Mein Kampf*, 273
Hogan, Homer: "Who Cooked the Canadian Goose?," 151, 153
Holocaust, xxxviii, 221–2, 235, 248
Honey Bunch Series, 102, 308n3
House of Anansi, 155
House of Hate (Janes), introduction by Laurence, xxviii, 184–8; on characters, 185–7; on narrator, 184–5; on Newfoundland dialect, 188, 313n2; on semiautobiographical nature, 187; on setting, 184; on structure, 187–8; on theme, 185
Hudson's Bay Company, 164
Hughes, Richard, 87
humility, 246–7
Huron-Wendat peoples, 307n4
Hurtig, Mel, 141, 155, 310n1
Hutchinson, Helen, 42, 303n1

Igbo (Ibo) people, 10, 54–5, 300n9, 301n11
Imperial Oil, xxxii–xxxiii
Indigenous peoples: on land, xxxii, 263; mercury poisoning in Asubpeeschoseewagong

(Grassy Narrows) First Nation, 237, 292, 317n5; railway and, 104; speculated ancestry from, xxxix, 310n2; support for, xxxvii–xxxviii, xxxix, xl, 267, 311n8. *See also* Métis
injuries and accidents, 80–2
International Year of Peace, xxxv, 239–40
Israel, Charles, 138; *The Hostages*, 138

Janes, Percy. *See House of Hate* (Janes), introduction by Laurence
Japan, 222, 227, 235, 248, 315n1
Japanese Canadians, xxxviii, 215–16, 263, 320n4
Jest of God, A (Laurence): composition, 305n1; defence of, xx; epigraph, 302n11; film adaptation, 34, 297n4; Governor General's Award, 311n6; narrative form and voice, xxiii, 32–4, 36, 134; revisions, 23; theme, 6–7, 12–13, 59
Jesus: on love of neighbours, 223, 226, 234, 240, 248, 298n10, 319n5; on peacemakers, xxxv, 240; summation of law by, xxxvi
Jewett, Pauline, 252, 319n8
Jews, xxxviii, 221–2, 235, 248
Jones, Judith, 21, 26–7, 85, 301n1
Journal of Canadian Studies, 200
Joyce, James, 28, 118
justice, struggle for, 223–5

Keable Inquiry into Illegal Police Activities, 320n1
Kennan, George, xxxiv, 250–1, 251–2
Kester, Marian: "The Awful Price of the Computer Age," 285, 286
King Lear (Shakespeare), 246
Kipling, Rudyard, 158, 161–2
Kitchener (Ontario), 116–17
Knopf (publisher), 20–1, 22, 25, 302n7
Kogawa, Joy: *Obasan*, xxxiv
Kriesel, Henry, 139; *The Betrayal*, 139
Kroetsch, Robert, 54; *But We Are Exiles*, 140; *The Words of My Roaring*, 132–3, 134, 140–1

Lakefield (Ontario), xxvi, 117–18, 310n3
Lake Wapakata (fictional), xxiii, 19
Lamp at Noon and Other Stories, The (Ross), afterword by Laurence, xxvii–xxviii, 173–7; on children, 176–7; on land, 174; on men, 175–6; on themes, 173, 177; on women, 174–5
"land" novel, 128
language: Canadian language, 261; demean-

ment of, 224, 239; dialect, 188; faith in, 270–
1; language rights for francophone Canadians, 266, 321n7; nuclear weapons and,
229, 235, 239, 249–50, 317n2; Pictish, 304n12
Laurence, David (son), 48, 119, 237, 268–9
Laurence, Jocelyn (daughter), xxi, 48, 108,
119, 163, 237, 309n7
Laurence, John Fergus (Jack; husband), xxiii,
107, 165, 214, 292, 302n3, 309nn5–6, 315n2
Laurence, Margaret: introduction, xix; on
aging, 246–8, 256; ancestry and roots,
xxxvii, xxxix, 4–5, 63–6, 67–8, 260–1,
304n10, 310n2; appearance, 121; Atwood on,
xxvi–xxvii, xxxix; beginnings of writing
career, 8–9; birth of son, 268–9; cabin on
Otonabee River, 41, 67, 87–91, 92–6, 98–100;
CanLit writers, relations with, xxvi, xxx, 91,
262, 293, 313n8; character of, 293–4, 295;
childhood reading experiences, 158–60,
161–3; on Christmas, 74–9; city experiences,
80–6; David Laurence on, xv–xvi; education, 311n2; as essayist, xix–xxi, 291–2; first
encounters with, 291; honorary degrees
and convocation addresses, 150; life experience, 292; on mail-order catalogues, 101–3;
marriage, xxiii, 214; name, 45, 46, 48, 303n5;
national recognition, xix; on railway, 104–
13; reflections on writing career, 9–14; religious background, xxxvi, 74, 94–5, 307n3,
317n1; signature on letters, 303n1; social
gospel and, xxxvi, 226, 234–5, 248; themes
in works, 12–13, 57, 58–9; travels, 299n5; on
typewriters, 45–9; van Herk on, 291–5;
women in childhood of, 162–3
– CHILDREN'S FICTION: The Christmas
Birthday Story, xxi; Jason's Quest, 145,
310n2; Six Darn Cows, xxi
– ESSAYS: afterword to The Lamp at Noon
and Other Stories (Ross), xxvii–xxviii, 173–
7; "Are Holocaust Victims Expected to Die
Again and Again …?," xxxviii, 298n15;
"The Artist Then, Now, and Always," xxxi,
xxxvii, 231–3; "Books That Mattered to
Me," xxix–xxx, 161–70; "Canada Still Too
Canada-Focused," xxix, 137–42, 310n2;
"Canadian Novels: Change in the Past
Decade," xxviii–xxix, 127–36; "Canadian
Third Track," xxxiv, 298n8; "Canadian
Writers: From Neglect to Special Treat-
ment," xxix, 154–7; "The Case for Canadian
Literature," xxvii, xxx, 150–3; "Clara
Thomas … Biographer, Teacher, Critic …

and Pioneer," 203–6; "A Constant Hope:
Women in the Now and Future High Tech
Age," xl–xli, 283–90, 323n3; "Don't Whisper
Sudden; I Scare Easy," xxv, xxxii, 80–6;
"Down East," xxv, xxxii, 114–18, 309n1; "Eye
on Books: The Writer as Performer," xxiv,
40–4; "A Fantasy Fulfilled," xxv, 101–3;
"Gadgetry or Growing: Form and Voice in
the Novel," xxiii, 28–37; "The Greater Evil:
Pornography or Censorship?," xli, 272–9;
"Half War—Half Peace: A Writer's Working Relationship with Publishers" xxiii, 20–
7; "I Am a Taxi," xxvi, 305n4; introduction
to Above Ground (Ludwig), xxviii, 178–83;
introduction to Crackpot (Wiseman),
xxviii, 189–95; introduction to House of
Hate (Janes), xxviii, 184–8; "Ivory Tower or
Grassroots?: The Novelist as Socio-political Being," xxiv, xxxvi, xli–xlii, 50–60;
"Journey from Lakefield," xxvi, 119–23;
"Listen, Just Listen," xxvi, xxxii, xxxvi, xl,
259–64; "Living Dangerously … by Mail,"
20, 302n5; "Lois Wilson," 207–9; "Love and
Madness in the Steel Forest," xxiv–xxv,
69–73; "Man of Our People," xxxii, xxxvii–
xxxviii, xxxix–xl, 212; "For Marian Passmore Engel," 210–11; "A Matter of Life or
Death," xxxi, xxxiii, xxxiv, 226–30; "A Message to the Inheritors," xxxvi–xxxvii, 221–5;
"The More Interesting Country," xxv–xxvi,
104–13; "My Final Hour," xxxiii, xxxvi,
246–56, 319nn6–7; "North Main Car,"
313n4; "On 'The Loons,'" xxii–xxiii, 38–9;
"Open Letter to the Mother of Joe Bass,"
xxxviii, 268–71, 321n1; "Operation Dismantle," xxxiii, xxxiv, 242–5; "'Peace': A
Word's Meaning," xxxi, xxxiii–xxxiv, 239–
41; "The Poem and the Spear," xxxvii;
"Quebec's 'Freedom' Is a Vital Concern,
but Freedom Itself Is That and More," xl,
265–7, 298n16; "Reply to the Toast to Canada," xxxvi, 298n9; "The River Flows Both
Ways," xxv, 87–91; "Road from the Isles,"
304n10, 307n1; "Salute of the Swallows,"
xxv, 92–6; "The Shack," xxv, 97–100, 307n1,
308n2; "Sources," xxii, xxviii, xxxi, 3–7; "A
Statement of Faith," 234–8; "Statement –
PEN," 280–2; "A Tale of Typewriters," xxiii–
xxiv, 45–9; "Ten Years' Sentences," xxii,
xxxvii, 8–14; "Time and the Narrative
Voice," xxii, 15–19; "Tribalism as Us Versus
Them," xxxviii, 298n14, 321n1; "Tribute to

Malcolm Ross," 201–2; "Upon a Midnight Clear," xxvi, 74–9; "Voices from Future Places," xxx, 143–9; "When You Were Five and I Was Fourteen," xxvii, 158–60; "Where the World Began," xxiv, xxxii, 63–8; "W.L. Morton – A Tribute," 199–200; "YWCA Woman of the Year Award," xl, 214–17
– LITERARY CRITICISM: *Long Drums and Cannons*, xxii, 10, 50, 56, 168, 299n2; *A Tree for Poverty*, xxii
– NONFICTION: *Dance on the Earth*, xxi; *Heart of a Stranger*, xxi, xxiii, 297n1, 319n2; *The Prophet's Camel Bell*, xxii, 9–10, 22–3, 25, 166, 299n5, 302n7, 309n6, 311n5
– NOVELS: "Dance on the Earth" (unfinished), xxi, xxxviii, 298n13; *Pillars Of The Nation* (juvenilia), 107, 308n4. See also *The Diviners* (Laurence); *The Fire-Dwellers* (Laurence); *A Jest of God* (Laurence); *The Stone Angel* (Laurence); *This Side Jordan* (Laurence)
– POETRY: "Via Rail and Via Memory," xxvi, 309n10
– SHORT STORIES: *A Bird in the House*, xxii, xxviii, 6, 17, 24, 59, 299n6, 310n2; "The Drummer of All the World," 202, 313n2; "The Loons," 18–19, 38–9; "A Queen in Thebes," 313n5; *The Tomorrow-Tamer and Other Stories*, xxii, xxv, 9–10, 57, 300n6, 302n7, 317n4; "To Set Our House in Order," 17–18; "The Voices of Adamo," 166, 311n7
Layton, Irving, 83, 138
Lee Ling, 78
Le Jour (newspaper), 266, 321n6
Lemelin, Roger, xxix, 130–1; *The Town Below*, 130–1
Lennox, John, 204
Le Pan, Douglas: *The Deserter*, 135
Lévesque, René, 266, 321nn5–6, 321n8
Lifton, Robert, 317n1
Lindsay, John, 306n5
Litton Industries, xxxiv, 229, 236, 253, 316n5, 318n5
Ludwig, Jack, xxx, 144, 293; *Confusions*, 132, 134. See also *Above Ground* (Ludwig), introduction by Laurence
Luxembourg, 151

McClelland, Jack: about, 306n1; contributions to CanLit, 141, 155; *Heart of a Stranger* and, xxiii; New Canadian Library series and, 202, 205; *The Prophet's Camel*

Bell and, 22–3; sign for Laurence's cabin, xxxii, 91
McClelland and Stewart, 20–1, 53, 155
McClung, Nellie, xxx, 128, 163; *Sowing Seeds in Danny*, 163
Macdonald, John A., 108, 166, 259, 309n8, 312n10
McLaughlin College, 83, 306n3
Maclean, Alan, 23
MacLennan, Hugh, xxvii, xxix, 53, 128, 129, 152, 164; *Barometer Rising*, 129; *Each Man's Son*, 129; *The Precipice*, 129; *Two Solitudes*, 129; *Voices in Time*, 170; *The Watch That Ends the Night*, 129
Macmillan (publisher), 20–1, 23, 26, 36, 141, 155
Mailer, Norman, 21
mail-order catalogues, 101–3, 292
malaria, 237, 240, 269
Manawaka (fictional town), 5, 7, 39, 165, 299n4
Manawaka Saga, xix, xxi, xxiv, xxvii, xxx, xlii. *See also specific works of fiction*
Mandel, Eli, 83, 139; *An Idiot Joy*, 310n1
Manitoba, 5, 166–7, 200, 266
Mannoni, O.: *Prospero and Caliban: The Psychology of Colonization*, 166
Maritimes, 115
Maskos, Karl, 49
Massey College. *See* writer-in-residence, Massey College
media appearances, 41–2, 72–3, 123
Mellwraith, Morag, 94–5, 307n2
Mennonites, 116–17, 320n3
mercury poisoning (Minamata disease), 237, 292, 317n6
"Method Writer," xxii, 17, 301n1
Métis, xxxvii–xxxviii, 59, 104, 121–2, 166–7, 259–60, 301n3, 319n1
Middleton, Fredrick, xxxix, 213, 259, 319n1
Mill, John Stuart, 167, 225, 274, 312n13
Milton, John: *Areopagitica*, 275, 278, 279
Minamata disease (mercury poisoning), 237, 292, 317n6
Mistahimaskwa (Big Bear), 166, 169–70, 311n9
Mitchell, Margaret: *Gone With the Wind*, 159
Mitchell, W.O., xxvii–xxviii, 53, 275; *Who Has Seen the Wind?*, 165
Molander, Roger, 228, 236, 244, 316n3, 318n4
Montgomery, L.M., xxix–xxx, 163; *Anne of Green Gables*, 163; *Emily of New Moon*, 163
Montreal, 133, 137–8

Moodie, Susanna, 95, 117, 216, 306n4; *Roughing It in the Bush*, 95, 117, 306n4
Moore, Brian, 313n3; *The Luck of Ginger Coffey*, 133
Morag Gunn (fictional): autobiographical element in, 311n1; bird watching and, xxv, 92; Catherine Parr Traill and, 307n5; comparison to *Crackpot* (Wiseman), 313n1; employment, 303n4; fictional character of, 308n2; flies' sex life and, 273; foremother of, xxxix, 315n3; name, 307n2; self-empowerment of, xlii, 59
Morton, Peg, 199
Morton, W.L., 199–200, 204; *Manitoba: A History*, 166–7, 200
Mowat, Farley, 139; *The Curse of the Viking Grave*, 139; *Westviking*, 139
Munro, Alice, 54, 275; *Lives of Girls and Women*, 322n1
Murphy, Emily, xxix–xxx, 163
Musgrove, Mildred, 45, 158–9, 303n3, 311n1
Myrdal, Alva, 244, 318n3

Nabokov, Vladimir: *Lolita*, 274
Nagasaki, xxxiv, 227, 235, 248, 315n1
narrative form: approach to, 29, 37; *The Fire-Dwellers*, xxii, xxiii, 13–14, 16, 34–7; influence from contemporaries, 29; *A Jest of God*, xxiii, 32–4, 36; novels and short stories, 17; reinvention of, 28; *The Stone Angel*, 30–2, 134; *This Side Jordan*, 29–30
narrative voice: character's role in, 16–17, 19, 32; *Crackpot* (Wiseman), 193–4; first-person narrative, 16, 30–1, 32, 33, 134; "The Loons," 18–19; *The Stone Angel*, 30–2; *This Side Jordan*, 30; "To Set Our House in Order," 17–18
Nathaniel Amegbe (fictional); xxii, 10, 29, 30, 34
nationalism, 66, 131, 152–3, 156, 321n1
NATO (North Atlantic Treaty Organization), 241, 252
Neepawa (Manitoba): about, 299n3; childhood memories, 63–6; Christmas in, 75–8; Manawaka and, 5; name and incorporation, 166–7, 312n11; public library, xxvii, 158–9, 161, 164; railway, 106
New Canadian Library (NCL), xxvii, 53, 139, 141, 202, 205
New Democratic Party (NDP), xxxvi, 252, 303n6, 319n8
New Land, A (TV series), xxxiii

New Left, 147, 311n4
New Press, 155
New York City, xxv, 84–6
Nigeria: Biafra, 11, 55, 56, 301n11; colonialism in, 52; Igbo (Ibo) people, 10, 54–5, 300n9, 301n11; *Long Drums and Cannons* (Laurence), xxii, 10, 50, 56, 168, 299n2; writers from, 4, 10–11, 53. *See also* Achebe, Chinua; Soyinka, Wole
non-hero, 131–3
North Atlantic Treaty Organization (NATO), 241, 252
North-West Rebellions, 166, 169, 311n9
nuclear disarmament: artists, responsibility for, 231–2, 245, 254–5; essays on, xxxiii–xxxv; future and, 283; movement, growth of, 243–4; potential Canadian role, 229–30, 236–7, 241, 244, 252–3; reasons for, 227–8, 232–3, 235–6, 237–8, 240–1, 242–3, 249–50, 253–4, 255; referendum proposal, 244–5; religious faith and, 237, 238, 253
nuclear weapons and war: destructive powers, realization of, 227, 235, 248; dropped on Japan, 222, 227, 235, 248, 315n1; government expectations, 222–3; language and, 229, 235, 239, 249–50, 317n2; Precipice Theory, 242; US-Russia relations and, 250–2
Nwapa, Flora, 53

Oberon Press, 155
October Crisis, 320nn3–4
O'Hagan, Howard, 53
Okara, Gabriel, 53, 313n2; *The Voice*, 191
Okigbo, Christopher Ifekandu, 10, 11, 300n8
"Old Hundredth" (hymn), xxxv, 317n8
Olsen, Tillie: *Silences*, 169; *Tell Me a Riddle*, 169
Ontario, 115–18, 223, 266, 321n7
Operation Dismantle, 244, 318n6
Orwell, George: "Politics and the English Language," xxxiv
Otonabee River, cabin at: about, xxv, 306n8; bird watching, 88, 92–5, 98; boat outings, 89–90; daily life at, 67, 87–8, 91, 98–9, 100; furnishings from catalogue, 103, 292; garden and wildflowers, 88–9, 99–100; muskie fishing, 67, 89, 92–3, 96; neighbours, 88–9, 90, 99; purchase of, 41, 86; river watching and recollections, 95–6; sign for, xxxii, 91

Parti Québécois (PQ), 266, 320n1, 321n5
Paul (saint), xxxvi, 211, 225

PEN International, 280, 322n1
people: influence on writing, 5–6, 14; value of individual, xxxv–xxxvi, 58, 226, 232, 234, 255
performances, by writers, 40–4
Peterborough (Ontario), 117–18, 216
Peter Martin Associates, 155
Phelps, Arthur, 164, 311n4
Physicians for Social Responsibility, 243, 253, 318n1
Pictish language, 304n12
Piquette Tonnerre (fictional), 19, 38
Pitikwahanapiwiyin (Poundmaker), 166, 311n9
place: being grounded in, 63–4, 67–8; cities in CanLit, 128, 133–4; influence on writing, 5; in *The Lamp at Noon and Other Stories* (Ross), 174
police, 269–70. *See also* Royal Canadian Mounted Police
politics, 51–2
pollution, xxxi–xxxiii, 66–7, 86, 115–16
pornography: arguments against, 274–5, 277–8; censorship and, xli, 275–6; Criminal Code and, 276–7, 322n2
Poundmaker (Pitikwahanapiwiyin), 166, 311n9
Prairies, xxv–xxvi, 5, 63–4, 66, 109, 114, 166–7, 260–1
Prism International, 9, 140, 155, 300n5
Project Ploughshares, xxxv, 208, 243, 253, 314n4
psychic numbing, xxxiv, 230, 232, 238, 244, 255, 317n1
publishers, 20–7; editing process, 21–4; relationship with, 20–1, 27; titles and, 24–7
Purdy, Al, 138, 299n7; *The New Romans*, 268; "Roblin's Mills," 7, 299n7

Quebec: geographic understanding of, 115; Keable Inquiry into Illegal Police Activities, 320n1; oppression of Québécois, xl, 261–4; separatism, xl, 265–7, 321n9
Queen's Quarterly, 8–9, 201–2, 300n3
Quill & Quire, xxvi, 159–60

Rachel, Rachel (film), 34, 297n4
Rachel Cameron (fictional), xlii, 6–7, 12–13, 33–4, 59
railway, 104–13; benefits of travel by, 105–6; childhood memories, 106–7; construction of, 108; family trips by, 107–8; impact on Canada, 104, 105; passenger trains, challenges facing, 104–5; in Scotland, 108; significance for Canadians, 112–13, 294; solo trips as adult, 108–12
Reagan, Ronald, 230, 251, 254, 316n7
Richler, Mordecai, 54, 132, 133, 143–4, 154; *The Apprenticeship of Duddy Kravitz*, 132; *The Incomparable Atuk*, 135
Riel, Louis, xxxvii, 122, 166–7, 213, 259–61, 301n4, 308n1
Robles, Alfonso Garcia, 244, 318n3
Ross, Malcolm, xxvii, 9, 141, 201–2, 205, 300n4
Ross, Sinclair, xxvii, xxix, 53, 129–30, 137, 152, 154, 173; *As For Me and My House*, xxvii, 91, 129–30, 137, 154, 159, 164, 173, 175; "Cornet at Night," 175, 176; "A Field of Wheat," 175, 176; "The Lamp at Noon," 175, 176, 177; "Not by Rain Alone," 174; "One's a Heifer," 176; "The Outlaw," 176–7; "The Painted Door," 174, 175, 177; "September Snow," 176. See also *The Lamp at Noon and Other Stories* (Ross), afterword by Laurence
Roy, Gabrielle, xxvii, xxix, xl, 128, 152, 164, 169, 261, 320n2; *The Road Past Altamont*, 140; *The Tin Flute*, 128, 169, 320n2; *Where Nests the Water-Hen*, 140
Royal Canadian Mounted Police (RCMP), 265, 320n1, 320n3
Rule, Jane, 140; *The Desert of the Heart*, 134, 140
Russia (Soviet Union), xxxiv, 223–4, 228, 235, 243, 249, 250–2
Ryerson (publisher), 155
Ryga, George: *Ballad of a Stonepicker*, 141

St Martin's Press, 22
Salinger, J.D.: *Catcher in the Rye*, 281
Sandburg, Carl, 312n1; *Losers*, 26–7, 183, 302n11
Saskatchewan, 139
Saturday Night: Belmont Award, 141
schools. *See* education
Scorerin, Mary, 141
Scotland, 5, 68, 108, 304n4, 304n10, 307n1
Scott, F.R.: *Essays on the Constitution*, 167, 225, 274, 277
Second World War, xxxviii, 59, 164, 221–2, 235, 248, 304n6
sex, 181, 223, 273, 274, 278. *See also* pornography

Sherman, Kenneth, 190
Shields, Carol, xli; "Canadian Writing,"
xxviii; *The Stone Diaries*, 313n3
Silversides, Ann: "Literature Goes Electronic
from Coast to Coast," 287
Simpson, John (maternal grandfather),
xxviii, 6, 299n6
Simpson, Ruby (aunt), 45, 106–7, 308n3
sins, seven deadly, 317n2
snake dancer/artist, 70–1
social gospel, xxxvi, 226, 234–5, 248
social justice, 59, 247, 256
Somaliland, xxxvii, xli–xlii, 165, 166, 237,
309n6
Soviet Union (Russia), xxxiv, 223–4, 228, 235,
243, 249, 250–2
Soyinka, Wole, xxii, xl, 11, 53, 262, 300n10
Speaking Our Peace (film), xxxv
Stacey Cameron MacAindra (fictional), xxiii,
xlii, 6–7, 13–14, 27, 34–5, 36–7, 59
Stein, David Lewis: *Scratch One Dreamer*, 134
Steinbeck, John: *The Grapes of Wrath*, 159
Stern, Stewart, 34
Stevenson, Robert Louis: *Kidnapped*, 162
Stone Angel, The (Laurence): about, 304n3;
Atwood on, xxvii; autobiographical ele-
ments, 39; controversy over, xxi; Hagar
character, 4–5, 11–12; narrative form and
voice, xxiii, 30–2, 134; publication, xxv; re-
visions, 23; theme, 6, 12, 59; title, 25–6; van
Herk on, 291; Wilson and, 300n6. *See also*
Hagar Shipley (fictional)
Storm Warning (anthology), 91
Stovel, Nora Foster, 291, 295
Stratton-Porter, Gene: *Laddie*, 159
Strickland, Samuel, 95, 307n6
structure. *See* narrative form
Stuart, Charles Edward, 307n1
style, 29. *See also* narrative form
subway, 70
Such, Peter, 52
suicide, 286, 322n1
survival, theme of, 6–7, 12–13, 59, 73
Swift Current (electronic literary magazine),
287–8, 322n2
Symons, Scott, 138; *Place d'Armes*, 138

Tamarack Review, 139, 141
Tanabe, Takao, 216, 315n3
taxi drivers, xxvi, 72, 118, 305n4
Taylor, Carole, 42, 303n1

technologies, new: children and, 285–6; computers and women writers, 286–8; women
and, 283–5, 289–90
Telford, Jim, 322n1
Third World writers, xxiv, 52
This Side Jordan (Laurence): Beta Sigma Phi
First Novel Award, 202; inspiration for,
317n4; narrative form and voice, 29–30,
302n6; publication, xxv, 301n2, 302n7; reflections on, xxii, 9–10, 57; revisions, 8, 22;
theme, 12; title, 25
Thomas, Clara: about, 306n2; as biographer,
204; as critic, 203–4; on *The Diviners*, 200;
friendship with, 203, 293; meeting at York
University, 83–4; as pioneer, 205–6; as
teacher, 204–5; tribute to, 203–6; works:
*The Manawaka World of Margaret Lau-
rence*, 203; *Our Nature, Our Voices*, 204
Thorndyke, Helen Louise: Honey Bunch
Series, 102, 308n3
time, 15–16, 18, 19
titles, 24–7
Toronto: Canadian writers in, 138–9; reflections on, xxiv–xxv, 69–70, 72–3, 81–4, 86,
115–16, 119
Traill, Catherine Parr, 95–6, 117, 216, 248,
307n5; *A Canadian Settler's Guide*, 95
travel: air travel, 70–1, 85–6; bus travel, 71–2,
119–23; by railway, 104–13; subway, 70; taxi
drivers, xxvi, 72, 118, 305n4
Trent University, xxx, 199, 297n7
tribalism, 11
Trudeau, Pierre Elliot, 252, 265, 266, 320n2,
321n7
Tundra Press, 155
Tutuola, Amos, xxii
Twain, Mark, 158
typewriters, 45–9

United Church of Canada, 208, 307n3, 314n6
United College, xxxvi, 164, 207, 311n2, 311n3
United Nations, xxxv, 239–40, 243–4, 314n5,
318n2
United States of America: American writers,
168–9; nuclear war and, 228, 235, 243, 249,
250–2
University of Toronto. *See* writer-in-
residence, Massey College
University of Western Ontario, xxx
University of Winnipeg, 164, 207, 311n3
Ustinov, Peter, xxv

Vancouver (British Columbia), 140
Vanessa MacLeod (fictional), xlii, 17–19, 38–9, 59
van Herk, Aritha, xxvi
Verbascum thapsus (Common Mullein/Aron's Rod), 42, 303n2
Verduyn, Christl: "(Es)saying It Her Way," xx
VIA Rail, 104, 109–10, 113, 308n2. *See also* railway
Victoria (British Columbia), 80–1
Vietnam, xxxiv, 223, 270, 311n4
Villerup, Jack, xxv
Vizinczey, Steve: *In Praise of Older Women*, 134, 141
voice. *See* narrative voice
Vonnegut, Kurt: *Slaughterhouse Five*, 169

Waddington, Miriam, 83
Wah, Fred, 322n2
war, struggle against, 224–5. *See also* nuclear disarmament; Second World War
Ward, Barbara, 237, 317n3
War Measures Act, 67, 263, 265–6, 320n4
Waterloo (Ontario), 116–17
Watson, Sheila, 313n3; *The Double Hook*, 135, 139
Waves (journal), 190
Weaver, Robert, 141
Wemyss, Bob (Robert; brother), xxv–xxvi, 76–7, 111
Wemyss, John (paternal grandfather), 48, 76, 167, 302n10, 304n10, 312n11
Wemyss, Margaret Simpson (stepmother), xxvii, 45, 65, 77, 158–9, 161, 162, 164, 303n2
Wemyss, Robert (father), 38–9, 66, 76, 77, 78, 158
Wemyss, Robert (great-grandfather), 67
Wemyss, Verna (mother), 66, 158
White, Patrick, 168
Wiebe, Rudy, xxxviii, xl, 54, 169, 264; *The Scorched-Wood People*, 264; *The Temptations of Big Bear*, 169–70, 264
Wilder, Thornton, 223
Williams, Alice, xxxix, 310n2
Wilson, Ethel, xxvii, xxix, 9, 53, 130, 140, 154, 293, 300n6; *The Equations of Love*, 130; *Hetty Dorval*, 130; *The Innocent Traveller*, 130; *The Swamp Angel*, 130
Wilson, Lois, 207–9, 314n1, 314n3; *Like a Mighty River*, 208, 238

Wilson, Roy, 208
Winnipeg (Manitoba): in *Crackpot* (Wiseman), 133, 193; motto, 195, 313n7; Old Left, xxxvi, 58, 147, 226, 310n3; writers in, 139; YWCA, 214–16
Winnipeg Citizen, 214
Wiseman, Adele: about, 137, 300n2; on electric typewriters, 47; friendship with, 8, 165–6, 293, 295; Holocaust and, xxxviii; literary culture and, 54; Malcolm Ross and, 201; *The Sacrifice*, xxviii, 133, 137, 165, 189, 311n6. See also *Crackpot* (Wiseman), introduction by Laurence
Wiseman, Chaika, 48, 165, 304n13
women: in *Above Ground* (Ludwig), 180–1; in academia, 206; censorship and feminism, 275; childbirth, 268–9, 284–5; comparison to colonialism, 58–9; computers and women writers, 286–8; domestic help for, 288–9; fictional portrayals of, 13; in *The Lamp at Noon and Other Stories* (Ross), 174–5; in Laurence's childhood, 162–3; Laurence's feminism, xxxix, xl–xli, 292, 311n8; new technologies and, 283–5, 289–90
Woodcock, George, 140; *The Métis Chief and His Lost World*, xxxii
World Council of Churches, 208
World War II, xxxviii, 59, 164, 221–2, 235, 248, 304n6
writer-in-residence, Massey College, xxx, 143–9; advice sought by Laurence, 143–4; availability advertised, 144–5; as change of pace, 310n1; discussions with students, xxx, 82–3, 145–7; memorable students, 147–8; office, 145; talks for groups and clubs, 40–1; tasks of, 148–9, 293
writers: computers and, 286–8; need for support against persecution, 280–2; nuclear disarmament responsibility, 231–2, 245, 254–5; as performers, 40–4
Writers' Union of Canada, xxvi, 43, 152, 210, 293, 303n3
writing. *See* fiction

York University, xxv, 83–4, 287
YWCA, 214–17, 315n1

Zieroth, Dale, 91, 164, 306n2